NOVELL'S

Novell's ZENworks™ for Servers 2 Administrator's Handbook

NOVELL'S

Novell's ZENworks™ for Servers 2 Administrator's Handbook

RON TANNER AND BRAD DAYLEY

Novell.
PRESS

Novell Press, Provo, UT

Novell's ZENworks™ for Servers 2 Administrator's Handbook
Published by
Novell Press
1800 S. Novell Place
Provo, UT 84606
Copyright © 2001 Novell, Inc. All rights reserved. No part of this book, including interior design, cover design, and icons, may be reproduced or transmitted in any form, by any means (electronic, photocopying, recording, or otherwise) without the prior written permission of the publisher.
ISBN: 0-7645-4732-1
Printed in the United States of America
10 9 8 7 6 5 4 3 2 1
1O/RW/QT/QR/IN
Distributed in the United States by Hungry Minds, Inc. Distributed by CDG Books Canada Inc. for Canada; by Transworld Publishers Limited in the United Kingdom; by IDG Norge Books for Norway; by IDG Sweden Books for Sweden; by IDG Books Australia Publishing Corporation Pty. Ltd. for Australia and New Zealand; by TransQuest Publishers Pte Ltd. for Singapore, Malaysia, Thailand, Indonesia, and Hong Kong; by Gotop Information Inc. for Taiwan; by ICG Muse, Inc. for Japan; by Intersoft for South Africa; by Eyrolles for France; by International Thomson Publishing for Germany, Austria, and Switzerland; by Distribuidora Cuspide for Argentina; by LR International for Brazil; by Galileo Libros for Chile; by Ediciones ZETA S.C.R. Ltda. for Peru; by WS Computer Publishing Corporation, Inc., for the Philippines; by Contemporanea de Ediciones for Venezuela; by Express Computer Distributors for the Caribbean and West Indies; by Micronesia Media Distributor, Inc. for Micronesia; by Chips Computadoras S.A. de C.V. for Mexico; by Editorial Norma de Panama S.A. for Panama; by American Bookshops for Finland.

For general information on Hungry Minds' products and services please contact our Customer Care department within the U.S. at 800-762-2974, outside the U.S. at 317-572-3993 or fax 317-572-4002.
For sales inquiries and reseller information, including discounts, premium and bulk quantity sales, and foreign-language translations, please contact our Customer Care department at 800-434-3422, fax 317-572-4002 or write to Hungry Minds, Inc., Attn: Customer Care Department, 10475 Crosspoint Boulevard, Indianapolis, IN 46256.
For information on licensing foreign or domestic rights, please contact our Sub-Rights Customer Care department at 650-653-7098.
For information on using Hungry Minds' products and services in the classroom or for ordering examination copies, please contact our Educational Sales department at 800-434-2086 or fax 317-572-4005. For press review copies, author interviews, or other publicity information, please contact our Public Relations department at 650-653-7000 or fax 650-653-7500.
For authorization to photocopy items for corporate, personal, or educational use, please contact Copyright Clearance Center, 222 Rosewood Drive, Danvers, MA 01923, or fax 978-750-4470.

Library of Congress Cataloging-in-Publication Data
Novell's ZENworks for servers 2 administrator's handbook / Ron Tanner and Brad Dayley.
p. cm.
Includes index.
ISBN 0-7645-4732-8 (alk. paper)1
1. Z.E.N.works. 2. administrator's handbook(Computer systems)
I. Title: ZENworks administrator's handbook..
II. Dayley, Brad.
QA76.9.U83 T38 2001
005.4'38—dc21   2001018706
                                          CIP

LIMIT OF LIABILITY/DISCLAIMER OF WARRANTY: THE PUBLISHER AND AUTHOR HAVE USED THEIR BEST EFFORTS IN PREPARING THIS BOOK. THE PUBLISHER AND AUTHOR MAKE NO REPRESENTATIONS OR WARRANTIES WITH RESPECT TO THE ACCURACY OR COMPLETENESS OF THE CONTENTS OF THIS BOOK AND SPECIFICALLY DISCLAIM ANY IMPLIED WARRANTIES OF MERCHANTABILITY OR FITNESS FOR A PARTICULAR PURPOSE. THERE ARE NO WARRANTIES WHICH EXTEND BEYOND THE DESCRIPTIONS CONTAINED IN THIS PARAGRAPH. NO WARRANTY MAY BE CREATED OR EXTENDED BY SALES REPRESENTATIVES OR WRITTEN SALES MATERIALS. THE ACCURACY AND COMPLETENESS OF THE INFORMATION PROVIDED HEREIN AND THE OPINIONS STATED HEREIN ARE NOT GUARANTEED OR WARRANTED TO PRODUCE ANY PARTICULAR RESULTS, AND THE ADVICE AND STRATEGIES CONTAINED HEREIN MAY NOT BE SUITABLE FOR EVERY INDIVIDUAL. NEITHER THE PUBLISHER NOR AUTHOR SHALL BE LIABLE FOR ANY LOSS OF PROFIT OR ANY OTHER COMMERCIAL DAMAGES, INCLUDING BUT NOT LIMITED TO SPECIAL, INCIDENTAL, CONSEQUENTIAL, OR OTHER DAMAGES.

Trademarks: Novell, NetWare, the Novell Press logo, GroupWise, ManageWise, Novell Directory Services, and NDPS are registered trademarks; Novell Press, NDS, Novell BorderManager, ZENworks, and Novell Distributed Print Services are trademarks; CNE is a registered service mark; and CNI and CNA are service marks of Novell, Inc. in the United States and other countries. All brand names and product names used in this book are trade names, service marks, trademarks, or registered trademarks of their respective owners. Hungry Minds, Inc. is not associated with any product or vendor mentioned in this book.

John Kilcullen, *CEO, Hungry Minds, Inc.*
Bill Barry, *President, Hungry Minds, Inc.*
Richard Swadley, *Senior Vice President & Publisher, Technology*

Hungry Minds™ is a trademark of Hungry Minds, Inc.

Novell. Marcy Shanti, *Publisher, Novell Press, Novell, Inc.*
Novell Press and the Novell Press logo are trademarks of Novell, Inc.

Welcome to Novell Press

Novell Press, the world's leading provider of networking books, is the premier source for the most timely and useful information in the networking industry. Novell Press books cover fundamental networking issues as they emerge — from today's Novell and third-party products to the concepts and strategies that will guide the industry's future. The result is a broad spectrum of titles for the benefit of those involved in networking at any level: end user, department administrator, developer, systems manager, or network architect.

Novell Press books are written by experts with the full participation of Novell's technical, managerial, and marketing staff. The books are exhaustively reviewed by Novell's own technicians and are published only on the basis of final released software, never on prereleased versions.

Novell Press at Hungry Minds is an exciting partnership between two companies at the forefront of the knowledge and communications revolution. The Press is implementing an ambitious publishing program to develop new networking titles centered on the current versions of NetWare, GroupWise, BorderManager, ManageWise, and networking integration products.

Novell Press books are translated into several languages and sold throughout the world.

Steve Rife
Publisher,
Novell Press, Novell, Inc.

Novell Press

Publisher
Steve Rife

Hungry Minds

Acquisitions Editor
John Gravener

Project Editors
Linda Turnowski
Christopher Johnson

Technical Editors
Jason Petty
James Talbot

Copy Editors
Cindy Lai
Dennis Weaver

Proof Editor
Cindy Lai

Project Coordinator
Nancee Reeves

Production
Indianapolis Production Services

Quality Control
Nancy L. Reinhardt

Proofreading and Indexing
York Production Services, Inc.

About the Authors

Ron Tanner is a networking professional who has been with Novell since 1993; he currently is working in the CTO office designing next-generation products at Novell. Prior to being with Novell, Ron worked at AT&T Bell Laboratories developing advanced networking systems. Ron has been involved with several ZENworks projects since their inception. He is also the coauthor of *Novell's ZENworks for Desktops 3 Administrator's Handbook*.

Brad Dayley is a software engineer on Novell's Critical Problem Resolution team. He has nine years of experience installing, troubleshooting, and coding Novell's products. He codeveloped an advanced debugging course used to train Novell's support engineers and customers and is the coauthor of *Novell's Guide to Resolving Critical Server Issues* and *ZENworks for Desktops Administrator's Handbook*.

To my soul mate and sweetheart. May the next 20 be as good as the last.

—Ron Tanner

For D, A, & F!

—Brad Dayley

Foreword

Computers and their use are extremely pervasive in our world. Indeed, almost every aspect of business has become dependent on the smooth functioning of computer systems. As we embark into the new millennium, the use of networks and computers are even moving into the home world. We are becoming a connected society, which will place an even greater burden and expectation on networks across the world.

The cornerstone device of the worldwide network and any business or community network is the powerful server. The server provides the muscle that is required to keep the network functioning and provide the features and resources that a hungry connected community requires. If the server were to fail or not function at peak performance, the entire system would cease to function and the potential for the loss of data and business vitality is threatened. The smooth running of the servers in your network must be paramount for your business, especially as e-business is placing more and more demands on company servers.

IT departments have a great responsibility to keep the network functioning and in keeping the servers accessible to all of those in the system. They require a solution that is powerful enough to provide the ease of traditional centralized management of their servers and yet still monitor and maintain control at each of the diverse server locations. The IT departments must have the management functionality they have enjoyed with a centralized mainframe computer system, and yet have this ability over their sprawling networks where their servers may reside in many different locations across the world.

Novell, Inc. in ZENworks for Servers 2 has taken its superior eDirectory solution and combined it with its knowledge of server management to provide a simple approach to centrally managing such a vital resource. This capability has been proven and shown useful with the desktop in Novell's ZENworks for Desktops product. Now the same ease of administration and reliability has been introduced to the server environment.

In this latest release of ZENworks for Servers 2, Novell has combined its SNMP management of network devices with its eDirectory-enabled management to provide an all-encompassing product to fully support the servers in your network. Indeed, this product provides SNMP and trap management, alarm monitoring, policy-based server management where the server keeps itself at administered performance, and Tiered Electronic Distribution that enables you to transfer your important data files efficiently to any other server in the network.

Novell's ZENworks for Servers 2 Administrator's Handbook is concentrated exclusively on the deployment and use of ZENworks for Servers 2 in any computing environment. This book covers many aspects and features of ZENworks for Servers 2, including the more advanced subjects, and can make the installation, deployment, troubleshooting, and use of the product a smooth and rewarding process. This book should be in every administrator's and server manager's library.

Craig Miller
Vice President and General Manager
Net Management Service
Novell, Inc.

Preface

The computer industry has made incredible progress with information sharing since the introduction of local area networks (LANs) in the 1980s. These advancements have produced services and tools that increase user productivity while decreasing their workload. Since the very infancy of the LAN industry, sharing of resources has been at the very root of the value of the use of LANs. One of the most vital resources in the network is the server — the large, expensive computer system that can supply facilities to many thousands of users, giving them access to capabilities that they do not have available on their desktops.

Since the introduction of ZENworks for Desktops, Novell has recognized the value in managing resources through the directory. This significantly reduces the cost of managing any resource, enabling the administrators of the network to handle more services and focus on the needs of the business. Novell has now moved this concept into managing the server. Within the directory, the administrator can set system parameters and policies to govern the behavior of their servers in the tree. These policies can affect as little as one server, or as many servers as are in the tree. With a single instruction to the directory literally all servers in the network can be modified.

In addition to managing the behavior of the servers, Novell with ZENworks for Servers 2 has given us a scalable distribution service that can efficiently transfer bundles of files to any or all servers in the network. Administrators can construct packages and bundles of files and have them efficiently distributed across the hall or across the world. The servers unpack and store these bundles on their local file systems. We no longer have to spend our time forever copying applications and files all across our servers in the network.

This book is your guide to leveraging ZENworks for Servers 2 to distribute files across the network and to maintain and manage your NetWare servers. This book provides steps to set up and use the advanced features of ZENworks for Servers to cut your administrative efforts and costs, while making the network environment much more effective for your company.

Who Should Read This Book

This book is for anyone responsible for setting up or maintaining a Novell network. If you are a network administrator, support technician, CNE, or consultant, this book gives you the edge you need to effectively manage servers and distribute files across all the servers in the network. You will save valuable time by using the advanced features of ZENworks for Servers that keep your servers exactly at the settings you specify; even if someone walks up to the server and changes the settings, they will be automatically changed back to your administered value.

This book also shows you how to effectively use the distribution services to send all of your files anywhere on the network and have them placed on the servers you wish—making them available to all the users of the servers, wherever they may be.

How This Book Is Organized

This book is organized into the following chapters to guide you through installing ZENworks for Servers, setting up ZENworks for Servers in NDS, and then leveraging the advanced features of ZENworks for Servers to reduce your network management costs.

Chapter 1: Introduction to ZENworks for Servers 2

This chapter discusses the basic high-level components of ZENworks for Servers, the purpose for the system, and the benefits of installing ZENworks for Servers in your network.

Chapter 2: Installing ZENworks for Servers 2

Chapter 2 discusses the steps that you need to take to install ZENworks for Servers 2 on your servers and in your network. It walks you through the pre-installation steps as well as each process of the install to get your system up and running.

Chapter 3: Understanding What Is Placed on Your Servers

This chapter discusses each of the components that you can choose in the install process (discussed in Chapter 2) and describes where the files are placed on the server. This chapter also reviews the processes that need to run on your server in order for the components of the system to function.

Chapter 4: Setting Up ZENworks for Servers in Your Tree

This chapter reviews, at a high level, the various objects that will be introduced into your tree and what basic function they perform. Additionally, Chapter 4 reviews the high-level steps that you need to take in order to get ZENworks for Servers 2 functioning in your tree.

Chapter 5: Setting Up Server Policies

This chapter discusses each of the various server policies that are introduced into the network with ZENworks for Servers 2. Chapter 5 reviews each policy carefully and describes how to set up these policies and make the most of directory-enabled management.

Chapter 6: Setting Up Tiered Electronic Distribution

Chapter 6 discusses the general architecture of Tiered Electronic Distribution (TED) and describes each of the components of the system. The chapter also describes each of the management processes that are required to get files properly distributed efficiently across any tree and any size network. It also covers the manipulation of the objects in the tree to use TED effectively.

Chapter 7: Understanding and Creating Server Software Packages

This chapter reviews the process to create server software packages, which constitute a set of files that are to be placed into the server and installed into the system. These packages can use TED to be distributed across the network and then automatically installed on any destination server.

Chapter 8: Understanding ZENworks for Servers 2 Management Services

Chapter 8 reviews and describes all of the various applications and tools provided with ZENworks for Servers 2 that will help you manage and monitor your network more effectively.

Chapter 9: Preparing and Using ZENworks for Servers 2 Network Discovery

This chapter discusses the use of the network discovery tools that scan your network to create and store network topology maps, which will help ZENworks and you be aware of all the devices that are attached to your network.

Chapter 10: Using ZENworks for Servers 2 Traffic Analysis

Chapter 10 discusses how to set up a system to monitor the traffic that is crossing a segment of your network. This monitoring information will help you in analyzing your traffic patterns in an effort to keep your network functioning at peak performance.

Chapter 11: Understanding and Using ZENworks for Servers 2 Server and Alarm Management

Chapter 11 delves deeper into the SNMP system. It reviews how to set up the system and make it work efficiently so that you can be notified when a server is experiencing problems or reaching administered thresholds on their resources.

Chapter 12: Using ZENworks for Servers 2 Server Management

This chapter reviews the features that are in ZENworks for Servers 2 that can be used specifically in managing any NetWare or NT/2000 servers in your network. This includes the ability to monitor resources, perform hardware and software inventory, and remote management of server configuration.

Chapter 13: Making the Most of ZENworks for Servers 2 Reporting

This chapter reviews the various reporting capabilities that are available in the ZENworks for Servers 2 product. This chapter also discusses how to manage and customize these reports for your specific needs.

Chapter 14: Troubleshooting ZENworks for Servers 2

This chapter reviews several of the components of ZENworks for Servers 2 and how to perform some diagnostics to determine why these components are not functioning as expected. This chapter also walks you through several repair procedures that you can follow to get the system back up and running.

Appendix A: Understanding NDS Changes for ZENworks for Servers 2

Appendix A identifies all of the objects and attribute changes that ZENworks for Servers 2 performs on your Novell NDS tree.

Appendix B: ZENworks for Servers 2 Database Schemas

This appendix discusses the several different databases, the various tables, and the attributes of these tables, all of which are used in ZENworks for Servers.

Appendix C: ZENworks for Servers 2 Console Commands

This appendix covers the commands that can be entered on the various consoles that are present on the NetWare server, or in an NT/2000 box. Currently, only the ZENworks for Servers 2 policy engine, TED distributor, or TED subscriber can receive console commands.

Appendix D: ZENworks for Servers 2 Resources

This appendix lists other places one can go to find out and get more help with their ZENworks for Servers 2 implementation.

Appendix E: ZENworks for Servers 2 Support Packs

This appendix discusses the expected release of the first support pack for the ZENworks for Servers 2 product.

Acknowledgments

Our sincere gratitude goes out to the following persons, without whom this book could not have come in to being:

To John Gravener, thanks for kick starting this book after it was put on hold for other more pressing publications. It was an accelerated process once you got hold of the project.

To Linda Turnowski, thanks for doing the worrying for all of us and for keeping us on our toes.

To the ZENworks for Servers 2 team, thanks for introducing the directory to the server — making administration of the most vital network resource, the server, even easier and more reliable. And thanks for giving us a great distribution service to make getting files there a snap. We're looking forward to many new versions to make the product even better.

To all of those in Novell who allowed us to pick their brains, thanks. Specifically, we would like to mention the following individuals (with apologies to any whose names we have forgotten): Ty Ellis, Ken Muir, Roy Studyvin, Ann Marie Miller, Krishnan R, Brian Vaughan, and Jon Pomeroy.

To our technical editors James Talbot and Jason Petty, our thanks for rooting out our errors and putting ZENworks for Servers through its paces. We know this book is a significantly better book thanks to your careful review.

Contents at a Glance

Foreword		ix
Preface		xi
Acknowledgments		xvii
Chapter 1	Introduction to ZENworks for Servers 2	1
Chapter 2	Installing ZENworks for Servers 2	9
Chapter 3	Understanding What Is Placed on Your Servers	33
Chapter 4	Setting Up ZENworks for Servers in Your Tree	41
Chapter 5	Setting Up Server Policies	51
Chapter 6	Setting Up Tiered Electronic Distribution	111
Chapter 7	Understanding and Creating Server Software Packages	187
Chapter 8	Understanding ZENworks for Servers 2 Management Services	219
Chapter 9	Preparing and Using ZENworks for Servers 2 Network Discovery	241
Chapter 10	Using ZENworks for Servers 2 Traffic Analysis	261
Chapter 11	Understanding and Using ZENworks for Servers 2 Server and Alarm Management	301

Chapter 12	Using ZENworks for Servers 2 Server Management	**333**
Chapter 13	Making the Most of ZENworks for Servers 2 Reporting	**367**
Chapter 14	Troubleshooting ZENworks for Servers 2	**399**
Appendix A	Understanding NDS Changes for ZENworks for Servers 2	**415**
Appendix B	ZENworks for Servers 2 Database Schemas	**425**
Appendix C	ZENworks for Servers 2 Console Commands	**439**
Appendix D	ZENworks for Servers 2 Resources	**455**
Appendix E	ZENworks for Servers 2 Support Packs	**459**
Index		**465**

Table of Contents

Foreword ix

Preface xi

Acknowledgements xvii

Chapter 1   Introduction to ZENworks for Servers 2   1

What Is the Purpose of ZENworks for Servers 2? 2
    Server Management through Policies. 2
    Tiered Electronic Distribution. 3
    Server Software Packages 3
    SNMP Services 4
    Alarm Management Services 4
    Server Inventory and Trending. 4
    Portal Services 5
    Common Management Console 5
What Is the Relationship between ManageWise
and ZENworks for Servers 2? 5
What Is the Relationship between ZENworks
for Desktops and ZENworks for Servers 2? 6
What Are the Benefits of Using ZENworks for Servers 2? 6

Chapter 2   Installing ZENworks for Servers 2   9

Prerequisite Steps for Installing ZENworks for Servers 2 10
    Installing ZENworks for Servers 2 from a Workstation 10
    Management and Monitoring Services. 11
Installing Server Components 16
    Log in to Tree as Admin 16
    Map Drives to Servers 17
    Install Supporting Software 17
    Launching the Install from the CD. 18
    Extending NDS Schema 18
    Selecting the ZENworks for Servers 2 Install 18
    Select Component Categories to Install 18
Installing Management and Monitoring Services 20
    Installing Site Management Services and Agent 20
    Install Site Management ConsoleOne Snap-ins 25
    Install Site Management Server License. 25

Installing Policy and Distribution Services 25
  Select Tree for Installation 25
  Install Licenses 25
  Select Server(s) for Installation 26
  Select to Modify Autoexec.ncf 27
  Enter Volume for Database 27
  Defining Distribution Routes 27
  Create Channel Objects 27
  Define Configuration Information for Distributors 28
  Define Configuration Information for Subscribers 28
  Complete the Install.. 29
Migration Tools 30
  Migration from ManageWise 2.x 30
  Migration from ZENworks for Servers 1.0 31
Understanding Product Guides 32
Browsing the CD 32

Chapter 3 Understanding What Is Placed on Your Servers   33

Management and Monitoring Services................................. 34
  Management Site Services 34
  Server Management 35
  Traffic Analysis 36
  Inventory Management.. 36
  Remote Management 37
  ConsoleOne Snap-ins... 37
Policy and Distribution Services 37
  Server Policies and Packages 37
  Remote Web Console 38
  ConsoleOne Snap-ins... 39
  Policies Database 39
  Tiered Electronic Distribution.................................... 39

Chapter 4 Setting Up ZENworks for Servers in Your Tree   41

Understanding General ZENworks for Servers 2 Architecture 42
  Learning about ZENworks for Servers 2 Objects................... 42
  Existing Objects Modified in the Tree 45
  Administration through Novell ConsoleOne 45
  Discussing Policy Packages and Policies.......................... 46

xxi

NOVELL'S ZENWORKS FOR SERVERS 2 ADMINISTRATOR'S HANDBOOK

Starting Up ZENworks for Servers in Your Network.................. 46
   Starting Up Management and Monitoring Services................ 47
   Starting Up Policy and Distribution Services..................... 48

Chapter 5   Setting Up Server Policies   51

Discussing ZENworks for Servers 2 Policies......................... 52
   Understanding Platform-Specific Policies........................ 52
   Plural versus Cumulative Policies............................... 53
Setting up a Container Policy Package............................. 54
   Introducing the Policies Page.................................. 55
   Understanding the Associations Property Page................... 56
   Defining the NDS Rights Property Pages 56
   Looking at the Other Property Page............................ 58
   Using the Rights to Files and Folders Property Page 60
Setting Up a Service Location Policy Package....................... 60
   Explaining the Policies Property Page 62
   Understanding the Associations Property Page................... 63
Setting Up a Server Policy Package 63
   Using the Policies Property Page............................... 64
Setting Up a Container Policy Package — Search Policy 67
   Looking at the Search Level Page............................... 68
   Describing the Search Order Page 69
   Understanding the Refresh Interval Page 70
Setting Up a Service Location Policy Package —
The SMTP Host Policy.. 70
Setting Up a Service Location Policy Package —
The SNMP Trap Target Policy..................................... 71
Setting Up a Service Location Policy Package —
The Tiered Electronic Distribution Policy 73
   Understanding the Settings Policy Page......................... 73
   Defining the Messaging Property Page.......................... 75
   Introducing the Variables Property Pages 77
   Looking at the Schedule Property Page......................... 78
Setting Up a Service Location Policy Package —
The ZENworks Database Policy 80
Setting Up a Service Location Policy Package —
The ZENworks for Servers License 82
Setting Up the Server Policy Package —
The NetWare Set Parameters Policy............................... 83
Setting Up the Server Policy Package —

xxii

TABLE OF CONTENTS

The Scheduled Down Policy 85
Setting Up the Server Policy Package —
The Scheduled Load/Unload Policy 86
Setting Up the Server Policy Package — The Server Down Process 88
    Describing the Down Procedure Page 88
    Discussing the Ordered Unload Page 90
    Looking at the Reporting Page............................. 91
    Introducing the Broadcast Messages Page.................... 92
    About the Targeted Messages Page 92
    Discussing the Conditions Page............................. 94
Setting Up the Server Policy Package — The Server Scripts Policy 96
Setting Up the Server Policy Package — The SNMP Community Strings... 98
Setting Up the Server Policy Package —
The SNMP Trap Target Refresh 101
Setting Up the Server Policy Package — The Text File Changes Policy.... 102
    Prepend to File.. 103
    Append to File 104
    Search File.. 104
    Policy Schedule Page 106
Setting Up the Server Policy Package — ZENworks for Servers 2....... 106
    Adding Users to the List 108
    Discussing the Configuration Page.......................... 108

Chapter 6   Setting Up Tiered Electronic Distribution   111

Understanding the General Architecture for TED 112
    Introducing the Components............................... 112
    NDS Objects 113
Discussing TED Configuration in Your Network...................... 115
    Examining a Simple Layout................................ 115
    Looking at a Complex Layout 117
    Examining Capacities and Restrictions 122
Configuring TED Systems....................................... 123
    Construction of a Routing Hierarchy 124
    Signing Distributions.................................... 124
    Scheduler Interactions 125
About the TED Distributor 127
    Introducing the Settings Property Page...................... 129
    Looking at the Messaging Property Page..................... 130
    Introducing the Distributions Property Page.................. 133
    About the Routing Hierarchy Property Page 133

xxiii

About the Schedule Property Page 135
NDS Rights Property Pages.................................... 138
About the Other Property Page 142
Discussing the Parent Subscriber.................................. 143
Discussing the TED Subscriber 144
About the Settings Property Page 146
Focusing on the Messaging Property Page..................... 147
Thinking about the Channels Property Page................... 149
About the Extract Schedule Property Page..................... 150
Variables Property Pages 153
Placing a Subscriber on Windows NT/2000 154
External Subscriber 155
About the General Property Page............................. 157
Discussing the Channels Property Page 157
Looking at the Network Address Property Page 157
About TED Distribution... 158
Looking at the General Property Page 159
About the Channels Property Page............................ 160
Looking at the Agent Property Page 161
Looking at the Schedule..................................... 162
About Manual Distribution 165
About TED Agents 167
About the NAL Application Distribution Agent 168
The HTTP Agent 170
The FTP Agent 171
The Server Software Package Agent 173
Discussing the File Agent 174
About the TED Channel.. 177
Discussing the Settings Property Page......................... 178
Looking at the Distributions Property Page 178
About the Subscribers Property Page.......................... 178
About the Schedule Property Page 178
Looking at the Remote Web Console............................... 179

**Chapter 7   Understanding and Creating Server
             Software Packages   187**

Understanding Server Software Packages 188
About Installation Requirements............................... 188
Focusing on .SPK and .CPK Files............................... 189

Rollback 189
Creating and Managing .SPK Files in ConsoleOne 190
Discussing Installation Failures. 190
Introducing the Remote Web Console 190
A Little about Variables 193
Creating a Server Software Package 194
Creating a New Server Software Package. 194
About Package Management 195
Managing Components. 202
About Prepend to File 209
About Append to File. 210
About Search File. 210
Compiling the Software Package 215
Installing a Server Software Package on the Target Server 216
Sending the File with TED 216
Copying the File Manually 216
Updating Server Software Packages. 217

Chapter 8 Understanding ZENworks for Servers 2 Management Services   219

Understanding ZENworks for Servers Management Components 220
Introducing Management Site Services 220
About Server Management 224
Analyzing Traffic 225
Information About Remote Control 226
Viewing the Server Inventory 226
About the Management Console. 226
Using the ZENworks for Servers 2 Console. 227
Navigating the ZENworks for Servers 2 Namespace 227
Setting ZENworks for Servers Console Options 228
Managing Console Views 230
Planning Your Network Management Services 235
Defining Management Groups and Needs. 235
Planning Your Network Management Strategy 235
Configuring Your Network. 236
Defining Administration Roles 238

NOVELL'S ZENWORKS FOR SERVERS 2 ADMINISTRATOR'S HANDBOOK

Chapter 9 Preparing and Using ZENworks for Servers 2 Network Discovery 241

Understanding Network Discovery. 242
    Understanding the Discovery Components 242
    Understanding the Discovery Process. 245
    Understanding What Is Discovered. 246
Using Network Discovery 249
    Starting and Stopping Network Discovery 249
    Checking the Status of the Initial Discovery 250
    Changing the Default Configuration 251
    Checking the Results of a Network Discovery. 257
Using the Atlas 257
    Accessing the Atlas. 258
    Using the Atlas to Troubleshoot. 260
    Using Atlas Manager Command-Line Options 260

Chapter 10 Using ZENworks for Servers 2 Traffic Analysis 261

Understanding LAN Traffic Analysis. 262
    Understanding LAN Traffic Components. 262
    Understanding Communication between Components 263
    Understanding Agent Functionality 264
Setting up LAN Traffic Analysis. 268
    Creating a Baseline Document 268
    Selecting the Preferred RMON Agent. 269
    Setting up SNMP Parameters. 270
Analyzing Network Traffic 272
    Analyzing Traffic on Network Segments 272
    Analyzing Traffic on Nodes Connected to a Segment. 279
    Capturing Packets from the Network 284
    Analyzing Captured Packets. 287
    Analyzing Protocol Traffic. 292
    Analyzing Switch Traffic 293
Setting Up ZENworks for Servers 2 Traffic Analysis Agents 295
    Setting up the Traffic Analysis Agents for NetWare. 295
    Setting up the Traffic Analysis Agents for NT. 298

TABLE OF CONTENTS

Chapter 11 Understanding and Using ZENworks for Servers 2 Server and Alarm Management   301

Understanding Alarm Management Components 302
    About the SNMP Trap Receiver. 302
    Discussing the SNMP Trap Forwarder. 303
    Understanding the SNMP Trap Injector. 303
    About the Alarm Injector. 303
    Discussing the Three Types of Alarm Processors 303
    Understanding the Alarm Manager Database 304
    Information About Database Archivers 304
    Discussing Alarm Viewers. 305
Managing ZENworks for Servers 2 Alarms 305
    Enabling and Disabling Alarms 306
    Understanding Alarm Indicators 307
    Working with Alarm Views. 308
    Managing Alarms. 315
    Setting Alarm Actions. 316
    Deleting Alarms 323
Using ZENworks for Servers 2 Monitoring Services 325
    Monitoring Services on Target Nodes. 325
    Setting up Monitoring Services on Monitored Nodes 330

Chapter 12 Using ZENworks for Servers 2 Server Management   333

Using ZENworks for Servers 2 SMNP Agents to Manage Servers 334
    Understanding SNMP-Based Server Management. 334
    Discussing the ZENworks for Servers 2 Management Views 335
    Planning Server Management. 336
    Displaying Server Configuration Information 338
    Showing Server Summary Data 339
    Viewing Trend Data 342
    Managing Trend Samplings 346
    Configuring Server Parameters 349
    Executing Server Commands. 351
    Managing Remote Servers 351
    Optimizing Server Management. 354

Using ZENworks for Servers 2 Server Inventory 360
    Understanding the Inventory Server Components 360
    Scanning Inventory of Servers 361
    Customizing Software Application Scanning 363

Chapter 13   Making the Most of ZENworks for Servers 2 Reporting   367

Reading ZENworks for Servers Reports. 368
    Understanding Server Inventory Reports 368
    Analyzing Topology Reports. 371
    Understanding Network Health Reports 373
    Appreciating Tiered Electronic Distribution Reports 379
Using ZENworks for Servers Reports. 381
    Generating Server Inventory Reports. 381
    Creating Topology Reports 384
    Generating Network Health Reports 386
    Using Tiered Electronic Distribution Reports. 394

Chapter 14   Troubleshooting ZENworks for Servers 2   399

Troubleshooting Policy and Distribution Services. 400
    Reviewing Server and Agent Object Associations 400
    Distributor Hangs if License not Installed 400
    Subscriber May Timeout with Patching 401
    Distributor Only Sends to Concurrent Connections 401
    Distributor Building Corrupt Path Files. 402
    ZENworks for Servers 2 Policy Engine and Distributor State
    Cannot Find Database 402
    Software Package Distribution Files Are Received But Not Extracted. 402
    Error-Extending Schema in a NetWare 4.*x* Tree 402
    Extraction Fails on Subscriber Because Files Not Found 404
    Installing ZFS Agent Without Appropriate Java on NetWare 404
    Installing JVM Twice Causes Loading Problems 405
    RWC Port Remains Open after Exit 405
    Reports Print in Portrait Mode 405
Troubleshooting Traffic Analysis 405
    Verifying That LAN Traffic Agents Are Loaded on Devices 406
    Verifying RMON Agent Settings. 406
    Verifying Settings in the LANZ.NCF File. 406

TABLE OF CONTENTS

Verifying Settings in the LANZCON Utility 406
Additional Debugging Tips 406
Troubleshooting Alarm Management................................ 408
Verifying That SNMP Agents Are Loaded on Devices 409
Verifying Status of Alarm Manager Database..................... 409
Verifying SNMP Connectivity Between Management
Console and SNMP Devices 409
Verifying Alarm Thresholds..................................... 409
Receiving and Using Unknown Alarms 409
Troubleshooting Server Management 410
Verifying Connectivity between the Management Console
and Server 410
Verifying Remote Management Agent Is Loaded on the Server 410
Verifying Port Number for RCONSOLEJ 410
Troubleshooting NetWare Errors.................................. 410
NetWare Server File System Errors 411
Troubleshooting NDS Errors..................................... 412

Appendix A   Understanding NDS Changes for ZENworks for Servers 2   415

Identifying New Objects for ZENworks for Servers 2................ 416
Modified Objects for ZENworks for Servers 2....................... 422

Appendix B   ZENworks for Servers 2 Database Schemas   425

Understanding the Inventory Database Schema 426
About the TED Database Schema 432
Using the MIB Browser 436
Understanding MIBs... 436
Starting the MIB Browser..................................... 436
Viewing Tables of Scalar Objects 437

Appendix C   ZENworks for Servers 2 Console Commands   439

ZENworks for Servers Policy Engine............................... 440
TED Distributor.. 446
TED Subscriber 450

xxix

Appendix D ZENworks for Servers 2 Resources 455

Novell Support and Online Documentation 456
ZENworks Cool Solutions. 456
Novell Consulting Services 457

Appendix E ZENworks for Servers 2 Support Packs 459

Support Pack 1 460
    Problem: 460
    Current Solution: 460
    Resolution: 460
    Problem: 461
    Current Solution: 461
    Resolution: 461
    Problem: 461
    Current Solution: 461
    Resolution: 462
    Problem: 462
    Current solution: 462
    Resolution: 462
    Problem: 462
    Current Solution: 462
    Resolution: 463
    Problem: 463
    Current Solution: 463
    Resolution: 463
    Problem: 463
    Current Solution: 463
    Resolution: 463
    Problem: 463
    Current Solution: 464
    Resolution:. 464

Index 465

CHAPTER 1

Introduction to ZENworks for Servers 2

NOVELL'S ZENWORKS FOR SERVERS 2 ADMINISTRATOR'S HANDBOOK

This guide helps you through the potential rough spots along your delivery of ZENworks for Servers 2 to your system. It also explains a little bit about how ZENworks for Servers 2 functions and affects your Novell network and your servers. Chapter 1 introduces you to the purpose and advantages of using ZENworks for Servers 2 on your servers and in your network.

What Is the Purpose of ZENworks for Servers 2?

ZENworks for Servers 2 is a server management system that has been introduced by Novell. ZENworks stands for zero effort networks; the name reflects the minimal effort required for you to manage the servers in your network. By reducing the effort necessary to manage servers, the end result goal is to reduce the total cost of ownership (TCO) of dealing with the network.

ZENworks for Servers 2 focuses on several areas of server management, which are discussed in the following sections.

Server Management through Policies

A problem that many server administrators have to deal with is ensuring that all of the parameters on a server are appropriate and that no one has been messing around with those server's parameters. Additionally, they may need to change a server parameter on each of hundreds of servers. With ZENworks for Servers 2, the administrator can change that one parameter on all of the servers in your network with a single mouse click.

In ZENworks for Servers 2, the administrator can manage selected servers or all of the servers in the network through policies that are stored in your directory. These policies enable you to specify such items as server parameters and how a server should shut down (called a downing policy). As ZENworks for Servers 2 continues to mature, many policies that describe server behavior and response will be implemented into the product.

By placing these policies in Novell eDirectory (the new name for Novell's NDS product), ZENworks for Servers 2 allows you to enforce a common set of values and behaviors for the servers in the tree. You can associate these policies to any individual server, a group of servers, or to a container higher in the tree and affect all servers below that container. Changing a single value in the policy automatically effects change on all of the servers that are associated with that policy — either by direct association or by containment.

Currently, policies are only effective on NetWare servers. In the future, ZENworks for Servers 2 is expected to expand into Windows NT, Linux, and other server environments.

Tiered Electronic Distribution

In many environments, files and systems need to reside on many servers across a diverse network. Often an administrator must spend many hours or write many tools to transmit files across the network to many different servers. For example, you may have several application servers in your network — many in different parts of the world — and you need to make sure that the application files on each of these servers are identical to the golden image that you have in the network. Today, you have to manually copy these files around or write some homemade tool to do the work for you. With ZENworks for Servers 2, and, more specifically, Tiered Electronic Distribution (TED), these files can be easily transmitted across the world to all of the required servers.

In ZENworks for Servers 2, the administrator goes into eDirectory and administers a set of agents called distributors and subscribers. These agents, through the directory, discover the files that need to be transmitted across the network and efficiently transmit them across to the specified servers in your network. All administration of these agents is stored in eDirectory objects, allowing you to effect change efficiently and completely through the directory.

Once these files are received on the target server, the system invokes a local agent to unpack the bundle and deliver it to the specified file directories. TED can move any type of file through the network. TED can distribute files to both NetWare and Windows NT/2000 environments.

Server Software Packages

TED, described above, is a terrific way to move files through your network to be placed on your servers in the tree. One type of file group that TED can move is called a server software package. These Server Software Packages are sets of files and scripts that describe how the server files are to be automatically installed on a server. Can you imagine the savings if you can move a support pack for your servers through your network with TED and have it automatically installed on all of your servers? It's going to save a tremendous amount of time having the system automatically upgrade all your servers with a few commands in the directory.

You, as the administrator, simply go into ConsoleOne. Once there, you administer a server package. This includes the ability to generate a script to load or unload NLMs, log out users, and so forth, before and after exercising the installation of the files. You can describe when the Server Software Packages should be installed, on what versions of the server, and so forth. With all of this control, you are able to install the package with confidence.

As Novell moves ZENworks for Servers 2 to support other platforms, this functionality is expected to move along.

SNMP Services

The services that you have become accustomed to in ManageWise are in the ZENworks for Servers 2 product. The SNMP services that enable you to receive SNMP alerts and then act on them are included in the ZENworks for Servers product.

From within ConsoleOne, you can navigate through an updated map of your network, browsing for alerts and looking at the current status of any server or router in your network. This physical view of the world is seamlessly merged with the logical view presented in eDirectory, enabling you to move effortlessly between the two in order to quickly make any administration changes that require your attention.

Alarm Management Services

ZENworks for Servers 2 continues to provide the alarm management services that were provided in the ManageWise product. ZENworks for Servers 2 enables you to continue to set alarm thresholds on each of the measured attributes for your network or individual server. When these alarm thresholds are hit, the console in ConsoleOne displays the information and follows the procedures that you have outlined with regard to notifying the proper personnel.

Server Inventory and Trending

ZENworks for Servers 2 also performs inventory for each of the NetWare 5 and NT servers that are in your network. This inventory is stored in a ZENworks database stored on your designated server in the network. From this inventory information you can generate reports, with various options to help you get a handle on the hardware that you have in your network.

Additionally, the trending information is stored in ZENworks for Servers 2, enabling you to get some longer-term information on the performance and behavior of your servers. This enables you to anticipate problems before they happen and get the changes into your network before you see the effects of the problem.

INTRODUCTION TO ZENWORKS FOR SERVERS 2

Portal Services

A majority of the functionality of ZENworks for Servers 2, particularly dealing with a specific server, is manageable via the portal system that is supplied in the NetWare 5 product. Portal is an HTTP service that runs on a NetWare 5 server and enables the administrator to manage many aspects of the NetWare 5 server via a browser on any desktop. This can prove extremely useful when you need to quickly make a fix to a server while you are on your Hawaii vacation (couldn't pass up the chance to capitalize on the commercials!).

ZENworks for Servers 2 delivers the plug-ins necessary to be placed on the NetWare server that enable its functionality to be viewed and managed through the Portal interface. Not all functionality is available through this mechanism, but the ones that are specific to a server are usable from Portal.

Common Management Console

Ever since the development of ManageWise and its functionality that manages servers, users have asked why one has to run a different administration tool to manage it versus the tools used to manage NetWare and NDS. Over time, the ManageWise product has evolved and moved its database to the server, but the majority of its work has been on a dedicated workstation. Now its functionality has been moved completely to the server and the network, and its interfaces have been updated to run in the ConsoleOne interface.

ConsoleOne is the common administration tool that Novell is using to manage all of their products. NetWare is now managed through ConsoleOne, and now ManageWise functionality is also in ConsoleOne. Now you have to use and understand only a single tool to use and understand in order to manage all of Novell products. Also, by having all of the administration functionality in a single place, there can be some synergy between the server management and eDirectory management, enabling you to move seamlessly between the logical and physical views of your network.

What Is the Relationship between ManageWise and ZENworks for Servers 2?

ManageWise has been upgraded and moved into the ZENworks for Servers 2 product line. All of the server functionality that you have come to expect with ManageWise is present in the ZENworks for Servers product, plus some new features.

It is expected that the ManageWise functionality of ZENworks for Servers 2 will continue to be enhanced over time, and the ManageWise product itself will be phased out.

What Is the Relationship between ZENworks for Desktops and ZENworks for Servers 2?

The name "ZENworks" originally was released as the name of a desktop management system. Since then, ZENworks has turned into a product brand name for Novell, and the original ZENworks is referred to as ZENworks for Desktops.

ZENworks for Desktops is considered a separate product and will continue to have its own independent releases, development cycles, and feature sets. However, some overlap exists between the two products. For example, the ZENworks for Desktops 3 version has shipped with the ability to interact with the Tiered Electronic Distribution portions of ZENworks for Servers 2, enabling you to transmit application objects and files throughout your network.

ZENworks for Servers 2 uses the same Sybase database engine that ZENworks for Desktops uses to store its inventory and other information. ZENworks for Servers 2 actually automatically creates tables in its own database files (ZFSlog.dB) and uses the same Sybase engine that the ZENworks for Desktops installs. The two ZENworks products reuse several of the objects in the tree, and they both follow the same concepts of the policies. The only difference is that ZENworks for Desktops introduces workstation policies whereas ZENworks for Servers 2 brings server-related policies into the system.

We would expect as these products continue to mature that the relationships between the various ZENworks products will become more and more integrated.

What Are the Benefits of Using ZENworks for Servers 2?

Using the ZENworks for Servers 2 product in your network environments has significant advantages. The greatest benefit comes from the effect of leveraging existing information that is currently in your directory and combining this with the new components and tree extensions provided in ZENworks for

Servers 2. By building relationships in the directory between servers and policies that govern their behavior, enormous management potential is gained and is easily available to the administrator. Using the eDirectory tree and its hierarchical nature enables you to manage all of the servers in your tree from one place in the tree, or delegate to local administrators in subcontainers.

ZENworks for Servers 2 also is an easy extension of the current administration system. All of the administration requirements for ZENworks for Servers 2 may be administered via snap-ins that are provided and plug directly into the ConsoleOne administration utility. Additionally, ZENworks for Servers 2 uses the familiar rights associated with your tree to govern the accessibility of the features, protecting them from unauthorized users.

The total cost of ownership (TCO) dealing with servers can be significantly reduced through ZENworks for Servers 2. Not only can you be proactive in monitoring and repairing your systems, but you can also ensure that the latest patches and system parameters are being delivered and installed automatically on your systems. By this alone you should have considerably less downtime with your systems. Additionally, the work required to keep common files across the network up-to-date will be minimized as TED is implemented in your system.

CHAPTER 2

Installing ZENworks for Servers 2

One of the biggest keys to using software tools effectively is properly installing them. Properly installing a software product enables you to get started faster and avoids problems later. This chapter helps you get set up to install ZENworks for Servers 2 and then install its components.

We have broken down the installation of ZENworks for Servers 2 into the following main sections, which will help you prepare and install the product quickly and correctly:

- Prerequisite steps for installing ZENworks for Servers 2
- Installing supporting server software and extending the eDirectory schema
- Installing Management and Monitoring Services
- Installing Policy and Distribution Services
- Installing Migration Tools
- Understanding product guides
- Browsing the CD

Prerequisite Steps for Installing ZENworks for Servers 2

The first step you should take to make sure you're ready to install ZENworks for Servers 2 is to make certain your hardware and software are correctly set up. Before installing ZENworks for Servers 2, you should spend some time making certain that the following criteria have been satisfied and that your environment is ready for the install.

ZENworks for Servers 2 is divided into two general components: Management and Monitoring Services, and Policy and Distribution Services. A separate installation is done for each of these categories of programs — in fact, you can separately install each agent from each of these categories. Hardware and software requirements for both types of installation are described in each of the following sections.

Installing ZENworks for Servers 2 from a Workstation

The installation of ZENworks for Servers 2 occurs from a workstation connected to the network. The following minimum hardware requirements must be placed on the installation workstation:

- 200-MHz Pentium Pro processor

- 128MB of RAM
- 60MB of free disk space.

The following minimum software must be running on the installation workstation:

- Windows 95/98 with Novell Client 3.3, or
- Windows NT 4.0 with SP6a or later and Novell Client 4.8, or
- Windows 2000 with SP1 or later and Novell Client 4.8

Management and Monitoring Services

Management and monitoring services is comprised of several agents that are placed on various servers throughout your network. You may place all or a single agent on any of these target servers, depending on your desired level of monitoring for the target server. The following sections describe the requirements that must be minimally met for each of the different agents that comprise management and monitoring services. If you are installing multiple agents on the same server, the greatest requirement of all the agents is used. For example, if one agent requires 16MB and another 32MB, then you must have 32MB for any of the installation to take place even though some agents may not require it.

The following describes the minimum server and workstation hardware and software requirements to get the management and monitoring services components working on the designated system.

Management Server

The management server is the collection point for management data across the network. All of the information, alarms, inventory, and so forth that are captured from other servers are stored on this management server. You may have more than one management server in the network, and then segment your other servers to send information to their respective management server. Traditionally, there is only a single management server in a geographic area. If you have more than one server running the Sybase database for site management, you cannot merge them or report on them together. The management server must satisfy the following hardware requirements:

- 200-MHz Pentium Pro processor
- 256MB of RAM
- 165MB of free disk space. It is recommended that you have at least 8GB of free space if the server is the server designated to store the discovery, alarm and inventory information.

The following minimum software must be placed on the management server:
- NetWare 5.1 with support pack 1, or
- NetWare 5 with support pack 5; and
- JVM 1.1.7b dated 9/19/00 or later. A copy of this Java Virtual Machine (JVM) is found on the ZENworks for Servers 2 Companion CD, a CD in the ZENworks for Servers 2 CD set.

Server Management Agent for NetWare

The target server contains the server management agent, which collects statistics about the server and generates alarms, sending this information to the management server when administered targets are exceeded. This server may also collect statistics about itself and store the data for trending analysis. The following hardware requirements must be met to hold the agent:
- 600K of RAM
- 2.5MB of free disk space. You will need more disk space should you wish to perform trending on this server.

The following software requirements need to be satisfied for the agent:
- NetWare 5.x with support pack 1, or
- NetWare 4.11 with support pack 8a, or
- NetWare 4.2 with support pack 8a, or
- NetWare 3.2 with the latest support pack, or
- NetWare 3.1x with the latest support pack, or
- NetWare for Small Business 4.11, or
- NetWare IP with the latest support pack if using NetWare IP.

Traffic Analysis Agent for NetWare

This agent monitors the segment and performs statistical analysis on the traffic on the segment. You should only place one traffic analysis agent on a segment. The following are the hardware requirements for this agent:
- Processor meeting the NetWare requirements
- 620KB of RAM above the NOS requirements
- 1.5MB of free disk space. You will need additional space if you wish to perform trending analysis on the traffic data.

The following software requirements need to be satisfied for the agent:
- NetWare 5.x with support pack 1, or
- NetWare 4.11 with support pack 8a, or
- NetWare 4.2 with support pack 8a, or
- NetWare 3.2 with the latest support pack, or
- NetWare 3.1x with the latest support pack, or
- NetWare for Small Business 4.11, or
- NetWare IP with the latest support pack if using NetWare IP.

Traffic Analysis Agent for Windows NT

This agent monitors the segment and performs statistical and analysis on the traffic on the segment. You should only place one traffic analysis agent on a segment. The following are the hardware requirements for the agent:
- Processor meeting the NT requirements
- 620K of RAM
- 2.5MB of free disk space. You will need additional space if you wish to perform trending analysis on the traffic data.

The software needed for the agent is a Windows NT 4.0 Server.

Management Console

The management console is a desktop that runs ConsoleOne and contains the plug-ins necessary to manage the service and the servers. The ConsoleOne and the plug-ins for Management and monitoring services can be installed on the server rather than a workstation. The following hardware requirements are placed on the management console workstation:
- 200-MHz Pentium Pro processor
- 128MB of RAM
- 60MB of free disk space

The following software requirements need to be satisfied for the management console:
- Windows 95/95 with Novell Client 3.3, or
- Windows NT 4.0 with SP3 or later and Novell Client 4.8, or
- Windows 2000 with SP1 or later and Novell Client 4.8.

Policy and Distribution Services

Policy and distribution services comprise several components that can be installed separately on different servers. These components are such items as a distributor, a subscriber, or the database. Each of these components is not described separately, as was done previously in the "Management and Monitoring Services" section, because the requirements for the policy and distribution services components are all the same.

The following describes the minimum server hardware and software requirements to get the specified components working on the target server for these services.

NetWare Target Server

The NetWare server running these services must satisfy the following hardware requirements:

- Processor requirements for the NOS
- 128MB of RAM
- 135MB of free disk space. You will need more disk space depending on the number of distributions that this server is expected to handle.

The following software must be on the server:

- NetWare 5.1 with support pack 1, or
- NetWare 5 with support pack 5. SLL must be also installed and active for Remote Web Console, or
- NetWare 4.11 with support pack 8a. NLS must also be installed. Additionally, the IP stack needs to be loaded on the server. The following DSTRACE setting must be on: DSTRACE=LIMBER IP ON, or
- NetWare 4.2 with support pack 8a. NLS must also be installed. Additionally, the IP stack needs to be loaded on the server. The following DSTRACE setting must be on: DSTRACE=LIMBER IP ON; and
- JVM 1.1.7b dated 9/19/00 or later. A copy of this JVM is on the ZENworks for Servers 2 Companion CD.
- If you are going to install multiple agents on a single server, you need to take that into consideration as the system requirements will be higher.

Windows NT/2000 Target Server

The Windows NT/2000 server may only contain a subscriber as part of the distribution services. No policy management is currently available for Windows NT servers. The following are the hardware requirements:

INSTALLING ZENWORKS FOR SERVERS 2

- 35MB of free disk space. You may need more disk space, depending on the number of distributions that this server is expected to handle.
- There must be a share named SYS where the software will be installed.

The following software must be on the server:

- Windows NT 4.x with Service Pack 6a, or
- Windows 2000 with service pack 1, and
- JRE 1.1.8. The installation of the JRE can be done from the ZENworks for Servers Companion CD.

JVM Installation

ZENworks for Servers 2 requires that you install/update the Java Virtual Machine (JVM) on the server. The correct version of the JVM is included on the ZENworks for Servers 2 companion CD and can be installed from there (just launch the java\jvm.exe file).

NOTE To avoid an extremely long install of the JVM, you may want to consider renaming the JAVA directory at the root of the SYS volume. The JVM may take an extensively long time to install on servers with compressed SYS volumes. Be aware that some other Java applications may have added files under the JAVA directory and may not work correctly if the directory is renamed. An alternate way to get the install to go more quickly is to copy the SYS:\JAVA directory from each server to a workstation. This uncompresses all the files in the JAVA directory. Then, copy the whole directory, from the workstation, back over the top of the one on the SYS volume. When all the files are back on the server, they no longer are marked as compressed files and the install of the JVM will go faster.

NDS Connection for Installation

The client from which you install ZENworks for Servers 2 must have an authenticated NDS connection to a server that has NDS installed on it.

NOTE The ZENworks for Servers 2 install must use an authenticated NDS connection to install components. Even though a mapped drive using bindery emulation may give an administrator file access to the SYS: volume, the ZENworks for Servers 2 install will not complete without an NDS authentication because of the schema extension operations it performs.

15

NOVELL'S ZENWORKS FOR SERVERS 2 ADMINISTRATOR'S HANDBOOK

Installation Prerequisite Checklist

Once you have verified that your network has the required hardware and software, you should run through the following prerequisite checklist prior to installing ZENworks for Servers 2:

- Make certain that you are authenticated to the network as either Admin or equivalent to the tree. It is recommended to be the [Root] Admin to your tree.
- Make certain that you are authenticated to all servers you wish to install ZENworks for Servers 2 to.
- If you are running the install on a NetWare server, make certain that Java is unloaded by typing **java –exit** at the console prompt.
- Exit any programs that use files in the SYS:\PUBLIC directory.
- If you are installing Sybase, make certain that it is not running on the server during the install.
- If you are installing from a client, exit any applications currently being run.
- Set the screen resolution on the workstation from which ConsoleOne will be run to be at least 1024×768 or you will not be able to view the entire application screen.

Installing Server Components

Once you have verified the hardware and software prerequisites for the server(s) and network you plan to install ZENworks for Servers 2 to, you can begin the installation procedure to install ZENworks for Servers 2. The following sections detail the steps to install ZENworks for Servers in your network.

Log In to Tree as Admin

The first step to installing ZENworks for Servers 2 is to log in to your NetWare tree as Admin or as a user with supervisor rights to the NetWare servers and NDS containers where you wish to install ZENworks for Servers 2. You need to have Admin rights to the tree for the install to be able to extend the schema properly.

Map Drives to Servers

Because the installation process only installs to servers to which your workstation has a connection, you need to connect to these destination servers. Map some drives to these servers to ensure that you have a connection that is recognized by the installation process.

Install Supporting Software

To ensure that your JVM and ConsoleOne are the appropriate versions, you will most likely need to install both of these from the companion CD provided with ZENworks for Servers 2.

JVM for NetWare

Insert the companion CD and install the JVM onto any destination servers. Launch the JVM installation by executing the file java\jvm.exe on the companion CD. This prompts you for the server where you wish the JVM to be installed. Unfortunately, this install is for a single server at a time. You need to rerun the JVM install for each server.

ConsoleOne

From the companion CD, you will also want to either install ConsoleOne onto your workstation, if you are going to manage the system from the workstation, or you will want to install ConsoleOne on each of the servers where you may manage the system.

ConsoleOne is installed by launching the consoleone\ConsoleOne.exe file on the companion CD. Unfortunately, this install is for a single server at a time and you need to rerun the installation for each server. The drive mapping is important for this process because the install asks you for a directory to install ConsoleOne. On a NetWare server, ConsoleOne is placed in the sys:\public\mgmt\ConsoleOne\<version> directory. The ConsoleOne on the companion CD is version 1.2d and must be placed on the sys:\public\mgmt\ConsoleOne\1.2 directory on your NetWare servers. The same idea applies to installing this as the JVM for speed of installation. Some files are marked as compressed and may take a while to install to the server. Follow the same suggestions as were previously given to prevent the slow install of the JVM.

Launching the Install from the CD

Once you are logged in as Admin or an Admin equivalent, and you have drives mapped to each server, you are ready to launch the ZENworks for Servers 2 install. The ZENworks for Servers 2 installation CD-ROM is supplied with an autorun feature, which is automatically launched when you insert the CD-ROM into your client.

Extending NDS Schema

Once you have launched the install, a screen appears. From this screen, you must select the item you wish to install. The first step in installing ZENworks for Servers 2 is to extend the NDS schema to accommodate the new objects and attributes that ZENworks for Servers 2 requires. Press this menu choice and you are prompted for the trees that should have their schema extended.

Once you have extended the schema, depending on the size of your network, you may wish to wait to ensure that the schema has been synchronized to all of the servers where you expect to install ZENworks for Servers 2 components.

Selecting the ZENworks for Servers 2 Install

Once you have extended the schema, you should choose to install ZENworks for Servers 2. Before selecting the ZENworks for Servers 2 option, as shown in Figure 2.1, you should do the following:

1. Make certain that no other Windows applications are running on your client. This can cause problems later on in the install, which may force you to restart the install.

2. Make certain that none of the files in sys:\public or its subdirectories are in use. This can cause problems for both the ZENworks for Servers 2 install and the applications using those files.

3. Unload Java and Sybase on the servers you wish to install ZENworks for Servers 2 to.

4. Make certain that ConsoleOne is installed on the servers and workstations you are installing ZENworks for Servers 2 to.

Select Component Categories to Install

Once you have selected the ZENworks for Servers 2 install, a window similar to the one in Figure 2.2 appears. From this window, you have the option of selecting one of two categories of ZENworks for Servers 2 components. The following sections discuss the two options.

INSTALLING ZENWORKS FOR SERVERS 2

FIGURE 2.1 *Main installation screen for the ZENworks for Servers install*

FIGURE 2.2 *Installation category screen for the ZENworks for Servers install*

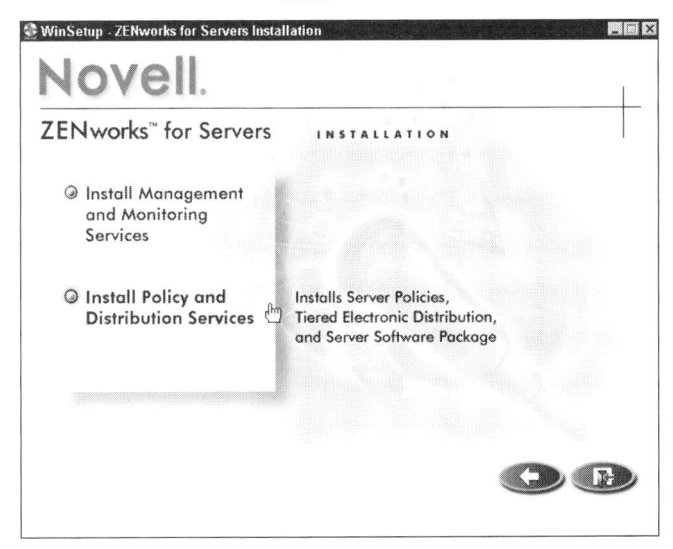

Installing Management and Monitoring Services

When you choose to install the Management and Monitoring Services, you are first presented with a screen that enables you to choose to install three parts of management and monitoring services. These choices include the following:

- **Install Site Management Services and Agents** — This includes the bulk of the services that can be installed on each of the different servers.
- **Install Site Management ConsoleOne Snap-ins** — This choice installs the snap-ins required to administer and manage the management and monitoring services.
- **Install Site Management Service License** — This installs the license required for management and monitoring services. This license is different than the license required for the Policy and Distribution Services and needs to be installed in order to have the management monitoring services functional.

Installing Site Management Services and Agent

This option installs the components required to perform the management and monitoring services. When you make this choice, you are first put in an introductory screen that reminds you to have extended the schema and to be logged into NDS or eDirectory with administration rights. You will next be shown the license agreement for the ZENworks for Servers 2 product.

Select Component Page

The next page that you are given enables you to choose which component of the ZENworks for Servers 2 management and monitoring services you wish to install. Figure 2.3 shows a sample of this page.

The following subsections discuss the installation of each of these components (Management Site Services, Server Management, Traffic Analysis, Inventory Management, and Remote Management).

INSTALLING ZENWORKS FOR SERVERS 2

FIGURE 2.3 *Component screen for the ZENworks for Servers Management and Monitoring Services install*

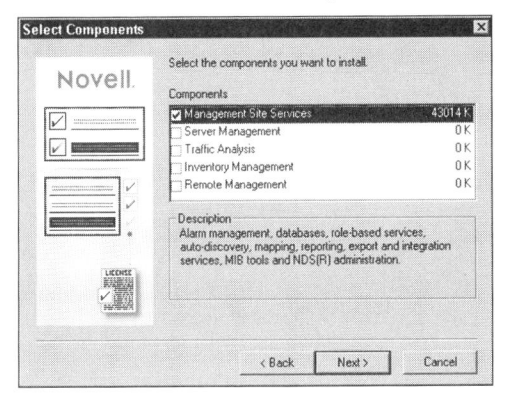

Management Site Services

Management and Site services are the software components that comprise the site server. The site server is the location where the collection of the database, discovery, alarms, and reporting are concentrated. This is the central server that is used to manage a site. Select this component and press Next.

> **NOTE** This cannot reside on the same server that has ZENworks for Desktops 3 inventory database.

License Path You are prompted to enter the path where the license is in the CD to activate the ZENworks for Servers 2 management and monitoring services. The default path should be fine, as long as the drive is the program CD.

Select Site Server You are next required to select the server that is to be the site server. Do this by pressing the Browse button and selecting the server object in NDS or eDirectory. You can select a volume object, which places the server into the server name and the volume into the chosen volume location. You also need to identify a site server number. Each site must have a unique site number. This site number is used in the consolidation of inventory and alarm data into a central database. The site number can then identify which site the data represents. The site number range is from 0–255.

21

Service Locator Objects   A service locator object in NDS or eDirectory identifies the site. To retrieve data and administer behavior of the site, you have to go through this object, so be sure and choose a container for the object that is within the physical locale of the site — keeping you from having to cross a WAN link to get to the object.

Database Accounts   When the database is created on the site server, there are three accounts: administrator, updater, and reader. The administration account has full access and the updater account has read and write rights, while the reader account can only view the data. Based on the various roles used in ZENworks for Servers, these accounts may be used. This screen enables you to specify passwords for each of these accounts. The passwords do not have to be the same, and they are stored in NDS or eDirectory and used by the services processes to access the data. You should change the passwords so that your database cannot be accessible by the defaults of the system.

Complete the Install   Once you have completed the setup options you are given the Summary screen. Once you press Finish, the system checks the Sybase database to make sure it is compatible and then makes the changes on the server in the mgmtdbs.ncf file to launch Sybase with this database. It also creates the NDS or eDirectory objects and copies the files to the identified management site server.

Once the files are copied, the install asks if you wish to begin the autodiscovery process. This can be a lengthy process, so it is recommended to not perform the autodiscovery at this time. (See Chapter 9 for more information.)

The system then asks if you wish to launch the back-end services on the server — these are items such as the inventory server, database, and so forth.

You are then prompted to view the README file and the installation of the management site services is completed.

Server Management

Server Management constitutes the software components that monitor and send alarms about a server. These are basically the SNMP agents that reside on the server to monitor the system and respond to commands from the site server.

Select NetWare Servers   On this screen, you can select the destination servers in the network where the agent should be placed. You must also select the agent, if it is not already selected, and modify the folder (under the volume selected) where the agent will be placed.

Select NT Servers   You can next select any NT servers that you want to also be monitored from this system. This also installs an NT agent to perform the management and alarm monitoring for NT.

Complete the Install   Once you have completed the setup options, the summary screen appears. When you press Finish, the system contacts the servers and installs the agent software on the system.

Traffic Analysis

Traffic Analysis constitutes the agent software that monitors a segment of the network. Its responsibility is to monitor and provide data alarms concerning the performance and traffic on the segment. You should only have one traffic analysis agent on a segment.

Select Site Server   You must first select the site server that is responsible for receiving alarms and collecting data from the given servers. Browse NDS or eDirectory to select the site locator object.

Select NetWare Servers   On this screen, you can select the NetWare server in the network that should run the traffic agent and monitor the segment. The NetWare server will need to have the agents restarted.

Select NT Servers   You can next select any NT servers that you want to run the agent to monitor the segment. Remember to only have a single server monitor the traffic in each segment. The NT servers will need to be rebooted in order to get the agent (service) running.

Complete the Install   Once you have completed the setup options, the summary screen appears. When you press the Finish button, the system contacts the servers and installs the agent software on the system.

Inventory Management

The inventory management system performs a hardware and software inventory process on the selected servers and places this inventory information in the Sybase database located on the site server.

Select Site Server   You must first select the site server that is responsible for receiving and collecting data from the given servers. Browse NDS or eDirectory to select the site locator object.

Select NetWare Servers   On this screen, you can select the target servers on which the agent is installed and running and have their inventory recorded in this system. You must also select the agent, if it is not already selected, and modify the folder (under the volume selected) where the agent will be placed.

Select NT Servers   You can next select any NT servers that you want to also run the inventory process and store the data into this system.

Complete the Install   Once you have completed the setup options, the summary screen appears. When you press the Finish button, the system contacts the servers and installs the agent software on the system.

Remote Management

Remote management software enables you to perform a remote control on the servers in your network. The remote control can be launched to communicate with a NetWare and an NT server.

Select Site Server   You must first select the site server that is responsible for receiving and collecting data from the given servers. Browse NDS or eDirectory to select the site locator object.

Remote Password   Enter the password that will be required from anyone who wishes to perform remote control on these servers.

Select NetWare Servers   On this screen, you can select the servers that will have installed on them the remote control agent and consequently will be able to be remotely controlled. You must also select the agent, if it is not already selected, and modify the folder (under the volume selected) where the agent will be placed.

Select NT Servers   You can next select any NT servers that you want to manage via remote control. You will also need to modify the share destination folder if necessary.

Complete the Install   Once you have completed the setup options, the summary screen appears. When you press the Finish button, the system contacts the servers and installs the agent software on the system.

Install Site Management ConsoleOne Snap-ins

This choice copies the additional snap-ins that are required in ConsoleOne to install the management system. The ConsoleOne listed on the page should be the ConsoleOne where you expect to perform your management. The path to ConsoleOne is dictated by the registry key:

HKEY_LOCAL_MACHINE\SOFTWARE\Windows\CurrentVersion\App Paths\ConsoleOne.exe

under the Path name. This registry key is placed in the registry when you install ConsoleOne from the companion CD.

Install Site Management Server License

This installs the license on the site server selected, enabling the site server system to function properly.

Installing Policy and Distribution Services

When you choose to install the policy and distribution services, you are first presented with a license agreement that you must accept.

Select Tree for Installation

The next screen in the install enables you to specify the tree in which you wish to install policy and distribution services. The ZENworks for Servers 2 install is only able to install ZENworks for Servers to one tree at time. Therefore, if you are authenticated to multiple trees, you must select one tree to update with NDS or eDirectory objects, programs, and files, and then repeat the install on other trees.

Install Licenses

Several of the policy and distribution components require that an NLS license be in the tree. If the licenses have not been installed from a previous install into this tree, check that the licenses should be installed and select the container(s) that will hold the license object. You can — and in many cases you'll want to — install multiple copies of the license to different locations in the tree.

Select Server(s) for Installation

Once you have selected the container(s) that will hold the license objects, you are given a list of servers to install the ZENworks for Servers 2 Policy and Distribution component to. You can select which server(s) to install Policy and Distribution Services to by pressing the Add button at the bottom and browsing in the tree and selecting servers to add to the list. There only needs to be one license object in the tree for all the servers to use, unless you have WAN links. In this case, you can put one license object at each WAN site.

You do not need to install ZENworks for Servers Policy and Distribution Services to every server in your tree—just the ones that you wish to participate in TED or manage with policies. Once you determine which servers you wish to use, select which components to install on the servers and click the Next button to continue.

> **NOTE** Make certain that you have verified the server hardware and software prerequisites for installing ZENworks for Servers 2 on all of the servers you check in this menu before proceeding.

The following components can be selected for each server by selecting the checkbox for the item:

- **Server Policies** — This installs the server policy engine on this server. This option must be checked for any server you wish to distribute server software packages to or want to be managed by policies.

- **Remote Web Console** — This installs the remote Web console on the server. You traditionally have only one RWC per geographic area, as it can manage several servers. This option is only available to servers running NetWare 5.0 and higher.

- **ConsoleOne Snap-ins** — This installs the snap-ins for ZENworks for Servers into the sys:\public\mgmt\ConsoleOne\1.2 directory on the server. Make sure that you install the ConsoleOne from the companion CD in this same place.

- **Database** — This installs a Sybase database on the server to hold logging of events from the various components in the network. This is a different database than the site management database. The Sybase engine still loads it, but it is a different .DB file.

- **Distributor** — This installs the distributor code on the server, enabling the server to run a distributor. The server may be both a distributor and a subscriber.

- **Subscriber** — This installs the subscriber code on the server, enabling it to run as a subscriber or a parent subscriber.

Select to Modify Autoexec.ncf

The next part of the install asks you to decide if you just want to create the objects for the selected components (because you may have installed the code there previously) or to do both the creation of the objects and copying of files.

In addition, you may choose to have the autoexec.ncf file on the server modified to launch the components after each restart. Also, there is a flag to pause the install if the JVM is running on the server. You will not want the JVM running, because that may cause the installation process to fail to copy some files to the server. You should stop the JVM on the servers now, if you have not done so yet, by typing **java –exit** at the server console.

Enter Volume for Database

Next, you need to select the volume where the Sybase database will be placed. It is not recommended that you store the database on the SYS volume because of the issues with the system should that volume become full. You should either enter in the name of the volume or browse for it by clicking the Browse button on the right.

Defining Distribution Routes

The next screen allows you to specify distribution hierarchy routes, enabling a subscriber to forward distributions on to other subscribers, increasing the scalability of the Tiered Electronic Distribution services. As you move subscribers from the right side into a route on the left, you are asking that the root subscribers on the left become parent subscribers and distribute to the subscribers they contain. You can specify a different route for each distributor you have selected. You do not need to define the distribution routes down to every single subscriber, only to the last set of subscribers that will act as parent subscribers.

These routes can also be constructed and modified later in ConsoleOne, should you not wish to define any routes at this time.

Create Channel Objects

As part of the distribution process, a distribution must be placed in a channel. A channel constitutes a set of subscribers. All subscribers hooked to a channel will receive all distributions in that channel. This page enables you to have the Installation Wizard create channels for you in NDS or eDirectory. You may also create, delete, and manage channels in ConsoleOne after the installation has completed.

Define Configuration Information for Distributors

The information on the screen enables you to set up the configuration information that is placed in the distributor objects. This information can also be administered in ConsoleOne after the installation has been completed.

For each distributor object, you can define the following configuration items:

- **OU** — The container where the distributor object will be created. Traditionally, this is the container where the server object is stored, but you are free to put it in any container. You should not move the distributor objects after they are created.

- **Working directory** — This is the directory on the server where the distributor places its files. Because of the issues with filling the SYS volume, you traditionally do not want to use this volume.

- **Log file** — This specifies the log file where the distributor records events. In addition to the log file, the distributor logs information into the database if it is associated with a ZENworks database policy. Because the log file may grow to be quite large, it is recommended that you do not place it on the SYS volume.

- **Console message levels** — This specifies the level of messages you want displayed on the distributor console on the NetWare server.

- **Log file message levels** — This enables you to choose the level of messages you desire to be logged into the file.

Define Configuration Information for Subscribers

The information on the screen enables you to set up the configuration information that is placed in the subscriber objects. This information can also be administered in ConsoleOne after the installation has been completed.

For each subscriber object, you can define the following configuration items:

- **OU** — The container where the subscriber object is created. Traditionally, this is the container where the server object is stored, because there is usually a subscriber for each server. You are free to place the subscriber objects anywhere in your tree. You can even move them around after installation is complete.

- **Working directory** — This is the directory on the server where the subscriber may place its files. Because of the issues with filling the SYS volume, you traditionally do not want to use this volume.

- **Log file** — This specifies the log file where the subscriber records events.
- **Console message levels** — This specifies the level of messages you want displayed on the subscriber console.
- **Log file message levels** — This enables you to choose the level of messages you desire to be logged into the file.
- **Parent subscriber** — You may choose a previously defined subscriber to be the parent subscriber for this subscriber. A parent subscriber receives distributions on behalf of the subscriber, off-loading work from the distributor, and then forwards them onto the subscriber. Every parent subscriber should have been added to a distributor's routing hierarchy previously in the installation.

Complete the Install

Once you have completed the setup options, the summary screen appears. This screen shows you the product components you selected and the size they take up on the server. If you need to make any changes, you can click the Back button; otherwise, click Finish and the ZENworks for Servers 2 install performs the following tasks.

Check File System

The ZENworks for Servers install checks for available disk space on the servers you requested to install to. If there is insufficient disk space, you are given the option to proceed. The ZENworks for Servers 2 install may install some files that already exist on the server. The older files will be overwritten. Therefore, there may be enough disk space to install ZENworks for Servers even if the available showing is less than needed.

Check Schema

The ZENworks for Servers install also checks that the NDS schema has already been updated. If no problems are found, the install proceeds.

Copy Files

Once the file system, schema, and NDS objects are checked and any problems are resolved, the ZENworks for Servers 2 install copies the files to each server selected in the previous menu in sequential order. A status screen lets you know which server is being installed and a percentage of progress to completion. Once the file copy is done, you can click the Finish button and the ZENworks for Servers install is complete.

Log Problems

All problems with the file system, schema, or NDS or eDirectory objects are reported in a log file and displayed on the screen. You can review the log file and correct any errors prior to continuing. The user only has the option of reviewing the log file if an error occurred during the installation process. If the install was successful, the log file is not displayed.

> **NOTE**
> We highly recommend that you carefully review the log file for all errors and review the readme file (available from the same screen). If any errors occur, at this point they will be much easier to correct than later.

Migration Tools

This option on the product CD enables you to access tools to migrate the database from ManageWise 2.x into the ZENworks for Servers 2 database. An additional tool on the product CD also enables you to migrate from a ZENworks for Servers 1.0 database into a ZENworks for Servers 2.0 database.

You may wish to do this if you have an exceptionally large tree and the discovery process is very long or you wish to keep your alarm data that is in the database.

Migration from ManageWise 2.x

Perform the following steps to migrate from ManageWise 2.x to ZENworks for Servers 2 management and monitoring services:

1. Extend the NDS schema to the new ZENworks for Servers 2 schema.

2. Install the Site Management Services Component of the management and monitoring services. During the installation, the system detects the presence of MW and updates the NCF files, and then prompts to restart the server.

> **WARNING**
> Do not restart the discovery or back-end processes during this installation.

3. Make sure the database engine is started on the site server. If it has not, run the mgmtdbs.ncf file. The database must be empty on the server.

4. Go to the ManageWise console and login as admin. Insert the program CD and install a license on the site management server.
5. Go to Migration Tools on the CD menu and select the Migration of ManageWise 2.x database.
6. Select the ZFS site server to receive the migration data.
7. You may restart the `netxplor` and `sloader` processes on the site server to continue populating the database with autodiscovery.
8. Start ConsoleOne after the migration is complete and choose the Atlas namespace menu, selecting Rebuild Topology. This rebuilds the maps into the new database.

Migration from ZENworks for Servers 1.0

Perform the following steps to migrate from ZENworks for Servers 1.0 into the new system. The Migration Wizard migrates all of the old distributor, subscriber, and proxy objects into the new distributor and subscriber objects. Perform the following steps:

1. Extend the schema to the new ZENworks for Servers 2 NDS or eDirectory objects.
2. Unload Java on each of the target servers by typing **java –exit** at the server console.
3. Choose this migration option on the program CD.
4. Select the tree to migrate.
5. Choose to install a license and give the wizard the container to hold the new NLS license.
6. To accept both options — migrating and removing — select the Next button. These options migrate the objects and then remove the TED 1.0 schema and software. You do have other choices for the migration tool:
   - **Migrate Now – Remove Later** — This migrates the data to the new object, leaving the original TED 1.0 objects and system in the tree. You will need to remove the objects at a later time.
   - **Remove Only** — This removes the entire TED 1.0 system from the tree. You will need to set up the distribution and new TED system from scratch, unless you have already done so.
7. Select the distributors to be migrated.

8. Select the target servers for the ConsoleOne snap-ins, the remote Web console, and the database.

9. The Migration Wizard now analyzes the selections and displays the results. When you are satisfied, press the Finish button to proceed with the migration.

Understanding Product Guides

This option on the product installation CD enables you to view additional documentation on the installation and product administration for ZENworks for Servers 2, in PDF format. If you do not have the Adobe Acrobat reader, selecting these options automatically installs the reader.

Browsing the CD

This option enables you to browse the contents of the CD in Windows Explorer.

CHAPTER 3

Understanding What Is Placed on Your Servers

This chapter and the following sections discuss the files and changes that occur on the server when you install various feature sets of ZENworks for Servers 2. The hardware and software requirements of the servers are discussed in Chapter 2. It is often important to understand the changes that occur on your systems in order to make good evaluations on where to install the system and to better know how the changes impact the service being provided by your servers.

Management and Monitoring Services

The management and monitoring services features of ZENworks for Servers 2 are broken into several categories for installation. Each of these categories may have different requirements and installs various system files on each of the designated servers. The following subsections discuss the changes for each area of the system.

Management Site Services

These services enable you to perform SNMP trap monitoring, which is using an SNMP management console to receive and interpret SNMP traps, on the systems and also provide the ability to view status and inventory information about each of your servers. The management site server contains the databases and the services software that is responsible for collecting the SNMP trap information and placing it into the database. Additionally, the management site server runs the discovery and the reporting software to provide information on the servers. Management Site Services are made up of the following components.

Alarm Management

Alarm Manager is a software module in Java that collects the alarms that are sent to it from the various server agents across the network. The responsibility of the Alarm Manager is to take the SNMP alarms that are sent from the various server agents and categorize them and place them into the database on the site server.

Installing this component places the agent on the server and provides changes in the AUTOEXEC.NCF to get the agent started. This agent is the host for the SNMP messages.

For more detailed information about alarm management, refer to Chapter 11.

UNDERSTANDING WHAT IS PLACED ON YOUR SERVERS

Databases

Several portions of the database for the management services are stored on the site server. An atlas or mapping database keeps track of the topology maps. In addition, entries in the database keep track of the alarms that are stored by the Alarm Manager.

This service installs an empty Sybase database onto the server and prepares it to receive topology, logging, and inventory information about the network.

Role-Based Services

In addition to the objects that are stored in the tree, some code in the system checks your authentication object and sees what roles you have in the system. Based on these roles, specific SQL statements are used to retrieve only specific items in the database. This effectively limits the scope of the devices that individuals can manage.

Additionally, selected functions can be given to these roles to enable users to perform management functions.

For additional information on role-based services, see Chapter 8.

Autodiscovery

As part of the installation, the Net Explorer discovery modules are stored on the management site server. These modules launch various NLM and Java components to perform the discovery of all of the devices on the network. Once the full discovery of the network is done and stored in the database, the discovery can be placed into automatic mode. Automatic mode enables the system to monitor the network to keep the topology and system up-to-date.

To discover more information about autodiscovery, see Chapter 9.

MIB Tools

Several MIB tools are also stored on the management site server. These tools are used to create and compile MIBs for inclusion into the monitoring and alarming services. MIBs are management information base text files that define what certain SNMP traps are and how to resolve them into English. This enables the ZENworks for Servers 2 system to be able to understand any SNMP device and decipher its communication and data information.

For additional information on the MIB tools, see Chapter 8.

Server Management

Server management is achieved by placing an agent onto the server. This agent samples various components of the operating system and device and then, based on the administered information in the fault management system, it sends SNMP traps to the Alarm Manager to notify the system when a reading is out of alignment. Additionally, this agent takes measurements of the system when requested and saves that information for use in trending and remote monitoring of the servers.

This agent also responds to SNMP messages that are sent to it from the management console to perform various tasks, including sending data for immediate views or modifying configuration parameters on the server.

Traffic Analysis

Selecting Traffic Analysis places a traffic agent on the server. This agent monitors the packets sent on its segment and records information about the performance of the system. Traditionally, you should only have a single traffic agent on a segment. The agent can be placed on either NetWare or Windows NT/2000.

Inventory Management

Inventory Management enables you to perform hardware and software scanning of your servers and has this information stored in the inventory database. This information can then be retrieved via ConsoleOne views on the screen or through reports that the system has performed. You can perform inventory management for both NetWare and Windows NT/2000 servers. Inventory Management is composed of the following.

Inventory Agent

The inventory agent is either an NLM or an EXE that is executed on the server and performs both the hardware and software scanning of the server. An additional agent is installed on Windows systems that, when contacted by the management system, performs the scan. When the scanning is completed, the information is stored in the inventory database.

Database

The inventory database is located with the management site services and is stored in the zeninv.db database file. This database is also loaded with the Sybase system on the management site server by adding the zeninv.db entry into the mgmtdbs.ncf file, which loads the Sybase engine. As the inventory agents collect data from the servers, their information is stored in the database. A report of the inventory information can be requested via the ConsoleOne snap-in.

Remote Management

ZENworks for Servers provides a Java remote console program. This program runs from ConsoleOne and enables you to perform a remote console, much like RCONSOLEJ. This requires that the agent for remote console be running on the servers you wish to control.

ConsoleOne Snap-ins

The management of your servers and the alarms associated with them is performed via ConsoleOne. In order for the system to properly manage the NDS or eDirectory objects, and to interface with the topology and logging database, several ConsoleOne snap-ins must be loaded. These snap-ins are stored in the ConsoleOne snapins\mw directory at installation.

Policy and Distribution Services

This set of services enables you to manage the server via policies in NDS or eDirectory. Additionally, these services enable you to activate the electronic distribution capabilities of ZENworks for Servers. With TED, you can transmit files across the network and have them placed on any server in the network that has a TED subscriber agent loaded. The Policy and Distribution Services are made of from the following components.

Server Policies and Packages

This set of software from the system enables you to manage your NetWare servers from NDS or eDirectory. These features include the ability to create policies in a server policy package and then have these policies applied to the servers that are associated with the policy package (see Chapter 5 for more detailed information).

The server software packages represent a set of software files that are constructed into bundles of server software (NLMs and so forth) that can be distributed with TED and then installed on the NetWare server. The package enables such controls as unloading and loading NLMs prior to installation and so forth (see Chapter 7 for more information).

The following sections discuss the items that are installed on the identified servers when this option is chosen.

Server Manager Engine

The Server Manager engine is a Java program that walks the tree looking for and applying policies to the server where this engine is running. The files that are required for the Server Manager Engine are stored on the SYS volume in the SManager directory.

The files in the SManager directory are a set of Java libraries and modules that, when run on the server, construct the engine. Additionally, several NLMs are also stored in this directory. These NLMs are helper programs that the Java applications call to perform actions on the server.

To be able to run the Server Manager Engine, each of the servers must be able to run the Java environment and load the several helper NLMs.

AUTOEXEC.NCF Modifications

In the process of the install, the AUTOEXEC.NCF file may be modified. It is modified to add the SYS:\SManager directory to the search path on the server and to load the ZFS.NCF file.

The ZFS.NCF file, when executed, starts up the NLMs required for the server to communicate with other servers participating in the ZENworks for Servers system and also starts up the Java system with the programs to perform the management functions that control policies being set on servers and software packages being extracted on the subscribers.

The system also starts up the pbroker.ncf, which loads the port broker system that allows all of the services to communicate over the same port number (1229), and then the port broker redirects the communication to the correct port for the registered service (distributor, subscriber, and so forth).

Remote Web Console

Remote Web Console is an HTTP service that enables you as an administrator to attach with a browser and receive HTML screens with information from the various distributors and subscribers in your network. The Remote Web Console communicates with the distributors and subscribers via the port broker software that is located on each of the remote servers in the network where a subscriber or distributor is located.

You can have as many remote Web consoles in the network as you want, but you do not need a remote Web console on every server that you are managing. You only need one in each geographical location, and from there you can manage all of the servers in the system. The Remote Web Console is started on the server with the sys\rwc\rwc.ncf file. If you chose to allow the installer to modify AUTOEXEC.NCF, this command is also added to start the RWC process each time the system restarts.

ConsoleOne Snap-ins

ConsoleOne snap-ins for administration of policy and distribution services are installed on the server or local workstation based on the installation choices. The various snap-ins for policy services are stored in the snapins\zen directory (ZENworks for Desktops 3 also stores some snap-ins in this same directory) while the Distribution services snap-ins are stored in the snapins\ted directory of ConsoleOne.

Policies Database

When you request that a database be placed on the server, the install checks if the proper Sybase engine has been installed on the server and if the ZENworks for Servers database is present.

The system makes sure that the Sybase database engine is installed on the server. This database engine is stored in the \zenworks\database directory of the volume you chose during installation. Additionally, the system installs the ZENworks for Servers database called zfslog.db. Although several different databases are stored for the ZENworks for Servers product, this one is the repository for logging the events and activities of the server management engine that enforces and applies policies and for the TED distributors and subscribers. This database can coexist on a server that has ZENworks for Desktops 3 inventory database, unlike the site management database file. The site management database uses a different version of the Sybase engine to load it.

During the install, the file SYS:\SYSTEM\MGMTDBS.NCF is created or modified to launch the Sybase database with the zfslog.db database files. There may be several databases open on the server at the same time. This is to enable the various aspects of ZENworks for Servers to access their separate databases at the same time. There is only one instance of the actual Sybase NLM, but the several different databases are simultaneously accessible.

Tiered Electronic Distribution

Tiered Electronic Distribution, also referred to as TED, is the system that enables the network to transfer bundles of files, called distributions, across the network to several server destinations. TED has been designed and implemented to be efficient in the network and to handle the scalability needed for the enterprise networks.

The behavior of the TED system is managed via NDS or eDirectory objects in the tree. From there, you can identify the sets of files to move and the destinations where the files should arrive. More details concerning the functionality of TED can be found in Chapter 6.

The TED system is made up of several Java components and some NLMs and DLLs that help in providing direct file support. From a high level, TED is composed of a distributor that sends distributions to entities called subscribers. The subscribers, when completed with the reception of the distributions, verify their contents and then activate software modules called agents who are responsible for the unpacking and installation of the distributions. The distributor and subscribers need to be active on the server at all times, whereas the agents are only launched when needed and are terminated when their work is complete.

Distributor

The distributor is responsible for sending files to subscribers throughout the network. The distributor is launched on the server by loading the SYS:\TED2\DIST. file. This NCF file starts up the Java system, if it is not already running, and starts up threads for the distributor process. The distributor then authenticates into NDS or eDirectory and collects the configuration information for itself and all of the subscribers to which it sends distributions. If you chose to allow the installer to modify AUTOEXEC.NCF, this command is also added to start the distributor process each time the system restarts.

Subscriber

The subscriber is responsible for receiving files from distributors or "parent" subscribers, which are subscribers who are told to forward files on to another subscriber. The subscriber is launched on a NetWare server by loading the SYS:\TED2\SUB.NCF file and is a service on a Windows NT/2000 server that is launched automatically at startup. If you chose to allow the installer to modify AUTOEXEC.NCF, this command is also added to start the subscriber process each time the system restarts.

Database

The TED system logs information into the logging database to enable you to run reports against the system. The TED system shares the zfslog.db database with the policy services.

CHAPTER 4

Setting Up ZENworks for Servers in Your Tree

This chapter provides a quick overview of the ZENworks for Servers system and a high-level view of the changes that occur within your tree when you install ZENworks for Servers. Be sure and understand this system and how it impacts your current Novell Directory Services installations. Other chapters get into the details of installation (see Chapter 2) and feature execution.

Understanding General ZENworks for Servers 2 Architecture

Novell ZENworks for Servers 2 requires some changes to your directory tree structure (namely, new objects and attributes in the schema) and installs the latest ConsoleOne along with the snap-in extensions to ConsoleOne that ZENworks for Servers requires. Additionally, several components are required on your servers to be able to use the system. This section details the changes that are needed to implement ZENworks for Servers 2 into your network.

Learning about ZENworks for Servers 2 Objects

When you install ZENworks for Servers 2 into your tree, it not only copies the executable files necessary to run the software, but it also extends the schema in your tree. The schema extension in your tree introduces several new objects and attributes to your system. Following is a high-level list of the changes to your schema. For a more detailed view of the schema changes, refer to Appendix A.

- **Application TED site distribution object** — When TED distributes application objects on behalf of ZENworks for Desktops 3, it constructs this object to help identify the distribution set to help TED automatically build the site lists for the remote application objects that are created. When TED unpacks an application, it stores the files on the server and creates an application object locally for that application. This object is then used by that service to construct and associate the various application objects into the site list.

- **Container package object** — This object collects for your administration all of the policies that are available to be associated with a container. You create one of these objects when you wish to affect a container policy. One such policy is the search policy, which affects the limit and order of searching for all ZENworks services in and below the container.

- **Database object** — This object represents the database in the network where you are storing such information as logs of ZENworks activity and events, as well as hardware and software inventory information. The service location package object refers to this object and can represent the same database used by ZENworks for Desktops. ZENworks for Desktops and ZENworks for Servers share the same database object, however, they each have their individual configuration parameters that can be independently configured for each product. There are separate configuration attributes of this object. You get to the configuration by pressing the "details" button.
- **MW account object** — This object contains the username and password that is used by the services to retrieve information from the management domain.
- **MW domain object** — This object represents the management domain of information (that is, the database that contains the discovered components in the network). All queries and reports against management information are referenced relative to this domain.
- **MW scope object** — This object holds an SQL query that retrieves out of the domain (database) the set of devices that a particular associated user may view and manage.
- **MW service object** — This object is an extension of the SAS object and contains additional information to identify the specific ZENworks for Servers 2 management service and relationships with the domain and other management objects. The services on the various servers, which need access to the system, log into NDS or eDirectory using this object.
- **NT server object** — This object is being introduced to represent an NT server in the network. Other NDS or eDirectory objects, to identify the server that has their service, can then reference this NT server object. Currently, this object stores the DNS name of the server along with the other traditional server fields.
- **Policy objects** — Several policy objects are introduced into the tree, representing policies that are contained in the Server policy packages. Currently in ZENworks for Servers 2, over seven different policies are created and used in the ZENworks for Servers system.
- **RBS module object** — This object is a container object that can contain task objects. This is basically a grouping of task objects.

- **RBS role object** — This role object identifies the set of tasks that a role can perform. The set of tasks is referenced to the task object or to a module object that contains a set of tasks.
- **RBS task object** — This object enables you to identify the specific task or functionality that can be performed in this role.
- **Remote Web Console object** — This object controls the configuration for the Remote Web Console used in communicating via a browser to the policy and distribution services such as a distributor and a subscriber. The object can specify such items as requiring SSL for the connection.
- **SAS service object** — This object may already be in the tree if you have SAS installed (which is normal for NetWare 5, but not in NetWare 4). This object provides a Directory Services authentication method for the agents and services that are running on the servers. The agents and services log into the directory via these objects. We discuss it here because it will be new for some systems.
- **Server group object** — This object enables the creation of a group of servers. This is useful when you want to apply a Server Policy package to a group of servers.
- **Service location package object** — This package collects the policies that are in the system that are related to locating services in the network. Currently these policies include the ZENworks Database Location Policy, ZENworks License Policy, TED Policy, and others.
- **Server package object** — This object collects all of the policies that are available for servers. The policies for servers in the ZENworks for Servers 2 product include such policies as the Server Downing Policy, the Scheduled Down Policy, and the Set Server Parameters Policy. Other server policies that are compatible with this object are also included in the ZENworks for Desktops 3 product.
- **TED channel object** — This object represents and holds configuration parameters for the channel, which is a logical grouping of distributions. A subscriber subscribes to a channel in order to receive distributions that are placed into the channel.
- **TED distribution object** — This object represents and holds information about the files to transmit through the network. The channel object refers to this object to identify the distributions that are sent. In a distribution object, you must identify the distributor that is performing the transmission.

- **TED distributor object** — This object represents and holds configuration parameters for the distributor on the specified server. As the distributor activates, it retrieves information from its object in the tree to autoconfigure itself. The distributor is responsible for sending files from itself to any subscribers specified in the system.
- **TED external subscriber object** — This object represents a subscriber that is *not* an integral part of the tree. This is a subscriber that is governed by an object in another tree. This object stores the IP address of the remote subscriber.
- **TED subscriber object** — This object represents and holds configuration information for the subscriber that is running on the specified server. The subscriber receives its configuration information out of this object through the distributor. The subscriber itself does not authenticate and retrieve this information from the Directory.

Existing Objects Modified in the Tree

Installing ZENworks for Servers 2 modifies the following objects that are already in your tree to enable the new attribute zenpolPolicy to be part of these objects: country, locality, organization, organizational unit, group, server, and server group. The zenpolPolicy attribute enables each of these objects to be associated with a ZENworks for Servers policy or policy package. These changes should not increase these objects more than 128 bytes.

In addition to the above changes, the server object is modified to also contain a group membership attribute. This enables the server to be associated with groups and maintain links from the server object back to the various groups with which it has membership. Depending on the number of groups with which the server is associated, this attribute consumes approximately 128 bytes for each group membership.

The NCP server object is modified so that it may contain an associated SAS service object. The service object is used to enable agents on the server to authenticate into Directory Services. This attribute should only take about 128 bytes.

Administration through Novell ConsoleOne

ZENworks for Servers 2 delivers all of its administration plug-ins into the new ConsoleOne management program.

Novell, Inc. has moved to ConsoleOne to provide a newer architecture for the administration of network resources. ConsoleOne provides a better programming interface for snap-in developers, easier management of plug-ins for administrators (no registry keys or memory problems), and, because it is written in Java, it facilitates the move of administration capabilities to non-Windows platforms. ConsoleOne is already available for NetWare, Linux, Solaris, and Windows environments, but the snap-ins for ZENworks for Servers 2 currently do not work on non-Windows machines.

The administration of ZENworks for Servers 2 follows the familiar method of administrating Novell directories. ZENworks for Servers 2 leverages all of the features of the directory, including inheritance, rights, and standard associations.

Discussing Policy Packages and Policies

To help in the administration of all of the features and policies of ZENworks for Servers 2, the various policies are conveniently grouped into policy packages. These policy packages are logical groupings of policies that are valuable for a server or service.

Policy packages may be associated to the various appropriate objects. For example, server packages may be associated with a single server, a group of servers, or a container. A single policy package may also be associated with several servers, groups, and containers.

Because each ZFS service looks for policies by searching up the tree from its corresponding object in the directory, it is desirable to keep this search from proceeding too far up the tree. Therefore, ZENworks for Servers 2 (along with its companion ZENworks for Desktops 3) includes a search policy found in the Container policy package. This policy limits the number of container levels and the search order that all ZENworks for Server systems use to discover and apply policies.

Various services are used by the ZENworks for Servers 2 system, and these services are located by the Service Location Policy package. This package is associated with a container and identifies where SNMP traps and the database are located, for example. The applications in the system then use the database that is specified in the location policy.

Starting Up ZENworks for Servers in Your Network

Once you have installed ZENworks for Servers into your tree and onto your servers, you need to do some administration to get the product really rolling in your system. This section talks about the basics that you need to do to get the product working in your environment. Subsequent chapters will discuss these areas in greater detail.

Starting Up Management and Monitoring Services

Several steps must be accomplished before you can begin the management and SNMP monitoring services for your servers in the network. The management and monitoring services require that several components of the system be up and active. These components are as follows:

- **Management Site Services** — This is the server that holds the database and receives all of the discovery information and the SNMP traps. This information is stored in the database and then other agents are activated to perform actions on the information. This must be a NetWare 5 server. This site server also holds the discovery and MIB tools.
- **Management Console** — This is the desktop that is running ConsoleOne and enables you to view the maps, statistics, data, and alarms that have been discovered in the system. ZENworks for Servers 2 installs a local copy of ConsoleOne on the administrator's workstation at installation time. This application is run on a Windows 32 desktop.
- **Server Management** — This is an agent that is responsible for monitoring the server and watching for events that warrant an SNMP trap. These traps are then sent to the management server. These agents are run on each NetWare or Windows NT/2000 server that you wish to monitor.
- **Traffic Analysis** — This is an agent that can run on either a NetWare or a Windows NT/2000 server and only needs to be run on one server for each managed segment. The data from this agent is also sent to the management server.
- **Inventory Management** — An inventory agent exists for both a NetWare and a Windows NT/2000 server. These agents need to be installed on each server and the inventory is transmitted to the inventory database, stored on the management site server.
- **Remote Management** — This is an agent that enables you to perform a remote control of the managed servers (that is, servers with the management agent on them). The Windows NT/2000 server agent is the same as the remote control agent shipped in ZENworks for Desktops 3, and the NetWare agent is a Java remote control agent you place on your NetWare servers. Both of these agents are controlled by an interface in ConsoleOne, available on your management console.

Other components make up these services — for example, the Explorer component that is necessary to run in order to discover the devices that are available on the network and construct a network map used in navigation in ConsoleOne.

To get the basics for management and monitoring services going in your tree, perform the following steps:

1. Install and create the management site server that holds the databases and is the target SNMP address. The target SNMP address would be either the IP or IPX address of the site management server.

2. Install the appropriate licenses to enable the services to begin functioning. You are prompted during the installation process to install licenses.

3. Install the management and monitoring services components into the tree and on each server you wish to monitor. This includes the management agent, inventory agent, and remote control agent (if you want all three).

4. Install the ConsoleOne snap-ins into your Management Console (that is, the workstation that runs ConsoleOne).

5. Create a SNMP Trap Target policy, if you wish to manage your trap targets through policies, and associate the policy with your managed servers.

6. Perform the discovery of the network by running the NetExplorer agent on the NetWare Management Server. Allow the system to find the devices (this usually takes hours, depending on the size of the network) and construct the topology map.

7. Log into the network via ConsoleOne on your Management Console workstation and drill down into the maps to view information about your servers.

See the additional chapters that deal with management and monitoring servers for more details and discussion on additional features.

Starting Up Policy and Distribution Services

Policy services enable you to control many behaviors of the server via policies that are defined in NDS and then associated with the servers. Distribution Services of ZENworks for Servers 2 enables you to transmit files through the network to various server destinations and have those files placed on the remote servers. The distribution is controlled via NDS, enabling you to easily manage the distribution services.

SETTING UP ZENWORKS FOR SERVERS IN YOUR TREE

To get policy management running in your network, perform the following basic steps:

1. Install the policy agents on each of the servers that you want to be able to manage from NDS via policies. Just because an agent is running does not mean that a policy will be applied — the policy must be associated with the server object in NDS before it is applied to the server.
2. Ensure that the file SYS:\SMANAGER\ZFS.NCF is part of your AUTOEXEC.NCF file so that the server starts up the policy engines on the server at each boot.
3. Create a Server Policy Package in NDS using ConsoleOne and turn on the specific policy that you wish to have applied to your server or servers.
4. Associate the Server Policy Package, using ConsoleOne, with the servers that enforce the activated policies.

Once you have the policy package in NDS and have it associated with servers in your tree, these policies are enforced on those servers the next time the agents refresh their policies from NDS. At a very minimum, you should set up a ZENworks License Policy in a Service Location Package and associate it to the containers where your Servers reside. This enables the policy services agents to find and access the ZENworks for Servers license. Without a license, the policy and distribution services agents do not function.

To activate the distribution services in your tree, perform the following high-level steps in your system:

1. Install the Distribution Services from the CD. When you install the services, you can specify where you want the distributor and the subscriber for your distributions. Traditionally, you have a single distributor send the data to several subscribers. The install also creates the objects in the directory for administering the system.
2. Make sure the distributor and the subscriber are running on the systems. The distributor runs from the SYS:\TED2\DIST.NCF file and the subscriber from the SYS:\TED2\SUB.NCF file.
3. Create a distribution. The distribution has a set of files that you would like to have distributed across the network. When you create the distribution, you associate it with the distributor (a particular server).

NOVELL'S ZENWORKS FOR SERVERS 2 ADMINISTRATOR'S HANDBOOK

4. Create a channel. The channel contains a logical grouping of distributions that subscribers can subscribe to. Make sure to associate at least one distribution and at least one subscriber to the channel.

5. Resolve certificates. The first time you start the distributor, it creates a public and private certificate set. The public certificate must be copied to the SYS:\TED2\SECURITY directory on every subscriber that receives or passes along distributions from the distributor. This is a simple process, but very important. You can right-click the distributor object in ConsoleOne and choose Resolve Certificates to have ConsoleOne automatically copy the distributor's public certificate to all the subscribers that need it.

The system should now activate the distributor, which collects the files defined in the distribution and then sends them on to the subscribers of the channel. The subscribers should then receive the distribution and unpack it on their respective servers. This happens according to the schedules for the various objects. Remember that the distributor agent needs access to a ZENworks for Servers license in order to function. For more information about TED, see Chapter 6.

CHAPTER 5

Setting Up Server Policies

This chapter provides discussion on setting up policies in the directory and administering them so they are effective on servers. Additionally, we discuss each of the various policies that are available with ZENworks for Servers 2 and how they each function.

Discussing ZENworks for Servers 2 Policies

ZENworks for Servers 2 introduces policies to the servers in your network. These policies are configuration or functional behaviors that may be applied to one or many elements or devices in the network. These policies function similarly to those introduced to the network environment by the ZENworks for Desktops product. The policies are placed into any container in the directory and then are either associated with a container, a group of servers, or an individual server. The agents running on the server walk the tree looking for the policies that are associated directly or indirectly to the server. The agents then apply the configuration and other features that are activated in the policies.

The agents in ZENworks for Servers 2 that look for and apply policies use the Search Policy that may be activated in the Container Policy package to determine the behavior of the search. The Search Policy may notify the agents to only walk to a container, for example, rather than to walk all the way to the root of the tree (potentially crossing WAN boundaries) looking for all of the policies. You need to be careful how you place policies and where the search policy is located in order to ensure an efficient and minimal walking of the NDS tree.

In addition to the server policies and the search policy (in the container policy package) the agents in ZENworks for Servers 2 also look for information concerning resources they wish to use in the directory. These resources are identified in the Service Location Policy package. This package is traditionally created directly after installation, but we also discuss this policy package and what resources are used in this package for ZENworks for Servers 2.

Understanding Platform-Specific Policies

ZENworks for Servers 2 allows the administration of specific policies for each platform that is supported in the ZENworks for Servers 2 system. By having a policy that is categorized for each type of platform, the administrator can make unique policies for each system. Each server finds the policies associated with it and executes the administrative configurations for that platform.

Sometimes you may want to associate a particular, unique policy to a set of servers that may be contained in containers along with other servers of the same type. You can then create a server group and then associate specific policies to those servers by associating the policy package to the group. You can then set up a Search Policy in a Container Policy Package to define that these servers receive the policies associated with the server group rather than those associated with the container.

Currently, ZENworks for Servers 2 has policies *only* for NetWare. Although policies are displayed in the General and Windows NT/2000 servers category, currently no policies are going to be effective on Windows NT/2000 — they are all be ignored because no policy engine is available for Windows NT/2000.

Plural versus Cumulative Policies

ZENworks for Servers 2 has both plural and cumulative policies available in the system.

Cumulative policies are policies that can be activated in multiple policy packages effective for the server. All of these policies would be applied to the server regardless of how they become effective for the server. For example, if a server had two effective server policy packages (one directly associated with it, one through a server group membership) and both of these policy packages have set parameters activated, then all of the set parameters in both of the policy packages could be applied to the server, depending on how you set up the effective search policy. Not all policies are cumulative policies. Not all cumulative policies are plural policies.

Plural policies are policies where there may exist more than one instance of the policy within the same policy package. For example, text file changes policy is a plural policy. You may create multiple text file changes policies so that several files may be changed by a single policy package. The plural policies have an Add button on their tab, enabling you to add multiple instances of the policy. All plural policies are cumulative, meaning that the plural policies from all of the associated policy packages are applied to the server.

Now you are probably wondering how conflicts in policies are handled. What happens if I have the same set parameter, for example, in several policies that are effective for a specific server in NDS? The result is that the last policy that is applied to the server wins. The algorithm to determine the last policy applied is as follows:

1. The policy engine walks the tree looking for a search policy in a Container policy package.

2. As soon as a search policy is found associated with the container of the server or any parent container (the first one found), the algorithm takes the search order that is specified in the search policy. The search policy specifies which types of policy package associations should be applied, which should be ignored, and in what order the associated policy packages should be applied.
3. If a search policy is *not* found, the policy engine assumes the default search order of object, group, container. It walks all the way to the root of the tree, looking for cumulative policies. You can see that it is important to set up a search policy to limit the policy engine from walking across WAN links.
4. The policies are then applied to the server in *reverse* order from the search order. In the default case, this causes the container policies, then the group policies, and then the object policies to be applied in this order. This makes the object policies the overwriting policy. If the search order is specified in the search policy, the policies are applied in reversed order listed in the search policy.

Setting up a Container Policy Package

In order to have a container policy package to affect the policies, you must first create the policy package. To create a Container Policy Package, do the following:

1. Start ConsoleOne.
2. Browse to the container where you would like to have the policy package. Remember that you do not have to create the policy package in the container where you are doing the associations. You can associate the same policy package to many containers in your tree. It is a good idea to have at least one Container Policy Package on every segment of your WAN.
3. Create the policy package by pressing the right mouse button and choosing New ⇨ Policy Package or by selecting the Policy Package icon on the toolbar.
4. Select the Container Policy Package object in the Wizard panel and press Next.

SETTING UP SERVER POLICIES

5. Enter the desired name of the package in the Policy Package Name field and select the container where you want the package to be located. The Container field will already be filled in with the selected container, so you should not have to browse to complete this field. If not, press the Browse button next to the field and browse to and select the container where you want the policy package stored. Press Next.
6. Select the Define Additional Attributes field in order to go into the properties of your new object and activate some policies. Press Finish.
7. Check and set any policies you desire for this Container Policy package and press OK.

The following subsections describe each of the fields and property pages that are available in the Container Policy package.

Introducing the Policies Page

The Policies page lists the set of available policies and those that are active. Figure 5-1 shows this policy page. Because no platform-specific policies are currently in the Container package, only the General page of the Policies tab is available.

FIGURE 5.1 *The Container Package policy page*

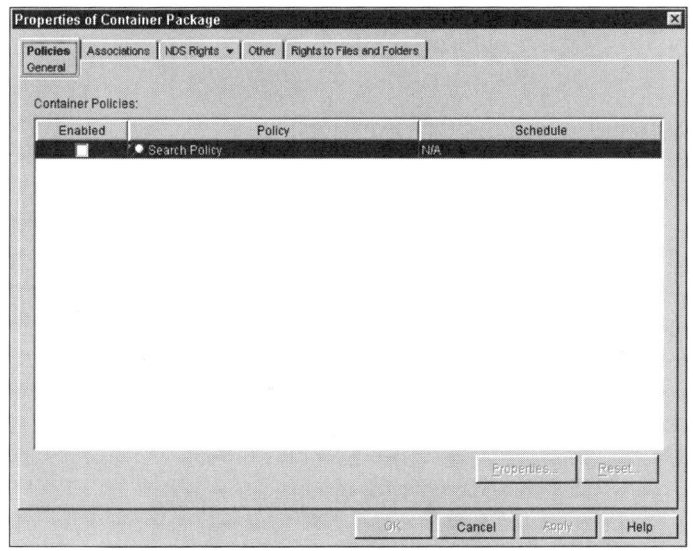

NOVELL'S ZENWORKS FOR SERVERS 2 ADMINISTRATOR'S HANDBOOK

Once you have created a Container Package, you can now activate policies. By clicking on the checkbox to the left of a policy within the policy package, that policy becomes active. An active policy is designated by a check in the check box. The details of any particular policy can be modified by selecting the policy and pressing the Properties button.

The Reset button on the Policies page resets the selected policy back to the system defaults for that policy.

Understanding the Associations Property Page

The Associations page of the Container Policy Package displays all of the locations in the tree (containers) where the policy package has been associated. These associations do not necessarily reflect where the policy package is located in the directory. The agents that are associated with servers that are in or below those containers have this policy package enforced. Pressing the Add or Remove buttons enable you to add or remove containers in the list that are associated with this policy package.

Defining the NDS Rights Property Pages

The NDS Rights property page is made up of three pages. You can get to each of the pages by clicking on the small triangle to the right of the page name, and then selecting the desired page to be displayed.

These pages allow you to specify the rights that users have to this object in the directory. The following subsections briefly discuss each of these pages. These NDS Rights pages are displayed for every object in the tree.

Trustees of This Object Page

On this page you can assign objects as trustees of the Container Policy Package. These trustees have rights to this object or to attributes within this object.

If the user admin.novell has been added to the trustee list, this user has some rights to this object. To get into the details of any trustee assignment (in order to modify the assignment), you would need to press the Assigned Rights button.

When you press the Assigned Rights button, after selecting the user you want to modify, a dialog box appears that allows you to select either [All Attribute Rights] (meaning all of the attributes of the object) or [Entry Rights] (meaning the object, not implying rights to the attributes).

From within the Assigned Rights dialog box, you may set the rights the object may have on this package. You can set those rights on the object as well

SETTING UP SERVER POLICIES

as any individual property in the object. The rights that are possible are the following:

- **Browse** — Although not in the list, this right shows up from time to time (especially in the effective rights screens). This represents the ability to view this information through public browse capabilities.
- **Supervisor** — This identifies that the trustee has *all* rights, including delete, for this object or attribute.
- **Compare** — This provides the trustee with the ability to compare values of attributes.
- **Read** — This allows the trustee to read the values of the attribute or attributes in the object.
- **Write** — This provides the trustee with the ability to modify the contents of an attribute.
- **Add Self** — This right allows the trustee to add himself or herself as a member of the list of objects of the attribute. For example, if this right were given on an attribute that contains a list of linked objects, the trustee could add himself or herself (a reference to their object) into the list.

If you wish to add the object as a trustee to an attribute you would need to press the Add Property button to bring up a list of properties or attributes that are available for this object.

From this list, you may select a single attribute. This attribute is then displayed in the Assigned Rights dialog box. From there, you can select the attribute and then set the rights you want the trustee to have for that property. A user does not require object rights in order to have rights on a single attribute in the object.

Remember that rights flow down in the tree and if you give a user or an object rights at a container level, those rights continue down into that container and any subcontainers until that branch is exhausted or another explicit assignment is given for that user in a subcontainer or on an object. An explicit assignment changes the rights for the user at that point in the tree. Inheritance rights filters may also be placed to restrict this flow of rights down into the tree.

Inherited Rights Filters Page

This page allows you to set the inherited rights filter (IRF) for this object. This filter restricts the rights of any user that accesses this object, unless that user has an explicit trustee assignment for this object.

You can think of the IRF as a filter that lets only items checked pass through unaltered. Rights that bump up against an IRF are blocked and discarded if the item is *not* checked. For example, if a user who had write privileges inherited at some point above (they were explicitly granted that right at some container at or above the one they're in) were to run into an IRF for an object or attribute that has the write privilege revoked (that is, unchecked), when they got to that object their write privilege would be gone for that object. If the object were a container, they would lose write privileges for all objects in that container and subcontainers.

You can effectively remove supervisor privileges from a portion of the tree by setting an IRF with the supervisor privilege turned off. You must be careful not to ever do this without someone being assigned as the supervisor of that branch of the tree (given an explicit supervisor trustee assignment at the container where the IRF is done) or you will make that part of the tree permanent (that is, you will never be able to delete any objects in that branch of the tree). ConsoleOne helps to keep you from performing this mistake by giving you an Error dialog box that keeps you from putting an IRF on the [Entry Rights] of the object with the supervisor right filtered away without having first given an explicit supervisor assignment on the same object.

Effective Rights Page

The Effective Rights property page allows you to query the system to discover the rights that selected objects have on the object you are administering.

Within this page (see Figure 5-2) you are presented with the distinguished name (DN) of the object whose rights you wish to observe. Initially, this is your currently logged-in user running ConsoleOne. You can press the Browse button to the right of the Trustee field and browse throughout the tree to select any object.

When the trustee object is selected, you may then move to the properties table on the lower half of the screen. As you select the property, the rights box to the right changes its text to reflect the rights that the trustee has on that property. These rights may be via an explicit assignment or through inheritance.

Looking at the Other Property Page

This page may or may not be displayed for you, depending on your rights to the plug-in that now comes with ConsoleOne. This page is particularly powerful and should not be used by those who do not have an intimate knowledge of the schema of the object in question and its relationships with other objects in the directory. The intention of this property page is to give you generic access to properties that you cannot modify or view via the other

SETTING UP SERVER POLICIES

plugged-in pages. The attributes and their values are displayed in a tree structure, allowing for those attributes that have multiple types (are compound types that consist of, say, an integer and a distinguished name, or a postal code that has three separate address fields).

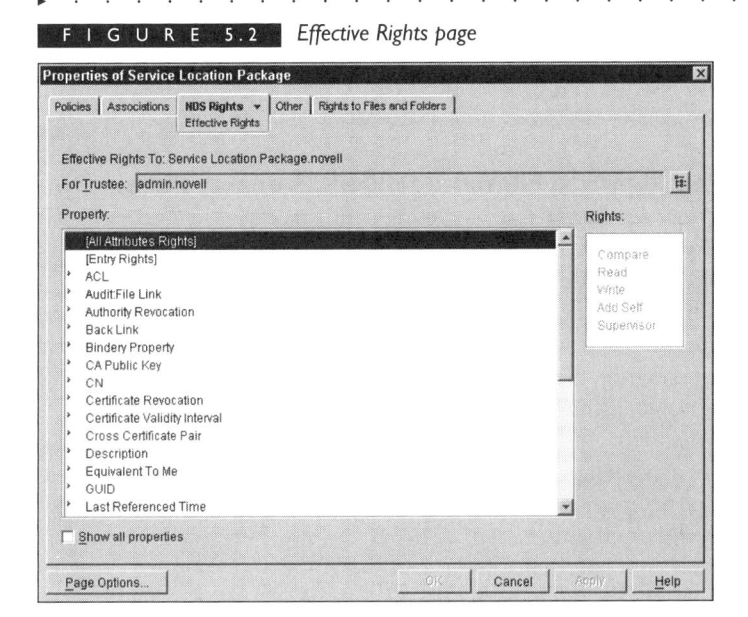

FIGURE 5.2 *Effective Rights page*

Every attribute in NDS is defined by one of a specified set of syntaxes. These syntaxes identify how the data is stored in NDS. For this page, ConsoleOne has developed an editor for each of the different syntaxes that are currently available in NDS. When an attribute is displayed on this page, the editor is invoked to display the data and then modify it should the user click on a specific attribute.

For example, if the syntax for an attribute were a string or an integer, an inline editor is launched enabling the administrator to modify the string or the integer value on the screen. More abstract syntaxes such as an octet string require that an octet editor be launched giving the administrator access to each of the bytes in the string, without interpretation of the data.

The danger with this screen is that some applications require that there be a coordination of attribute values between two attributes within the same object or across multiple objects. Additionally, many applications assume that the data in the attribute is valid, because the normal user interface checks for invalid entries and would not allow them to be stored in the attribute. If you should change a data value in the Other page, no knowledge of related attributes or objects or valid data values are checked since the generic editors know nothing about the intention of the field. Should you change a value without making all the other appropriate changes or without putting in a valid value, some programs and the system could be adversely affected.

Rights are still in effect in the Other property page and you are not allowed to change any attribute values that are read-only or that you do not have rights to modify.

Using the Rights to Files and Folders Property Page

This page in the property book is present in all objects in the directory. This property page allows you to view and set rights for this object onto the volumes and specific files and folders on that volume.

You must first select the volume that contains the files and folders in which you are interested. You can do this by pressing the Show button on the right and then browsing the directory to the volume object. Selecting the volume object places it in the window labeled Volumes. When that volume is selected, you can then go to the Add button to add a file or folder of interest. This brings up a dialog box enabling you to browse to the volume object, and then clicking the volume object moves you into the file system. You can continue browsing that volume until you select the file or directory you are interested in granting rights.

Selecting the file or folder in the lower pane displays the rights that the object has been granted on that file or folder. To modify the rights, simply click on or off the rights that you want to have explicitly granted for the object.

You can also see the effective rights that the object has on the files by pressing the Effective Rights button. This displays a dialog box, allowing you to browse to any file in the volume and having the effective rights displayed (in bold) for the object. These effective rights include any explicit plus inherited rights from folders higher in the file system tree. Remember that any user who has supervisor rights to the server or volume objects automatically gets supervisor rights in the file system.

Setting Up a Service Location Policy Package

A Service Location Policy package contains a set of policies that are associated with only containers. These policies are expected to identify the location

SETTING UP SERVER POLICIES

of resources that other ZENworks for Servers 2 agents, throughout the network, need. These resources are associated through the container to all agents that are working on behalf of the objects in the container and subcontainers.

For example, if you have set up a service location policy package associated with container A, and activated the database location policy specifying that the database is located on server A, then all of the server agents that are on the servers whose server objects are located in or below container A look in the tree and walk up the tree to find the service location policy package associated with container A. In this policy, they would find that the database where they should store their events or logging information is located on server A, because the database location policy in the service location package would be active. The agents would then contact the database on server A and send it their information.

In order to have a service location policy package to identify resources in the network, you must first create the policy package. To create a Service Location Policy Package, do the following:

1. Start ConsoleOne.

2. Browse to the container where you would like to have the policy package. Remember that you do not have to create the policy package in the container where you are doing the associations. You can associate the same policy package to many containers in your tree.

3. Create the policy package by pressing the right mouse button and choosing New ⇨ Policy Package or by selecting the Policy Package icon on the toolbar.

4. Select the Service Location Policy Package object in the Wizard panel and press Next.

5. Enter the desired name of the package in the Policy Package Name field and select the container where you want the package to be located. The Container field will already be filled in with the selected container, so you should not have to browse to complete this field. If not, then press the Browse button next to the field and browse to and select the container where you want the policy object stored. Press Next.

6. Select the Define Additional Attributes checkbox in order to go into the properties of your new object and activate some policies. Press Finish.

7. Check and set any policies you desire for this Service Location Policy package and press OK.

NOVELL'S ZENWORKS FOR SERVERS 2 ADMINISTRATOR'S HANDBOOK

The following subsections describe each of the fields and property pages that are available in the Service Location Policy package. NDS Rights, Other, and Rights to Files and Folders pages are described in the "Setting Up a Container Policy Package" section.

Explaining the Policies Property Page

All of the policies are activated within the Policies property page. Initially, the page is on the General policies. Currently in the Service Location Policy, no platform-specific policies are available, so no drop-down menu is present on this page. The Policies page lists the set of available policies and those that are active. Figure 5.3 shows this policy page.

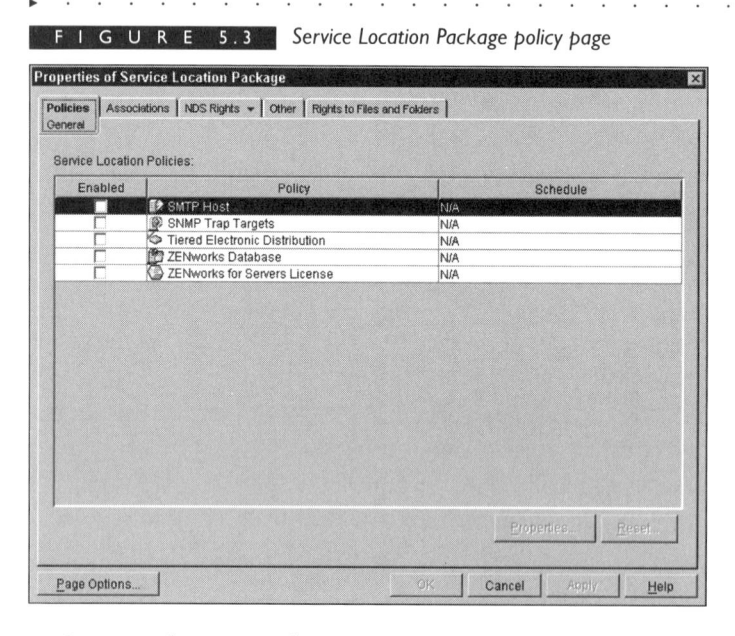

FIGURE 5.3 *Service Location Package policy page*

Once you have created a Service Location Package, you can activate policies. By clicking on the checkbox to the left of a policy within the policy package, that policy becomes active. An active policy is designated with a check in the checkbox. The details of any particular policy are modified by selecting the policy and then pressing the Properties button.

The Reset button on the Policies page resets the selected policy back to the system defaults for that policy.

SETTING UP SERVER POLICIES

Understanding the Associations Property Page

The Associations page of the Service Location Policy Package displays all of the locations in the tree (containers) where the policy package has been associated. These associations do not necessarily reflect where the policy package is located in the directory. The agents that are running on servers in or below those containers have this policy package enforced. Pressing the Add or Remove buttons enables you to add or remove containers in the list that are associated with this policy.

Setting Up a Server Policy Package

A Server Policy Package contains a set of policies that are associated with servers, either directly or by association with a server group or container.

In order to have a server policy package, you must first create the policy package. To create a Server Policy Package, do the following:

1. Start ConsoleOne.
2. Browse to the container where you would like to have the policy package. Remember that you do not have to create the policy package in the container where you are doing the associations. You can associate the same policy package to many containers, server groups, or servers in your tree.
3. Create the policy package by pressing the right mouse button and choosing New ⇨ Policy Package or by selecting the Policy Package icon on the toolbar.
4. Select the Server Policy Package object in the Wizard panel and press Next.
5. Enter the desired name of the package in the Policy Package Name field and select the container where you want the package to be located. The Container field will already by filled in with the selected container, so you should not have to browse to complete this field. If not, then press the Browse button next to the field and browse to and select the container where you want the policy object stored. Press Next.
6. Select Define Additional Attributes checkbox in order to go into the properties of your new object and activate some policies. Press Finish.
7. Check and set any policies you desire for this Server Policy package and press OK.

63

The following subsections describe each of the fields and property pages that are available in the Server Policy package. NDS Rights, Other, and Rights to Files and Folders pages are described in the "Setting Up a Container Policy Package" section.

Using the Policies Property Page

All of the policies for servers are activated within the Policies property page. Initially, the page is on the General policies. As other platforms are selected, additional policies are displayed. You can select which platform to display by placing the mouse over the small triangle to the right of the word "Policies" in the tab (see the next few sections for specifics). This activates a drop-down menu that enables you to select which platform-specific page you wish to display. Remember that no policy engine for Windows NT/2000 servers currently is available, even though a platform-specific page for Windows NT/2000 servers is.

Once you have created a Server Policy Package, you can activate policies. By clicking on the checkbox to the left of a policy within the policy package, that policy becomes active. An active policy is designated with a check in the checkbox. The details of any particular policy are modified by selecting the policy and then pressing the Properties button.

The Reset button on the Policies page resets the selected policy back to the system defaults for that policy.

The following sections briefly discuss each of the policy pages, and then we cover the specifics of each policy.

General Policies

When you first go into the properties of the server policy package, you are presented with the Policies property page. The policy page first displays the General category. All of the policies that are activated in the General category will be active for *all* server platforms supported by ZENworks for Servers 2 (currently, NetWare is the only supported platform for policies — distributions can be sent to both NetWare and Windows NT/2000) that have this policy package associated, either directly or indirectly. Currently, the policies that are available for all platforms are Server Down Process and ZENworks for Servers 2 policies. The plural policies that are available for all platforms (by pressing the Add button) are Scheduled Down Policy, Scheduled Load/Unload Policy, Server Scripts Policy, and Text File Change Policy.

Figure 5.4 shows the initial property page of the workstation policy package.

SETTING UP SERVER POLICIES

FIGURE 5.4 *Server Policy Package, Policies General property page*

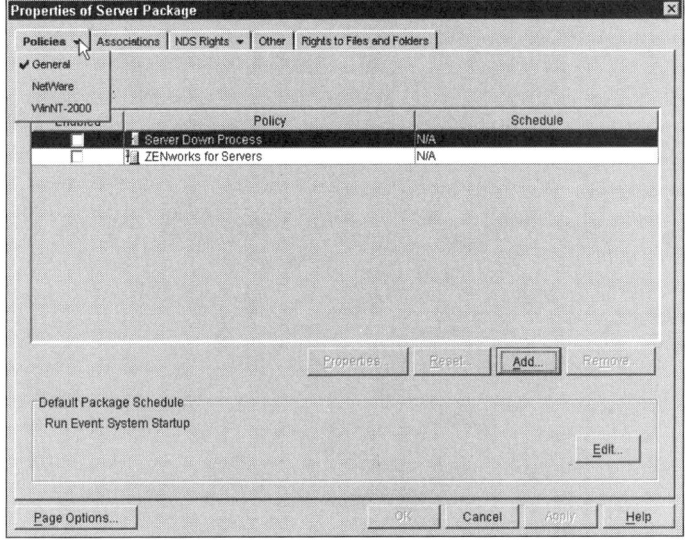

[Screenshot: Properties of Server Package dialog showing Policies tab with General subtab selected. Lists "Server Down Process" and "ZENworks for Servers" policies with N/A schedule. Default Package Schedule: Run Event: System Startup.]

As you can see from the image, currently two policies are available to all of the platforms supported by ZENworks for Servers 2: Server Down Process and ZENworks for Servers (configuration policy). These, as well as all of the other policies, are discussed later in this chapter.

In order to activate a policy, you simply need to check the box to the left of the policy by clicking on the box with the left mouse button. You can then go into the details of the policy and set additional configuration parameters on that specific policy.

NetWare Policies

Within the Policies tab, you can select the NetWare policy page. This page displays the policies that are available for NetWare servers. These policies include Server Down Process, SNMP Community Strings, SNMP Target Refresh, and ZENworks for Servers. The plural policies that are available for the NetWare platform (by pressing the Add button) are NetWare Set Parameters Policy, Scheduled Down Policy, Scheduled Load/Unload Policy, Server Scripts Policy, and Text File Change Policy. See Figure 5.5 for a sample of the NetWare policies page.

FIGURE 5.5 *Server Policy Package, NetWare Policies property page*

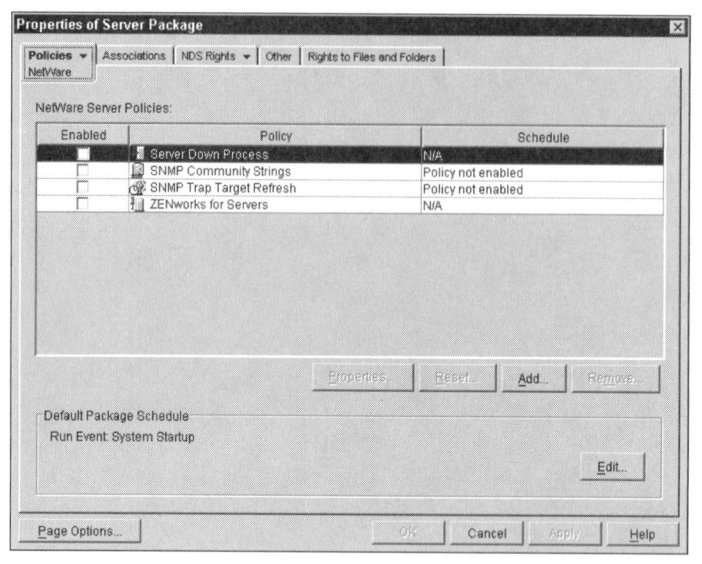

As you can see, some of the same policies are available under both the General and the NetWare policies pages. When you select a policy in the NetWare page, it supersedes any selections that may have been on the General tab for that platform. The policies are not merged together, but only the platform-specific policy is used instead of the policy set in the General category. Also, only the policies selected in the platform-specific tab are used in place of the General policies. For example, if the Server Down Process policy is selected in the General tab and in the NetWare tab, agents on a NetWare system use the NetWare-specific Server Down Process policy rather than the policy in the General tab.

Windows NT/2000 Policies

Although this page is shown in Figure 5.6, for ZENworks for Servers 2, no policy engine for Windows NT/2000 is available, so these policies will not function.

SETTING UP SERVER POLICIES

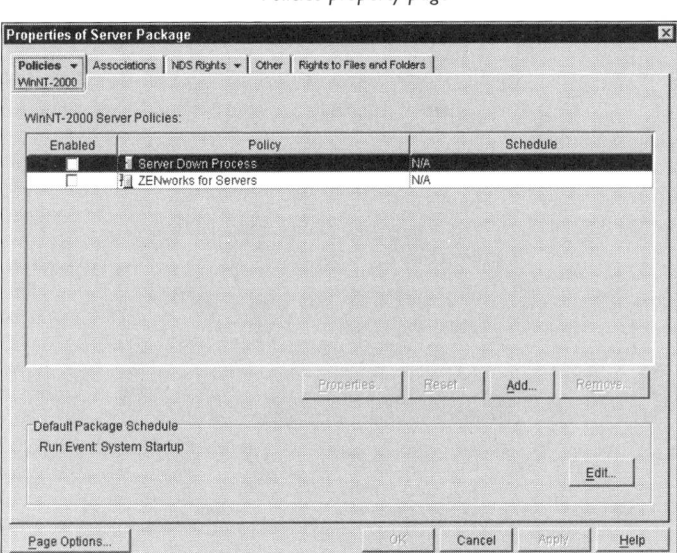

FIGURE 5.6 *Server Policy Package, Windows NT-2000 Policies property page*

Setting Up a Container Policy Package — Search Policy

A Search Policy governs the behavior of the ZENworks for Servers 2 agents as they search for all other policies. With all of the ZENworks for Servers 2 agents, there could be some significant walking of the tree as they search for the policies, especially if the tree is of a significant depth. This is the reason why ZENworks for Servers 2 has this search policy. Often, the performance of your network searching with ZENworks for Servers 2 is not significant until you cross a partition boundary. When you cross a partition boundary, the system must make a connection and authenticate to another server. This is particularly time-consuming should the system need to cross a WAN link.

The search policy tells the ZENworks for Servers 2 agents how far up the tree they should search and what order (object, group, container) should be followed to find the policies. Remember that the order is significant because often the first policy found governs the behavior of the system.

67

NDS Rights, Other, and Rights to Files and Folders pages are described in the "Setting up a Container Policy Package" section.

Looking at the Search Level Page

This page allows the administrator to identify how far up the tree the ZENworks for Servers agents should traverse in their search for policies. Figure 5.7 shows this page.

FIGURE 5.7 *Search Level page of a Search Policy within a Container Policy package*

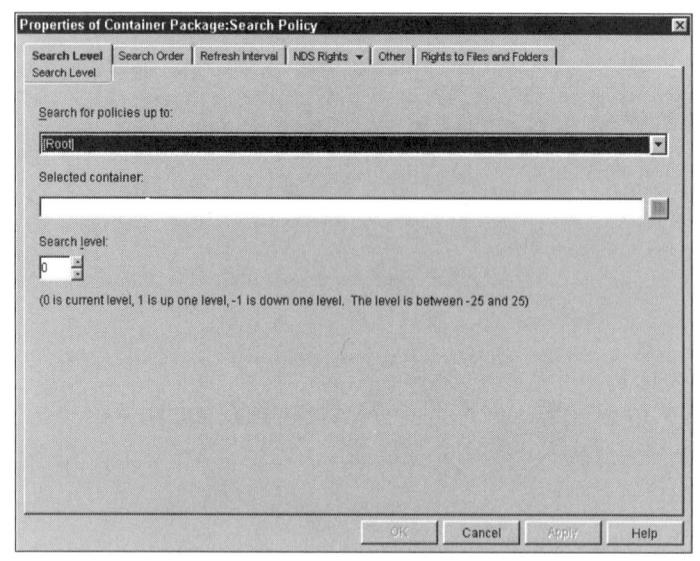

The following fields may be administered in the Search Level features of the Search Order policy:

- **Search for policies up to** — This field allows you to specify the container in the tree that will complete the search. The choices that can be made through the drop-down list may be any of the following:
  - **[Root]** — Search up to the root of the tree.
  - **Object Container** — Search up to the container that holds the object that is associated with the policy. For example, if you were searching for a server policy package, the object container would be the context of the server object.

- **Partition** — Search up the tree to a partition boundary. Crossing a partition boundary causes connections to other systems in the tree. This option is available for performance considerations.
  - **Selected Container** — This searches up to the specified container. When this option is chosen, the "Selected container" field is activated and you can then browse in this field to the desired container.
  - **Search level** — This field enables you to specify an additional level of containment beyond that given in the "Search for policies up to:" field. A search-level value of 0 causes searches to be limited to the specified container. A search level of a positive numerical value enables searching up to the specified container and then continues searching upward the number of levels specified by the positive number. Should the search level be a negative number, the search only proceeds up to the number of levels specified below the specified container. For example, if the value of Object Container were selected and the object is in the Provo.Utah.Novell container and the search level is 0, the searching stops at the Provo.Utah.Novell container. If the search level is 2, the searching continues to the Novell container. If the search level is –1, no policy is found because the object container is already above the search level.

At first, it may seem that no reason exists for having a negative search level, but there is some value in having this option. Suppose that your tree is set up such as Organization.Region.Company, where Organization is the container that is given to each organization in the company and Region represents the area of the company. Now suppose that you want policies to only be effective for each organization. You could set up one single search policy at the Region.Company level with a selected container as Region.Company and a search level of –1. This would enable each organization to have a customized policy and ensure that no organization's policies would impact another because the search would stop at the Organization level.

Describing the Search Order Page

This page allows the administrator to identify the order that the agents should go looking for policies. The default is object, then group, then container. This policy enables the administrator to change this order.

You can modify the search order by selecting the item in the search order list and then pushing the up or down arrows to rearrange the list. Pressing the Remove button removes the selected association type. Pressing the Add button adds that association type to the search order.

Since the first policy that is found has the greatest significance in the behavior of the system, you should be sure that you have the order set (from top to bottom) in the way that you want to find that first policy.

You should be aware that it is a good idea to use the search order policy. Because many ZENworks for Servers 2 features stop walking up the tree when a policy is found, it is wise to make policies search on object, container, and then group. This is because the proximity of these objects in the tree is always going to be closer to the partition on the server. The object is obviously always the closest in the tree to the server object. Next, the container is the closest in the tree-walking scenario because the container must be known in order for the object to be found in the tree. Consequently, the container is very close in the local replica to the object. Groups, however, can be stored in any container, and they could be in a completely different part of the tree than the object. Therefore, the amount of walking of the tree that is potential with a group is significant. With any significant walk of the tree there is a corresponding performance cost, and you should consider this as you manage your tree and search policies.

Understanding the Refresh Interval Page

This policy page enables the administrator to identify if the Policy Manager should refresh the set of policies from NDS and how often to check NDS for new or changed policies. The Policy Manager in ZENworks for Servers 2 is an agent that resides on the server and is responsible for getting ZENworks for Servers 2 policies and enforcing them on the server. This page gives this refresh interval configuration to this agent. If the checkbox is off, meaning the agent should not refresh from NDS, the agent only gets the policies at initialization time — and only again should the server or the agent be restarted. If the checkbox is checked, the agent checks for any changes or new policies every time the interval has passed.

Setting Up a Service Location Policy Package — The SMTP Host Policy

Several of the features in ZENworks for Servers 2 include the ability to have information and events e-mailed to identified users. In order to send the e-mail, the agents must contact the SMTP server in your environment and will send the e-mail through that system. This policy allows you to specify the IP

SETTING UP SERVER POLICIES

address of the SMTP host that the agents associated with this policy (through inheritance) will use.

The "Setting Up a Container Policy Package" section describes NDS Rights, Other, and Rights to Files and Folders pages.

The SMTP Host page allows the administrator to identify the IP address of the SMTP mail server in their environment. Figure 5.8 shows this page.

FIGURE 5.8 *SMTP Host page in the SMTP Host Policy of the Service Location Policy Package*

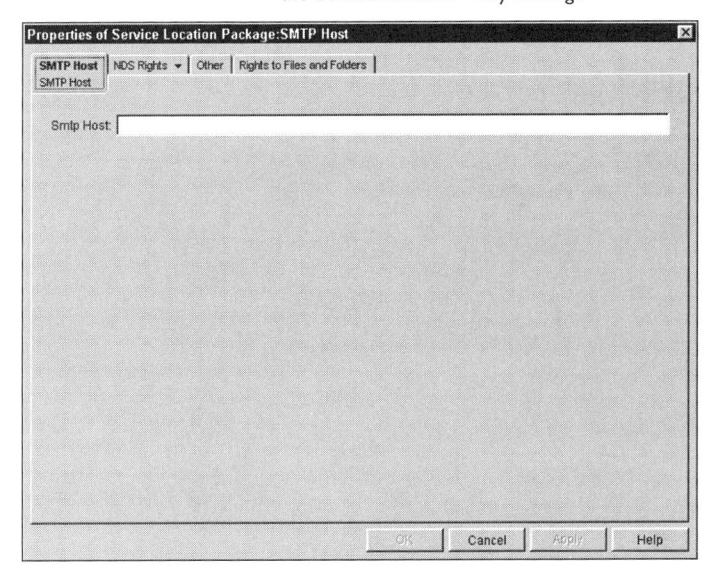

Just place your cursor on the SMTP Host field and enter the IP address of the SMTP mail host. This field saves only the IP address. You can type in the DNS name of the SMTP host, but it will be saved as the IP address. The field queries DNS to resolve the IP address and then saves that address here.

Setting Up a Service Location Policy Package — The SNMP Trap Target Policy

In ZENworks for Servers 2, several agents send an SNMP message to a central server that stores these messages and enables you to print reports on the

71

NOVELL'S ZENWORKS FOR SERVERS 2 ADMINISTRATOR'S HANDBOOK

traps. These traps can identify whether a policy has been successfully applied, whether a distribution was sent successfully, and other potential successes and failures.

The SNMP Trap Target policy identifies the location of the service that is accepting and recording the SNMP messages from the server agents.

NDS Rights, Other, and Rights to Files and Folders pages are described in the "Setting up a Container Policy Package" section.

Figure 5.9 displays the Trap Target policy page. The service on the workstation walks the tree to find this policy and uses the service location stored in this policy as the destination of the SNMP messages.

FIGURE 5.9 *SNMP Trap Target policy page of the Service Location Policy Package*

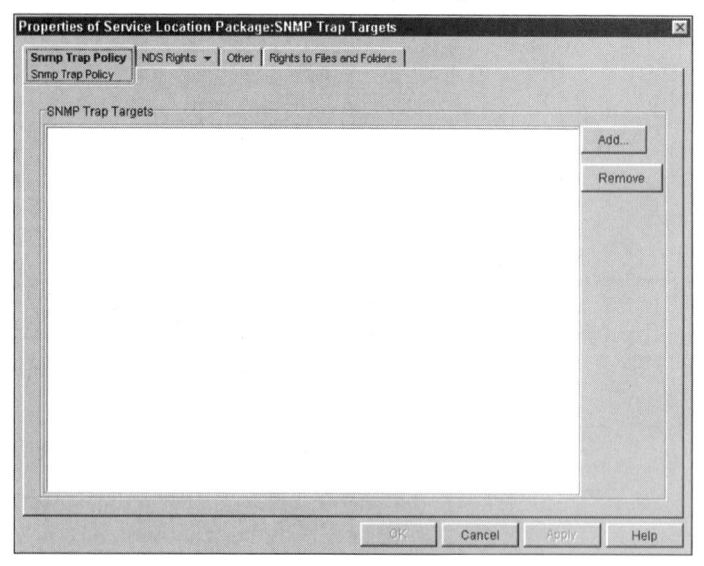

Once you have brought up the policy page, you may add as many trap targets as you desire. The service on the server sends the SNMP message to all of the specified trap targets. Press the Add button and specify whether the destination can be achieved with an IP address, an IPX address, or a DNS name. After selecting the type, a dialog box appears in which you can enter either the address or the DNS name of the target service.

Setting Up a Service Location Policy Package — The Tiered Electronic Distribution Policy

In a ZENworks for Servers 2 TED system, you can define several configuration items in this policy that will be applied to the components in the TED system. Using this policy keeps you from having to administer these items in each of the subscribers or distributors that you create in the network.

The "Setting Up a Container Policy Package" section describes NDS Rights and Other pages

Understanding the Settings Policy Page

This page is found under the General tab and represents some general configuration settings that are effective for any associated distributors and/or subscribers. Figure 5.10 shows this page.

FIGURE 5.10 *Settings property page of a Tiered Electronic Distribution policy object*

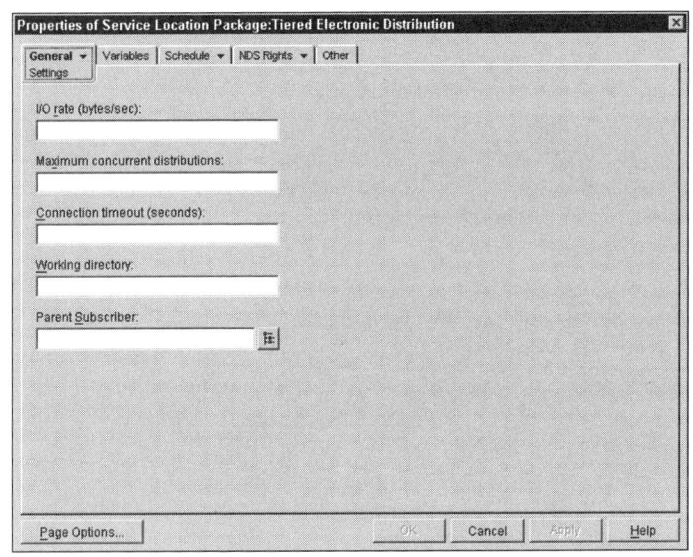

On this property page, you may enter the following settings:

- **I/O rate** — This represents the number of bytes per second that you will allow a distributor or subscriber to consume for all distributions for input and for output, independently. The default is for the system to send at the maximum rate possible on the server. For example, if you choose to enter 4096, associated subscribers and distributors will not exceed sending 4K per second to all subscribers (each subscriber gets the quantity, 4K divided by the number of subscriber threads, amount of I/O), regardless of the capacity of the subscriber, and it will not exceed receiving 4K bytes per second for incoming messages. (That's a total of 8KB — the amount you specify is for each, so the total consumed for both input and output is double the specified amount.) This setting does not change the I/O rate for the distributor when gathering distributions via the FTP or HTTP agents, which always consume as much bandwidth as possible.

- **Maximum concurrent distributions** — Each time the system is going to perform a distribution, it creates a java thread that handles the distribution to the subscriber. This value identifies the maximum number of threads that you will allow the distributor or subscriber to create to service the sending of the distributions.

- **Connection timeout** — The default for this is 300 seconds. You can also enter your own timeout value. When the timeout value is exceeded, the distributor fails the distribution and retries the distribution every 2 minutes for the next 30 minutes (as long as it is still in its scheduled window). If, after all 15 retries, the distribution still has not succeeded, the distributor fails and cancels the distribution and does not attempt to distribute it again until the next scheduled time for the channel to be distributed.

- **Working directory** — This identifies the directory where the distributor or subscriber stores its distribution files. The agents on the distributor, when they are called to collect the files and compress them into the distribution file, store the files in this working directory. The agents on the subscriber use this working directory to uncompress the files before copying them to their final destination. It is not recommended to use the SYS volume because of the potential system problems should that volume become full.

- **Parent subscriber** — This enables you to identify if the associated subscribers should receive distributions from the specified parent subscriber (as opposed to getting them directly from the distributor).

SETTING UP SERVER POLICIES

Defining the Messaging Property Page

The Messaging property page is under the General tab and can be configured by pressing the active tab and selecting the messaging under the drop-down on the tab (by pressing the small triangle in the tab). Figure 5.11 shows a sample of a messaging page. Unless you are having some problems and are diagnosing some issues, it is not recommended to request a level higher than 4.

FIGURE 5.11 *Messaging property page of a Tiered Electronic Distribution policy object*

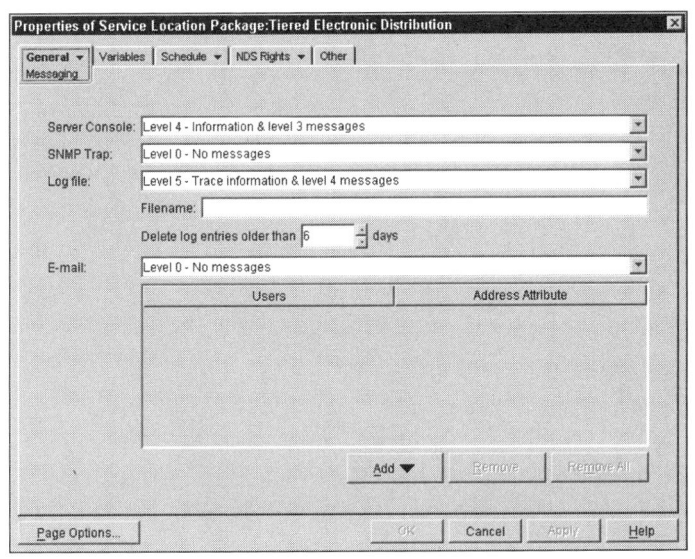

For each of the appropriate fields, you may enter one of the following message levels:

- **Level 6** — This level includes all of the other levels plus developer trace information.
- **Level 5** — This level includes all level 4 messages in addition to trace information, which notify the observer of the modules that are being executed. This level also captures and displays all Java exceptions.
- **Level 4** — This level includes all of the level 3 messages and, in addition, informational messages that identify key points in the system.

NOVELL'S ZENWORKS FOR SERVERS 2 ADMINISTRATOR'S HANDBOOK

- **Level 3** — This level displays any warnings that were encountered in the system in addition to all of the level 2 messages.
- **Level 2** — This level displays the successes that were satisfied by the system and will also include all of the level 1 messages.
- **Level 1** — This level only displays errors that were encountered in the system.
- **Level 0** — This level displays no messages.

You can administer the following configuration parameters on the Message property page:

- **Server Console** — This item identifies the level of messages that are displayed on the distributor or subscriber console (not the main server console).
- **SNMP Trap** — This identifies the level of messages that should be sent as an SNMP trap to the SNMP host. The SNMP Host policy must be defined and active in an effective (for the distributor or subscriber object) Service Location package for traps to be sent.
- **Log file** — This identifies the level of messages that should be stored in the log file. Additionally, you can configure the following about the log file:
  - **Filename** — This is the filename of the log file. The default location for a distributor is SYS:\TED2\DIST\DIST.LOG and SYS:\TED2\SUB\SUB.LOG for a subscriber. You should probably change the location of the log file, because it can grow as well and may adversely affect the system since it is located on the SYS volume by default.
  - **Delete log entries older than X days** — In this parameter, you identify the number of days (X) worth of log entries that should remain in the log file. The default is six days. Therefore, any log entries that are older than six days are cleared from the log file. The process of removing the old entries from the log happens once every 24 hours.
- **E-mail** — With the e-mail option, you may specify the level of messages that are sent in an e-mail to the identified users. The SMTP Host policy in the ZENworks for Servers 2 Service Location policy package must be active and the package must be effective for the distributor or subscriber object in order to enable it to discover the address of the SMTP host to send the e-mail. If this is not specified, the e-mail will not be sent.

In addition to identifying the level of messages, you must also specify who should receive these messages. To add users to the list, and have them receive the message, you must press the Add button and select whether you wish to add an NDS User or Group, or specify an e-mail address. When you select a user, you are asked to browse to the user in the directory and the system takes the e-mail address attribute from the user and uses that as the address for the user. Should you choose a group, all of the users in the group will be sent the e-mail message and the e-mail attribute will be used for each of those users. Should you not want to use the e-mail address attribute in the user object, you may select the down arrow in the Address Attribute field and select which of the NDS User attributes you wish to identify as containing the e-mail address. It is expected that the attribute you identify will contain a valid e-mail address.

If you choose to enter an explicit e-mail address, rather than selecting a user or a group, you may choose the E-mail Address choice from the Add button. You are prompted to enter a valid e-mail address. The entered e-mail address is assumed to be valid and is shown as the User Name field in the table with an "N/A" in the Address Attribute field.

Introducing the Variables Property Pages

Variables enable you to substitute a variable name in the distribution with the value specified for the subscriber. When you create a distribution, you may use variables in the volumes and directory names, for example. When the distribution is sent to the subscriber and the extraction agent is called, the agent replaces these variables with their defined value in the subscriber object. If no value is given, the variable name (including the % [percent sign]) is used for that value.

The variables defined in this policy are additions to the variables defined in any associated subscriber. If you define the same variable in the effective policy and directly in the subscriber object, the variable definition found directly in the subscriber object is used.

Unlike ZENworks for Servers 2 policies and software distribution packages, the TED software only performs basic substitution of variable to value and does not allow you to reference an NDS object or its attribute. This is done to eliminate the requirement that the subscriber have access to NDS and all of the objects in the tree. This would be especially difficult if the subscriber is an external subscriber — not even in the same tree as the distributor!

For example, if you created a distribution and specified %DEST_VOLUME% as the volume name, when the subscriber extracts the files, the agent substitutes the variable DEST_VOLUME defined in this property page with the value. If DEST_VOLUME is not defined, a directory called %DEST_VOLUME% is created in the SYS volume.

Remember to be consistent in your conventions and your variable names. You should probably come up with a set of common variables that you define with each subscriber that you set up. When you create a distribution, you can then use these variables in defining the directories in which the distribution will be placed. Remember, the subscribers that receive the distribution are purely based on who subscribes to the channels where you place the distribution. If you are not consistent in your variables across all subscribers, you may inadvertently send a distribution to a subscriber that does not have the variable defined. This results in the distribution being extracted in a place you do not expect (probably on the SYS volume). Some variables that you should consider defining in each of your subscribers are as follows:

- **DEST_VOLUME** — Define this variable as the volume that receives the distribution after it is extracted.
- **DEST_APPVOL** — Define this to be the volume where your applications are stored.
- **DEST_APPDIR** — Define this to be the directory under the application volume where you place your applications.

Looking at the Schedule Property Page

This policy page enables you to specify how often the associated distributor software on the server goes to NDS and reads the configuration information for itself, the distributions for which it is responsible, the channels with which its distributions are associated, and the subscribers that are subscribed to those channels. The default value is Never, which means that the associated distributors only read information from NDS when it is first loaded on the server, anytime you reboot or restart the server or distributor process, or if you explicitly refresh the distributor from the distributor console or from the distributor object in ConsoleOne.

This page enables you to select when the configuration should be read and applied: Never, Daily, Monthly, Yearly, Interval, or Time.

Once you have selected when you want the configuration applied, you have additional fields to select in the lower portion of the screen. The following sections discuss the various options you have.

Never

This option only loads the distributor with the configuration information when it is first loaded on the server, or after each reboot or restart.

Daily

When you choose to have the configuration applied to the system daily, you need to also select when the changes will be made.

This schedule requires that you select the days when you want the configuration applied. You select the days by clicking on the days you desire. The selected days appear as depressed buttons.

In addition to the days, you can select the times the configuration is applied. These start and stop times provide a range of time where the configuration will be applied.

You can have the configuration also reapplied within the time frame specified per hour/minute/second by clicking the "Repeat the action every" field and specifying the time delay.

Monthly

Under the monthly schedule, you can select which day of the month the configuration should be applied or you can select "Last day of the month" to handle the last day, because all months obviously do not end on the same calendar date (that is 30 days hath September, April, June, and November, all the rest have 31 except for February . . .).

Once you have selected the day, you can also select the time range when the configuration will be reread and applied.

Yearly

You would select a yearly schedule if you want to apply the configuration only once a year.

On this screen, you must choose the day that you wish the configuration to be applied. This is done by selecting the Calendar button to the right of the Date field. This brings up a Monthly dialog box where you can browse through the calendar to select the date you wish. This calendar does not correspond to any particular year and may not take into account leap years in its display. This is because you are choosing a date for each year that will come along in the present and future years.

Once you have selected the date, you can also select the time range when the configuration should be read and applied.

To keep all the distributors from simultaneously accessing NDS, you can select "Randomly dispatch policy during time period." This causes each server to choose a random time within the time period when they will retrieve and apply the configuration.

Interval

This schedule type enables you to specify how often to repeatedly read and apply the configuration. You can specify the interval with a combination of days, hours, minutes, and seconds. This type of schedule waits for the interval to pass before applying the configuration for the first time and then for each sequence after that.

Time

This allows you to specify a specific calendar date and time when the configuration will be applied. When the current date on the server is beyond the identified date, the configuration will be applied.

Setting Up a Service Location Policy Package — The ZENworks Database Policy

Many of the agents in the system want to record information into the ZENworks database that is installed on your system. The ZENworks for Servers 2 agents record logging and other information directly to the database and do not rely on the SNMP system to record events. In order for these agents to discover which database they should place their information in, they walk the tree from the object representing the system they are supporting until they find an active ZENworks Database Location policy in an associated Service Location policy package or as far up the tree as their effective Search Policy allows.

The Database Location policy then refers to a ZENworks database object in the directory (that was created at installation time), which in turn contains the DN or the IP address of the server that is supporting the database. The system also uses other information in the database object.

The Database Location page enables you to browse to the database object in the directory that represents the database that you wish to use. All policy engines and distributor agents associated with this policy then log information into this database. Figure 5.12 is a snapshot of this page.

FIGURE 5.12 *Database Location page of the Database Location policy in a Service Location Policy Package*

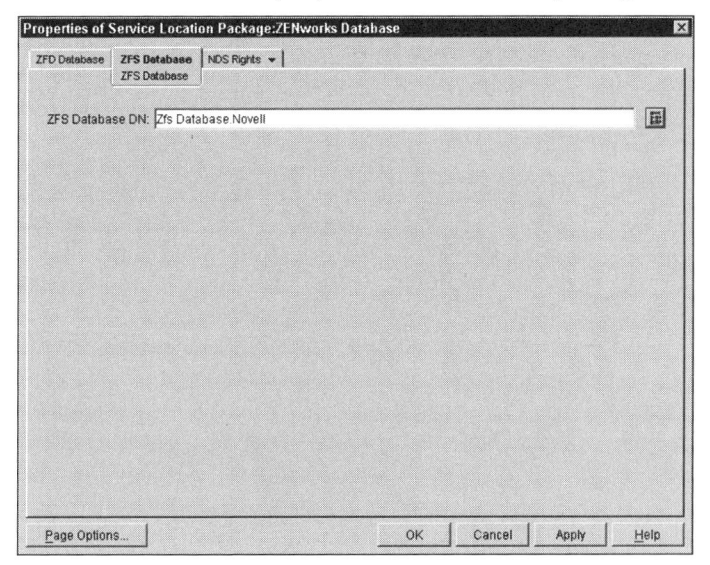

NDS Rights, Other, and Rights to Files and Folders pages are described in the "Setting up a Container Policy Package" section.

To set the database, you must go to the ZFS (ZENworks for Servers) Database tab and click the Browse button to the right of the field and then browse to and select the database object that you wish. This places the DN of the database object into the field.

> **NOTE** ZENworks for Servers 2 cannot use the database until a database location policy is set and found by the policy engines and distributor agents. Remember that Service Location Packages can only be associated with containers, not directly with servers or with server groups.

Setting Up a Service Location Policy Package — The ZENworks for Servers License

The following agents in ZENworks for Servers 2 look for an appropriate license in the directory before they begin processing any requests: ZENworks for Servers policy engine and TED distributor.

The ZENworks for Servers License policy then refers to the NLS license for the ZENworks for Servers product in NDS. The license would have been placed in the directory when the product was installed. If you determine later that you need more copies of the license (to avoid agents crossing WAN links, and so on), you can install the license to new locations by running the Installation Wizard again.

The ZENworks for Servers 2 License Location page allows you to browse to the NLS object in the directory that represents the licenses that you placed in the tree at install. All agents associated with this policy go to the specified license DN to retrieve and validate the product. Figure 5.13 is a snapshot of this page.

FIGURE 5.13 ZENworks for Servers License Location page of the ZENworks for Servers License policy in a Service Location Policy Package

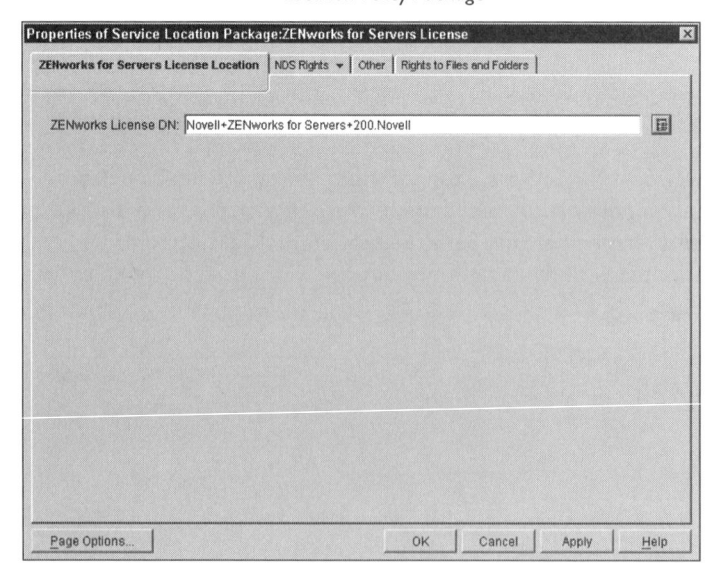

SETTING UP SERVER POLICIES

The "Setting Up a Container Policy Package" section describes NDS Rights, Other, and Rights to Files and Folders pages.

To set the license, you must go to the ZENworks License DN field and click the Browse button to the right of the field and then browse to and select the NLS object that you wish. This places the DN of the NLS object into the field.

> **NOTE** The NLS object behaves like a container, because it holds within it licenses that have been allocated to a particular system. You want to select the container for this field and not browse into the NLS object looking for the specific license.

Setting Up the Server Policy Package — The NetWare Set Parameters Policy

This policy is a plural policy, which means that you can create multiple instances of this policy in a single policy package. You create this policy by pressing the Add button on the bottom of the main Server Policy Package screen. When you press the Add button, you are prompted to select a policy and to name the policy. You need to select NetWare Set Parameters for the policy and enter a unique policy name.

Once you have added the policy, you are guided through a wizard to collect potential parameters. Because the set parameters on NetWare are dynamic and can be enhanced by various sets of NLMs, there is not a known set of set parameters. Consequently, ZENworks for Servers 2 walks you through a wizard that goes to an identified NetWare server (the server must be running the ZENworks for Servers Policy engine) and queries the server for the set of parameters. This list is then transmitted back to the wizard.

Perform the following steps to complete the wizard and to administer the policy:

1. Press the Add button and select the NetWare Set Parameters policy. Select Set Parameter policy and press the details button. Press the Add button in the Set Parameters Policy window to activate the wizard. The Wizard screen is displayed, as shown in Figure 5.14.

2. Press the Browse button and browse the NDS tree to the server that has a representative set parameter list. Select that server. Press the Next button. This causes the wizard to query the server and retrieve all possible set parameters. The screen shown in Figure 5.15 is displayed with the list of potential parameters

NOVELL'S ZENWORKS FOR SERVERS 2 ADMINISTRATOR'S HANDBOOK

FIGURE 5.14 *In ZENworks for Servers Wizard, select server page for set parameters policy in a Service Location Policy Package.*

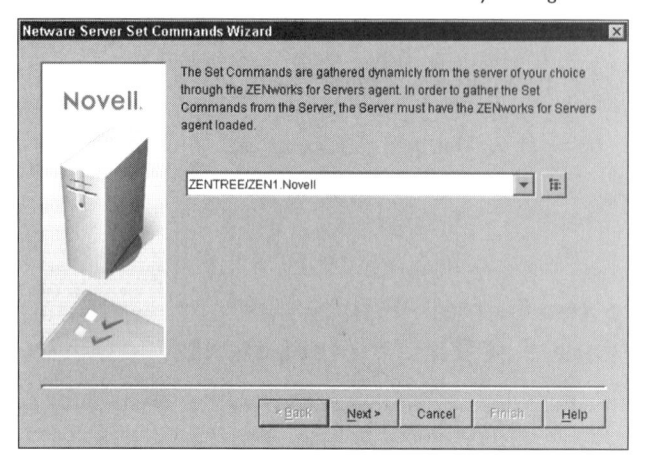

FIGURE 5.15 *In ZENworks for Servers Wizard, select parameters for set parameters policy in a Service Location Policy Package.*

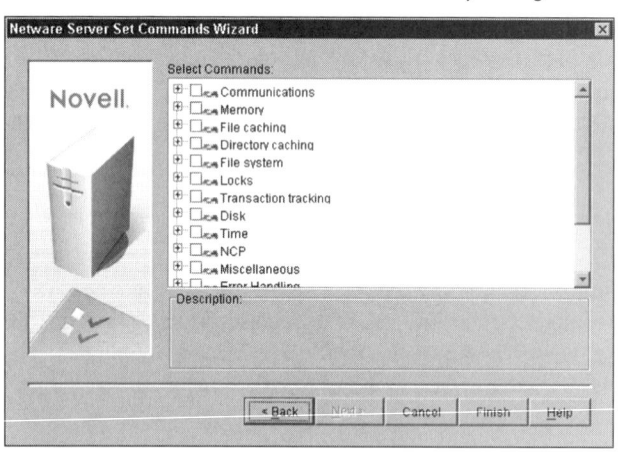

3. Select the set of parameters that you wish to have contained in the policy. You can select an entire category by clicking on the checkbox next to the category, or you can open the category and select individual

set parameters. Once you have selected the set of parameters you wish to administer with the policy, press the Finish button.

4. You are placed back in the policy with the list of only the categories and/or the parameters that you had selected in the wizard. To administer an individual parameter, select the parameter and press the Edit button.

5. When you press the Edit button, you are presented with a dialog box that is unique for each parameter type. From this dialog box, you may administer the value of the parameter. You may also select one of the following choices: console, `autoexec.ncf`, `startup.ncf`. These choices administer how the parameter is given to the server. Each of these choices is defined as follows:

   - **Console** — The command is passed to the server console by the policy engine.
   - **Autoexec.ncf** — In addition to passing the command to the console for immediate activation, the set parameter is placed into the autoexec.ncf file so that, following a reboot, the server will set the parameter.
   - **Startup.ncf** — In addition to passing the command to the console for immediate activation, the set parameter is placed into the startup.ncf file so that, following a restart, the server will set the parameter.

6. Complete the list of parameters and press the OK button to apply the policy. The policy engine, on its next refresh cycle, collects this policy and applies it to the servers that are associated with this policy.

Setting Up the Server Policy Package — The Scheduled Down Policy

This policy is a plural policy, which means that you can create multiple instances of this policy in a single policy package. You create this policy by pressing the Add button on the bottom of the main Server Policy Package screen. When you press the Add button, you are prompted to select a policy and to name the policy. You need to select Scheduled Down for the policy and enter a unique policy name. Once you do this, you can activate and modify the policy. Figure 5.16 displays a sample scheduled down policy.

This policy allows you to schedule that the server either reset, restart, or down at a particular time.

FIGURE 5.16 *Procedure page of the scheduled down policy in a Server Policy Package*

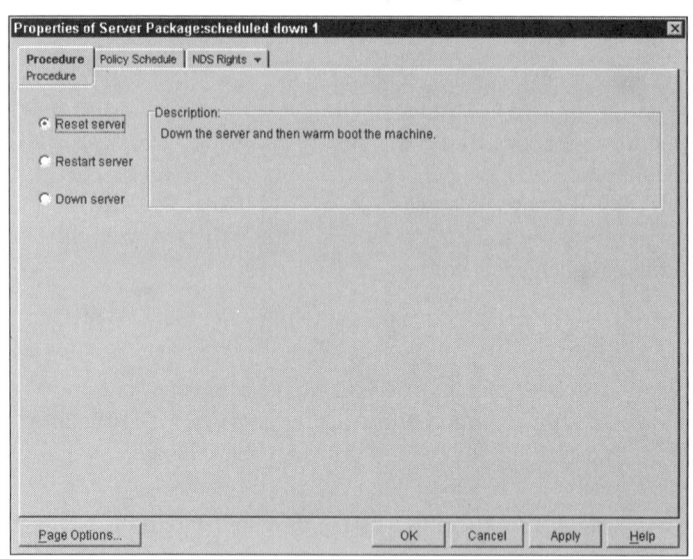

You can select one of the following server options:

- **Reset server** — This downs the server and performs a warm boot of the machine.
- **Restart server** — This downs and then restarts the server.
- **Down server** — This downs the server.

On the Policy Schedule page, you may specify the time frame when you want the server to be reset, restarted, or downed. The details concerning your choices for the schedule are described in the "Setting Up the Server Policy Package — SNMP Community Strings" section.

Setting Up the Server Policy Package — The Scheduled Load/Unload Policy

This policy is a plural policy, which means that you can create multiple instances of this policy in a single policy package. You create this policy by pressing the Add button on the bottom of the main Server Policy Package

SETTING UP SERVER POLICIES

screen. When you press the Add button, you are prompted to select a policy and to name the policy. You need to select Scheduled Load/Unload for the policy and enter a unique policy name. Once you do this, you can activate and modify the policy. Figure 5.17 displays a sample scheduled load/unload policy. This policy enables you to specify when you wish to have a selected set of NLMs or Java processes loaded or unloaded on the server.

FIGURE 5.17 *Scheduled Load/Unload page of the Scheduled Load/Unload policy in a Server Policy Package*

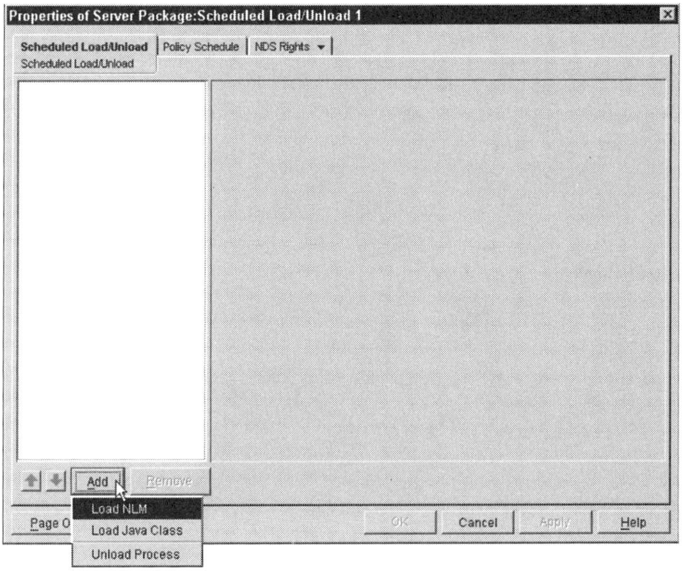

In this policy, you press the Add button and select whether you wish to load an NLM or Java class, or unload a process. Once you have made your selection, an entry is placed on the left side of the screen. Corresponding to this entry are some parameters that are displayed and edited on the right. By selecting the entry on the left, you can administer the values on the right. You can edit the entries on the left by selecting the entry (like you do in Windows), and this enables you to change the name to something more useful.

On the fields on the right, you enter the name of the NLM or Java class and any parameters that are needed for the process.

When you are loading a process, you can enter the NLM or class name and also specify the parameters that you want passed to these processes. Additionally, you can specify if you wish to wait for the loaded NLM or Java class to terminate before continuing onto the next item in the list. Make sure you only check this box if you are expecting the process to complete and exit on its own; if you are just loading monitor.nlm, the policy will be waiting for a long time to be able to move onto the next item.

When you are unloading a process, you can enter the name of the NLM or the Java class name. Additionally, you can specify if you should wait for the termination to complete before proceeding in the list.

Once you have entered several items in the list, you can select an item and move it up and down the list. This is significant because the items are processed in the order specified, from top to bottom. By selecting any item and moving it about in the list, you can order the loads and unloads in a sequence that is necessary for your process.

On the Policy Schedule page, you may specify the time frame when you want the system to perform this policy. The details concerning your choices for the schedule are described in the "Setting Up the Server Policy Package — The SNMP Community Strings" section.

Setting Up the Server Policy Package — The Server Down Process

The Server down Process policy allows you to specify what should happen when the server receives a command to go down. This catches the instances when the user types the down command on the console; this process does not catch any other down request (done programmatically). You can even specify that other servers notify you if the downed server does not come up after a certain amount of time.

The "Setting Up a Container Policy Package" section describes NDS Rights.

Describing the Down Procedure Page

The Down Procedure page enables you to specify the procedure that should be followed when the server is downed. Figure 5.18 displays this ConsoleOne page.

SETTING UP SERVER POLICIES

FIGURE 5.18 *Down Procedure page of the Server Down Process policy in a Server Policy Package*

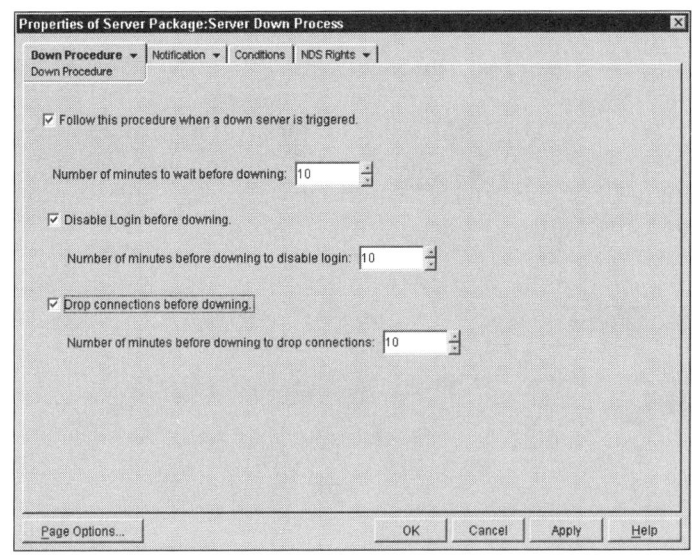

The following options on the page are activated when the checkbox is checked:

- **Follow this procedure when a down server is triggered** — This activates or not activates the procedure identified on this page. If this checkbox is not checked, this policy will not be in effect for the associated servers. You can specify, when activated, how many minutes the server must wait before it actually performs the down process.

- **Disable Login before downing** — This effectively runs the `disable logins` command on the server, disallowing anyone to be able to log into the server. You can specify how many minutes before the downing process you want to disallow anyone to log into the server. If the number of minutes specified in this field is greater than the ". . . when a down server is triggered" field, the disabling of logins occurs immediately when the down request is given.

- **Drop connections before downing** — This drops all the current connections on the server before downing the server. You can specify the number of minutes before the actual downing of the server when you want the connections dropped. If the number of minutes specified in this field is greater than the ". . . when a down server is triggered" field, the connections are dropped immediately when the down request is given.

Discussing the Ordered Unload Page

By selecting the small triangle drop-down control on the Down Process page, you can select the Ordered Unload page. This page enables you to specify a set of NLMs and Java processes that you want killed or unloaded and the order in which to kill or unload them before the downing of the server actually begins. Figure 5.19 displays this property page.

FIGURE 5.19 *Ordered Unload page of the Server Down Process policy in a Server Policy Package*

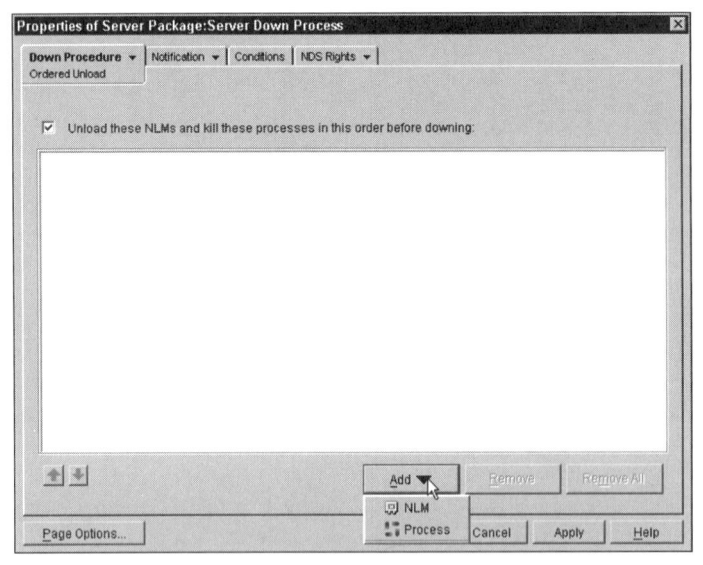

When you select with the Add button either to unload an NLM or kill a process, a dialog box prompts you to enter the name of the NLM or the process. After entering the name of the NLM or process, press the OK button on the dialog box and the NLM or process name appears in the Ordered Unload page. Once you have more than one process or NLM in the list, you can select an item in the list and then move it up or down in the list by pressing the up or down arrows, after selecting an item.

SETTING UP SERVER POLICIES

Before the server is downed, these systems are unloaded or killed on the server. This is useful if you have such processes or NLMs as databases or other programs that are caching items in memory and need to flush those buffers onto disk. This can be done, usually, by unloading the process or NLM. This can keep your data integrity solid instead of pulling the server out from under these processes, not allowing them to save their data.

Looking at the Reporting Page

Under the Notification tab, the Reporting page can be found. The purpose of this page is to identify some companion servers, whose responsibility it is to send notifications if the server that is associated with this policy does not come up after a specified time. When the server is told to go down, it contacts these companion servers and places a scheduled entry to send a notification message. When the server comes back up, and the policy engine is restarted, it contacts these servers again and removes the scheduled entry for the notifications. If the server and the policy engine do not come up in the specified time, these companion servers fire the scheduled entry and send the specified notification messages. These companion servers must also be running the policy engine for this to work. Figure 5.20 displays this page.

FIGURE 5.20 *Reporting page of the Server Down Process policy in a Server Policy Package*

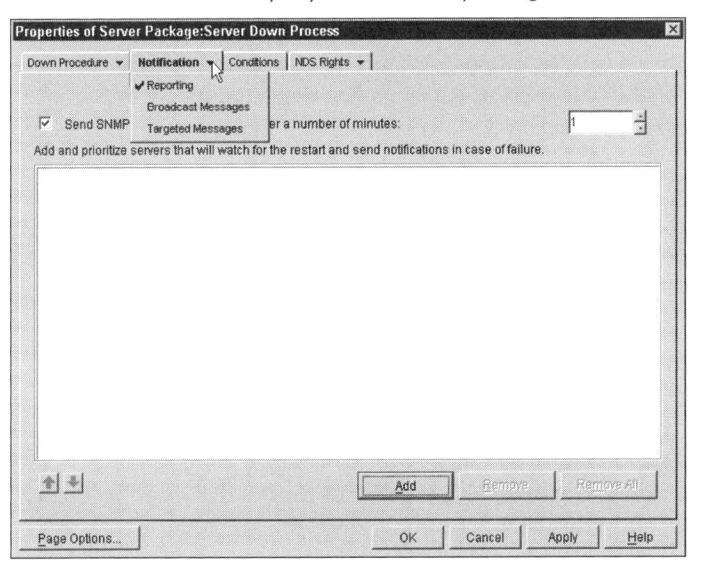

The checkbox on "Send SNMP alert if server is not up after a number of minutes" turns on or off the monitoring of the server. You can specify the number of minutes that these other "watcher" servers will wait before they send their SNMP alerts notifying you that the server that was downed is not coming back up.

You then must press the Add button and then browse the tree to identify the servers that are to monitor this behavior. Once you have specified more than one server, you can order the servers to identify which server has first responsibility to monitor the downed server. When the ZENworks for Servers engine gets the event that signals the down, it attempts to contact the servers in this list (in order) to notify them to watch for when the server comes back up. If the server in the list cannot be contacted, the engine goes to the next server in the list.

Introducing the Broadcast Messages Page

The Broadcast Messages page can be found under the Notification tab. This page enables you to specify the broadcast messages that are sent to the connected users as the system is being taken down. You can specify if the message should be sent, how many times you want the message sent before the system goes down, the contents of the message, and an additional trailer that tells the user how long before they will be disconnected from the server. Figure 5.21 shows a snapshot of this page.

The number of times to send the message is divided evenly into the number of minutes specified in the Down Procedure page before dropping connections or downing the server (if "dropping connections" is not checked). For example, if you stated that the server should go down ten minutes after the request and you specify that the connections should be dropped four minutes before downing, the number of minutes that a user has left on the server is six minutes (10 – 4). The number of messages are divided into the six minutes and spaced evenly across that time.

If you include the line that states the number of minutes left, the "x" in the line is calculated the same way as above, minus a broadcast cycle. You subtract one cycle so that the last message is displayed at the beginning of the last cycle (rather than the end).

About the Targeted Messages Page

The Targeted Messages page enables you to send specific e-mail messages to a selected set of users, to notify them of the downing of the server. Figure 5.22 displays a sample of this page.

SETTING UP SERVER POLICIES

FIGURE 5.21 *Broadcast Messages page of the Server Down Process policy in a Server Policy Package*

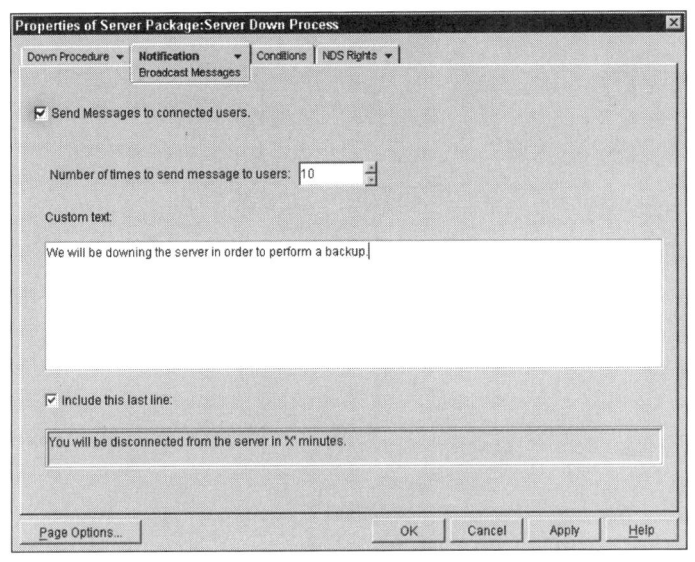

The checkbox on the "Send Email to selected users when server is going down" turns off or on this feature. The "Email message" box displays the message that is sent to each of the specified users. You are not able to change or customize the message that is sent.

To add users to the list, and have them receive the message, you must press the Add button and select whether you wish to add an NDS User or Group, or specify an e-mail address explicitly. When you select User, you are asked to browse to the user in the directory, and the system takes the e-mail address attribute from the user and uses that as the address for the user. Should you choose a group, all of the users in the group are sent the e-mail message and the e-mail attribute is used for each of those users. Should you not want to use the e-mail address attribute in the user object, you may select the down arrow in the Address Attribute field and select which of the NDS User attributes you wish to identify as containing the e-mail address. It is expected that the attribute you identify contains a valid e-mail address.

93

NOVELL'S ZENWORKS FOR SERVERS 2 ADMINISTRATOR'S HANDBOOK

FIGURE 5.22 *Targeted Messages page of the Server Down Process policy in a Server Policy Package*

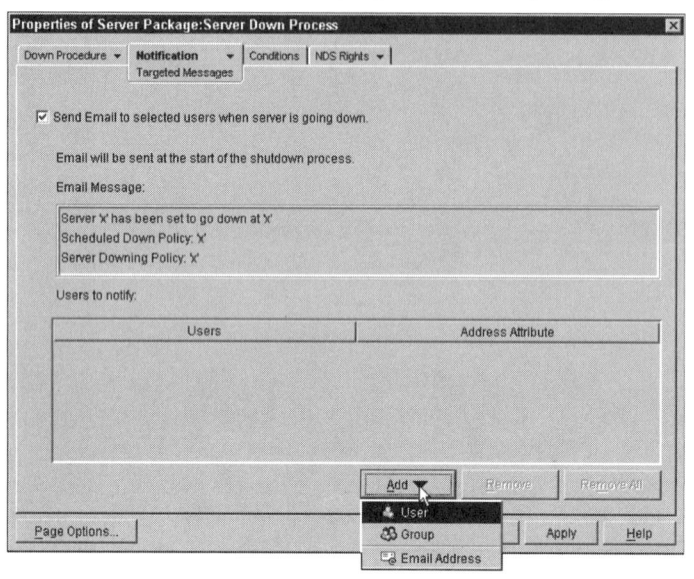

If you choose to enter an e-mail address explicitly, rather than selecting a user or a group, you may choose the "Email Address" choice from the Add button. You are prompted to enter a valid e-mail address. The entered e-mail address is assumed to be valid and is shown as the User Name field entry in the table with N/A in the Address Attribute field.

You can place any number (based on the limits of NDS) of users, groups, or e-mail addresses into the page and each of them are sent the e-mail message when the server has been requested to go down. The e-mail users just get one message, at the very beginning of the downing process. This gives these users the maximum amount of time to connect to the server and stop the downing process should they desire. They can connect to the server and, via the policy engine console or via Remote Web Console, cancel the down process.

Discussing the Conditions Page

This page enables you to specify conditions when the down server request should *not* be honored. Figure 5.23 displays this page.

94

SETTING UP SERVER POLICIES

FIGURE 5.23 *Conditions page of the Server Down Process policy in a Server Policy Package*

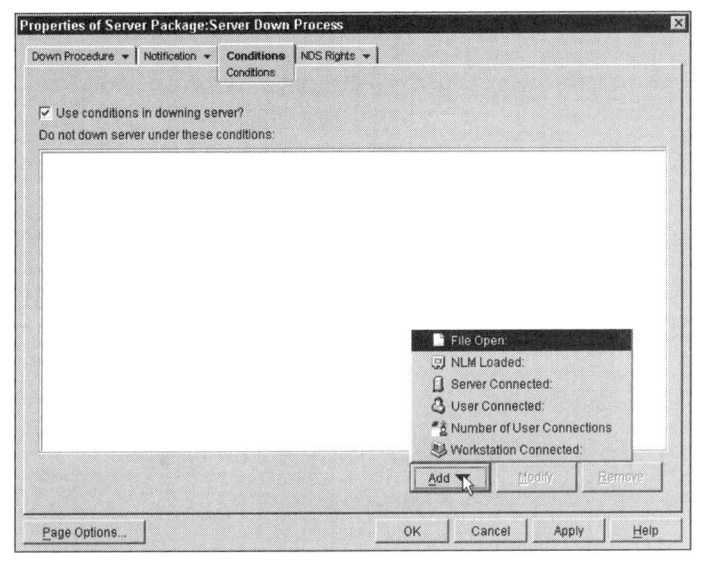

You must check the checkbox on the "Use conditions in downing server?" statement to make the conditions effective. Then you may add any number of conditions that you wish to identify. If any of these conditions are true, the server does not honor the down server request. Press the Add button to select any of the following choices:

- **File Open** — Specify if an identified file is currently open on the server. If that file is open, the system does not allow the down request.
- **NLM Loaded** — Specify if a particular NLM is currently loaded on the server. The system checks to see if the NLM is loaded before it performs any unload of NLMs that were specified in the Ordered Unload page. So, if you have an NLM in the Unload page and in the conditions, the down is halted if the NLM is loaded.
- **Server Connected** — If the identified server is currently connected to the server, the down request is denied.
- **User Connected** — If the identified user has a current connection to the server, the down request is denied.

95

▶ **Number of User Connections** — Specify the number of active connections whereby, if exceeded, the down will not be allowed. For example, if you specify 15 as the number of active connections, and there are 16 or more connections, the down request is denied.

> **NOTE** These are active connections, which include server and agent connections, not just authenticated user connections.

▶ **Workstation Connected** — Identify the workstation that, when connected, halts the down request. You cannot specify a group of workstations, but must identify them individually.

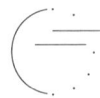

> **NOTE** This feature functions only when you have ZENworks for Desktops installed in your tree.

Setting Up the Server Policy Package — The Server Scripts Policy

This policy is a plural policy, which means that you can create multiple instances of this policy in a single policy package. You create this policy by pressing the Add button on the bottom of the main Server Policy Package screen. When you press the Add button, you are prompted to select a policy and to name the policy. You need to select Server Scripts for the policy and enter a unique policy name. Once you have done this, you can activate and modify the policy. Figure 5.24 displays a sample Server Script policy.

This policy enables you to specify a set of scripts that you wish to have run on your server.

You add a script to the policy by pressing the Add button. When you press the Add button, an entry is placed in the left window and you can edit the name of the script. Once you have named the script, you can choose on the right the type of script that you will be creating. The choices of script types are currently NCF, NETBASIC, and PERL. Once you have identified the script type, you are free to type in the script in the provided window. ZENworks for Servers provides no syntax checking or validation for the script you enter. You may enter ZENworks for Servers variables into the script and they will be processed prior to the script being executed.

SETTING UP SERVER POLICIES

FIGURE 5.24 *Script policy page of the scheduled load/unload policy in a Server Policy Package*

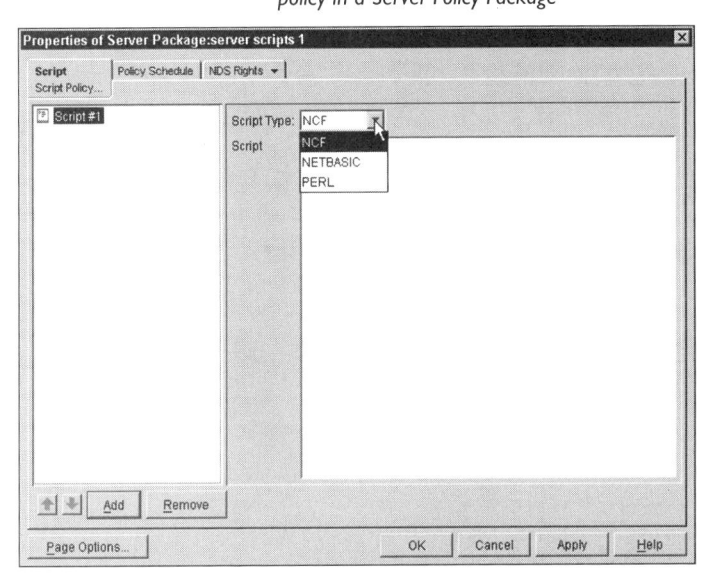

You can add multiple scripts of any of the available types into this one policy. The scripts are executed in the order shown on the administration screen (from top to bottom). If you wish to reorder the running of the scripts, you must select a script name on the left pane and press the up or down arrows to move the script into a different order.

When the ZENworks for Servers policy engine launches this policy, it creates a temporary script file (in its working directory) that contains the specific script and then launches the corresponding NLM that works with the identified script, passing the NLM the name of the script to run. Consequently, netbasic.nlm and perl.nlm must already exist on the server where the script is to be run. These are normally installed with the standard NetWare 5 system. Regardless whether a script fails or succeeds, the engine proceeds onto the next script.

On the Policy Schedule page, you may specify the time frame when you want the system to enforce this policy. The details concerning your choices for the schedule are described in the "Setting Up the Server Policy Package — The SNMP Community Strings" section.

97

Setting Up the Server Policy Package — The SNMP Community Strings

This policy enables you to specify the various SNMP community strings that are used in your system for the various levels: Monitor, Control, and Trap. Figure 5.25 displays a snapshot of this simple screen. NDS Rights are described in the "Setting up a Container Policy Package" section.

FIGURE 5.25 *SNMP Community Policy page of the SNMP Community Strings policy in a Server Policy Package*

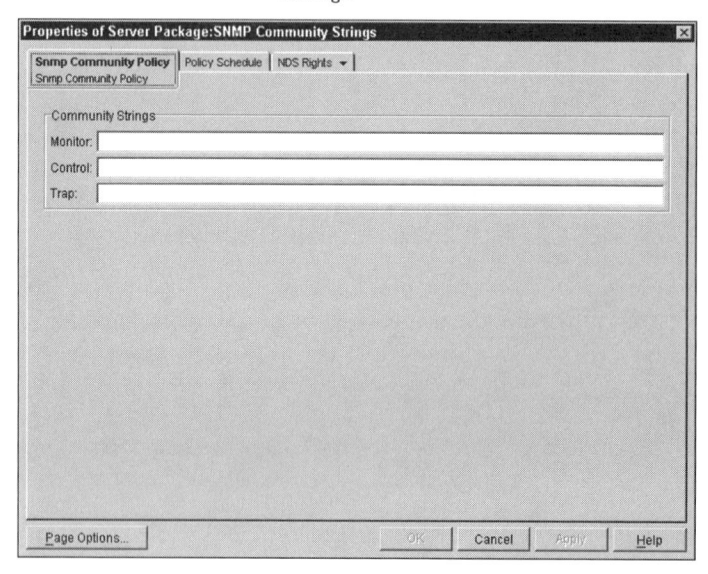

In this page, you simply need to go to each of the fields and enter in the community string that you want configured. These community strings are placed into the SNMP agents on the server, causing the SNMP agents to reset their strings to these values.

The Policy Schedule page enables you to customize (outside of the package default schedule) when you want the community strings applied to the system.

This page enables you to select when the package should be applied: Daily, Weekly, Monthly, Yearly, Relative, Run Immediate, Event, Interval, or Time.

Once you have selected when you want the package applied, you have additional fields to select in the lower portion of the screen. The following sections discuss the various options you have with scheduling the package.

Package Schedule
This option runs this policy based on the schedule that has been identified for the entire policy package. This is the default for all policies.

Daily
When you choose to have the policy applied to the system daily, you need to select when the policies will be enforced.

This schedule requires that you select the days when you want the policy applied. You select the days by clicking on the days you desire. The selected days appear as depressed buttons.

In addition to the days, you can select the times the policies are applied. These start and stop times provide a range of time where the policies will be applied.

You can have the policy also reapplied within the time frame every specified hour/minute/second by clicking the "Repeat the action every" field and specifying the time delay.

Weekly
You can alternatively choose that the policies be applied only weekly.

In this screen, you choose which day of the week you wish the policy to be applied. When you select a day, any other selected day will be unselected. Once you have selected the day, you can also select the time range when the policy may be applied.

To keep all the policies from simultaneously applying to the servers, you can select the "Randomly dispatch policy during time period" option. This causes each server to choose a random time within the time period when they will retrieve and apply the policy.

Monthly
Under the monthly schedule, you can select which day of the month the policy should be applied or you can select "Last day of the month" to handle the last day, because all months obviously do not end on the same calendar date (that is, 30 days hath September, April, June, and November, all the rest have 31 except for February . . .).

Once you have selected the day, you can also select the time range when the policy may be applied.

To keep all the policies from simultaneously applying to the servers, you can select the "Randomly dispatch policy during time period" option. This causes each server to choose a random time within the time period when they will retrieve and apply the policy.

Yearly

You would select a yearly schedule if you want to apply the policies only once a year.

On this screen, you must choose the day that you wish the policies to be applied. This is done by selecting the Calendar button to the right of the Date field. This brings up a Monthly dialog box where you can browse through the calendar to select the date you wish to choose for your policies to be applied. This calendar does not correspond to any particular year and may not take into account leap years in its display. This occurs because you are choosing a date for each year that will come along in the present and future years.

Once you have selected the date, you can also select the time range when the policy may be applied.

To keep all the policies from simultaneously applying to the servers, you can select the "Randomly dispatch policy during time period" option. This causes each server to choose a random time within the time period when they will retrieve and apply the policy.

Relative

This option enables you to repeat the policy every X unit of time. The specified time can contain days, hours, minutes and/or seconds. You may specify each length of time by entering the number of each unit in each of the respective fields.

Once you have identified the intervals, the policy is applied, and the system does not apply the policy until the next specified interval has passed.

Run Immediately

In the Run Immediately choice, the system runs the policy immediately upon administration (or refresh of the server). You can then also specify how often to repeat the policy by selecting the "Repeat the action every" field and identifying the delay time. After the policy is applied, the system reapplies the policy after each of the intervals have passed.

Event

When you choose this option, the policy is applied when certain events have occurred. The events that you can select are one of the following:

- **System Startup** — This applies the policy just after the system has started up.
- **System Shutdown** — This applies the policy just before the system is shut down.
- **Custom Event ID** — This is a third-party event. This is to be a Java class event that is identified by a third party that they can plug into the ZENworks for Servers policy engine. This feature is currently not documented in ZENworks for Servers. At some future time, the team may provide documentation on the methods to register with the system.

Interval

This schedule type allows you to specify how often to repeat the policy. You can specify the interval with a combination of days, hours, minutes, and seconds. This is very similar to the Run Immediate type except that this type waits for the interval to pass first before applying the policy for the first time.

Time

This enables you to specify a specific calendar date and time when the policy will be applied. When the current date on the server is beyond the identified date, the policy will be applied.

Setting Up the Server Policy Package— The SNMP Trap Target Refresh

This policy is associated with the SNMP Trap Target policy that is found in the Service Location Policy Package. That policy allows you to identify the addresses of the SNMP host services that will be accepting SNMP trap messages. This policy, the SNMP Trap Target Refresh policy, allows you to specify how often that policy should be applied to the SNMP agents on the server. Figure 5.26 is an example of this screen.

In this policy, you simply identify the policy schedule type that you want to apply. When the scheduled time arrives, the system retrieves the SNMP Trap Target policy and applies it to the agents on the server. The details concerning your choices for the schedule are described in the "Setting Up the Server Policy Package — The SNMP Community Strings" section.

FIGURE 5.26 *SNMP Trap Target Refresh Policy Schedule page in a Server Policy Package*

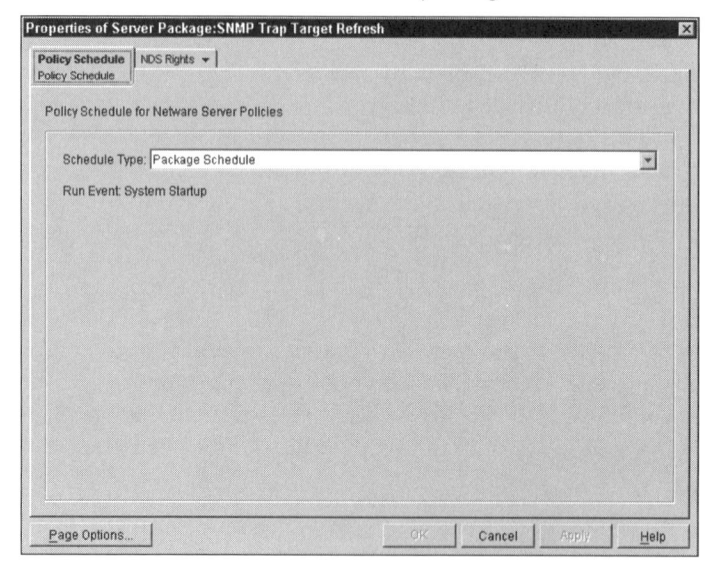

Setting Up the Server Policy Package — The Text File Changes Policy

This policy is a plural policy, which means that you can create multiple instances of this policy in a single policy package. You create this policy by pressing the Add button on the bottom of the main Server Policy Package screen. When you press the Add button, you are prompted to select a policy and to name the policy. You need to select Text File Changes for the policy and enter a unique policy name. Once you do this, you can activate and modify the policy. Figure 5.27 displays a sample Text File Changes policy.

This policy enables you to specify a set of text changes that you wish done on ASCII text files on your server.

SETTING UP SERVER POLICIES

FIGURE 5.27 *Text File Policy page of the text file changes policy in a Server Policy Package*

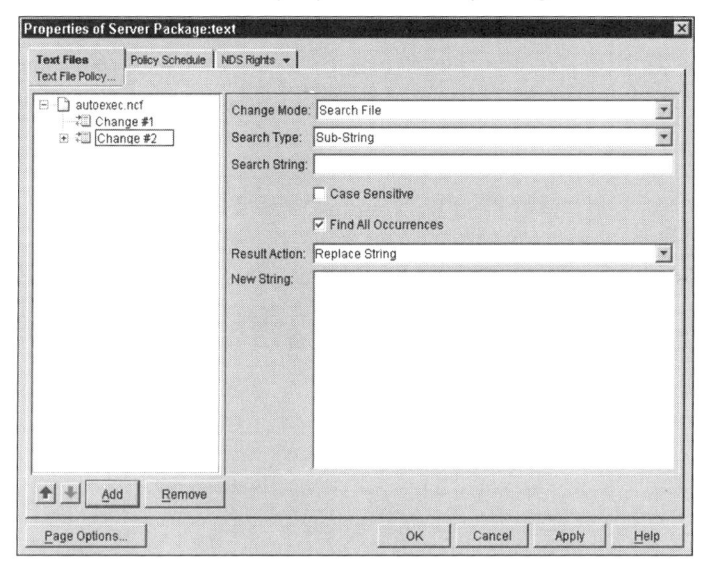

You enter a requested text file change by pressing the Add button. After pressing the Add button, you are prompted to identify the name of the text file and the name of the change script. You can have multiple change scripts for each file you identify. Make sure you enter the complete filename (including path) for the name of the text file to change. The changes are applied to the specified file in the order shown. Should you wish to change the order of the changes or the order of the files, select the item and move it in the list by pressing the up or down arrows.

The first to be done is to choose the change mode that corresponds to this change policy. You may choose either Search File, Prepend to File, or Append to File as one of your modes.

Prepend to File

When you choose to prepend text to the file, the right side of the Administration page changes to display a large text box. You may enter any text strings that you wish in the text box and press OK to store this entry. When the policy is applied, the exact strings that you typed are placed as the first lines in the file.

103

Append to File

When you choose to append text to the file, the right side of the Administration page changes to display a large text box. You may enter any text strings that you wish in the text box and press OK to store this entry. When the policy is applied, the exact strings that you typed are placed as the last lines in the file.

Search File

Should this change be a Search File change, you need to administer the following additional information to make the change effective:

1. Identify the search type that you need for this change. The search type may be Sub-String, Whole Word, Start of Line, End of Line, or Entire Line. The following describes the meaning of each of these search types.

    - **Sub-String** — Search for the search string in any of the text. The text specified may be contained anywhere in the file, even in the middle of a word. For example, if we have the substring of "day", the following text would all match with this substring: today, day, yesterday, daytime, and so forth.

    - **Whole Word** — Search for the string such that it is surrounded by white space or beginning or end of line. For example, if we have the string of "day", only the word "day" would be a match. The words today, yesterday, daytime, and so forth do not constitute a match.

    - **Start of Line** — This is a successful match if the beginning of a line (first line of file, or characters following a carriage return) starts with the string, regardless of whether the string is a whole word or not. To continue our example, if we had the string "day", this type would only match with the following lines: daytime is set, day by day, and so forth.

    - **End of Line** — This is a successful match if the end of a line (characters preceding the carriage return or end of file) contains the string, regardless of whether the string is a whole word or not. With our example, if we had the string "day", this type would only match with the following lines: the time to act is today, day by day, and so forth.

    - **Entire Line** — The entire specified string must consume the entire line of text (from text following a carriage return, or beginning of the file, to the next carriage return, or end of the file), including any white space. It must be an exact match of every character, other than the carriage returns, on the line. If our string were "day", only a line with the single word "day" on it will match.

2. Specify the search string that you're trying to match. Enter this into the Search String field.

3. Identify if you wish the search to be case sensitive by checking the checkbox to make the search only match if the case matches.

4. Change the Find all Occurrences field if you wish to only find the first occurrence of the string in the file. The default is to have this field checked, meaning that all occurrences in the file will have this policy applied to them.

5. Choose a result action that will be applied to the string once it is located in the file. The possible actions are Delete All Lines After, Delete All Lines Before, Prepend to File if not Found, Append to File if not Found, Replace String, Replace Word, Replace Line, Append Line. The following describes each of these choices and their resulting action:

- **Delete All Lines After** — All lines (characters following the next carriage return) are deleted from the file. The file will basically be truncated, ending with the line that held the first matching string. Obviously, searching for all occurrences is not effectual when this is the resulting action, as a match truncates the rest of the file.

- **Delete All Lines Before** — All lines (characters before and including the previous carriage return) are deleted from the file. The file is reset such that it begins with the line that held the first matching string. With this result action, another search continues and if another match is found, all the lines before it are deleted as well.

- **Prepend to File if not Found** — This action places the replacement text in the file at the very beginning of the file should the search string not be found in the file. This action only adds text, it does not delete or modify text.

- **Append to File if not Found** — This action places the replacement text at the end of the file should the specified search string not be found. This action only adds text, it does not delete or modify text.

- **Replace String** — This action takes the matching string and removes it from the file, placing the replacement string in the exact location of the deleted string. If the replacement string is of a different length than the search string, the surrounding characters are shifted to the left or right depending on whether less or more room is required. Basically, the new text is inserted in the location were the search string was removed.

* **Replace Word** — This action takes the word where a substring was matched and replace the whole word (from space or beginning of line to space or end of line) with the replacement text. For example, if the substring were "day", the following words would be replaced with the replacement text: day, today, daytime, and so forth.

- **Replace Line** — This action takes the line where the match has occurred and removes the complete line from the file. The replacement text is placed in the same location where the removed line was located in the file.

- **Append Line** — This action appends the replacement string to the line that contained the match. The matching string is not removed from the file; the only change is the addition of text to the end of the line.

6. Specify the new string. In the text box that is provided, you need to supply the text that will be applied to the file, based on the action that was specified.

Policy Schedule Page

On this page, you may specify the time frame when you want the system to apply this policy. The details concerning your choices for the schedule are described in the "Setting Up the Server Policy Package — The SNMP Community Strings" section.

Setting Up the Server Policy Package — ZENworks for Servers 2

This policy contains the configuration information that is used by the ZENworks for Servers 2 engine that is the controlling process on the server. The engine is responsible for taking care of communicating with NDS, watching the schedule of all policies and launching subprocesses to apply the various policies to the server. This policy applies to the configuration of the engine itself. Figure 5.28 shows this screen.

SETTING UP SERVER POLICIES

FIGURE 5.28 *Messaging page of the ZENworks for Servers policy in a Server Policy Package*

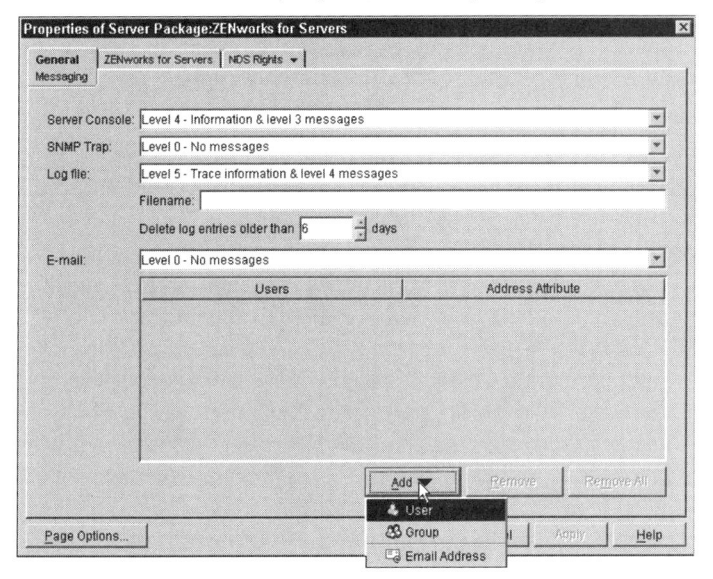

In this policy, you may set the messaging level you desire for each of the various components available to you for notification: Server Console, SNMP Traps, Log file, and E-mail message. You may set a different level of messages for each of the various notification conduits. The Server Console refers to the ZFS screen that is on the server when the engine is running. You may choose from any of the following choices:

- **Level 6** — This level includes all of the other levels plus developer trace information.
- **Level 5** — This level includes all level 4 messages in addition to trace information, which will notifies the observer of the modules that are being executed.
- **Level 4** — This level includes all of the level 3 messages and, in addition, informational messages that identify key points in the system.
- **Level 3** — This level displays any warnings that were encountered in the system in addition to all of the level 2 messages.
- **Level 2** — This level displays the successes that were satisfied by the system and also includes all of the level 1 messages.

- Level 1 — This level only displays errors that were encountered in the system.
- Level 0 — This level displays no messages.

When you specify that messages are going by e-mail, you can identify any number of users or groups of users or a specified e-mail address.

Adding Users to the List

To add users to the list, and have them receive the message, you must press the Add button and select whether you wish to add an NDS User or Group, or specify an e-mail address. When you select a user, you are asked to browse to the user in the directory and the system will take the e-mail address attribute from the user and use that as the address for the user. Should you choose a group, all of the users in the group are sent the e-mail message and the e-mail attribute is used for each of those users. Should you not want to use the e-mail address attribute in the user object, you may select the down arrow in the Address Attribute field and select which of the NDS User attributes you wish to identify as containing the e-mail address. It is expected that the attribute you identify will contain a valid e-mail address.

If you choose to enter an e-mail address explicitly, rather than selecting a user or a group, you may choose the "Email Address" choice from the Add button. You are prompted to enter a valid e-mail address. This entered e-mail address is assumed to be valid and is shown as the User Name field in the table with N/A in the Address Attribute field.

You can place any number (based on the limits of NDS and the Java control) of users, groups, or e-mail addresses into the page and each of them are sent the e-mail messages.

Discussing the Configuration Page

This page enables you to configure some additional parameters in the ZENworks for Servers 2 engine. Figure 5.29 displays this page.

In this page, you may configure the following information:

- **Console Prompt** — This enables you to specify the prompt that you wish to have displayed on the ZFS console screen.
- **Working Path** — This specifies the working path on the server that the engine should use for its temporary files.
- **Purge database entries** — You can specify the number of days old that a database log entry can be before it is removed from the ZFS database.

FIGURE 5.29 *Configuration page of the ZENworks for Servers policy in a Server Policy Package*

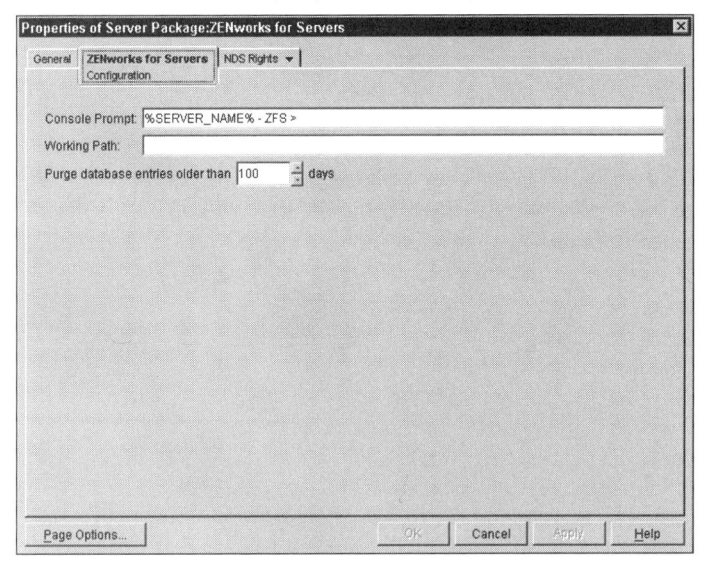

Several variables can be used in this and other places in ZENworks for Servers 2. These variables are enclosed in % (percent signs) and can be either a defined set, an environment variable from the server, an attribute of the server object, or an attribute of a specified NDS object. The order is as follows:

1. If the string between the percent signs is a predefined variable, that value is placed in that string. Predefined variables are one of the following:

    - LOAD_DIR — The directory where the NetWare server was loaded.
    - TREE_NAME — The name of the tree where ZENworks for Servers is located.
    - WORKING_PATH — The working directory for the temporary files.
    - SERVER_DN — NDS distinguished name for the server object.
    - IP_ADDRESS — IP address of the server.
    - BASE_PATH — The base path of where the ZENworks for Servers policy engine is located (for example, SYS:\SMANAGER).
    - SERVER_NAME — Name the server was given at install time.

2. If the string has the format `%object distinguished name;attribute%`, the attribute value of the specified object is placed in the string. For example, the string `%rtanner.novell:username%` would return the value of the attribute "username" in the object `rtanner.novell`.
3. If the string has no semicolon, the system looks for an environment variable of that name and replaces the value in the string.
4. If no environment variable exists with that name, the name is assumed to be a server attribute and the system attempts to place the attribute's value in the string.

CHAPTER 6

Setting Up Tiered Electronic Distribution

This chapter discusses the construction, deployment, and administration of the ZENworks for Servers 2 Tiered Electronic Distribution (TED) subsystem. As part of ZENworks for Servers 2, TED, provides a mechanism to enable you to reliably transmit files from one server to another throughout your entire network. TED is designed to be a high-end distribution service that can handle the complexity of a very large network.

Understanding the General Architecture for TED

This section discusses the components of TED and how to consider placing them into your network.

Introducing the Components

Tiered Electronic Distribution in ZENworks for Servers 2 is composed of the following components:

- **Distributor** — This is a Java software process that runs only on a NetWare server. This software is responsible for distributing the files to the subscribers in the network. The distributor also calls on some TED agents to collect the files and bundles them into a distribution that can then be sent to the subscribers (see the next item).

- **Subscriber** — This is a Java software module that may run on a NetWare or a Windows NT/2000 server. The subscriber is responsible for receiving software distributions from distributors or parent subscribers. The subscriber also calls TED agents, when appropriate, to perform additional actions on the distributions after they are received.

- **Parent subscriber** — A Java software package that runs on a NetWare or a Windows NT/2000 server. This module fulfills two purposes. The parent subscriber is first a subscriber and can receive and extract distri-butions for the server on which it resides. However, it additionally has the responsibility of forwarding some distributions on to other subscribers, when instructed. This module is the same software as the subscriber; the only difference is that the requests sent to parent subscribers have additional information that instructs the subscribers to act as parent subscribers and pass the distribution on to at least one other subscriber. This means any subscriber can become a parent subscriber by simply listing it in the routing hierarchy on a distributor object, or by listing it as a parent subscriber in any subscriber object.

- **TED agents** — These are Java modules that are started by the distributor or the subscriber and have a specific function. For example, there are agents whose job it is to collect files and collapse them into a distribution package suitable for transmission to subscribers. There are also agents who are responsible for expanding these distributions and placing the extracted files on the servers that have received the distribution.

Several TED components may reside on the same server. For example, you may have a server that is both a distributor and a subscriber, which results in that server having and running a distributor module, a subscriber module, and agents when creating and extracting files from a distribution.

NDS Objects

TED uses objects in the directory to help direct and control its configuration and behavior in the network. The following objects are associated with TED components:

- **Distributor object** — This object may be placed anywhere in the tree and holds the configuration information for the distributor.

- **Subscriber object** — This object contains some configuration information that the subscriber uses. This object is never actually accessed by any subscriber (removing the need for a subscriber process to access NDS); instead, the distributor reads the configuration information from the subscriber objects and sends this configuration information to the subscriber agents with every distribution.

- **External subscriber object** — This object refers to a subscriber that is outside the distributor's tree. The configuration information for this subscriber is contained in a subscriber object in its own tree. This object is used to enable TED to distribute across tree boundaries.

- **Distribution object** — This object represents the collection of files that you wish to transmit as a bundle across the network to various subscribers. A distribution is owned by a single distributor. That distributor is responsible for collecting, packaging, and distributing all the files listed in the distribution object.

▸ **Channel object** — This object represents a set of distributions and subscribers that are grouped together. When you place a distribution into a channel, all subscribers associated with the channel receive the distribution. When you place a new subscriber into a channel, all distributions associated with the channel are sent to the subscriber.

When you install TED components, you can specify which servers in the network will be distributors and subscribers and their relationship with any channels. The channel relationship can also be constructed after the installation process through ConsoleOne.

The following list describes the relationships of the various components of TED:

1. Distributors are associated with distributions. The same distributor sends the distribution, regardless, to any of the subscribers (or parent subscribers) that will be receiving the files. Distributors are only indirectly associated with subscribers or channels because the distributions (to which distributors are associated) are associated with channels and the channels know the subscribers. Currently, the files that are going to be bundled in a distribution *must* be on the distributor that is handling the work or accessible via FTP or HTTP from the distributor server (depending on the TED agent used).

2. Subscribers are associated with channels. A subscriber may be associated with many channels and receive all the distributions that are placed in each of the channels to which it is associated.

3. Parent subscribers are identified as a parent either in the routing hierarchy list in any distributor object or as the parent subscriber in any subscriber object.

4. Channels are a collection of distributions and subscribers. Subscribers and distributions are associated with the channel. Essentially, the channel describes a set of subscribers that should receive the set of distributions. Distributions from many distributors can be placed in a single channel.

5. Distributions are collections of files that are sent in the TED system. Each distribution belongs to a single distributor and can be placed in multiple channels. A distribution may be placed in any number of channels, and the distributor is responsible for sending the distribution to all of the subscribers that are subscribed to the channels.

SETTING UP TIERED ELECTRONIC DISTRIBUTION

TED also uses digital certificates and MD5 message digests of the distributions to verify the contents and originator of the distributions. When a distributor is doing the gathering process (that is, the agent is actively collecting the files and placing them in the distribution file), it runs an MD5 message digest on the distribution. When the distributor is sending the distribution, it sends a header to the subscriber that includes the digest and other information — all digitally signed with the signature of the distributor. When the subscriber receives the header, it checks the digital signature of the distributor with the digital certificate that it has for the server (you need to install this certificate on the subscriber through ConsoleOne or manually). If the signatures match, the subscriber proceeds with the download. When the download is complete, the subscriber runs its own MD5 message digest on the file and compares the results with the digest the distributor placed originally in the header. If they match, the file is deemed valid and the subscriber proceeds to schedule the agents to handle the unpacking of the distribution.

> **NOTE** The generation of the MD5 message digest may take significant time, particularly with large distribution files. Be aware that this could increase, possibly by hours, the time it takes to perform the gathering and creation of the distribution file. The digest is optional, so be sure you decide whether you want it or not.

Discussing TED Configuration in Your Network

You need to consider how you wish to lay out TED into your tree and network. You need to take into account any WANs that you must use for your distributions and be careful to minimize the amount of traffic that is transmitted over a WAN link. TEDs from ZENworks for Servers 2 are designed to handle anything from the smallest network to large enterprises and can be configured to help minimize this traffic. However, you must set up TED and administer its functions in order to get these gains.

Examining a Simple Layout

To help in the explanation, let's take an example of a simple and then a complex tree and discover the best method to lay out TED components to get the best performance for your network. Let's first take a look at Figure 6.1, which shows a simple tree.

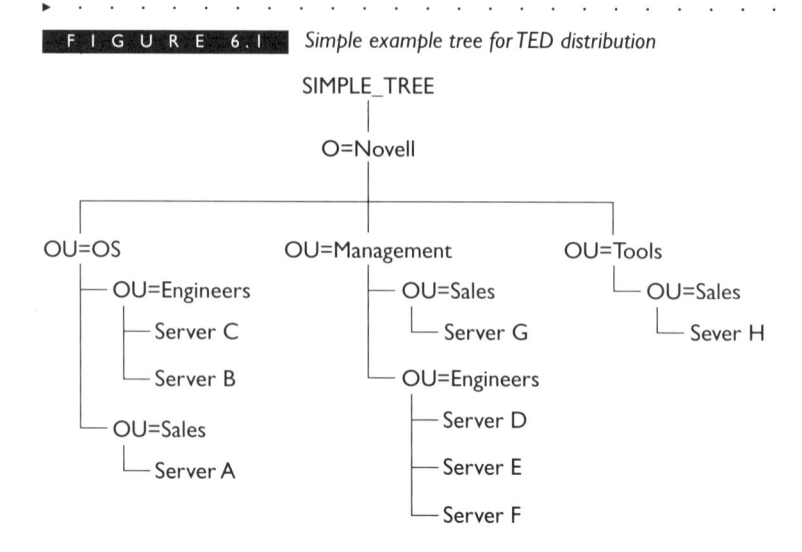

FIGURE 6.1 Simple example tree for TED distribution

```
                    SIMPLE_TREE
                         |
                      O=Novell
                         |
   ┌─────────────────────┼─────────────────────┐
 OU=OS              OU=Management            OU=Tools
   ├─ OU=Engineers      ├─ OU=Sales             └─ OU=Sales
   │    ├─ Server C     │    └─ Server G             └─ Sever H
   │    └─ Server B     └─ OU=Engineers
   └─ OU=Sales               ├─ Server D
        └─ Server A          ├─ Server E
                             └─ Server F
```

As you can see in Figure 6.1, the tree (SIMPLE_TREE) contains a tree that is assumed to be all in a single campus where no WANs are involved. The TED configuration for this setup can be fairly simple, because there are only eight servers in the system. In order to not overburden a distributor or a parent subscriber, you should not have a distributor or parent subscriber support more than 40 subscribers. Because there are not going to be more than eight subscribers in the network, we only need in this simple case a single distributor and eight subscribers (one on each server, including the distribution server).

The number of channels that you want is based on the types of distributions that you would expect to perform or the time schedules that you want the distribution sent. It is recommended that you base your channels on the types of distributions or schedules that you expect to send, rather than the destination. For example, you should name your channels Sales Data, Base Engineering Apps, Virus Patterns, Europe Off Hours, and so forth. By naming your channels this way (rather than Building1, for example), it will be clear by the name of the channel what type of distributions can be expected to be transmitted to the subscribers attached to the channel. You can have any number of channels in the directory and a subscriber can subscribe to any number of channels, so there is no reason to limit the channels that you create.

In the SIMPLE_TREE, we create three channels: Sales Apps, Eng Apps, and Sales Data. We place a distributor on server A because the sales data is written on this server, and a distributor on server B because it holds all of the golden

SETTING UP TIERED ELECTRONIC DISTRIBUTION

images of the engineering applications. We place a subscriber on each of the other servers and associate them with the appropriate channels. Figure 6.2 displays the same tree with all of the channels, distributors, and subscribers in place. Subscribers G and H both subscribe to channels Sales Data and Sales Apps. Subscribers B, C, E, F, and G subscribe to the Eng Apps channel.

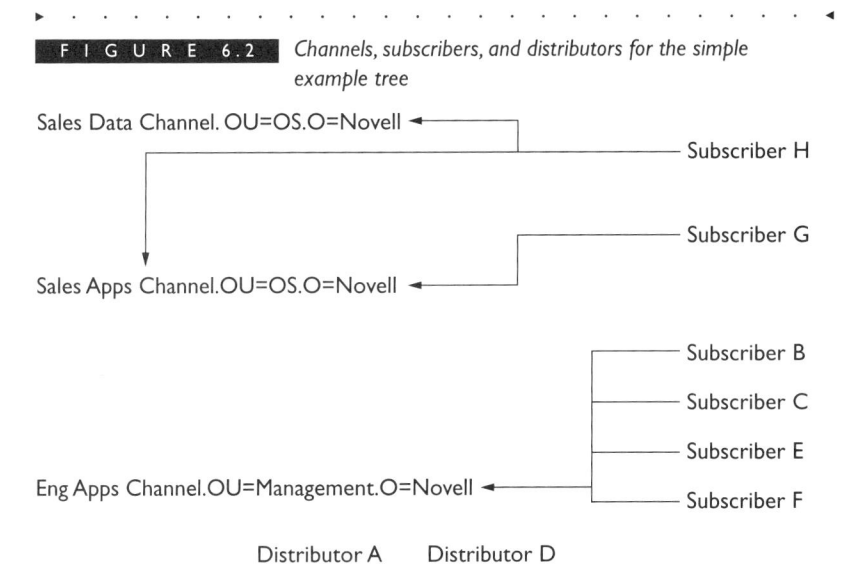

FIGURE 6.2 *Channels, subscribers, and distributors for the simple example tree*

```
Sales Data Channel. OU=OS.O=Novell ◄─────────┐
                                              │            ──── Subscriber H
                                              │
                                              │            ──── Subscriber G
Sales Apps Channel.OU=OS.O=Novell ◄──────────┘

                                                          ┌── Subscriber B
                                                          ├── Subscriber C
                                                          ├── Subscriber E
Eng Apps Channel.OU=Management.O=Novell ◄────────────────┤
                                                          └── Subscriber F

            Distributor A    Distributor D
```

This layout is done because of the needs of each of the servers, regardless of their location in the network or the tree.

Looking at a Complex Layout

Now lets take a look at a more complex tree, one that includes some WAN traffic to cross container boundaries. Figure 6.3 is a demonstration of this type of tree.

In the WAN, tree you can see Provo, Paris, Honolulu, and Sydney. Let's assume that Provo is in the United States, Paris in France, and Sydney in Australia, thus requiring a WAN to interconnect these sites. There is an added complexity that is not shown and that is, in order to get to Sydney from Provo you must first make a WAN hop in Honolulu and then the final WAN hop to Sydney. To throw in a twist, we'll have a sales server, server 7, in the mix that is getting information from a Sales channel from somewhere in the tree.

117

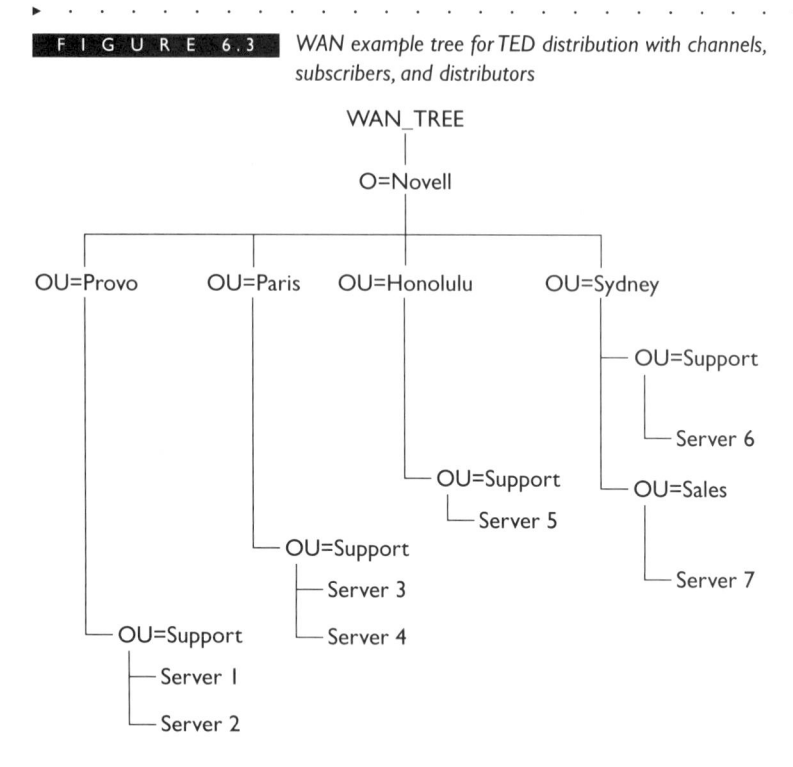

FIGURE 6.3 *WAN example tree for TED distribution with channels, subscribers, and distributors*

```
                            WAN_TREE
                               |
                           O=Novell
      ┌────────────┬──────────┴──────────┬────────────┐
   OU=Provo     OU=Paris            OU=Honolulu    OU=Sydney
                                                    ├── OU=Support
                                                    │     └── Server 6
                                         OU=Support └── OU=Sales
                                           └─ Server 5    │
                              OU=Support                  └── Server 7
                                ├── Server 3
               OU=Support       └── Server 4
                 ├── Server 1
                 └── Server 2
```

Because there are WANs involved, you wish to minimize the traffic that must go over the WAN lines. This can be accomplished by placing a parent subscriber at each of the WAN sites and then connecting each of the destination subscribers in the target WAN to that parent. In the case of Sydney, we need to have a parent subscriber send the distributions to another parent subscriber in Sydney, because it is a two-hop scenario.

We only look at two channels, one called Sales Data (collected and distributed by an unshown distributor) and one called TID Data that is used to transmit all of the TID files that are collected at the main Provo site and then transmitted to each of the support sites across the world. We would want to set up the following channels, distributors, and subscribers to support the WAN tree (see Figure 6.4).

SETTING UP TIERED ELECTRONIC DISTRIBUTION

FIGURE 6.4 *Subscribers, distributors, and channel configuration for the WAN example tree*

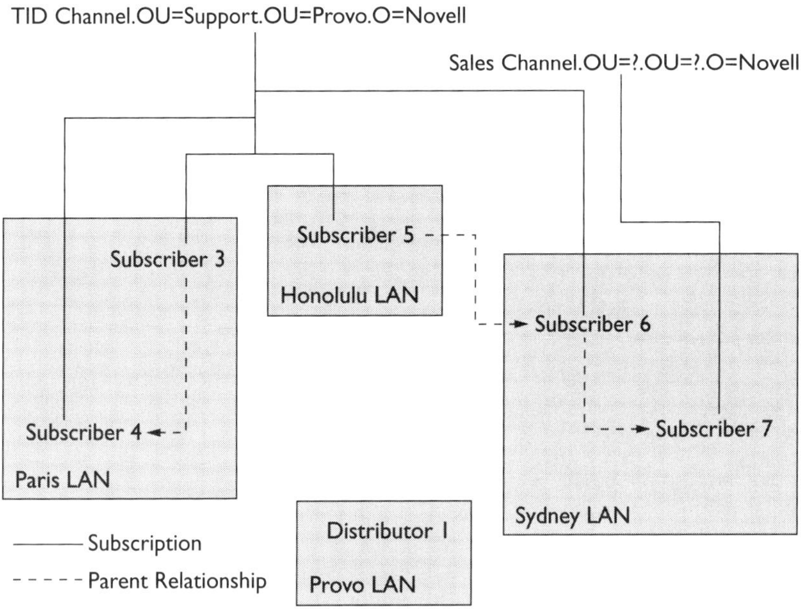

TID Channel.OU=Support.OU=Provo.O=Novell

Sales Channel.OU=?.OU=?.O=Novell

Subscriber 3

Subscriber 5
Honolulu LAN

Subscriber 6

Subscriber 4
Paris LAN

Subscriber 7
Sydney LAN

Distributor 1
Provo LAN

——— Subscription
- - - - - Parent Relationship

As we can see, there are two channels; the TID channel in Provo and the Sales channel that is somewhere in the tree (it is really not relevant where the channel is located). We have connected subscribers 3, 4, 5, and 6 to the TID channel in NDS. We have also made sure that subscriber 7 is connected to the Sales channel. The distributor is simply shown to exist in the Provo LAN and is not fully shown in the tree. Suffice it to say that it exists on a server in Provo in the same tree as shown.

Now we must define the parent subscribers in the network, in order for distributor 1 (in the Provo LAN) to be the most efficient in its use of the WANs. If we do not define parent subscribers, the distributor transmits to each subscriber directly. This results in the same files being transmitted to Paris twice, to Honolulu three times, and to Sydney twice, for a total of seven WAN transmissions. Let's see how this would work out by looking at Table 6.1. As you can see, they each take one hop except for Sydney, which requires a hop through Honolulu and then to Sydney.

TABLE 6.1 WAN Hops for WAN Tree Transmissions

LAN	# OF WANS	TO SUBSCRIBER
Paris LAN	1	Subscriber 3
Paris LAN	1	Subscriber 4
Honolulu LAN	1	Subscriber 5
Sydney LAN	2	Subscriber 6
Sydney LAN	2	Subscriber 7

Now we can describe in NDS the parent subscribers of our network. This can be done in one of two ways: as a routing hierarchy in the distributor object, or as a parent subscriber identification in each "child" or "leaf" subscriber (see Figure 6.5).

The quickest way to define this would be to go to distributor 1's object in the tree and define the following routing hierarchy:

1. Subscriber 3
    a. Subscriber 4
2. Subscriber 5
    a. Subscriber 6
        Subscriber 7

This would state to the distributor that when it is distributing its collections, subscriber 3 will service subscriber 4, and subscriber 5 will service subscriber 6, who then services subscriber 7. If we look at the behavior of TED when this is done, the following transmissions occur over the WAN (see Table 6.2).

TABLE 6.2 Optimized WAN Hops for WAN Tree Transmissions

LAN	# OF WANS	TO SUBSCRIBER
Paris LAN	1	Subscriber 3
Local, from subscriber 3	0	Subscriber 4
Honolulu LAN	1	Subscriber 5
Sydney LAN, passed from subscriber 5	1	Subscriber 6
Local, from subscriber 6	0	Subscriber 7

SETTING UP TIERED ELECTRONIC DISTRIBUTION

FIGURE 6.5 *Subscribers, distributors, and channel configuration for the WAN example tree*

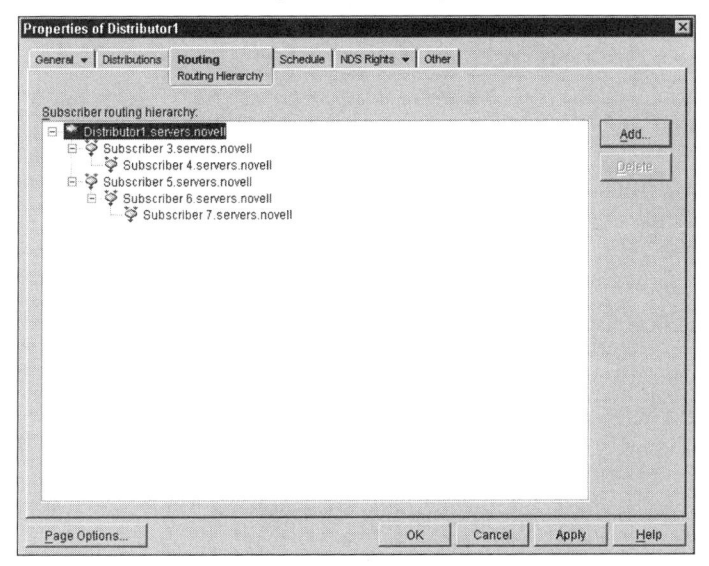

[Screenshot: Properties of Distributor1 dialog showing Routing Hierarchy tab with Subscriber routing hierarchy:
- Distributor1.servers.novell
  - Subscriber 3.servers.novell
    - Subscriber 4.servers.novell
  - Subscriber 5.servers.novell
    - Subscriber 6.servers.novell
      - Subscriber 7.servers.novell]

We see now that we will only transmit the files three times over a WAN and have saved almost 233 percent of the traffic that we would have consumed had we not done parent subscribers.

One annoyance is that, when you define the routing hierarchy in the distributor, *only* that distributor knows of this configuration. You have to go to all of the distributors in that LAN and put this same routing hierarchy into their objects. This can also be a great benefit, because it enables you to set up different distribution routes depending on the distributor that is sending the information. For example, you might have a financial information distributor, but you may not want that financial information passing through a certain subscriber. By defining a separate distribution hierarchy on the financial distributor, you can eliminate certain servers from ever getting the financial information. To save you some aggravation with having to describe your whole network, you can leave the leaf node subscribers out of the routing hierarchy definitions and identify their parent in their own object. The distributor automatically discovers this and includes it in the routing list. (See the section titled "Construction of a Routing Hierarchy" for more information.)

Examining Capacities and Restrictions

Now let's review some of the issues that you should watch in your network to make sure that you don't attempt to overburden your servers with distribution work. This concern is relative to the number of dependents a distributor must support and where distributors must be in the network.

Looking at Dependents

As was mentioned earlier, you should attempt to not overburden any distributor or parent subscriber with more than 40 direct dependents. This can be difficult to manage, and you will need to keep a careful eye on how you configure your subscribers and distributors to keep this from becoming a problem. The issue is that you really don't know at the beginning which distributors will be sending to which subscribers, because it is purely based on which channel you chose to place the distribution. The easiest way to keep this all working well is to think about your TED distribution network from the bottom up as you are constructing the system. As you place subscribers into the network, choose a hierarchy of well-known parent subscribers, making sure that no branch of your TED network is overburdened.

For example, let's say we start with the TED distribution network shown in Figure 6.6.

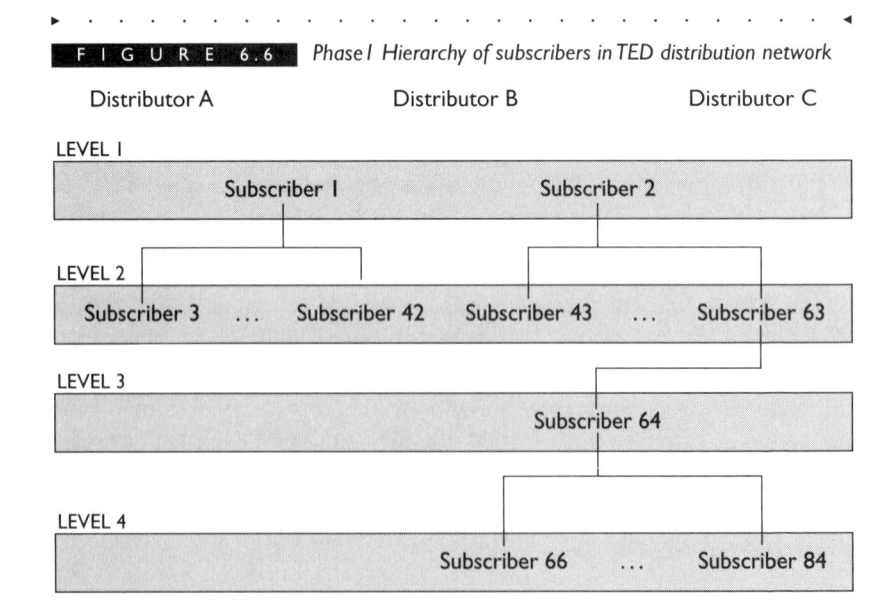

FIGURE 6.6 *Phase I Hierarchy of subscribers in TED distribution network*

| Distributor A | Distributor B | Distributor C |

LEVEL 1
- Subscriber 1
- Subscriber 2

LEVEL 2
- Subscriber 3 ... Subscriber 42
- Subscriber 43 ... Subscriber 63

LEVEL 3
- Subscriber 64

LEVEL 4
- Subscriber 66 ... Subscriber 84

In Figure 6.6, we have set up subscribers 3 through 63 so that they each use either subscribers 1 or 2 as their parent subscriber. We also set up subscribers 66 through 84 to use subscriber 64 as their parent subscriber. In the figure, we have labeled the levels of the hierarchy (levels 1–4) to help us understand where in the structure each of the subscribers reside. Now, when we wish to add more subscribers, we can either place them hierarchically, under some other subscribers at level 2, or we can create a new level 1 and go from there. Just keep in mind to keep the TED distribution hierarchical tree balanced somewhat so as to not overburden any one subscriber or distributor.

This leveling approach works well for a single LAN. When you move into multiple LANs and introduce a WAN link, you need to have this leveling in each of the LANs in your network and then describe in the distributors how you may efficiently move from one WAN to the next, based on their location. For example, distributor X may only have one hop to LAN Y, but distributor M may have two. So, the routing hierarchy defined in distributors X and M will be different with regard to how to most efficiently get to LAN Y.

Limits on Distributors

Additionally, in ZENworks for Servers 2, the TED distributor may only run on NetWare and can only distribute files that are found on its local volumes (file agent) or FTP/HTTP accessible from the NetWare server. This may require that you set up several distributors in your network, to place them on servers that keep the "golden" copies of the files. Be aware that you may not want to place all the burden of distribution on a single server unless it has the memory and disk capacities that can keep up with the demand. There is no limit to the number of distributors in the network; however, you should keep in mind the amount of work these distributors perform and their relationship with the subscribers and LAN/WAN placement. Traditionally, you would expect to have a relatively few number of distributors in your network.

Configuring TED Systems

There are several algorithms that you should know in order to help you in determining the best configuration of TED components. The following sections shed some light on how the internals of TED components function.

Construction of a Routing Hierarchy

The distributor is responsible for constructing a routing hierarchy when it sends each distribution. The following describes the steps that the distributor follows to construct the hierarchy:

1. The distributor discovers all of the subscribers (that is, leaf subscribers) that are to receive this distribution.

2. The distributor looks into the routing hierarchy that has been administered in its NDS object. For each subscriber, it looks to see if that subscriber is in its hierarchy list. If it is, it sends the distribution to that subscriber following the routing hierarchy defined in the distributor object.

3. If the subscriber is not found in the administered list, the distributor looks in the subscriber's object to see if it has identified a parent subscriber. If there is a parent subscriber identified, the distributor then looks for the parent subscriber in its routing hierarchy list.

4. If the parent subscriber is in the routing hierarchy list, the distributor follows the hierarchy described to get to the parent subscriber and then tack on the end-node subscriber into the route to get the distribution to the subscriber.

5. If the parent subscriber is not in the distributor's routing hierarchy list, the distributor sends the distribution directly to the identified parent subscriber (identified in the subscriber's object) or directly to the subscriber (when no parent subscriber is identified).

You should note that in the algorithm the distributor does not go to the subscriber and get its parent and then go to the parent and get its parent, and so forth, trying to construct the hierarchy of subscribers. The distributor only goes up one level in your TED distribution hierarchy. Therefore, you must, if you have more than one level of subscribers, describe $n - 1$ levels in the routing hierarchy in each distributor object. You can then leave the last level undefined in the distributor, defining it in each subscriber object (or in a TED policy that affects each subscriber) instead.

Signing Distributions

The following steps are taken by the distributor and the subscribers to check the validity of the distributor and the distribution file:

1. The distributor activates agents that collect the files off its volumes and collapse the files into a single, compressed distribution file.

2. The distributor then performs an optional MD5 message digest on the distribution file.
3. The distributor places the digest along with other information into a header packet and then sign the header with its digital signature.
4. The distributor then sends the header packet to the subscriber via the calculated distribution route.
5. The subscriber receives the header and checks to see if the distributor identified in the header is a distributor it will accept distributions from (because it has a digital certificate stored on its drives for this distributor).
6. If it is an accepted distributor, the subscriber validates the digital signature of the distributor; matching it with the signature stored in the certificate it has on file for this distributor.
7. If the signature's match, the subscriber saves the distribution digest and accepts the rest of the distribution.
8. The distributor sends the remainder of the distribution file to the subscriber.
9. Once the subscriber has received the entire distribution file, it performs its own MD5 message digest on the file. This digest is compared with the one sent in the header and signed by the distributor. If the digests match, the distribution is accepted, and when the extraction schedule starts, the agents are contacted to unpack the distribution.

Scheduler Interactions

As you introduce yourself to the various components of the TED system (distributor, subscriber, distribution, channel), you will discover that each component has its own independent scheduler to determine when its work is done. At first look you will say, okay, but then confusion will set in as you try to jumble how the schedules of these various components can keep or enable a successful distribution.

Here we examine, briefly, the various schedulers for each component and how they can play together to create a functioning TED system in your network. Let's first look at each of the components and the responsibility the scheduler plays:

▶ **Distributor schedule** — Determines when the distributor reads NDS for the configuration information for itself, its distributions, and any channels and subscribers it interacts with. It discovers the channels and subscribers by looking at any distributions that it has in any channels and the subscribers that are hooked to these channels. The distributor also looks for the NDS objects for any TED policies that may affect the configuration of itself, channels, or subscribers and includes them in its configuration information. The information for a subscriber is collected from NDS when the distributor schedule fires and it reads the information from NDS. Any changes to the subscriber objects or policies that affect the subscribers need to be made in NDS prior to the distributor refresh schedule firing. This information is then sent on to the subscribers when a distribution is given to them.

- **Distribution schedule** — This schedule determines when the agents on the distributor server will be activated to perform any gathering of the files and compacted into the single distribution file. This process must be completed before the channel begins its processing or the distribution needs to wait until the next channel cycle. The gathering does not occur if the distribution is inactive or does not belong to a channel with active subscribers. Once the gathering has started, it continues to completion even if it extends beyond the administered schedule.

- **Channel schedule** — Determines when the distributor transmits any previously constructed distribution files to any destination subscribers. Any distribution files that have not been constructed when the channel is activated (based on the schedule) will have to wait until the next firing of the channel schedule to be transmitted. The transmission is terminated if the time has expired for the channel, and the transmission picks up where it left off on the next scheduled time for the channel.

- **Subscriber schedule** — Determines when the subscriber activates the agents on the subscriber server to extract any files from distributions that have been received and have not been processed. The extraction continues once it has started on a particular distribution even if the time has expired for the extraction schedule.

Looking at the network, you would want the time frames to occur in your systems as represented in Figure 6.7.

SETTING UP TIERED ELECTRONIC DISTRIBUTION

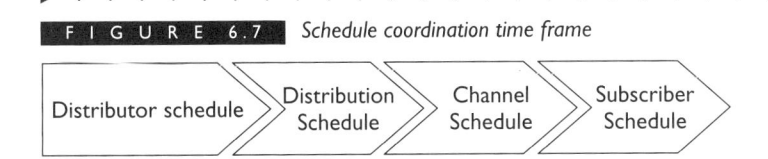

FIGURE 6.7 *Schedule coordination time frame*

Distributor schedule → Distribution Schedule → Channel Schedule → Subscriber Schedule

For example, if you schedule your distributor to refresh the configuration each day at the close of the day (say 5 p.m.), and then schedule the distribution to gather the files at 6 p.m., and the channels to begin their distributions at 10 P.M. and the subscribers to extract at 4 a.m., the cycle could be completed in the night. This obviously gets more complicated when you cross time zone boundaries. You could simplify this some by having, possibly, channels for each different area of the world, which would have a different local time to begin the distribution such that the remote site and the local site will be busy at appropriate levels.

NOTE The channel schedule is "translated" into the distributor's time zone. For example, if the channel schedule says 3 p.m. MST and the distributor is in California, it starts at 2 p.m. PST. If you have a distributor in New York that also has distributions in this channel, it starts at 5 p.m. EST. This means that all distributors with distributions in a channel start sending at the same time, regardless of time zone.

About the TED Distributor

The TED distributor has the responsibility for transmitting a distribution (collection of files) to subscribers throughout the tree and to external subscribers that are found outside of the distributor's tree. The distributor calls TED agents to collect the files and compact them into a distribution file that are then sent to the appropriate subscribers.

The distributor is installed on a server as part of the installation process and is launched by the following being placed in the autoexec.ncf file. The distributor uses the port broker to assist in the distribution process.

```
sys:\zenworks\java\lib\pbroker.ncf
sys:\ted2\dist.ncf
```

127

The distributor is managed by command-line commands (see Appendix C for more details) and by a distributor object that is placed in the tree. The following sections discuss each of the pages that can be administered on the distributor object. Traditionally, because the distributor is associated with the server (there is a distributor object expected for each server that is running a distributor), it should be named such that the server is clearly known. The default naming by the installation process is "Distributor_<SERVERNAME>" and the distributor object is created in the same container where specified.

> **NOTE** The TED distributor and subscriber objects should only be created through the installation program on the product CD. This ensures that the NCF files on the servers authenticate with the correct objects in NDS. If you move or rename a distributor object, you need to update the SYS:\TED2\DIST.NCF file with the new DN of the distributor object or it ceases to function. All other TED objects can be moved and renamed, but remember to refresh the distributor after any change to these objects.

> **TIP** Startup ConsoleOne with a `-tedcreate` option. If you do this, you can select the TED distributor and subscriber objects and ConsoleOne allows you to go ahead and create the objects. This does *not* place the distributor or subscriber code on the server, nor does it modify the autoexec.ncf file. You need to place the code (everything under the sys:\ted2 and sys:\smanager directories) on the server and modify the autoexec.ncf file manually. You may also need to manually modify the dist.ncf or sub.ncf if the paths to the Java components are not the same as the server where you copied the files.

The distributor is the only TED component that queries NDS and reads its object. The distributor reads its distribution object, the channel objects, and any policies when it starts on the server, when requested through the console with a `refresh` command, by right-clicking the distributor object in ConsoleOne and choosing the Refresh Distributor option, or as scheduled in the distributor object. The distributor also reads any subscriber related to the distribution they are to send and relay any updates in the subscriber object and policies (such as the Tiered Electronic Distribution policy in the Service Location Policy package) to the subscriber when the distribution is sent.

Introducing the Settings Property Page

This page is found under the General tab and represents some general configuration settings that are effective for this distributor. Figure 6.8 displays a capture of this screen.

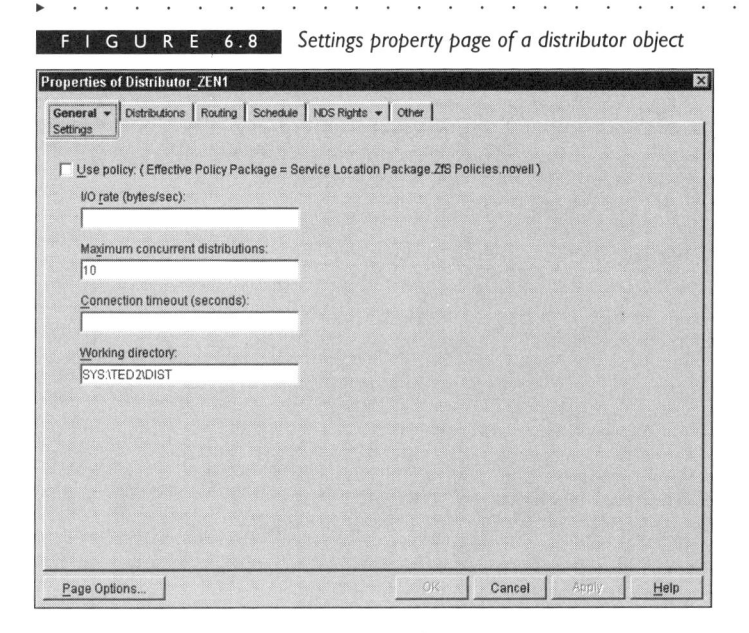

FIGURE 6.8 *Settings property page of a distributor object*

On this property, page you may make the following settings:

- **I/O rate** — This represents the number of bytes per second that you allow a distributor to consume for all distributions for input (acknowledgments and so forth) and for output, independently. The default is for the distributor to send at the maximum rate possible on the server. For example, if you choose to enter 4096, this distributor will not exceed sending 4K per second to all subscribers (each subscriber gets 4K/# of subscriber threads amount of I/O), regardless of the capacity of the subscriber, and it will not exceed receiving 4K bytes per second for incoming messages. (That's a total of 8K bytes — the amount you specify is for each, so the total consumed for both input and output is double the specified amount.) This setting does not affect the rate at which FTP and HTTP distributions are gathered. The distributor will always use as much bandwidth as is available when gathering distributions.

- **Maximum concurrent distributions** — Each time a distributor is going to perform a distribution, it creates a Java thread that handles the distribution to the subscriber. This value identifies the maximum number of threads that you allow the distributor to create concurrently to service the sending of distributions.
- **Connection timeout** — The default for this is 300 seconds. You can also enter a timeout value that, when exceeded, the distributor fails the distribution and retries it every two minutes for the next thirty minutes (as long as it is still in its scheduled window). If after the retries the distribution still has not succeeded, the distributor fails the distribution, and at the next scheduled distribution time for the channel the distributor will reattempt to send the distribution.
- **Working directory** — This identifies the directory where the distributor stores its distribution files. The agents, when they are called to collect the files and compress them into the distribution file, store the files in this working directory. It is not recommended to use the SYS volume because of the potential system problems should that volume become full.

Looking at the Messaging Property Page

The Messaging property page is under the General tab and can be configured by pressing the active tab and selecting the messaging value under the drop-down on the tab (by pressing the small triangle in the tab). The following is a sample of a Messaging page (see Figure 6.9). Unless you are having some problems and are diagnosing some issues, it is recommended to use level 4 or lower.

For each of the appropriate fields, you may enter one of the following message levels:

- **Level 0** — This level displays no messages. In the Messaging page, you can administer the following items regarding the behavior of the distributor.
- **Level 1** — This level only displays errors that were encountered in the system.
- **Level 2** — This level displays the successes that were satisfied by the system and also includes all of the level 1 messages.
- **Level 3** — This level displays any warnings that were encountered in the system, in addition to all of the level 2 messages.

SETTING UP TIERED ELECTRONIC DISTRIBUTION

- **Level 4** — This level includes all of the level 3 messages and, in addition, informational messages that identify key points in the system.
- **Level 5** — This level includes all level 4 messages in addition to trace information, which notifies the observer of the modules that are being executed. This level also captures and displays all Java exceptions.
- **Level 6** — This level includes all of the other levels plus developer trace information.

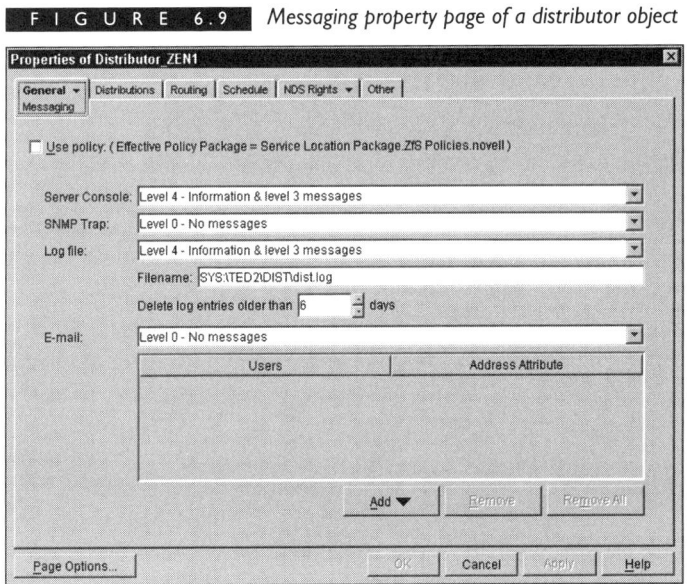

FIGURE 6.9 *Messaging property page of a distributor object*

You can administer the following configuration parameters on the Message property page:

- **Server Console** — This item identifies the level of messages that are displayed on the distributor server console (not the main server console).
- **SNMP Trap** — This identifies the level of messages that are sent as an SNMP trap to the SNMP trap target. The SNMP Trap Targets policy must be defined and active in an effective (for the distributor object) Service Location policy for traps to be sent.

131

- **Log file** — This identifies the level of message that should be stored in the log file. Additionally, you can configure the following about the log file:
    - **Filename** — This is the filename of the log file. The default location is SYS:\TED2\DIST\DIST.LOG. You should change the location of the log file, because it can grow as well and may adversely affect the system if it is located on the SYS volume.
    - **Delete log entries older than X days** — In this parameter you identify the number of days (X) worth of log entries should remain in the log file. The default is six days. Therefore, any log entries that are older than six days will be cleared from the log file. The process of scanning for and removing old log entries happens once every 24 hours and is not configurable.
- **E-mail** — With the e-mail option, you may specify the level of messages that will be sent as e-mail to the identified users. The SMTP Host policy in the ZENworks for Servers 2 Service Location policy package must be effective for the distributor object in order to enable it to discover the address for the SMTP host to send the e-mail. If this is not specified, the e-mail will not be sent.

In addition to identifying the level of messages, you must also specify who should receive these messages. To add users to the list and for them to be sent the message, you must press the Add button and select whether you wish to add an NDS User or Group, or specify an e-mail address. When you select a user, you are asked to browse to the user in the directory, and the system takes the e-mail address attribute from the user and uses that as the address for the user. Should you choose a group, all of the users in the group are sent the e-mail message and the e-mail attribute are used for each of those users. Should you not want to use the e-mail address attribute in the user object, you may select the down arrow in the Address Attribute field and select which of the NDS User attributes you wish to identify as containing the e-mail address. Many administrators store user e-mail addresses in the "internet e-mail address" attribute instead of the "e-mail address" attribute. It is expected that the attribute you identify contains a valid e-mail address.

If you choose to enter an explicit e-mail address, rather than selecting a user or a group, you may choose the E-mail Address choice from the Add button. You will are prompted to enter a valid e-mail address. The entered e-mail address is assumed to be valid and is shown as the Username field in the table with an N/A in the Address Attribute field.

Introducing the Distributions Property Page

This page of the distributor object identifies the defined distributions that this particular distributor is responsible for collecting and sending. You cannot add distributions on this page — they are only added or deleted in this list when the actual distribution object is created or deleted from NDS. You may look at the distribution object, however, by selecting the distribution in the list and pressing the Details button. This launches the property pages for the selected distribution object.

About the Routing Hierarchy Property Page

The Routing Hierarchy property page is one of the most important pages to administer, especially if you have WANs in your tree and you wish to be efficient in your distribution of files. Figure 6.10 shows a sample of this page.

FIGURE 6.10 Routing Hierarchy property page of a distributor object

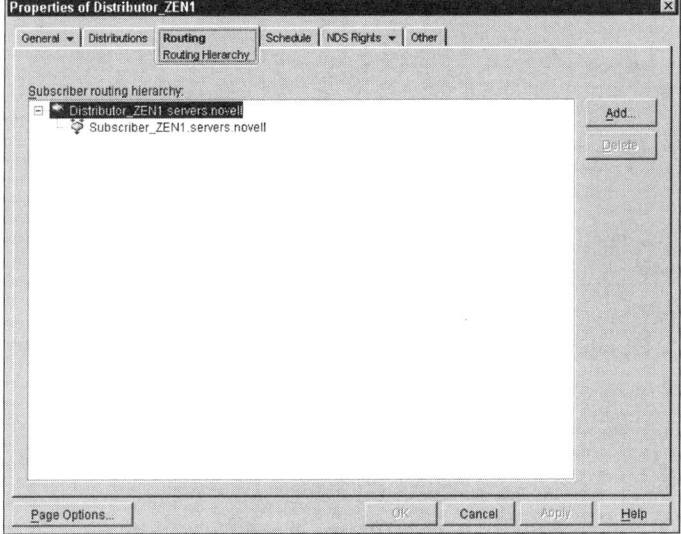

On this property page you can define the hierarchy associating the distributor to subscribers. This is the path that the distributor uses in sending distributions to the subscribers. As discussed in the "TED Configuration in Your Network" section, this page defines the route that you wish TED to follow when attempting to transmit a distribution from this distributor to any identified subscriber.

On this page you build a hierarchy tree that describes the routes that the distributor must follow. You place a child in the tree by selecting the parent and pressing the Add button. Once the add button is pressed, you are required to browse the NDS tree and identify the subscriber(s) you wish to insert. For example, if we wanted the routes shown in Figure 6.4 placed into this distributor, we would perform the following steps.

1. Select the distributor 1 object in the list (the topmost item). Press the Add button.
2. Browse NDS and select subscriber 3 in the tree.
3. Select subscriber 3 in the list and press the Add button.
4. Browse NDS and select subscriber 4 in the tree.
5. Select the distributor 1 object in the list and press the Add button.
6. Browse NDS and select subscriber 5 in the tree.
7. Select subscriber 5 in the list on this property page and press the Add button.
8. Browse NDS and select subscriber 6 in the tree.
9. Select subscriber 6 in the list and press the Add button.
10. Browse NDS and select subscriber 7 from the tree.

The hierarchy shown in Figure 6.11 should be displayed on the Routing page after you have completed the above steps.

Using the routing algorithm, the distributor now sends any distributions to subscriber 3 that are bound for either subscriber 3 or 4 and sends any distributions to subscriber 5 that are bound for either subscriber 5, 6, or 7.

NOTE The subscriber can be in the routing table and send distributions to other subscribers even if they are not participating in the channel for the end-target subscriber. They simply forward the distribution on and not extract it on their local system.

The routing hierarchy must be entered for each distributor object in the tree. If there are no entries in the hierarchy, the distributor only relies on the parent subscriber, which can be defined in the subscriber object to give any type of route other than direct. See the routing hierarchy algorithm described previously to understand how the distributor uses the routing hierarchy and the parent subscribers.

SETTING UP TIERED ELECTRONIC DISTRIBUTION

FIGURE 6.11 *Routing Hierarchy property page of a distributor object after entering route*

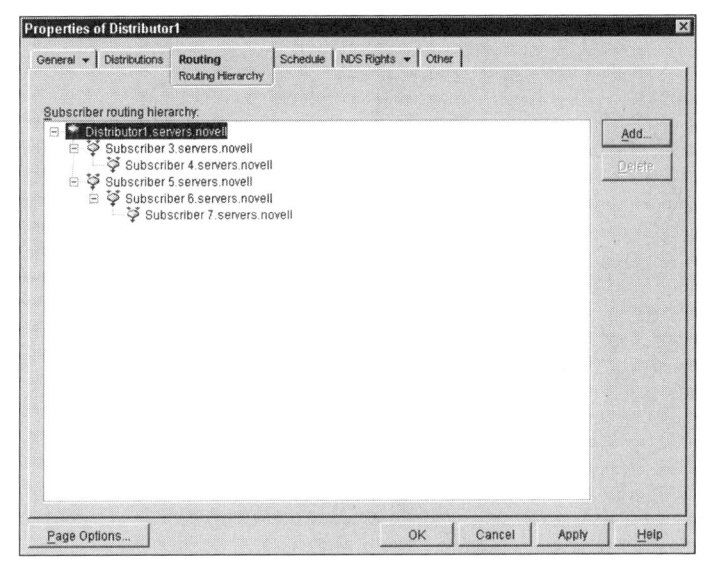

[Screenshot of Properties of Distributor1 dialog showing Routing Hierarchy tab with subscriber routing hierarchy:
- Distributor1.servers.novell
  - Subscriber 3.servers.novell
    - Subscriber 4.servers.novell
  - Subscriber 5.servers.novell
    - Subscriber 6.servers.novell
      - Subscriber 7.servers.novell]

About the Schedule Property Page

The Schedule page (shown in Figure 6.12) enables you to specify how often the distributor software on the server will go to NDS and read the configuration information in its object, the distributions assigned to the distributor, channel information, and subscriber configuration information. The default value is Never, which means that the distributor only reads its NDS object when it first is loaded on the server, or if told to with the console command (refresh), or in ConsoleOne if you right- click the distributor object and choose the Refresh menu option.

If there is a Tiered Electronic Distribution policy in a Service Location Policy package associated with the distributor, the checkbox for using the policy appears on this page. If there is no policy, the checkbox is not displayed. When this checkbox is activated, the schedule described in the policy is used for this distributor. When unchecked, this distributor has its own schedule and the Schedule Type field is available for administration. By default, this checkbox is checked if you have a TED policy.

135

FIGURE 6.12 *Schedule property page*

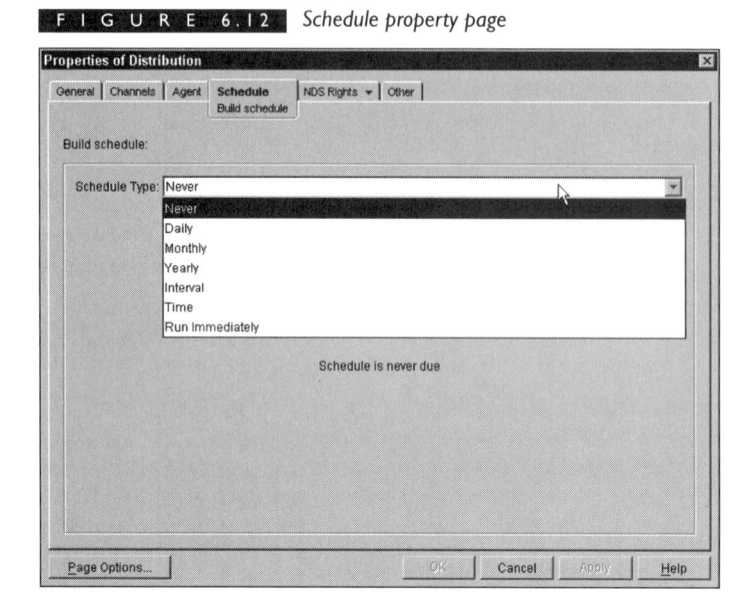

This page enables you to select when the configuration should be read and applied: Never, Daily, Monthly, Yearly, Interval, or Time.

Once you have selected when you want the configuration applied, you have additional fields to select in the lower portion of the screen. The following sections discuss the various options you have.

Never

This option only loads the distributor with the configuration information when it is first loaded on the server, after each reboot or restart.

Daily

When you choose to have the configuration applied to the system daily, you also need to select when the changes will be made.

This schedule requires that you select the days when you want the configuration applied. You select the days by clicking the days you desire. The selected days appear as depressed buttons.

In addition to the days, you can select the times the configuration is applied. These times — the start and stop times — provide a range of time when the configuration will be applied.

SETTING UP TIERED ELECTRONIC DISTRIBUTION

You can have the configuration also reapplied within the time frame every specified hour/minute/second by clicking the "Repeat the action every" field and specifying the time delay.

To keep all the distributors from simultaneously accessing NDS, you can select the "Randomly dispatch policy during time period" option. This causes each server to choose a random time within the time period when they will retrieve and apply the configuration.

Monthly

Under the monthly schedule, you can select which day of the month the configuration should be applied, or you can select "Last day of the month" to handle the last day, because all months obviously do not end on the same calendar date (that is, 30 days hath September, April, June, and November, all the rest have 31 except for February . . .).

Once you have selected the day, you can also select the time range when the configuration will be reread and applied.

To keep all the distributors from simultaneously accessing NDS, you can select the "Randomly dispatch policy during time period" option. This causes each server to choose a random time within the time period when they will retrieve and apply the configuration.

Yearly

You would select a yearly schedule if you want to apply the configuration only once a year.

On this screen you must choose the day that you wish the configuration to be applied. This is done by selecting the Calendar button to the right of the Date field. This brings up a Monthly dialog box where you can browse through the calendar to select the date you wish. This calendar does not correspond to any particular year and may not take into account leap years in its display. This is because you are choosing a date for each year that will come along in the present and future years.

Once you have selected the date, you can also select the time range when the configuration should be read and applied.

To keep all the distributors from simultaneously accessing NDS, you can select the "Randomly dispatch policy during time period." This causes each server to choose a random time within the time period when they will retrieve and apply the configuration.

Interval

This schedule type enables you to specify how often to repeatedly read and apply the configuration. You can specify the interval with a combination of days, hours, minutes, and seconds. This type waits for the interval to pass first before applying the configuration for the first time and then for each sequence after that.

Time

This enables you to specify a specific calendar date and time when the configuration will be applied. When the current date on the server is beyond the identified date, the configuration will be applied.

Run Immediately

The distributor does not use this schedule type, but it is used by other components. It is described here for the completeness of listing all possible schedulers.

With the Run Immediately schedule type, the first time that the associated object is activated the schedule causes the activity to occur. You may also specify a repeat interval in days, hours, minutes, and seconds. If no repeat interval is specified, the action only runs once until the object is restarted or refreshed.

NDS Rights Property Pages

The NDS Rights property page is made up of three pages. You can get to each of the pages by clicking the small triangle to the right of the page name and then selecting the desired page to be displayed.

These pages enable you to specify the rights that users have to this object in the directory. The following subsections discuss briefly each of these pages. These NDS Rights pages are displayed for every object in the tree.

Trustees of This Object Page

On this page (see Figure 6.13), you can assign objects to have rights as trustees of the distributor object. These trustees will have rights to this object or to attributes within this object.

If the user admin.novell has been added to the trustee list, then this user has some rights to this object. To get into the details of any trustee assignment (in order to modify the assignment), you would need to press the Assigned Rights button.

SETTING UP TIERED ELECTRONIC DISTRIBUTION

FIGURE 6.13 *Trustees of this Object page*

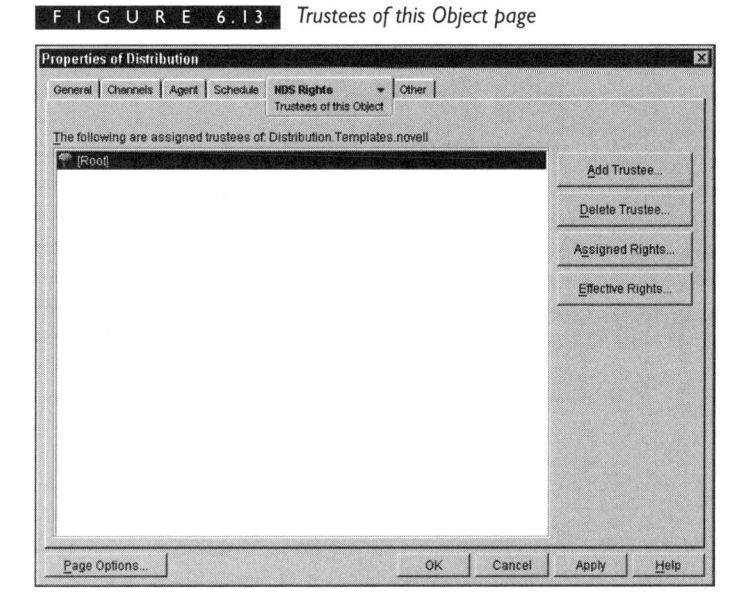

When you press the Assign Rights button, after selecting the user you want to modify you are presented with a dialog box that enables you to select either [All Attribute Rights] (meaning all of the attributes of the object) or [Entry Rights] (meaning the object, not implying rights to the attributes).

From within the Assigned Rights dialog box, you may set the rights the user may have on this object. You can set those rights on the object as well as any individual property in the object. The rights that are possible are as follows:

- **Browse** — Although not in the list, this right shows up from time to time (especially in the effective rights screens). This represents the ability to view this information through public browse capabilities.

- **Supervisor** This identifies that the trustee has *all* rights, including delete for this object or attribute.

- **Compare** — This provides the trustee with the ability to compare values of attributes.

- **Read** — This enables the trustee to read the values of the attribute or attributes in the object.

- **Write** — This provides the trustee with the ability to modify the contents of an attribute.

> **Add Self** — This right enables the trustee to add himself or herself as a member of the list of objects of the attribute. For example, if this right were given on an attribute that contains a list of linked objects, the trustee could add himself or herself (a reference to their object) into the list.

If you wish to add the object as a trustee to an attribute, you would need to press the Add Property button to bring up a list of properties or attributes that are available for this object.

From this list, you may select a single attribute. This attribute is then displayed in the Assigned Rights dialog box. From there, you can select the attribute and then set the rights you want the trustee to have for that property. A user does not require object rights in order to have rights on a single attribute in the object.

Remember that rights flow down in the tree and if you give user or an object rights at a container level, those rights continue down into that container and any subcontainers until that branch is exhausted or another explicit assignment is given for that user in a subcontainer or on an object. An explicit assignment changes the rights for the user at that point in the tree. Inheritance Rights Filters may also be placed to restrict this flow of rights down into the tree.

Inherited Rights Filters Page

This page (as shown in Figure 6.14) enables you to set the IRF (Inheritance Rights Filter) for this object. This filter restricts the rights of any user that accesses this object, unless that user has an explicit trustee assignment for this object.

You can think of the IRF as a filter that lets only items checked pass through unaltered. Rights that bump up against an IRF filter are blocked and discarded if the item is *not* checked. For example, if a user who had write privileges inherited at some point above (they were explicitly granted that right at some container at or above the one we're in) were to run into an IRF for an object or attribute that has the write privilege revoked (that is, unchecked), when they got to that object their write privilege would be gone for that object. If the object were a container, they would loose write privileges for all objects in that container or subcontainer.

You can effectively remove supervisor privileges to a portion of the tree by setting an IRF with the supervisor privilege turned off. You must be careful not to ever do this without someone being assigned as the supervisor of that branch of the tree (given an explicit supervisor trustee assignment at the container where the IRF is done) or you will make that part of the tree permanent (that is,

SETTING UP TIERED ELECTRONIC DISTRIBUTION

you will never be able to delete any objects in that branch of the tree). ConsoleOne helps keep you from performing this action by giving you an Error dialog box that will keep you from putting an IRF on the [Entry Rights] of the object with the supervisor right filtered away without having first given an explicit supervisor assignment on the same container.

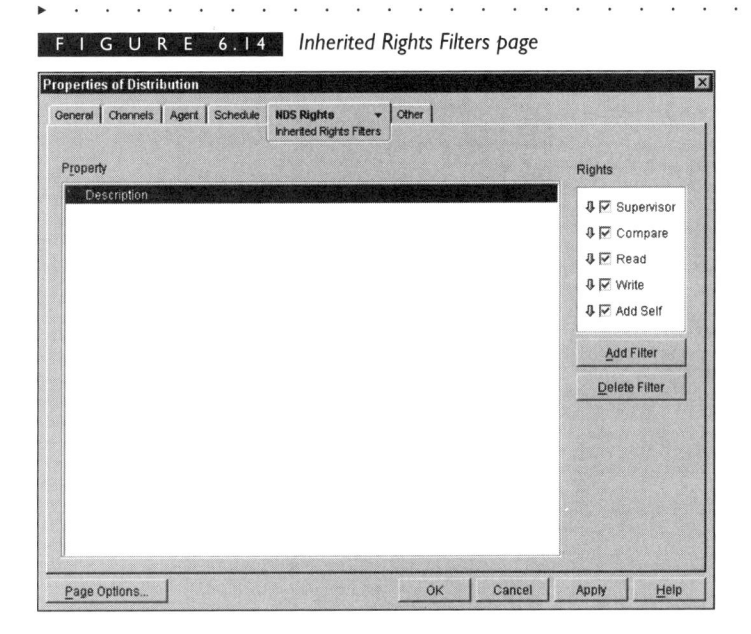

FIGURE 6.14 *Inherited Rights Filters page*

Effective Rights Page

The Effective Rights (as shown in Figure 6.15) property page enables you to query the system to discover the rights that selected objects have on the object you are administering.

Within this page you are presented with the distinguished name (DN) of the object whose rights you wish to observe. Initially, this is your currently logged in user running ConsoleOne. You can press the Browse button to the right of the Trustee field and browse throughout the tree to select any object.

When the trustee object is selected, you may then move to the Properties table on the lower half of the screen. As you select the property, the Rights box to the right changes its text to reflect the rights that the trustee has on that property. These rights may be via an explicit assignment or through inheritance.

141

FIGURE 6.15 *Effective Rights page*

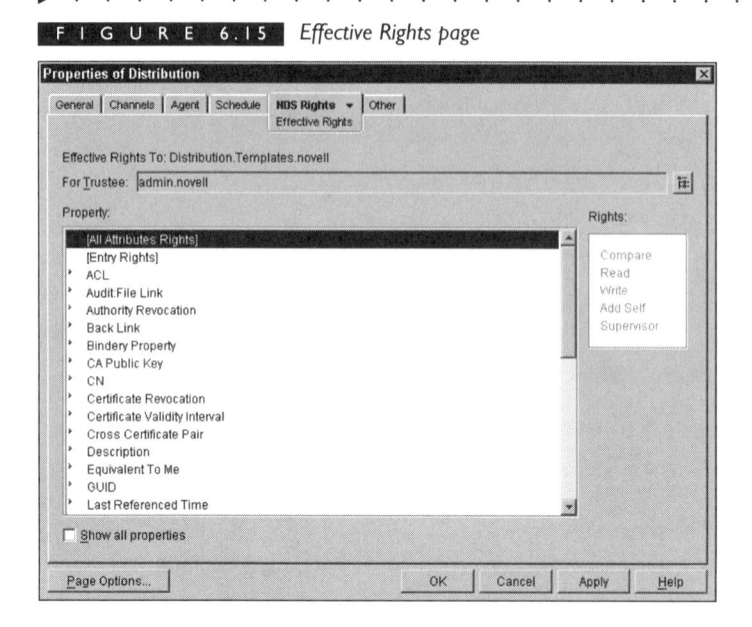

About the Other Property Page

This page may or may not be displayed for you, depending on your rights to the plug-in that now comes with ConsoleOne. This page is particularly powerful and should not be used by those who do not have an intimate knowledge of the schema of the object in question and its relationships with other objects in the directory. The intention of this property page is to give you generic access to properties that you cannot modify or view via the other plugged-in pages. The attributes and their values are displayed in a tree structure, allowing for those attributes that have multiple types (are compound types that consist of, say, an integer and a distinguished name, or postal code that has three separate Address fields).

Every attribute in eDirectory is defined by one of a specified set of syntaxes. These syntaxes identify how the data is stored in eDirectory. For this page, ConsoleOne has developed an editor for each of the different syntaxes that are currently available in eDirectory. When an attribute is displayed on this page, the editor is invoked to display the data and then modify it should the user click a specific attribute.

For example, if the syntax for an attribute were a string or an integer, then an inline editor is launched enabling the administrator to modify the string or the integer value on the screen. More abstract syntaxes such as octet string requires that an octet editor be launched, giving the administrator access to each of the bytes in the string without interpretation of the data.

The danger with this screen is that some applications require that there be a coordination of attribute values between two attributes within the same object or across multiple objects. Additionally, many applications assume that the data in the attribute is valid, because the normal user interface checks for invalid entries and not allow them to be stored in the attribute. If you should change a data value in the other page, no knowledge of related attributes or objects or valid data values is checked because the generic editors know nothing about the intention of the field. Should you change a value without making all the other appropriate changes or without putting in a valid value, some programs and the system could be affected.

Rights are still in effect in the Other property page, and you are not allowed to change any attribute values that are read-only or that you do not have rights to modify.

Discussing the Parent Subscriber

The TED parent subscriber is first a subscriber, and can receive distributions if they are subscribed to a channel. A parent subscriber has the additional responsibility to take the distribution and pass it along to a set of designated subscribers. In this manner, a parent subscriber acts as a relay transmitter for the distributor and relays the distribution onto other subscribers. Any subscriber can become a parent subscriber without any software change. The subscriber only needs to be designated a parent in either the distributor's routing hierarchy or in a subscriber object.

There is no parent subscriber object that is created in NDS. A subscriber acts as a parent subscriber any time that it is identified in either another subscriber object (as that subscriber's parent) or as an entry, with a child subscriber, in the routing hierarchy of any distributor.

A subscriber that receives a route with the distribution that identifies that it should forward the distribution on to other subscribers activates its parent subscriber code and forwards the distribution to all of the subscribers in the next level of the route. Identifying a subscriber as a parent only aids the distributor in the construction of the routing for a distribution.

Just like the distributor, a parent subscriber is responsible for sending configuration information to the end-node subscriber. When the distributor sends configuration information to the parent subscriber, it includes all configuration information for any other parent or end-node subscribers that this parent subscriber is responsible for forwarding distributions to. When this parent subscriber has a distribution for a destination subscriber (parent or end node), it bundles the configuration relevant for those destination subscribers and send it along with the distribution. All configuration information is stored in the ted.cfg binary file stored in the sys:\ted2 directory. This file is created or updated when the subscriber process exits.

Discussing the TED Subscriber

The TED subscriber is responsible for receiving and extracting distributions, validating that they come from an acceptable distributor and that the distribution file is accurate. The subscriber, when the extraction schedule starts, activates TED agents to unpack the distribution and handle the placement of the data in the distribution. If the subscriber should receive, with the distribution, a route that specifies that it send a distribution to other subscribers, the subscriber forwards the distribution to the next level of specified subscribers.

The subscriber system on a server never accesses NDS. The distributor, who is sending a distribution to this subscriber, is responsible for communicating any information from the subscriber object to the subscriber software. The distributor only sends configuration information to the subscriber if the distributor has a newer revision of the subscriber object, or the effective policy. The subscriber stores any changes in a configuration file (sys:\ted2\ted.cfg) so that the next time that it is started it loads the configuration information. You can manually configure a subscriber by creating a tednode.properties file in the sys:\ted2 directory. When the subscriber starts up, it reads this file and create a sys:\ted2\ted.cfg file from the tednode.properties. Any updates from a distributor or parent subscriber goes into the sys:\ted2\ted.cfg file, overwriting any previous configuration. The tednode.properties file is only used when the ted.cfg file cannot be found.

NOTE There is a sample tednode.properties file on the root of the ZENworks for Servers 2 companion CD. You can take this file and edit it for the particular subscriber and place it in the ted2 directory.

SETTING UP TIERED ELECTRONIC DISTRIBUTION

All subscribers must have a copy of the digital certificate of the distributor in order to receive distributions from the distributor. If there is a distribution in the channel that is coming from a distributor for which the subscriber does not hold a copy of the distributor's digital certificate, the subscriber rejects the distribution. You can transmit the digital certificate manually, or ConsoleOne will attempt to contact the subscribers with a UNC path when a distribution is placed in a channel from a new distributor or when a subscriber is added to the channel. Over this connection, the digital certificate of all distributors (that currently have distributions in the channel) are sent and placed on the file system of the subscriber. Perform the following steps to secure a copy of the digital certificates of the distributors that may be sent to the subscriber:

1. Launch ConsoleOne.
2. Browse to the distributor object of the distributor whose certificate you wish to retrieve. Select the distributor object.
3. Press the right mouse button and select Resolve Certificates. You are presented with a dialog box that will give you two radial buttons:
   - **Copy certificates to subscribers automatically** — This goes to all distributions associated with this distributor and then to all of the subscribers that are associated with all the channels that the distribution is in, and also to all subscribers that act as parent subscribers to pass the distributions to the subscribers that are associated with the channels. It attempts to gain access to the subscriber file system with a UNC path and write the certificate to the sys:\ted2\security directory on the subscriber server.
   - **Save certificates to disk** — This writes the certificates to the directory specified on the disk.
4. Choose "Save certificates to disk" and type in the directory name to copy the certificates on your local drive or floppy. Or, press the Browse button to browse to the directory where you want the certificates copied.
5. Press OK. The certificates will be placed in the directory specified.
6. Take the files written to the directory and copy them to the directory sys:\ted2\security on the subscriber system.

IMPORTANT
If you start the subscriber with the -nosecurity option, it does not require nor verify digital certificates. It accepts any distribution from any distributor and performs MD5 digests, if administered.

145

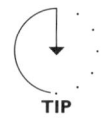

> **TIP**
>
> You can also use ConsoleOne to automatically resolve certificates for a specific subscriber, instead of a distributor. By right-clicking the subscriber object and choosing the Resolve Certificate option, the subscriber receives all certificates for all distributors that have distributions associated with the channels to which the subscriber is subscribed.

The NDS Rights and Other pages are described in the distributor sections of this chapter.

About the Settings Property Page

This page is found under the General tab and represents some general configuration settings that are effective for this subscriber. Figure 6.16 displays a capture of this screen.

On this property page, you may make the following settings:

- **I/O rate** — This represents the number of bytes per second that you allow a subscriber to consume for all subscriptions' input or output, independently. The default is for the subscriber to receive at the maximum rate possible on the server. For example, if you choose to enter 4096, this subscriber does not exceed sending 4K bytes per second to any other subscriber and 4K bytes per second receiving from any distributor, regardless of the capacity of the subscriber.

- **Maximum concurrent distributions** — Each time that a subscriber is going to relay a distribution (because it is a parent subscriber), it creates a Java thread that handles the sending of the distribution to the child subscriber. This value identifies the maximum number of threads that you will allow the parent subscriber to create to service relaying distributions.

> **NOTE**
>
> The subscriber always creates all the concurrent receiver threads that it needs regardless of this maximum value. There is currently no method to manage the total number of receiver threads.

- **Connection timeout** — The default for this is 300 seconds. You can also enter a timeout value that, when exceeded, the parent subscriber fails the distribution and retries the distribution every two minutes for the next thirty minutes (as long as it is still in its scheduled window). If after the retries the distribution still cannot succeed, the parent subscriber fails the distribution and the next time it tries is when the distributor reattempts the distribution. This value is also used for the

SETTING UP TIERED ELECTRONIC DISTRIBUTION

maximum amount of time a subscriber waits between packets while receiving a distribution from a distributor or parent subscriber.

- **Working directory** — This identifies the directory where the subscriber stores the distribution files it receives. The agents, when they are called to extract the files, go to this directory to find the distribution files. It is not recommended to use the SYS volume because of the potential system problems should that volume become full.

- **Parent subscriber** — This enables you to specify a parent subscriber from which this subscriber should receive all distributions (as opposed to getting it directly from the distributor). This can be overridden on a per-distributor basis by including the subscriber in the routing hierarchy on each distributor (see the TED Systems section for more information).

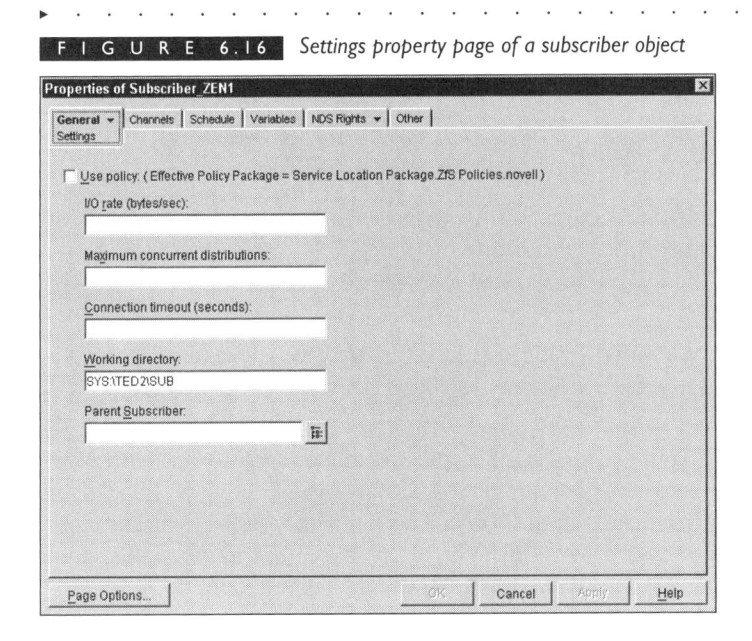

FIGURE 6.16 *Settings property page of a subscriber object*

Focusing on the Messaging Property Page

The Messaging property page is under the General tab and can be configured by pressing the active tab and selecting the messaging value under the drop-down on the tab (by pressing the small triangle in the tab). The following is a sample of a Messaging page (see Figure 6.17).

FIGURE 6.17 *Messaging property page of a subscriber object*

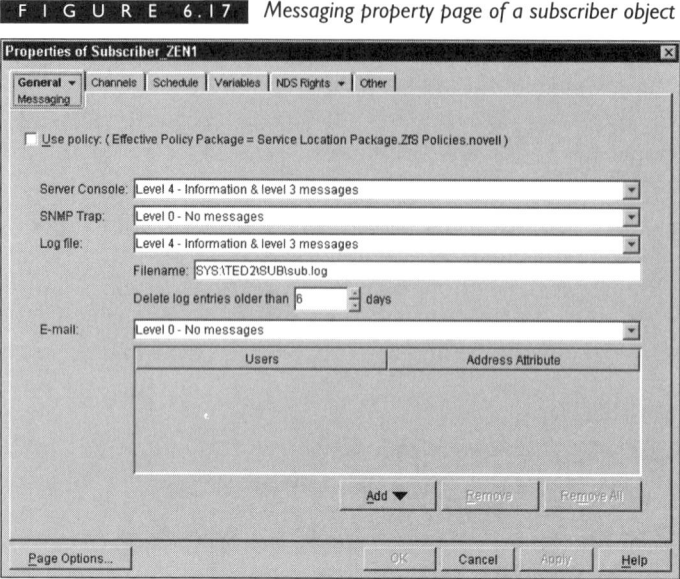

For each of the appropriate fields, you may enter one of the message levels described in the distributor section.

You can administer the following configuration parameters on the Message property page:

- **Server Console** — This item identifies the level of messages that are displayed on the subscriber server console (not the main server console).

- **SNMP Trap** — This identifies the level of messages that are sent as an SNMP trap being sent to the SNMP trap target. The SNMP Trap Targets policy must be set in the Service Location Policy Package effective for the subscriber object. This information is included in the configuration information sent to the subscriber from the distributor.

- **Log file** — This identifies the level of message that should be stored in the log file. Additionally, you can configure the following about the log file:
  - **Filename** — This is the filename of the log file. The default location is SYS:\TED2\SUB\SUB.LOG. You should change the location of the log file because it can grow, as well, and may adversely affect the system if it is located on the SYS volume.

- **Delete log entries older than X days** — In this parameter, you identify the number of days (X) worth of log entries that should remain in the log file. The default is six days. Therefore, any log entries that are older than six days will be cleared from the log file. The process of scanning the log for and removing old log entries happens once every 24 hours and is not configurable.

▶ **E-mail** — With the e-mail option, you may specify the level of messages that will be sent as an e-mail to the identified users. The SMTP Host policy in the ZENworks for Servers 2 Service Location policy package must be effective for the subscriber object in order to enable it to discover the address for the SMTP host to send the e-mail. If this is not specified, the e-mail will not be sent.

In addition to identifying the level of messages, you must also specify who should receive these messages. To add users to the list and for them to be sent the message, you must press the Add button and select whether you wish to add an NDS User or Group, or specify an e-mail address. When you select a user, you are asked to browse to the user in the directory, and the system takes the e-mail address attribute from the user and uses that as the address for the user. Should you choose a group, all of the users in the group are sent the e-mail message and the e-mail attribute is used for each of those users. Should you not want to use the e-mail address attribute in the user object, you may select the down arrow in the Address Attribute field and select which of the NDS user attributes you wish to identify as containing the e-mail address. Many administrators store user e-mail addresses in the "Internet e-mail address" attribute instead of the "e-mail address" attribute. It is expected that the attribute you identify will contain a valid e-mail address.

If you choose to enter an explicit e-mail address, rather than selecting a user or a group, you may choose the "E-mail Address" choice from the Add button. You are prompted to enter a valid e-mail address. The entered e-mail address is assumed to be valid and is shown as the Username field in the table with an N/A in the Address Attribute field.

Thinking about the Channels Property Page

This page of the subscriber object identifies the channels that this subscriber is going to receive distributions from. A subscriber may subscribe to many channels. To add a channel to the list, press the Add button and browse in NDS to the channel. Once this channel is added, it appears on the list.

NOVELL'S ZENWORKS FOR SERVERS 2 ADMINISTRATOR'S HANDBOOK

To delete a channel from the list, you must first select the channel and then press the Delete button. The subscriber will no longer accept distributions from this channel.

You can view/edit the property pages of the channel by selecting the channel and pressing the Details button.

The same distribution may be placed in more than one channel. It is possible that the same subscriber may be subscribed to multiple channels, and that more than one channel may want to distribute the same distribution. The distributor and subscriber keep a version number on each distribution and does not send the same distribution more than once to the same subscriber, no matter how many channels the distribution is in.

About the Extract Schedule Property Page

The Schedule property page enables you to specify when and how often the extraction agents are called to dissect the distribution file and extract the files within, placing them in the file system of the server as specified in the distribution. Figure 6.18 shows a sample of this page.

FIGURE 6.18 *Extract Schedule property page of a subscriber object*

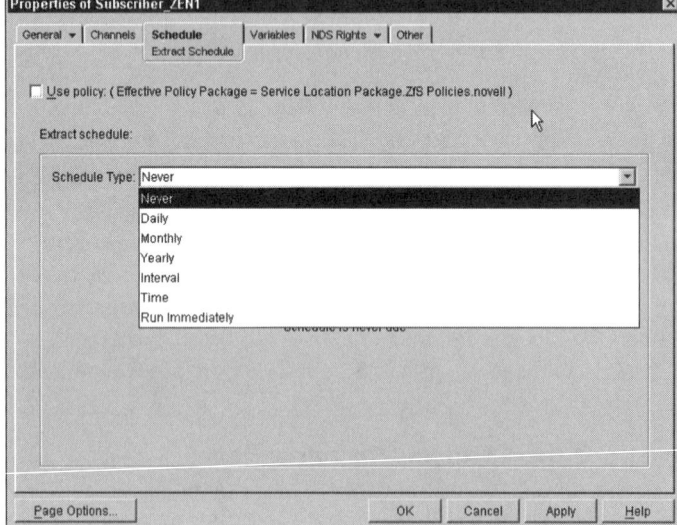

SETTING UP TIERED ELECTRONIC DISTRIBUTION

If there is a Tiered Electronic Distribution policy in a Service Location Policy package effective for the subscriber object, the checkbox for using the policy appears on this page. If there is no effective policy, the checkbox is not displayed. When this checkbox is activated, the schedule described in the policy is used for this subscriber. When unchecked, this subscriber has its own schedule and the Schedule Type field is available for administration. The checkbox is checked by default if there is an effective TED policy.

This page enables you to select when the extraction agents should do their work on the subscriber server: Never, Daily, Monthly, Yearly, Interval, Time, or Run Immediately.

Once you have selected when you want the configuration applied, you have additional fields to select in the lower portion of the screen. The following sections discuss the various options you have.

> **NOTE** The default is Never. Therefore, the subscriber never extracts the files until you change the schedule. Remember, the configuration of the subscriber does not change until the next distribution, when the distributor sends the new configuration.

Never

This option only loads the distributor with the configuration information when it is first loaded on the server, after each reboot or restart.

Daily

When you choose to have the configuration applied to the system daily, you have the additional need to select when the changes will be made.

This schedule requires that you select the days when you want the configuration applied. You select the days by clicking the days you desire. The selected days appear as depressed buttons.

In addition to the days, you can select the times the configuration is applied. These times—the start and stop times—provide a range of time when the configuration will be applied.

You can have the configuration also reapplied within the time frame every specified hour/minute/second by clicking the "Repeat the action every" field and specifying the time delay.

To keep all the distributors from simultaneously accessing NDS, you can select the "Randomly dispatch policy during time period" option. This causes each server to choose a random time within the time period when they will retrieve and apply the configuration.

Monthly

Under the monthly schedule, you can select which day of the month the configuration should be applied or you can select "Last day of the month" to handle the last day, because all months obviously do not end on the same calendar date (that is, 30 days hath September, April, June, and November, all the rest have 31 except for February . . .).

Once you have selected the day, you can also select the time range when the configuration will be reread and applied.

To keep all the distributors from simultaneously accessing NDS, you can select the "Randomly dispatch policy during time period" option. This causes each server to choose a random time within the time period when they will retrieve and apply the configuration.

Yearly

You would select a yearly schedule if you want to apply the configuration only once a year.

On this screen, you must choose the day that you wish the configuration to be applied. This is done by selecting the Calendar button to the right of the Date field. This brings up a Monthly dialog box where you can browse through the calendar to select the date you wish. This calendar does not correspond to any particular year and may not take into account leap years in its display. This is because you are choosing a date for each year that will come along in the present and future years.

Once you have selected the date, you can also select the time range when the configuration should be read and applied.

To keep all the distributors from simultaneously accessing NDS, you can select the "Randomly dispatch policy during time period" option. This causes each server to choose a random time within the time period when they will retrieve and apply the configuration.

Interval

This schedule type enables you to specify how often to repeatedly read and apply the configuration. You can specify the interval with a combination of days, hours, minutes, and seconds. This type waits for the interval to pass first before applying the configuration for the first time and then for each sequence after that.

Time

This allows you to specify a specific calendar date and time when the configuration will be applied. When the current date on the server is beyond the identified date, the configuration will be applied.

Run Immediately

The distributor does not use this scheduled type, but it is used by other components. It is described here for completeness in describing all the possible schedulers.

With the Run Immediately schedule type, the first time that the associated object is activated the schedule causes the activity to occur. You may also specify a repeat interval in days, hours, minutes, and seconds. If no repeat interval is specified, the action only runs once, until the object is restarted or refreshed.

Variables Property Pages

Variables enable you to substitute a variable name in the distribution with the value specified in the subscriber. When you create a distribution, you may use variables in the volumes and directory names, for example. When the distribution is sent to the subscriber and the extraction agent is called, the agent replaces these variables with their defined value in the subscriber object. If no value is given, the variable name (including the % [percent sign]) is used for that value.

If there is a Tiered Electronic Distribution policy in a Service Location Policy package effective for the subscriber, the checkbox for using the policy appear on this page. If there is no policy, the checkbox is not displayed. When this checkbox is activated, the variables described in the policy is used for this subscriber in addition to the variables that you define in the subscriber. When unchecked, this subscriber has its own independent variables. If there is a duplicate, the subscriber's definition is used. This enables you to override a specific variable from the policy, while still accepting the other variables from the policy.

Unlike ZENworks for Servers policies and software distribution packages, the TED software only performs basic substitution of variable to value and does not allow you to reference an NDS object or its attribute. This is done to eliminate the requirement that the subscriber have access to NDS and all of the objects in the tree. This would be especially difficult if the subscriber is an external subscriber — not even in the same tree as the distributor!

For example, if you created a distribution and specified %DEST_VOLUME% as the volume name, when the subscriber extracts the files, the agent substitutes the variable DEST_VOLUME defined in this property page with the value. If DEST_VOLUE is not defined, then a directory called "%DEST_VOLUME%" is created in the SYS volume.

Remember to be consistent in your conventions and your variable names. You should probably come up with a set of common variables that you define with each subscriber that you set up. Then when you create a distribution, you can use these variables in defining the directories where the distribution will be placed. Remember, the subscribers that receive the distribution are purely based on who subscribes to the channels where you place the distribution. If you are not consistent in your variable names across all subscribers, you may inadvertently send a distribution to a subscriber that does not have the variable defined; this results in the distribution being extracted in a place you do not expect (probably on the SYS volume). Some variables that you should consider defining in each of your subscribers are the following:

- **DEST_VOLUME** — Define this variable as the volume that receives the distribution after it is extracted.
- **DEST_APPVOL** — Define this to be the volume where your applications are stored.
- **DEST_APPDIR** — Define this to be the directory under the application volume where you place your applications.

Placing a Subscriber on Windows NT/2000

The subscriber process can be installed and executed on a Windows NT or Windows 2000 system. The subscriber system is the exact same system that is running on NetWare and functions in the same manner. To place the subscriber on NT, you must perform the following:

1. Install the Java JRE onto the Windows system. The JRE that is required for the subscriber process is located on the ZENworks for Servers companion CD. The file to execute is java\jre-1_1_8_004-win-i.exe. This installs the JRE and prepares the system to run Java applications. Make sure you install I18N support.

2. Create a shared directory with the share name of SYS. This is the directory where the subscriber and its required supplemental processes are installed. You should already have a directory (usually C:\Novell) shared as SYS if you have installed NDS for NT. NDS for NT is not required, but it enables you to install to NT machines that are in a

SETTING UP TIERED ELECTRONIC DISTRIBUTION

remote location. All Windows NT/2000 machines must have the latest NetWare client installed as well.

3. Install the subscriber on the local machine by running the installation process on the ZENworks for Servers program CD. This installs the files on the SYS share. You can also browse for and select to install the subscriber to NDS for NT machines, which will have NT server objects in NDS. Using the "Local Machine" option for installing eliminates the need for NDS for NT, but requires that each NT machine run the Install Wizard locally.

Once you have installed the subscriber, it can be started on the system by running the sub.bat file under the SYS\ted2 directory. This starts up the Java runtime environment and loads the dependent code and the subscriber. The console for the subscriber is placed in a DOS box on the system. From there, you may execute the identified console commands. The subscriber is started automatically as a service each time the machine reboots. It is only started as a service and cannot be controlled by the Service Control Manager. The subscriber process runs in the background until any user logs on to the machine locally. The subscriber console will be available to every user that initiates an interactive logon (someone sitting in front of the machine, not over the network). This means any user sitting at the machine can issue console commands on the subscriber console.

External Subscriber

An external subscriber is a TED subscriber that resides on a server not located in the tree of the distributor. The controlling subscriber object of an external subscriber is located in the external tree. The distributor's tree does contain an external subscriber object, which identifies the IP address of the remote subscriber.

An external subscriber object is basically just a pointer to the subscriber service running on a server that has its subscriber object in a different tree. Each subscriber should have exactly one subscriber object, but each may also have many external subscriber objects that point to. For example, if there were a subscriber object in the FORD tree, it would receive its configuration information from a distributor in the FORD tree. There could be an external subscriber object in each of the GM, NISSAN, and BMW trees, but distributors in those trees would only send distribution files, not configuration information, to the subscriber. This is an important distinction. A distributor cannot send a distribution to an external subscriber object until the configuration information (contained in the actual subscriber object) has been sent in a distribution from a distributor in the subscriber's tree. It's also important to remember that any variables you may be using in the definition of your distributions must be defined in the actual subscriber object, because anything defined in the tree where the external subscriber object exists is not passed on as part of distributions sent from distributors in that tree.

It is also possible to have an external subscriber that does not have a subscriber object. Because it does not have a subscriber object, it does not receive configuration information from a distributor. You can manage the configuration information for the subscriber by using a file called TEDNode.Properties. A sample configuration file is located at the root of the ZENworks for Servers 2 companion CD.

To successfully manage a subscriber without a subscriber object, you should do the following:

1. Make any modifications to the TEDNode.Properties file and copy it to the SYS\TED2 directory.

2. Stop and exit the subscriber service (issue the `exit` command from the subscriber console). This causes the subscriber to write its current configuration to a file called TED.CFG in the SYS\TED2 directory. The subscriber uses this file to load its configuration information the next time the subscriber is started.

3. Delete the TED.CFG file. This causes the subscriber to generate a new TED.CFG based on the attributes you have defined in the TEDNode.Properties file.

4. Restart the subscriber service.

You must follow this procedure every time you want to make changes to the configuration information (working directory, messaging levels, variables, and so forth) for an external subscriber that does not have a subscriber object.

Like all subscribers, the external subscriber must also have a copy of the digital certificate of the distributor in order to receive distributions from the distributor. If there is a distribution in the channel that is coming from a distributor, and the external subscriber does not hold a copy of the distributor's digital certificate, the external subscriber rejects the distribution. You need to transfer the digital certificate to the external subscriber manually.

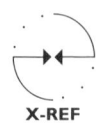

X-REF See the section on subscribers in this chapter for steps to obtain a distributor's certificate.

The details of the NDS Rights and Other property pages are described in the section above, discussing the distributor.

SETTING UP TIERED ELECTRONIC DISTRIBUTION

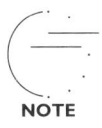

> **NOTE** If you start the external subscriber with the `-nosecurity` option, it does not require nor verify digital certificates from distributors. It still accepts any distribution from any distributor and performs MD5 digests, if administered.

About the General Property Page

On this page you may identify a parent subscriber for this subscriber. The parent subscriber would be a subscriber object in this tree. You need to press the Browse button to the side of the field and browse NDS to select the subscriber that is to be identified as the parent subscriber.

Discussing the Channels Property Page

On this property page you identify the channels from which this external subscriber will receive distributions. As you recall, any distribution that is placed in a channel subscribed by this external subscriber will be sent.

Looking at the Network Address Property Page

On this property page, represented in Figure 6.19, you specify the IP address of the server that is running the external subscriber.

FIGURE 6.19 *Network Address property page of an external subscriber object*

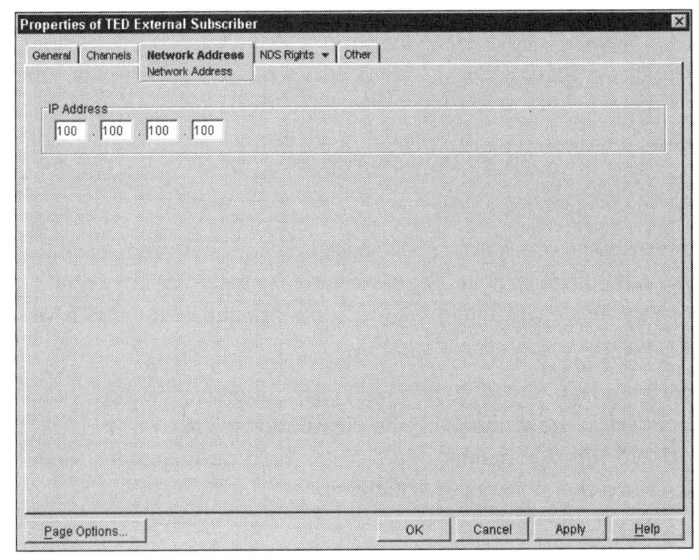

NOVELL'S ZENWORKS FOR SERVERS 2 ADMINISTRATOR'S HANDBOOK

To administer the address, simply place the cursor in the IP Address fields and enter the IP address. Currently, ZENworks for Servers 2 does not allow you to enter DNS names to be resolved to addresses.

About TED Distribution

The TED distribution object represents the collection of files that are compiled into a distribution file and then sent to the subscriber. Once at the subscriber, the distribution is extracted from the distribution file and placed in the locations specified in this distribution (with appropriate variable substitution).

All of the files that are specified in a TED distribution must reside on the file system of the distributor, or the server must have access to HTTP and FTP capabilities to retrieve the files for those agents. Once the distribution is defined, in order to get the distribution transmitted to a subscriber, it must be placed into a channel or a set of channels. The files that are specified in the distribution object are collected by the agents on the distributor system and placed into a single distribution file. This file is then transmitted to all of the subscribers that are subscribed to the channels where the distribution object is placed.

The distribution is a live object. The distribution object are sent each time the channel schedule is activated. When the gatherer schedule activates this distribution, the agent is called to collect the files specified and compare them to the previous distribution. If there are differences that have occurred in the files, a new delta package, or an entire distribution, of the distribution is generated and the new revision are sent to the subscribers of the designated channels. This happens each time the gatherer and send schedule activate the distribution. Unless a distribution is expressly identified as a one-time only distribution, it does not become inactive after it has been sent. The distribution continues to be reevaluated, recollected, and redistributed each time the schedule is activated.

NOTE The distribution does not rebuild based on any file system event, such as an update to a file. The distribution rebuilds strictly based on the gatherer schedule in the distribution, whether the files have changed or not.

If there is no subscriber to receive a distribution (that is, no subscribers in the channel) or the distribution is inactive, or is not associated with any channel, the distribution is never gathered and built, even if the gathering is scheduled.

SETTING UP TIERED ELECTRONIC DISTRIBUTION

The NDS Object and Other property pages are described in the distributor section of this chapter.

Looking at the General Property Page

The General property page enables you to specify some settings that are used in the deployment of the distribution. Figure 6.20 displays a typical snapshot of this page.

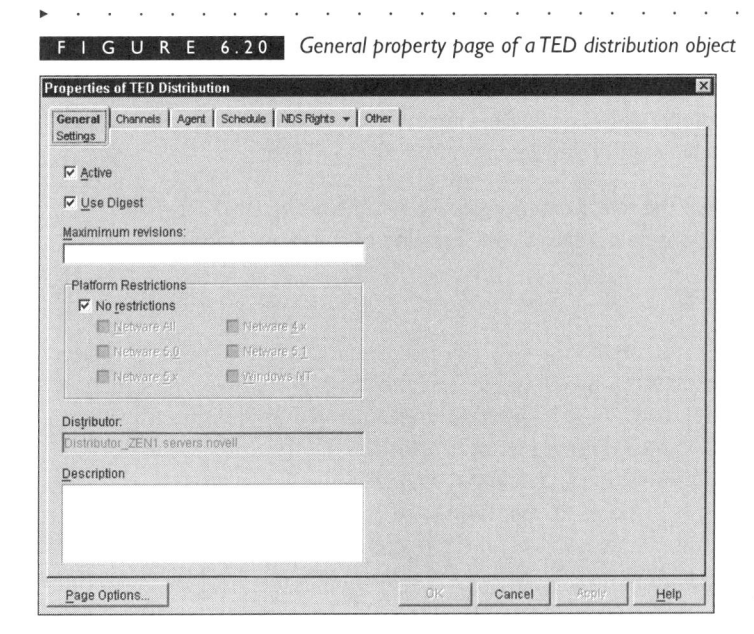

FIGURE 6.20 *General property page of a TED distribution object*

You can specify the following settings on this General property page:

- **Active** — The checkbox activates or deactivates the distribution. If a distribution is inactive, the distribution is not sent to subscribers even if it is in a channel.

- **Use Digest** — This checkbox activates the TED system to use a digest on the distribution file. The digest is used to verify that the contents of the distribution file have not changed from the distributor to the subscriber (during transmission). When the subscriber receives the distribution, it verifies the digest it calculates with the digest that the distributor computes and places in a header. If the digests match, the file is unchanged and the subscriber accepts the distribution.

> **NOTE**
> The generation of the MD5 message digest may take significant time, particularly with large distribution files. Be aware that this increases the time it takes to gather and create the distribution file.

- **Maximum revisions** — This value enables you to specify the number of revisions of the distribution that you will keep. Each time that a distribution is collected and a distribution file is created, this constitutes a revision. When the maximum number of revisions has been created, the oldest revision is discarded from disk (unless it is currently being sent to a subscriber, in which case it is discarded on the next distribution cycle). Each subscriber that receives this distribution will keep this number of revisions. This includes subscribers that act as parent subscribers but do not actually subscribe to the channel.

> **NOTE**
> When the maximum revisions is hit, the file agent deletes all revisions and create a new baseline of the distribution.

- **Platform Restrictions** — This section enables you to specify if there are restrictions that should be specified for the distribution. If there are no restrictions, the distribution is accepted by any subscriber and then extracted on that subscriber. If there are restrictions, uncheck the "No restrictions" checkbox and check the various checkboxes that correspond to the platforms that accept this distribution. The distribution only extracts on the platforms with a checked checkbox.
- **Distributor** — This is a display-only field that identifies the distributor that performs the collection and transmission of this distribution. This distributor is specified when the distribution object is created. This distributor is the owner of this distribution. The owner of a distribution cannot be changed.
- **Description** — This enables you to have a free-flowing text description of the distribution. This can be used to help in understanding the files and the purpose for the distribution package.

About the Channels Property Page

In the Channels property page the administrator can select the channels that contain this distribution. This distribution can be placed in any number of

SETTING UP TIERED ELECTRONIC DISTRIBUTION

channels. All of the subscribers associated with each channel are sent this distribution by the distributor associated with this distribution object. Figure 6.21 shows this page.

To add this distribution to a channel, press the Add button. You are next presented with a dialog box to browse through NDS to select the channel. Once you have selected the channel, it is placed in the list displayed in the Channels box. To delete the channel from the list (removing the distribution from being distributed), select the channel and press the Delete button. To go to the property pages of the channel object, select the object and press the Details button.

Any distributions that are associated with channels also appear in the channel object under the Distributions property page.

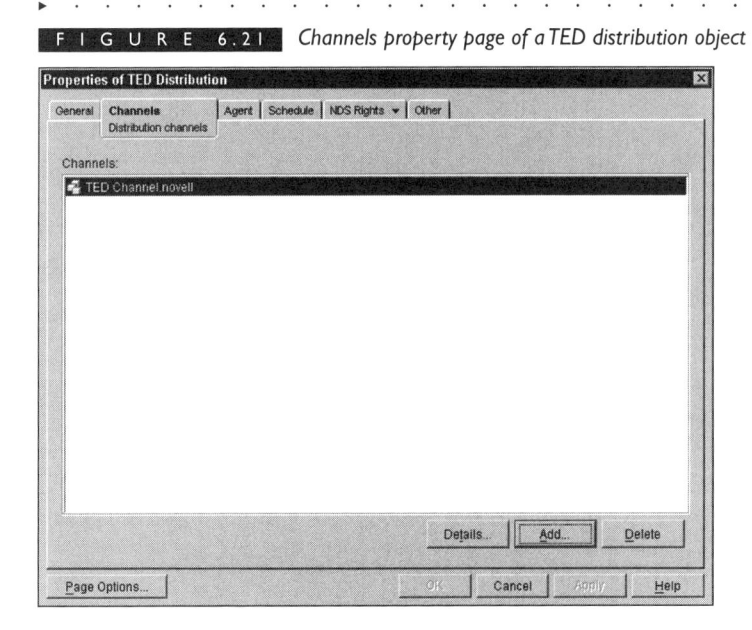

FIGURE 6.21 *Channels property page of a TED distribution object*

Looking at the Agent Property Page

In the Agent property page you specify the agent and the files that will be sent as part of this distribution. The agent determines the type of distribution (for example, local files from the file agent, remote files from the HTTP or FTP agent, software installations from the server software packages agent, and so forth). Figure 6.22 shows this page. Once you select the agent that this distribution will use (you can only select a single agent per distribution), the screen updates and you need to give files specification details.

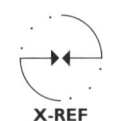

> See the section in this chapter on TED agents for more details about each agent.

X-REF

FIGURE 6.22 *Agent property page of a TED distribution object*

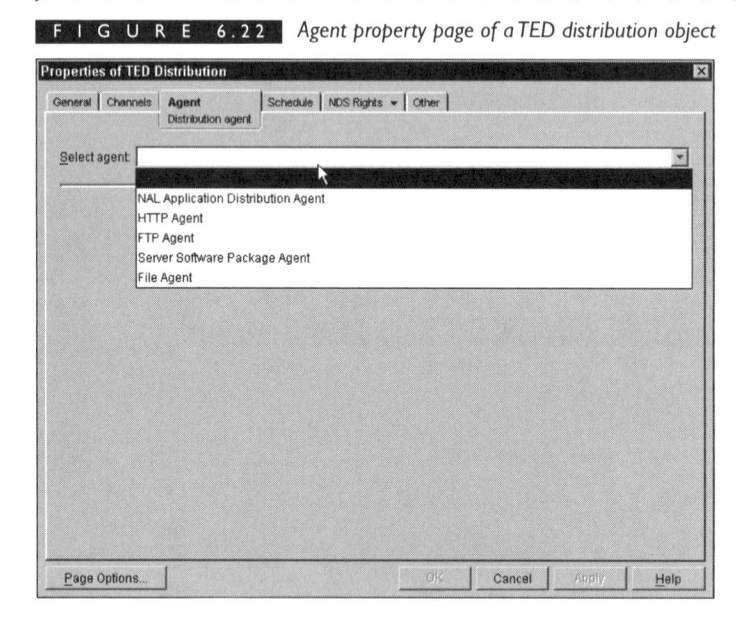

Looking at the Schedule

This property page enables you to specify how often and when this distribution should be gathered. Each time the server clock hits the specified scheduled time, the agents are activated and the distribution gathered and compared with the previous version to determine if any changes have been made. If there have been changes, a new version of the distribution file is created. The actual distribution of the file occurs based on schedules of the channels. Figure 6.23 displays the TED distribution Schedule page.

The following choices are available to you for the scheduling of the distribution: Never, Daily, Monthly, Yearly, Interval, Time, or Run Immediately.

SETTING UP TIERED ELECTRONIC DISTRIBUTION

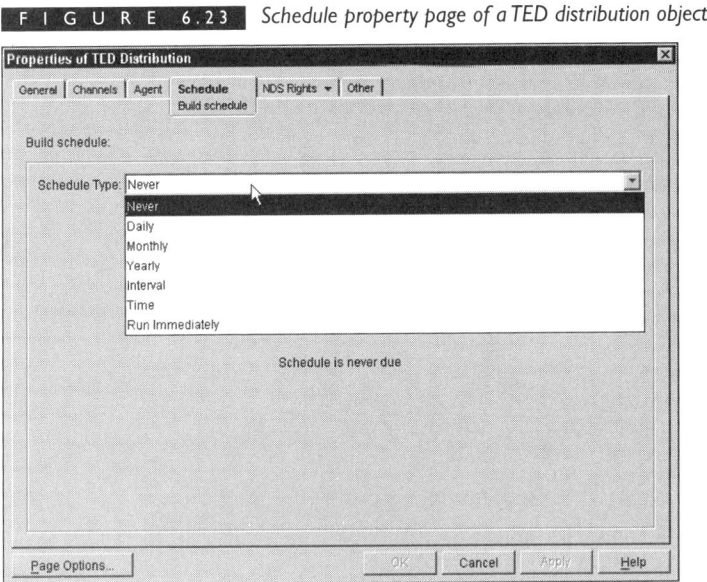

FIGURE 6.23 *Schedule property page of a TED distribution object*

Never

This option only loads the distributor with the configuration information when it is first loaded on the server, after each reboot or restart.

Daily

When you choose to have the configuration applied to the system daily, you have the additional need to select when the changes will be made.

This schedule requires that you select the days when you want the configuration applied. You select the days by clicking the days you desire. The selected days appear as depressed buttons.

In addition to the days, you can select the times the configuration is applied. These times — the start and stop times — provide a range of time where the configuration will be applied.

You can have the configuration also reapplied within the time frame every specified hour/minute/second by clicking the "Repeat the action every" field and specifying the time delay.

To keep all the distributors from simultaneously accessing NDS, you can select the "Randomly dispatch policy during time period" option. This causes each server to choose a random time within the time period when they will retrieve and apply the configuration.

Monthly

Under the monthly schedule you can select which day of the month the configuration should be applied or you can select "Last day of the month" to handle the last day, because all months obviously do not end on the same calendar date (that is, 30 days hath September, April, June, and November, all the rest have 31 except for February . . .).

Once you have selected the day, you can also select the time range when the configuration will be reread and applied.

To keep all the distributors from simultaneously accessing NDS, you can select the "Randomly dispatch policy during time period" option. This causes each server to choose a random time within the time period when they will retrieve and apply the configuration.

Yearly

You would select a yearly schedule if you want to apply the configuration only once a year.

On this screen you must choose the day that you wish the configuration to be applied. This is done by selecting the Calendar button to the right of the Date field. This brings up a Monthly dialog box where you can browse through the calendar to select the date you wish. This calendar does not correspond to any particular year and may not take into account leap years in its display. This is because you are choosing a date for each year that will come along in the present and future years.

Once you have selected the date, you can also select the time range when the configuration should be read and applied.

To keep all the distributors from simultaneously accessing NDS, you can select the "Randomly dispatch policy during time period" option. This causes each server to choose a random time within the time period when they will retrieve and apply the configuration.

Interval

This schedule type enables you to specify how often to repeatedly read and apply the configuration. You can specify the interval with a combination of days, hours, minutes, and seconds. This type waits for the interval to pass first before applying the configuration for the first time and then for each sequence after that.

Time

This enables you to specify a specific calendar date and time when the configuration will be applied. When the current date on the server is beyond the identified date, the configuration will be applied.

Run Immediately

The distributor does not use this scheduled type, but it is used by other components. It is described here for completeness in covering all of the possible schedulers.

With the Run Immediately schedule type, the first time that the associated object is activated the schedule causes the activity to occur. You may also specify a repeat interval in days, hours, minutes, and seconds. If no repeat interval is specified, the action only runs once, until the object is restarted or refreshed.

About Manual Distribution

TED provides a mechanism for you to send your distributions manually, avoiding the need to contact any subscribers over the wire. You may possibly use this to place a distribution across a WAN link that may not be reliable or where you are going to that location and want to bring the distribution with you. You must first run a wizard to create the distribution file and then rerun the wizard at the destination to bring the distribution into the remote system.

Creating a Manual Distribution

The manual distribution is created through a wizard. Perform the following steps to create the distribution that can be placed on portable media and then manually transported to the destination systems:

1. Launch ConsoleOne and create a normal distribution and place it into a channel.

2. Ensure that the distributor has gathered the distribution and the distribution file has been created.

> **TIP**
> The easiest way to know if a distribution has been created is to go to the distributor's working directory and see if a subdirectory has been created with the name of the distribution. Inside of this directory are subdirectories; each named with a time stamp. Each of these directories contains the files that are used in the distribution. The actual distribution file is called distribution.ted.

3. Launch ConsoleOne and choose TED Manual Distribution under the Tools Menu. This launches the wizard to create the manual distribution media.
4. Follow the steps of the wizard:
   a. Choose "Export a distribution from TED and copy to disk" on the first page. Press Next.
   b. Use the Browse button to select the channel that contains the distribution you wish to manually create. Once you have selected the channel, the wizard displays the list of distributions. Select the desired distribution. Press Next.
   c. Enter the desired name of the distribution file, including the path. You may press the Browse button to select a file that already exists on the disk. Press Next.
   d. A summary screen is displayed. Press Finish. At this time, the wizard creates the distribution file in the directory and with the name specified.
5. Take the file you have created and transport it to the destination location. Perform an import distribution to bring the distribution into the destination subscriber or parent subscriber.

Importing the Distribution

Once you have created the distribution and carried it to the destination site (a remote subscriber or parent subscriber), you need to run the wizard again to bring the distribution into the system. Perform the following steps to import the distribution into the remote system:

1. Make sure the distribution file created with the Export Wizard is accessible to the system. Also, make sure that you have access (through UNC paths) to the destination subscriber or parent subscriber that is to receive the distribution.
2. Launch ConsoleOne and choose TED Manual Distribution under the Tools menu. This launches the wizard to import the manual distribution media.
3. Follow the steps of the wizard:
   a. Choose "Import a distribution from disk to TED" on the first page. Press Next.
   b. Use the Browse button to browse to and select the distribution file you have brought to this site. Press Next.

SETTING UP TIERED ELECTRONIC DISTRIBUTION

   c. This page of the wizard displays all of the known subscribers and parent subscribers that have subscribed to the channel that you selected when you created the manual distribution file. Select the subscribers or parent subscribers that you wish to receive this distribution. If you select a parent subscriber, it automatically sends the distribution to all of its destination subscribers. Press Next.

   d. A summary screen is displayed. Press Finish. At this time, the wizard copies the distribution file to the subscriber's working directory through UNC paths.

5. The distribution is *not* automatically extracted on the subscriber. It is only extracted by one of the following methods:

   a. The channel schedule fires to send the distribution and the distribution is administered to have "Run Immediate" schedule. The distributor connects with the subscriber and sees that the latest version of the distribution is already on the subscriber, so it does not resend the distribution. If it is a "Run Immediate" selection, the subscriber next extracts the distribution. This is only possible when the distributor can communicate with the subscriber over the wire.

   b. The extraction schedule on the subscriber fires, which causes the subscriber to unpack all distributions that have not been done, including the one you just imported.

   c. Manually go to the subscriber console (or through Remote Web Console) enter the command to request that the distribution be extracted (for example, `extract -x tree,DN`). If the name of your distribution has a space, you need to put quotes around the entire parameter after the `-x` – for example, `extract -x "simple_tree,my distribution.ted.novell"`.

About TED Agents

TED agents are Java modules that are activated by either a distributor or a subscriber to either pack up or unpack a distribution files. Currently, there are the following agents available in ZENworks for Servers 2: the NAL Application Distribution Agent, the HTTP Agent, the FTP Agent, the Server Software Package Agent, and the File Agent. The following sections discuss each of the agents and what they do for TED.

> **WARNING** Once you have created a distribution and the agent has performed its gathering process, and then you change the agent used for the distribution (that is, you readminister the distribution object and change to a different agent type), unpredictable behavior may occur. This can impact the effect of versioning, which can lead to failures. You should, when changing to a different agent, go to the distributor's working directory and locate the subdirectory titled the same as the distribution, and then remove all time stamp subdirectories under this distribution directory. This causes the agent to perform a clean build of the distribution, ensuring that the distribution is complete and accurate for the new agent.

About the NAL Application Distribution Agent

This distribution agent enables you to specify the application object in NDS that represents the files that are associated with the application. You must have previously installed ZENworks for Desktops 3 Application Management and have at least one application object in your tree in order for this option to function properly.

As you recall, the files for the application object must reside on the distributor file system. The application object, when added, is analyzed, and the files that are specified in the application object are automatically bundled together into the distribution file, sent to the subscriber, and extracted into the same file directory structure that is identified in the source application object. This NAL agent also creates or updates an application object in the destination site area, making the application available to users in the subscriber location.

The NAL distribution is dependent on the existence of a new object called a site distribution object. This object is responsible for holding configuration data that is used in constructing and updating any application objects that are created or updated by the TED distribution process. The site distribution object is created through a wizard and is expected to be located in a container in your tree that is representative of a geographical area. For example, if your tree contained OUs that are Provo, San Jose, and Washington, you would want a site distribution object in each OU; one each in the Provo, San Jose, and Washington containers. The NAL distribution agent, when extracting the files and creating the object, locates the appropriate site distribution object by comparing its full DN with the subscriber's full DN and finding the one that more closely matches. Then, the configuration information stored in that site distribution object is applied to the new or updated application objects. For example, if there is a subscriber in subscriber1.servers.provo.novell and the

SETTING UP TIERED ELECTRONIC DISTRIBUTION

following site distribution objects are available — provo-site.provo.novell, sanjose-site.sanjose.novell, and washington-site.washington.novell — the agent will match the subscribers1.servers.provo.novell with provo-site.provo.novell because it is the only site distribution object with a similar path (that is, provo.novell) in its full DN.

Site distribution objects may only be created or edited from within the distribution object when you select the NAL distribution agent or within an application object, under the Site Distribution tab. The site distribution object is edited and created via a wizard that prompts you for the following information:

- Container where the site distribution should be created (for example, provo.novell).
- Name of the site distribution object (for example, provo-site).
- Container where the autocreated application objects should reside (for example, provo-apps.provo.novell).
- Destination volume or share where the application files should be copied. This value is really a list of potential volumes or shares. The agent goes down the list, from top to bottom, until it finds a matching volume or share on the subscriber. The first found volume or share is the one used by the agent to store the application files.
- Application directory path. This can be the default-application directory path specified in the application object or a defined one that you enter in the wizard. This path is placed after the destination volume or share to give the full path to the file location.
- The associated users, groups, or containers that should be given rights to these automated application objects and the default associations for these applications (e.g., force run, system tray, app launcher, and so forth).

The information stored in the site distribution object is then transferred to the newly created application objects when the distribution is extracted at the subscriber. If you modify these application objects, your changes remain, except that when an update distribution occurs, the information administered in the site distribution object is reapplied to the object. For example, if you removed a user from having permissions to the application but the site distribution still has that user associated, that user will be added back if the application is redistributed.

NOTE

ZENworks for Servers 2 blocks the site distribution objects from being visible in the main ConsoleOne window. You can only create and administer them through an application object or a distribution object. However, there are occasions when you may need to delete these site distribution objects. You cannot perform this action from either of the prescribed methods (application object or distribution object). You can start up ConsoleOne with the `showhiddenobjects` command-line option. When you do, you will be able to see all of the hidden objects — be careful, because there may be several. You will then be able to browse to and delete these objects, because they now appear in the ConsoleOne main windows.

WARNING

Do not edit the site distribution objects manually from the ConsoleOne main window (with the `-showhiddenobjects` option). Always go through the wizards to make changes to these objects.

The HTTP Agent

The HTTP agent connects to the specified target and attempts to retrieve the specified file via the HTTP protocol. The construction of the destination path is the same as described in the file agent section. The only difference is when an Add File button is pressed, you are prompted for the URL that will reference the file that the agent should retrieve. Multiple different URLs can be added to the list. The HTTP agent cannot authenticate to the HTTP server. Also, it cannot get files over a secure (SSL) connection.

By selecting the "Enable patching" checkbox, the system causes the TED components to perform a bit-wise patching examination of the distribution, compared with a previous distribution file. Before the patching starts the distributor communicates with the subscriber (or parent subscriber) and determines the latest distribution revision it has on file. The distributor then prepares a bit-wise patch file (actually in 4K blocks) that, when applied to the latest revision of the distribution that the subscriber has locally, produces the new distribution. Only the patch file is transmitted across the network, rather than sending the entire distribution file. Then, the subscriber applies the patch to its copy of the distribution, creating the new distribution file. If the subscriber does not have any previous distribution revision, the entire distribution is sent to that subscriber. If the distributor does not have a local copy of the latest distribution revision that the subscriber has, because it was deleted for exceeding the max revisions parameter, the system performs a bit-wise block compare over the network with the subscriber to create the patch file.

SETTING UP TIERED ELECTRONIC DISTRIBUTION

When the schedule causes this agent to be activated, it contacts each source HTTP system and attempts to retrieve each of the files by performing a `get` command on the URL specified. After the files are copied to the distributor's working directory, they are compressed into a single file for distribution. Each time that this agent runs, it generates a new, complete distribution file containing a full copy of each file gathered. This is due to the fact that the distributor cannot detect if any changes have happened to the files until it gathers the files from the remote Web server. After the ZENworks for Servers 2 support pack 1 is released, the agent will not create a new revision of the distribution if the files it collects from the HTTP server have not changed. Until that is released, you will probably see better performance with this agent when you turn the patching option on.

The FTP Agent

The FTP agent connects to an FTP server and transfer the specified files from that server into the distributor, and then collect these files into a single distribution file to be sent and extracted in the subscriber.

When you begin defining the files for the FTP agent, you must first specify a New FTP Source by pressing this button (see Figure 6.24). This prompts you for a server name, the login, and the password for this server to retrieve FTP files. Then, you continue to add destination folders as described in the section on file agents. When you attempt to add a file, ConsoleOne will immediately attempt to connect to the FTP server and enable you to browse the FTP server, selecting the files that you wish to gather at the designated time.

By selecting the "Enable patching" checkbox, the system causes the TED components to perform a bit-wise patching examination of the distribution, compared with a previous distribution file. Before the patching is begun, the distributor communicates with the subscriber (or parent subscriber) and determine the latest distribution revision it has on file. Then, the distributor prepares a bit-wise patch file (actually in 4K blocks) that, when applied to the latest revision of the distribution that the subscriber has locally, will produce the new distribution. Only the patch file is transmitted across the network, rather than sending the entire distribution file. Then, the subscriber applies the patch to its copy of the distribution, creating the new distribution file. If the subscriber does not have any previous distribution revision, the entire distribution is sent to that subscriber. If the distributor does not have a local copy of the latest distribution revision that the subscriber has, because it was deleted for exceeding the max revisions parameter, the system performs a bit-wise block compare over the network with the subscriber in an effort to create the patch file.

FIGURE 6.24 *FTP Agent property page*

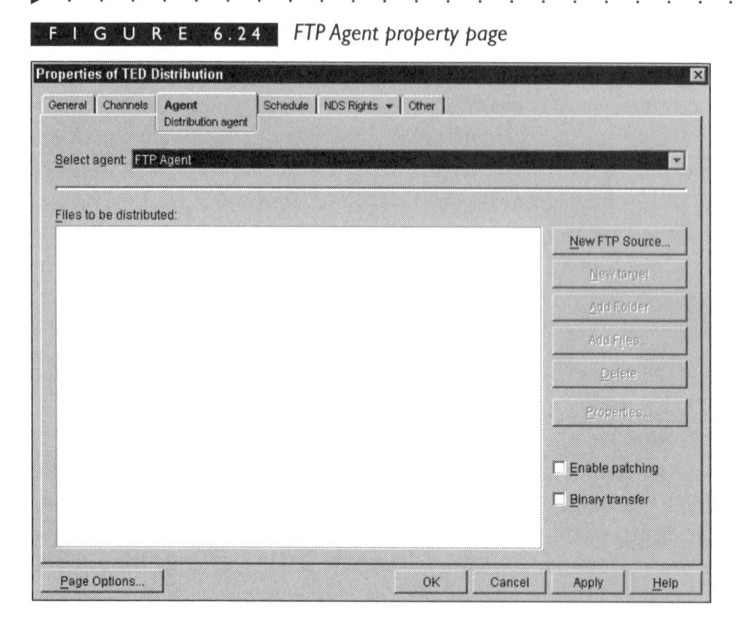

By default, the FTP agent retrieves the files in ASCII mode. If you wish to retrieve the files in binary mode, which is required when transferring any file that contains nontext characters, you need to select the "Binary Transfer" checkbox. You can only specify binary mode for the entire distribution, so if you need to get some binary files and some text files, you may need to use separate distributions. Using binary mode to transfer text files may corrupt the files if transferring from a UNIX FTP server, so be sure to use ASCII mode when getting text files from UNIX servers.

When the gatherer schedule starts, the agent connects with the FTP server, logging in with the username and password you administered, and retrieves the files that you have specified. This agent also generates a new, complete distribution file containing full copies of each file each time it is activated. This is due to the fact that the distributor cannot detect if any changes have happened to the files until it gathers the files from the remote FTP server. After the ZENworks for Servers 2 support pack 1 is released, the FTP agent does not create a new revision of the distribution if the files it collects from the FTP server have not changed. Until that is released, you will probably see better performance with this agent when you turn the patching option on.

SETTING UP TIERED ELECTRONIC DISTRIBUTION

The Server Software Package Agent

This agent is responsible for distributing Server Software packages, which are specific to ZENworks for Servers 2 policy management. In Figure 6.25, which shows the distribution object, you can identify the set of Server Software packages that you want included in the distribution. To construct a Server Software package, refer to the details described in Chapter 7.

NOTE A subscriber that is receiving a distribution that is a server software package must have the ZENworks for Servers 2 Policy and Package agent installed and running (ZFS.NCF). This agent assists in the extraction and installation of these packages.

FIGURE 6.25 *Server Software Package agent, distribution agent of a distribution object*

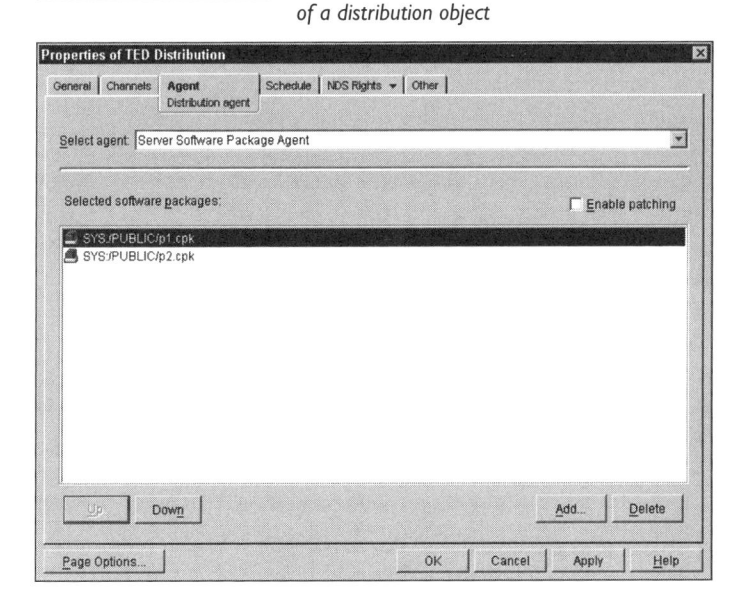

To add software packages to the distribution, press the Add button and browse to select the .cpk file. Once several packages are selected, you can specify the order that the software packages will be applied to the subscriber server. The order can be specified by selecting the package and pressing the Up or Down button to order the packages. To remove packages, select the package and press the Delete button.

By selecting the "Enable patching" checkbox, the system causes the TED components to perform a bit-wise patching examination of the distribution, compared with a previous distribution file. Before the patching is begun, the distributor communicates with the subscriber (or parent subscriber) and determines the latest distribution revision it has on file. Then, the distributor prepares a bit-wise patch file (actually in 4K blocks) that, when applied to the latest revision of the distribution that the subscriber has locally, will produce the new distribution. Only the patch file is transmitted across the network, rather than sending the entire distribution file. Then, the subscriber applies the patch to its copy of the distribution, creating the new distribution file. If the subscriber does not have any previous distribution revision, the entire distribution is sent to that subscriber. If the distributor does not have a copy of the latest distribution revision that the subscriber has locally, because it was deleted for exceeding the max revisions parameter, the system performs a bit-wise block compare over the network with the subscriber in an effort to create the patch file.

You may ask, how is it that the distributor does not have a revision of the distribution that the subscriber has? This can happen if the communication with the subscriber is sporadic and many distributions have been attempted by the distributor but failed to get to the subscriber, or if the subscriber was removed from the channel for a time and then added to the channel again. It can also happen if the distribution is scheduled to be gathered more often than the channel is scheduled to be sent. As a result, the distributor may remove some early versions of the distribution because of the max revisions parameter. Those early distributions may have been the only distributions that have successfully made it to the subscriber. One resolution to this type of problem is to up the max revisions for the distributor, or improve the communication link between the distributor and the subscriber (in the first situation). You may not want to increase the max revisions setting if the distribution is large, however. Remember that a 100MB distribution with a max revisions setting of 5 requires more than 600MB of free disk space on the distributor and every subscriber (including parent subscribers that are not even subscribed to a channel that includes the distribution).

Discussing the File Agent

This agent enables you to select any file on the distributor file system and place it in a defined directory on the subscriber system. The directories that are specified do not have to exist on the target server; they will be created at extraction time. Figure 6.26 shows a distribution using the File agent.

SETTING UP TIERED ELECTRONIC DISTRIBUTION

FIGURE 6.26 *File agent, distribution agent of a distribution object*

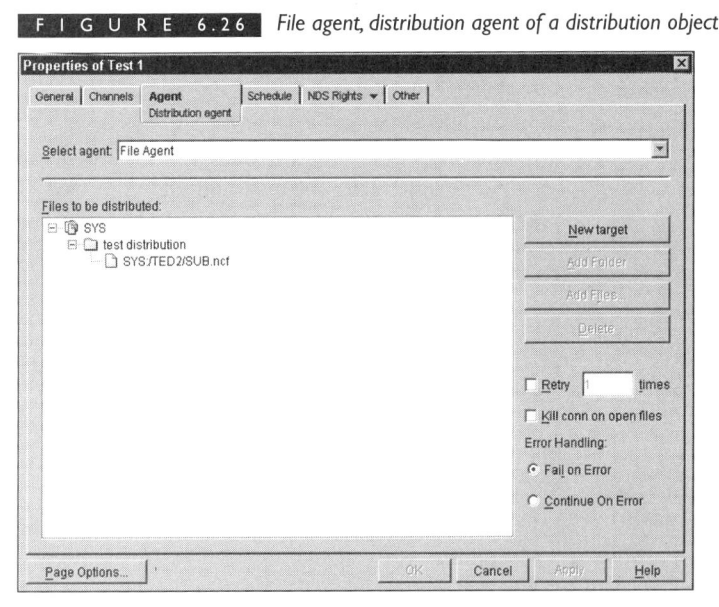

You begin identifying the target set of files to include in the distribution by pressing the "New target" button. This creates a root node displayed on the left panel. Traditionally, this represents the destination volume for the files. ConsoleOne initially places the string `%DEST_VOLUME%` in this field. You can change the string by selecting the text and pressing the left mouse button. The field clears and you can enter any text string you wish, including hard-coded volume names (on the target subscribers) or variable names (don't forget the surrounding percent signs).

You then construct a tree of the file system as you would like it created on the target subscriber. You can add subdirectories by highlighting a directory in the tree and pressing the Add Folder button. You can then highlight the folder name and press the left mouse button to edit the name of the folder (initially it is set as the string "New Folder").

When you wish to send a file to the destination subscriber, you first highlight the folder that is the file's parent on the destination subscriber and press the Add File button. This brings up a Browser dialog box, enabling you to browse through the file system of the distributor to the volume you desire and then down into the volume file system. Continue browsing until you find the file you desire. Select the file by double-clicking the filename, or by selecting the file and pressing the OK button on the dialog box. The full path name of the file (as found on the distributor) is displayed as the name of the file in the tree. The actual name of the file when it is transmitted and extracted from the distribution is the base name of the file (the file name without any directories), and the file is located under the directories and subdirectories that you have specified in the tree design in the left panel.

Continue doing the above until you have all of the desired files selected and placed in the desired locations on the target subscriber. Should you need to delete a file or directory, simply select the item and press the Delete button The file and/or the directory and all subdirectories will be removed from the tree display and will not be included in the distribution.

The following configuration flags can be placed on the distribution and only apply when the extraction process is occurring on the subscriber:

- **Retry X times** — Attempt to write the file the specified number of times. If the write fails — because the file is open, for example — the agent repeats the attempts the specified number of times before failing.

- **Kill conn on open files** — This flag enables the process to drop the connections to the subscriber server for the connection that has the file open, preventing the agent from writing the file. This terminates the session for the user that is currently using the file and they will have to re-login into the server.

- **Fail on Error** — This terminates the extraction should a failure occur in writing the files.

WARNING

The system does not roll back any files that have been installed at the point of failure.

- **Continue on Error** — This causes the agent to skip the file, logging the error if specified, and continue to extract the other files in the distribution.

These options are for the entire distribution and are not specified on a per-file basis.

The File Agent does not create a new distribution file in its entirety. If there is a previous distribution available, the agent performs a "file-wise" delta where only changed files are included in the new distribution. When the number of revisions reaches the administered max revisions, the agent removes all previously created versions and creates a completely new "baseline" of the distribution consisting of all the files specified in the distribution. This is important because each subscriber must extract the various revisions of the distribution

SETTING UP TIERED ELECTRONIC DISTRIBUTION

in order. If a new subscriber is brought online after the distributor has created eight revisions of a file agent distribution, it needs to send all eight revisions to the subscriber in order to bring it up to the latest revision. The good thing about this process is that the delta revisions are usually much smaller than the entire (baseline) distribution files. Other agents do not behave this way. The other agents either send the entire distribution file each time, or send a "bitwise" patch file. With these patching agents, the patch is calculated for and applied directly to the previous revision of the distribution to create a new complete revision of the distribution. When a new subscriber is brought online after the distributor has created eight revisions of a patching distribution, it only need to be sent one patch file to the subscriber, which will essentially be the entire distribution.

About the TED Channel

The TED channel basically identifies the group of subscribers that should receive the distributions in the channel. Multiple distributions from multiple distributors can be in the channel. Figure 6.27 displays this object.

FIGURE 6.27 *Channel object*

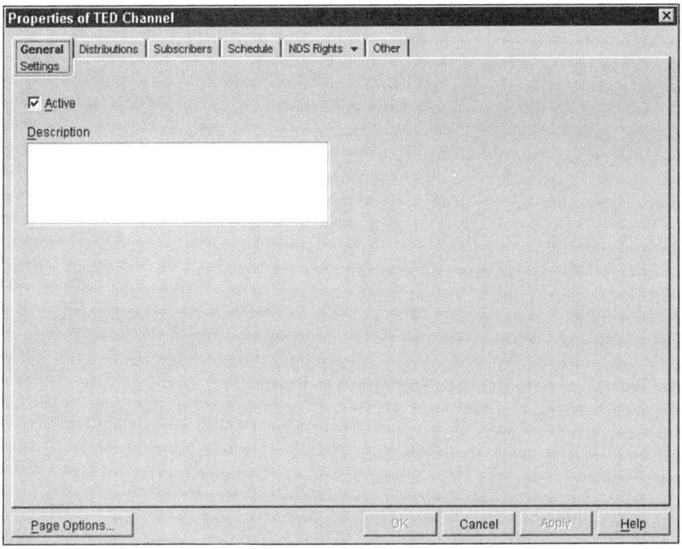

Discussing the Settings Property Page

On the Settings property page you can specify a description of the channel. This hopefully gives an indication of the type of distributions that are placed in the channel and the type of subscribers. For example, a channel for Engineering Applications would give a good signal that the distributions are applications that are used by engineers in the organization.

You can also activate or deactivate a channel. If a channel is active, the distributions are sent per the channel schedule.

Looking at the Distributions Property Page

This page enables you to specify the distributions that should be included in the channel. From this page, you can add distributions by pressing the Add button and browsing NDS to select the distribution objects. You can also look at the details or remove distributions from the channel in this property page. This can also be done in the distribution objects. If the distribution is associated to the channel in the distribution object, the distribution automatically appears in this list as well.

About the Subscribers Property Page

This page enables you to specify the subscribers that should be included in the channel. From this page, you can add subscribers by pressing the Add button and browsing NDS to select the subscriber or external subscriber objects. You can also look at the details or remove subscribers from the channel in this property page. This can also be done in the subscriber object. If the subscriber is associated to the channel in the subscriber object, the subscriber automatically appears in this list as well.

About the Schedule Property Page

This page enables you to specify the send schedule for all distributions within the channel. The channel schedule determines when the distributions are sent to the subscribers. See the section on distributors in this chapter for more details on the different types of schedule types available.

NOTE The channel schedule is converted into the time zone of the distributor. All distributors that own distributions that are in this channel start sending at once, regardless of what time zone they are in.

SETTING UP TIERED ELECTRONIC DISTRIBUTION

Looking at the Remote Web Console

The Remote Web Console is a small HTTP service that can be installed anywhere in your network and then, through administration, enables you to communicate and view the status of the distributors, subscribers, and policy engines throughout your network. You only need one RWC (Remote Web Console) per network in order to communicate with all the distributors, subscribers, and policy engines in your network, but you may want to have more than one to provide a closer access to the RWC from different locations. The RWC software communicates with the port brokers on each of the designated servers through the registered port of 1227 (it communicates through port 443 by default to the browsers on the administrators workstation). The port broker then forwards the requests on to the local policy engine, distributor, or subscriber.

RWC can be installed on any NetWare 5.x server from the installation CD. Once installed, there is an RWC_<SERVERNAME> object created in the directory, in the same container as the server object. You may start RWC by running the sys:\rwc\rwc.ncf file, which is placed in autoexec.ncf at installation. However, you will want to perform some administration on the object before you begin using the RWC software. Perform the following in order to get the RWC up and functional:

1. Launch ConsoleOne.

2. Browse to the RWC_<SERVERNAME> object and select to edit the properties. You will see the following screen (see Figure 6.28).

3. You need to determine and set the following items on the General Settings property page: Port, and Enable SSL.

    Edit the Port field (defaulted to 443, which is the standard SSL port) to another port if the server that is running RWC is already running a general purpose Web server or another system that may be conflicting with this port.

    Determine if you have SSL set up on the server. If you do, you can use the SSL system; however, you need to set up the Java components of the SSL system, following the documentation that came with the server on setting up the Java SSL system to do this. You may be able to perform the following shortcut to get it going:

    a. Determine the name of the SSL certificate object. This is probably found in the same container as the server object and would have a

179

name something like "SSL CertificateIP - <SERVERNAME>". You do not need the container (or full distinguished name) of the object.

   b. Create a file in the directory sys:\java\lib called nssl.properties and place the following text line in the properties file: **nssl.keystore = <SSL Certificate Object Name>**.

   You only need to enter the object name, and not the full name, with all of the containers.

   c. Save and close the file. You should now be able to use SSL through the Java system, allowing RWC to perform SSL functions.

   Running RWC over a secure (SSL) connection is *highly* recommended, as not doing so sends the complete username (including context) and password in clear text over the network for every action performed through the browser.

4. Select the Servers tab in the object and add all of the servers that you wish RWC to manage. If the server is not in this list, it does not appear on the screens with RWC. This is where you may want to have more than one RWC running in your system, having each independent RWC system managing different sets of servers.

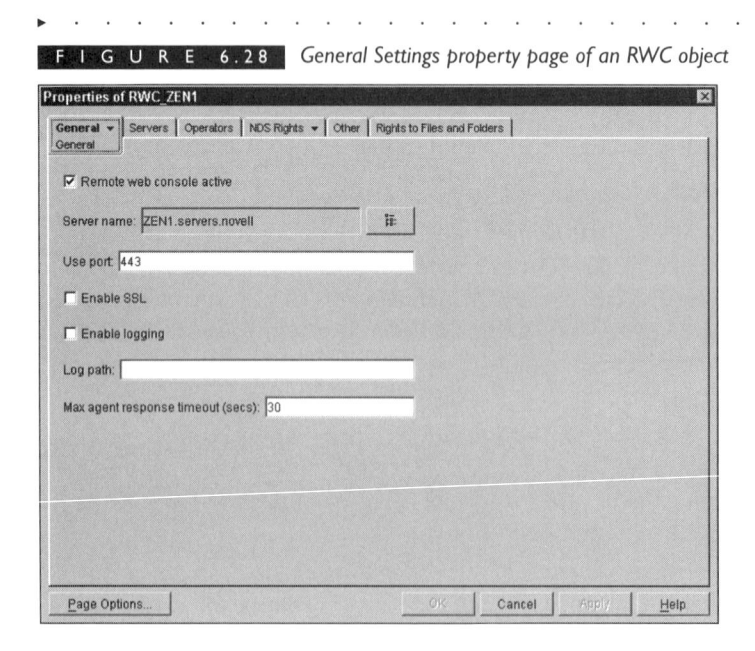

FIGURE 6.28 *General Settings property page of an RWC object*

SETTING UP TIERED ELECTRONIC DISTRIBUTION

NOTE Make sure the RWC software is running on the server. When you add servers to the list, the system must copy the digital certificates for the RWC server to these servers in order to enable communication. There is a dialog box that comes up to transmit the certificates after you have completed the object administration.

5. Select the Operators tab in the object and add any users that you want to be able to access RWC (this includes administrators). Just because administrators have supervisory rights to the objects, does not gain them access to RWC.

6. Save the object and restart the RWC process on the server by entering **EXIT** in the RWC console and then running the sys:\rwc\rwc.ncf file. You could also wait a few minutes for the RWC service to check NDS for any updates. The RWC service checks NDS for updates periodically and applies any changes immediately (this schedule is not configurable).

7. You can now get to RWC by opening a browser on your desktop and entering in the IP address of the server (running RWC), adding the port number (137.65.203.56:500) to the address. Remember, if you have enabled SSL, you need to use the HTTPS protocol in your address rather than the default HTTP protocol. When you start up RWC, you will see the introductory page, which will list the servers that this RWC is managing (see Figure 6.29).

After selecting the server and a server module to manage, you are prompted for a username and password. This is your user object name (including the full path — for example, admin.novell) and your NDS password. If your username and password are correct and you are on the RWC operator list, you are presented with information about the various ZENworks for Servers 2 components on that server.

You may perform the following functions from an RWC console: distributor, policy package engine, or subscriber.

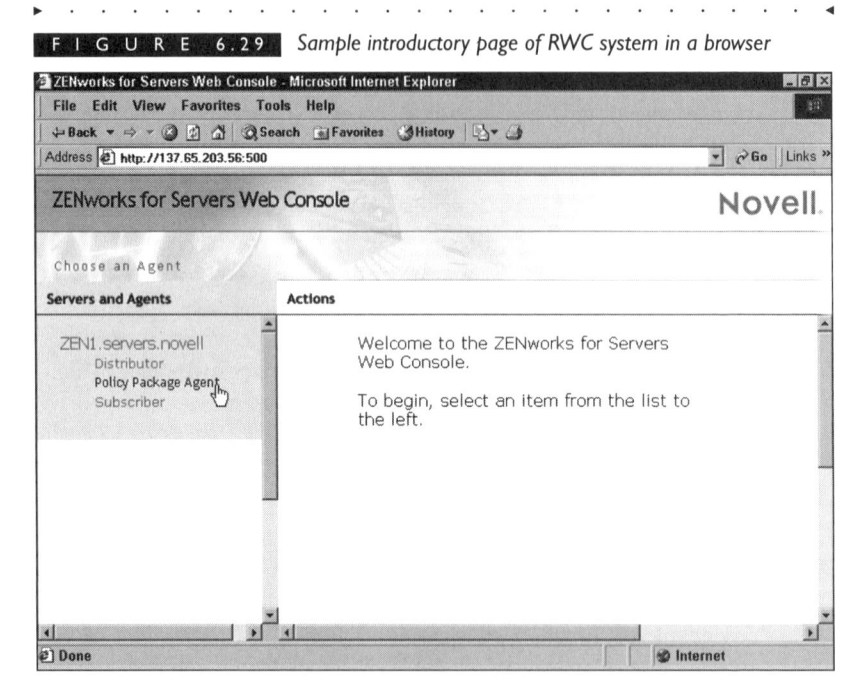

FIGURE 6.29 *Sample introductory page of RWC system in a browser*

The different distributor functions you can perform include:

- **Show distributor configuration** — Display distributor configuration information, including object name, object revision, current working directory, distribution timeout, concurrent distributions, console messaging level, logging level, log file path, I/O rate, schedule, and variables.

- **Show subordinate configuration for IP address** — You are presented with a drop-down list of known subscribers (to this distributor) and a Text field. You can select an IP address from the list or type in a subscriber IP address into the Text field, then press the OK displayed on the page. RWC then displays the configuration information for the subscriber, including object name, object revision, current working directory, distribution timeout, concurrent distributions, console messaging level, logging level, log file path, I/O rate, schedule, and variables.

SETTING UP TIERED ELECTRONIC DISTRIBUTION

- **Show subordinate configuration for object** — Same as the "Show subordinate configuration for IP address," except you need to enter the tree name and subscriber object DN.
- **Show currently scheduled events** — Show events waiting to be fired.
- **Exit** — This unloads the distributor from the server. You will get a confirmation request that you must select Yes before this will happen.
- **Refresh distributor from NDS** — You are asked to confirm this request. The distributor then refreshes the configuration information it holds (distributor, subscribers, channels, and so forth). This causes "Run Immediately" distributions to occur.
- **Show route to subscriber** — You are prompted to select the DN of the subscriber and the IP address of the subscribers are displayed in a simple routing hierarchy. This is a good way to verify that your parent subscriber relationships are functioning as you think they should be.
- **Show channel information** — You need to select a channel (known to this distributor, because it has a distribution in it) and then it displays the following configuration information about the channel: object name, object revision, schedule, subscribers, and distributions.
- **Distribute channel** — You are prompted to verify this action. Once you have, the distributor activates the channel, causing all the distributions that it is responsible for to be sent. Other distributions (owned by other distributors) may be in the same channel, but will not be sent.
- **Show distribution information** — You are asked to select a distribution. The following information is then displayed: object name, object revision, policy revision, schedule, max revisions, platform restrictions, and assigned channels.
- **Build distribution** — You are prompted to select a distribution. The distribution is then rebuilt on the distributor and a new version created, if required.

The different policy package engine functions you can perform are as follows:

- **Schedule Run** — This walks you through a couple of pages, enabling you to schedule when an NLM, a script, or a Java process should be launched.
- **Server Policies** — This displays the list of server policies and the last time they were enforced, status, and current actions on these policies.

- **Server Software Packages** — This shows the list of server software packages on the server, when they were installed, and the status and any actions associated with these packages.
- **Down Server Options** — This displays the current down state of the server and enables you to make changes in the state, including the following:
  - Cancel the down request
  - Down the server without using the down server policy (the server will not come back up)
  - Take the server down (same as downing without using the policy, but in this case it does follow the rules specified in the down server policy)
  - Down the server and restart it
  - Down the server and warm boot the machine (these also follow the rules specified in the down server policy)

  You are then prompted to confirm any of your requests.

The different subscriber functions you can perform are as follows:

- **Show subscriber information** — This displays the configuration information for the subscriber, including object name, object revision, current working directory, distribution timeout, concurrent distributions, console messaging level, logging level, log file path, I/O rate, schedule, and variables.

- **Show subordinate configuration for IP address** — You are presented with a drop-down list of known subscribers (because this could be a parent subscriber) and a Text field. You can select an IP address from the list or type in a subscriber address into the Text field, then press the OK displayed on the page. RWC then displays the configuration information for the remote subscriber, including object name, object revision, current working directory, distribution timeout, concurrent distributions, console messaging level, logging level, log file path, I/O rate, schedule, and variables.

- **Show subordinate configuration for object** — Same as the "Show subordinate configuration for IP address," except you need to enter the tree name and subscriber object DN.

- **Show currently scheduled events** — This displays the current events that are scheduled to fire.

SETTING UP TIERED ELECTRONIC DISTRIBUTION

- **Show distribution status** — You are prompted to select a distribution. Once selected, this displays the following information about the distribution: object name, version number (time stamp), IP address of distributor (or parent subscriber) who sent this distribution, and status.
- **Start distribution extraction** — You are prompted to select a distribution that has the extraction process started on it, if it has not already been extracted.
- **Reset distribution status** — This resets the status of the distribution back to the initial state, as if it has just been received. Then, you could, for example, request a distribution extraction and have the distribution re-extracted.
- **Show certificates** — You are prompted for the IP addresses of the distributors for which the subscriber has certificates. The following information is then displayed: IP address of distributor, guarantor (DN of distributor), and expiration date.
- **Exit** — Unload the subscriber from the server. You will get a confirmation request that you must select Yes to before this will happen.

CHAPTER 7

Understanding and Creating Server Software Packages

This chapter discusses the creation of Server Software Packages and how they can be used to manage your servers. With Server Software Packages, you can create a package that runs scripts for preinstallation and postinstallation, loading and unloading of NLMs and Java classes, installation prerequisites to restrict package installation, and for installing software on your servers after it has been successfully transmitted to the target server through TED, or placed on the server manually.

Understanding Server Software Packages

Server Software Packages currently only function in a NetWare server environment. The package is much like an installation package that you may be familiar with for other systems. This package system enables you to specify that certain features of the hardware and system be present (disk space, OS version , and so forth) and you can look for the existence of particular files and registry keys or set parameters. You may also specify variables that are substituted into the package when installation occurs, to enable you to customize the package for several different target machines. Additionally, you may include the loading and unloading of NLMs and Java classes and the execution of specified scripts both before and after the installation of the package.

A software package is made up of a set of components. You may have any number of components within a software package. Within a component, you may have any number of files and folders that are copied to the server.

About Installation Requirements

Before a software package may be installed on the server, the server must satisfy the requirements that have been administered as part of the package. In addition to package requirements, each component may have its own set of requirements that must be fulfilled before it is installed. If the requirements are not met for a particular component, that component will not be installed.

Consequently, only portions of a software package may actually be installed on the server. Additionally, because of the logic placed in the components and the fact that the component is installed prior to the rules for the next component being processed, you can put in some rules in a subsequent component that check for the existence of a previous package component on the server. By doing this, you can have subsequent components fail and not be installed if a previous component has not been installed. For example, you could have component 2 look for the existence of a file on the server that should have

UNDERSTANDING AND CREATING SERVER SOFTWARE PACKAGES

been installed if component 1 was successful. If component 1 does not install properly, component 2 will not run because the file from component 1 will not be found on the server.

Focusing on .SPK and .CPK Files

The specifications that you give are all stored in a file with the suffix of .SPK. This file is stored on the file system and contains the configuration information for all components of the package. The .SPK file cannot be sent to a server or installed on a server; it must first be compiled into a .CPK file. At compile time, the ConsoleOne snap-in takes the references to the files in the .SPK file and retrieves the files and places them into the .CPK file so that no references are in the file. All of the data for the installation is compacted and stored into the single .CPK file. This complete file can then be used to install the features onto your servers.

The compiled .CPK file may be sent over to the servers via the TED distribution system, or it may be manually copied to those servers (through CDs, Jaz, network, and so forth) and then executed locally. The TED system subscribers (see Chapter 6 for more information) receive the .CPK file and, if the ZENworks for Servers 2 Policy Manager is running on the server, activate that agent to have it unpack and execute the .CPK file. This can also be done manually by copying the file to the server (or having it accessible from the server drivers, for example, CD-ROM) and then entering the command PACKAGE PROCESS <path to .CPK file>. This performs the unpacking and execution of the .CPK file.

Rollback

ZENworks for Servers 2 provides the capability to roll back an installation that has occurred via a .CPK file. The rollback can remove any installation changes that have occurred on the last applied package. You can perform several rollbacks in order to get back to previous packages. For example, if packages A, B, and C have been applied, you can only roll back C. And once package C has been rolled back, you can roll back package B.

When ZENworks for Servers 2 applies a package, it creates a rollback package in the working directory of the policy engine, under the ROLLBACK subdirectory. Each rollback file is itself a .CPK file and is named by a GUID (globally unique identifier). When you request that a rollback occur, the rollback .CPK file is processed and then deleted. Rerunning the same installation .CPK file (unchanged version) does not create multiple rollback files. However, if you recompile the .SPK file, a new .CPK file is created, even if you

189

give it the same name, and the package will be installed again on the server even though the .SPK file was unchanged.

You can request a rollback by going to the ZENworks for Servers 2 console and entering the command `package rollback`. Additionally, you can go through the browser-based management system (see the section below on Remote Web Consoles for more details) and request that a rollback occur on the server.

Creating and Managing .SPK Files in ConsoleOne

You create and manage .SPK files in ConsoleOne. The ZENworks for Servers 2 install establishes a new *namespace* in ConsoleOne to manage these packages. A namespace in ConsoleOne results in a new rooted entry under your My World icon, at the same level as NDS in the ConsoleOne hierarchy display on the left panel.

When you create or insert an .SPK file, an entry is placed in ConsoleOne configuration files that, when ConsoleOne comes up, displays the known software packages without requiring the namespace to search all possible drives to find the .SPK file. Consequently, if you delete the .SPK file from the file system, ConsoleOne is not be aware of this and continues to display the software package entry in the Server Software Packages namespace. However, if you attempt to modify the package parameters, an error occurs because the file is not found. You need to manually delete the entry from ConsoleOne by choosing the "Remove package" entry from the menu.

NOTE Choosing the "Remove package" entry does *not* remove the .SPK or .CPK files that are associated with the package. You also need to manually remove them from the file system if you no longer desire to keep the packages.

Discussing Installation Failures

Should the processing of a .CPK run into problems installing the components (for example, run out of file space), the package installation is aborted, an error log is created, and a message is displayed. The components of the package that were installed are automatically rolled back and uninstalled.

Introducing the Remote Web Console

Remote Web Console is a small HTTP service that can be installed anywhere in your network, and it then, through administration, enables you to communicate and view the status of the distributors, subscribers, and policy

UNDERSTANDING AND CREATING SERVER SOFTWARE PACKAGES

engines throughout your network. You only need one RWC (Remote Web Console) per network in order to communicate with all the distributors, subscribers, and policy engines in your network, but you may want to have more than one to provide a closer access to the RWC from different locations. The RWC software communicates with the port brokers on each of the designated servers through the registered port of 1227. The port broker then forwards the requests on to the local policy engine, distributor, or subscriber.

RWC can be installed on any NetWare server from the installation CD. Once installed, an RWC_<SERVERNAME> object is created in the directory, in the same container as the server object. You may start RWC by running the sys:\rwc\rwc.ncf file, which is placed in autoexec.ncf at installation. However, you will want to perform some administration on the object before you begin using the RWC software. You need to perform at least the following in order to get the RWC up and functional:

1. Launch ConsoleOne.
2. Browse to the RWC_<SERVERNAME> object and select to edit the properties.
3. Determine and set the following items on the General Settings property page: Port, and Enable SSL:

    Edit the Port field (defaulted to 443, which is the standard SSL port) to another port if the server that is running RWC is already running a general-purpose Web server or another system that may be conflicting with this port.

    Determine if you have SSL set up on the server. If you do, you can use the SSL system; however, you need to set up the Java components of the SSL system. Follow the documentation that came with the server on setting up the Java SSL system to do this. You may be able to perform the following shortcut to get it going:

    a. Determine the name of the SSL certificate object for the server where RWC is running. This is probably found in the same container as the server object and would have a name like "SSL CertificateIP - <SERVERNAME>". You do not need the container (or full distinguished name) of the object.

    b. Create a file in the directory sys:\java\lib called nssl.properties and place the following text line in the properties file:

    nssl.keystore = <SSL Certificate Object Name>

    You only need to enter the object name and not the full name, with all of the containers.

c. Save and close the file. You should now be able to use SSL through the Java system, allowing RWC to perform SSL functions.

Using secure sockets (SSL) with RWC is *highly* recommended. If you choose to disable SSL for your RWC sessions, the username and password combination of the user using RWC is sent in clear text over the network for every action performed.

4. Select the Servers tab in the object and add all of the servers that you wish RWC to manage. If the server is not in this list, it does not appear on the screens with RWC. This is where you may want to have more than one RWC running in your system, having each independent RWC system managing different sets of servers.

5. Select the Operators tab in the object and add any users that you want to be able to access RWC (this includes administrators). Just because administrators have supervisory rights to the objects does not mean they can access RWC.

6. Save the object and restart or start up the RWC process on the server by running the sys:\rwc\rwc.ncf file. This is required when you change the port or toggle the SSL setting. Other changes made (adding or removing servers or operators) automatically become active when the RWC software queries NDS. The RWC software automatically queries NDS for any modifications every couple of minutes — this schedule is not configurable.

7. You can now get to RWC by opening a browser on your desktop and entering in the IP address of the server (running RWC), adding the port number (http://137.65.203.56:500) to the address. Remember, if you have enabled SSL, you need to use the HTTPS protocol in your address rather than the default HTTP protocol. An alternate way to view the RWC is to right-click the RWC object in ConsoleOne and choose the "Launch Web browser" option. This launches your default Web browser and brings it to the correct address to connect to the RWC software. When you start up RWC, you will see the introductory page, which lists the servers that this RWC is managing.

After selecting the server and server modules to manage, you are prompted for a username and password. This is your user object name (including the full path, for example, admin.novell) and your NDS password. If your username and password are correct and you have been added to the list of RWC operators, you are presented with information about the various ZENworks for Servers 2 components on that server.

UNDERSTANDING AND CREATING SERVER SOFTWARE PACKAGES

You may perform the following functions from an RWC console for the policy engine:

- **Schedule Run** — This walks you through a couple of pages, enabling you to schedule when an NLM, a script, or a Java process should be launched.
- **Server Policies** — This displays the list of server policies and the last time they were enforced, the status, and current actions on these policies.
- **Server Software Packages** — This shows the list of server software packages on the server, when they were installed, and the status and any actions associated with these packages, including rollback of any packages.
- **Down Server Options** — This displays the current down state of the server and enables you to make changes in the state, including the following:
  - Cancel the down request.
  - Down the server without using the down server policy (the server will not come back up automatically).
  - Take the server down (the server does not come back up automatically, but follows the rules defined in the down server policy before going down).
  - Down the server and restart it.
  - Down the server and warm boot the machine (these options also follow any rules defined in the down server policy prior to executing).

You are prompted to confirm any of your requests.

A Little about Variables

The details of variables are described fully in the "About Package Management" section of this chapter. However, it is noteworthy to mention that the Server Software Package system performs resolution of these variables in any place where manual text may be entered, including scripts. They process the text first to resolve the variables, before acting on the data.

Creating a Server Software Package

You may create server software packages inside of ConsoleOne. When you installed ZENworks for Servers 2 (policies and TED components), there was a snap-in into ConsoleOne that registers itself to ConsoleOne, displaying a new rooted entry under your My World icon in ConsoleOne. The name of this container under My World is called "Server Software Packages."

Two methods are used to introduce software packages into ConsoleOne and the system. You may create a new software package or you may insert a previously constructed software package. When you insert a software package (by choosing "Insert package" with the right-mouse button on the Packages container) you are prompted through the wizard to specify the location of the .SPK file. This file is then read, and the information is displayed and is modifiable in ConsoleOne as if the package was just created. This would be the one way that you may reintroduce a package that you had created and then removed from ConsoleOne.

At a high level, the steps to follow in administering a Server Software package include:

1. Create a server software package and administer any rules associated with installation of the package.
2. Create components in the software package and administer any additional rules (beyond the package rules), if necessary, for the component to install.
3. Compile the package and place the resulting .CPK file on the distribution server.
4. Deliver the package to the target server manually or through Tiered Electronic Distribution.
5. Install the package. This is done automatically by Tiered Electronic Distribution services and the ZENworks for Servers 2 agent. You can also install the package manually by typing **PACKAGE PROCESS <path to CPK file>** at the ZFS console.

Creating a New Server Software Package

To create a new server software package, you should perform the following:

1. Launch ConsoleOne.
2. Select the Server Software Packages container on the left panel of ConsoleOne (the hierarchical browser).

UNDERSTANDING AND CREATING SERVER SOFTWARE PACKAGES

3. Press the right-mouse menu to bring up the packages menu and select New Package. This launches the Software Package Wizard that prompts you through the initializations of the .SPK file.
4. Press Next.
5. Specify the name of the package and the filename of the .SPK file. You may browse through the file system to find an existing .SPK file to overwrite, or specify the name of a new file. You may give the file any extension you desire, but parts of the system expect the extension to be .SPK, so that is your best bet. If you do not enter a suffix, the system automatically puts the .SPK suffix on the package.
6. Press Next. The basic package is created and an entry is placed in the ConsoleOne Server Software Packages namespace for this new package. The new package is now displayed under the Server Software Packages container.
7. Select the new software package. Press the right-mouse button. From this menu, you may choose Properties to set up the package requirements and rules, or New Component to add a new component to the package. You may also choose Remove if you wish to delete this package from the namespace. Removing this package from the display in ConsoleOne does not remove the associated .SPK and .CPK files from the file system.

The following sections discuss the package rules administration and the addition of components to your software packages.

About Package Management

When you select a package under the Server Software Packages container, the path name to the package .SPK file is displayed on the right view window and you will see the administered description of the package (which is empty the first time). To administer the rules and features of the package as a whole, you must select the package in the container and then press the right-mouse button to bring up the menu choices. From that menu, you need to select the Properties menu item. When you select the Properties menu item, the screen shown in Figure 7.1 is displayed.

FIGURE 7.1 *Property pages for package management*

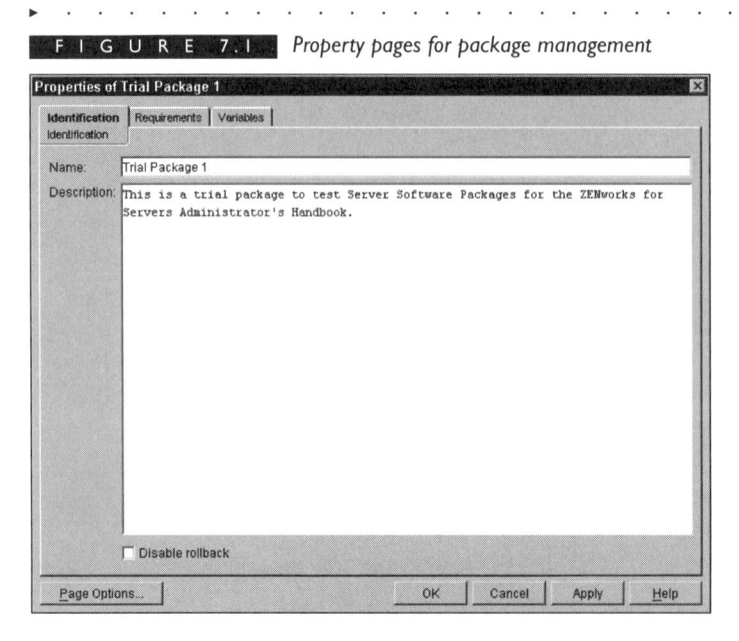

The following property pages are available for administration under the package.

Information on the Identification Property Page

Under the Identification property page you may administer the name and the description of the package. The name of the package is what is displayed under the Server Software Packages container in ConsoleOne, and the description is displayed on the right window of ConsoleOne when the package is selected.

If you select the checkbox "Disable rollback," this package will not be available for rollback on the installed servers. It will be installed and the rollback scripts and information will not be created.

Understanding the Requirements Property Page

The Requirements property page enables you to specify the requirements that must be satisfied for any portion of the package to be installed. If any requirement is not satisfied, no component will be installed from the package. The following is a sample page of the Requirements page (see Figure 7.2).

UNDERSTANDING AND CREATING SERVER SOFTWARE PACKAGES

FIGURE 7.2 *Requirements property page for Server Software Package management*

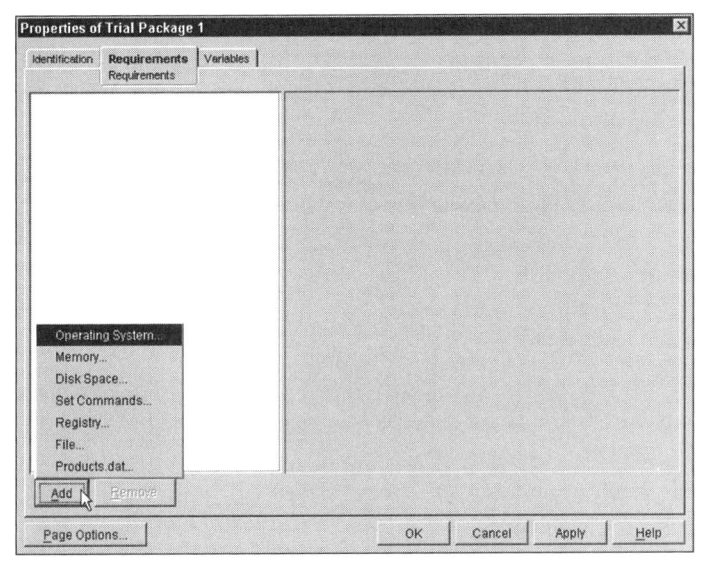

Within the Requirements property page, you may set up any number of requirements that must be satisfied for the package to be installed. You may even set up multiples of the same type of rule (e.g., two file requirements) for the requirements. Be careful not to place contradictory rules, as this causes the package to never install, because all rules must be satisfied for any portion of the package to be installed on the server.

To add a rule, press the Add button and select the type of rule that you desire. The rules are displayed on the left panel. To administer or modify a rule, select the rule on the left and administer its values on the right panel. To remove a rule, select it and then press the Remove button. The types of rules you can choose from are Operating System, Memory, Disk Space, Set Commands, Registry, File, and Products.dat. The following sections describe each type of rule.

About the Operating System Rule Currently within the Operating System requirement, you may only choose the NetWare operating system. As the product evolves, it is expected that other operating systems such as Windows, Solaris, and Linux will be supported.

197

Once you choose an operating system type, you may also keep the default, which states that it will install on any version of the operating system. Should you choose to be selective, you may enter the version number (major, minor, revision) of the NetWare operating system and then choose one of the appropriate rules to apply to the comparison between the administered value and the actual version number of the target servers. You may choose one of the following:

- **Any** — Ignore the version number of the operating system.
- **Less than** — The target server version number is less than the entered value.
- **Less than or equal to** — The target server version number is less than or equal to the administered value.
- **Equal to** — The target server version is exactly the same as the administered value.
- **Greater than** — The target server version is greater than the specified version number.
- **Greater than or equal to** — The target server is greater than or equal to the specified version.

To get the server version number, enter the command `version` on the main server console and then follow Table 7.1 to enter the right version.

TABLE 7.1 *List of NetWare Versions*

NETWARE VERSION	MAJOR	MINOR	REVISION
5.0 + SP5	5	0	5
5.0 + SP6	5	0	6
5.1 + SP1	5	1	1
5.1 + SP2	5	10	2
4.2 + SP8 or SP8a	4	20	0
4.2 + SP9	4	20	0
4.11 + SP8a	4	11	0

About the Memory Rule The memory rule enables you to specify the amount of RAM that must be present on the server. This is *not* the amount of current free space, but the total amount of RAM that is installed on the server.

UNDERSTANDING AND CREATING SERVER SOFTWARE PACKAGES

You may choose the following options on the rule and specify the amount to compare (e.g., 128) in megabytes:

- **Less than** — The target server has less installed memory then the specified amount of RAM.
- **Less than or equal to** — The target server has the same or less than the amount of RAM specified.
- **Greater than** — The target server has more RAM then the specified amount.
- **Greater than or equal to** — The target server has as much or more than the RAM specified.

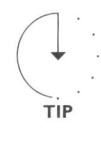

> **TIP** To get the amount of RAM from the server, enter the command memory on the main server console. This gives you the amount of memory in kilobytes, so divide that number by 1,024 to get megabytes.

About the Disk Space Rule This rule enables you to specify the amount of free disk space that must be available on the server prior to the package being installed. The amount of free space is specified in megabytes (MB) and you can specify either the SYS volume or a specific volume name. If the specified volume name (for example, VOL1) is not found on the server, the package will not be installed on the server. You may choose from the following rules:

- **Less than** — The target server volume has less space then the specified amount.
- **Less than or equal to** — The target server volume has the same or less than the amount of disk space specified.
- **Greater than** — The target server volume has more space than the specified amount.
- **Greater than or equal to** — The target server volume has as much or more than the amount of space specified.

About the Set Commands Rule Within this rule you may specify the expected value for any of the possible set parameters. When you select this rule, the Set Parameters Wizard walks you through contacting a server that is running ZENworks for Servers 2 Policy Manager, which retrieves from the specified server the list of potential set parameters. Because different servers with different software installed may have very different set commands, the wizard has you browse for a server running ZENworks for Servers 2 to use as the model server. The set commands from the server you select should represent the other servers in your network. From this list you may choose which set parameters (by category or specific parameter) you are interested in having contained in the rule. Once the list is selected, the wizard terminates and the list of chosen parameters is displayed on this page.

Then, you may create the rule by selecting the parameter and specifying the value that the parameter must have in order to enable the package to be installed. If any of the specified parameters are not set as administered, no component of the software package will be installed.

About the Registry Rule   This page enables you to place a rule on the existence or value of a registry key from the NetWare registry. You may first select if the registry interest is either a key, a name, or data. Currently, the data values may only be represented as strings and an exact match is the only type of compare supported.

When you select a key type, you may choose to accept the installation depending on if the key exists or not. Then, you must specify the name of the key.

By selecting the name type on this rule, you may also choose to accept the installation based on whether the name exists in the registry or not. You must also specify the name to be matched.

When you choose to look for a data value, you must specify if the data value equals or does not equal the specified value. Then, you must specify the key, the name, and the value of the data. The page is set up to enable you to compare based on several different types of values — currently, the only value type is string.

About the File Rule   With the file rule, you may specify that a particular file exists or does not exist on the server. You specify the name of the file (including the volume; SYS is assumed if not specified) and the flag to succeed if the file exists or not, or if you wish to base the rule on the date of the file. Should you choose to look at the date of the file, you may choose from the following:

- **Before** — The target server file has a date and/or time earlier than the specified date and time.
- **On or before** — The target server's file has a time stamp that is the same or before the specified date and time.
- **On** — The target server file has the same time stamp as specified.

UNDERSTANDING AND CREATING SERVER SOFTWARE PACKAGES

- ▶ **On or after** — The target server file has the same time stamp or later than the one specified.
- ▶ **After** — The target server file has a date that is after the given date and/or time.

Once you have chosen the comparison function, you need to press the Calendar button to be given a calendar control that enables you to select a date and enter a time value for the file.

About the Products.dat Rule   This rule enables you to match strings that are stored in the products.dat file on the server. The products.dat file identifies the various features and NetWare components that have been installed on the server.

This rule enables you to specify the name of the product ID and then look at the version and the description of the ID to see if a match exists. With both the version and the description, you may identify if the specified value contains, begins with, or matches the entry in the products.dat file. All comparisons of the values, including the ID, use case-sensitive matching. If the matched ID exists and has the value identified, the package will satisfy this rule.

Exploring the Variables Property Page

This property page enables you to specify variables that are used by the installation package to customize the filenames and locations in the software package.

Several variables can be used in this and other places in ZENworks for Servers 2. These variables are enclosed in % (percent signs) and can be either a defined set, an environment variable from the server, an attribute of the server object, or an attribute of a specified NDS object. The order is as follows:

1. If the string between the %s is a predefined variable, that value is placed in that string. Predefined variables are one of the following:

   - **LOAD_DIR** — The directory where the NetWare server was loaded.
   - **TREE_NAME** — The name of the tree where ZENworks for Servers is located.
   - **WORKING_PATH** — The working directory for the temporary files.
   - **SERVER_DN** — NDS distinguished object name for the server.

- **IP_ADDRESS** — IP address of the server.
- **BASE_PATH** — The base path showing where the ZENworks for Servers policy engine is located (e.g., SYS:\SMANAGER).
- **SERVER_NAME** — Name the server was given at install time.

2. If the string has the format `%object distinguished name;attribute%`, the attribute value of the specified object is placed in the string.

3. If the string has no semicolon, the system looks for an environment variable of that name and replaces the value in the string. The system looks in both the NetWare and the Java environments for this variable.

4. If no environment variable exists with that name, the name is assumed to be a server attribute and the system attempts to place the attribute's value in the string.

5. If the variable is not a server attribute, the unchanged variable string (including the % signs) is used as the value.

Managing Components

Once you have created a package, you need to add components to the package. The components that actually contain the files will be installed on the target server.

To add a component to a package, select the package in ConsoleOne and press the right-mouse button to bring up the menu. From the menu, choose the New Component option. After selecting the option, a dialog box prompts you for the name of the component. Remember, multiple files can be installed in a single component and a component can have its own set of rules to enable it to be installed independently in the package. Choose a name that will help you remember the types of files that are in the component. Once a name is supplied, the component is created and is displayed under the package title. When you select the component, its description is displayed on the right pane.

To manage a component, you must select the component and press the right mouse button and select the Properties entry from the menu. After selecting the Properties menu, you are presented with the property book for the component. Figure 7.3 shows a sample property book for a component.

UNDERSTANDING AND CREATING SERVER SOFTWARE PACKAGES

FIGURE 7.3 *Property book for a component of a Server Software Package*

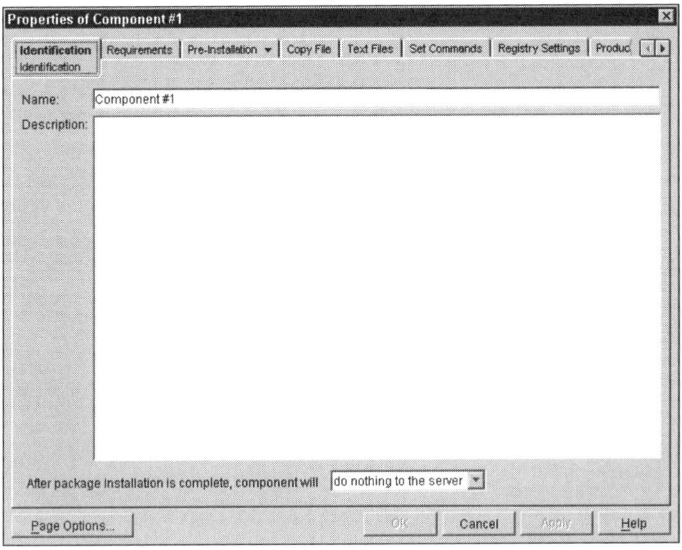

From this property book, you may administer the following pages in the component.

Looking at the Identification Property Page

As shown in Figure 7.3, you may administer the name of the component and the description of the component. The name of the component is displayed in ConsoleOne under the package and the description is displayed in the right panel of ConsoleOne when the component is selected.

Additionally, there is the ability to request that an action on the server be performed after the entire package is successfully installed on the server. This is administered at the bottom of the page and has the following values:

- **Do nothing to the server** — Continue and perform no particular action.
- **Down the server** — Down the server without restarting system.
- **Restart the server** — Down the server and restart it, which causes the server hardware to be rebooted.
- **Reset the server** — Down the server and reset it.

Examining the Preinstallation Requirements Property Page

This page enables you to specify various requirements that must be met in order for the component to be installed on the server. No component will be installed if the server does not meet the requirements of the package. In addition to the requirements of the package, the component preinstallation requirements must also be met in order for the component to be installed. Components may have different requirements, resulting in the possibility of only some components being installed on the server while other components are not installed.

See the section above on package management that discusses its property page. The same components are available to the package.

Discussing the Preinstallation Load/Unload Property Page

From this page you can request that the system load or unload an NLM or Java process. Despite what some documentation states, you can unload/kill an NLM process with the unload process request. A sample of this property page can be seen in Figure 7.4.

FIGURE 7.4 *Preinstallation Load/Unload property page for a component of a Server Software Package*

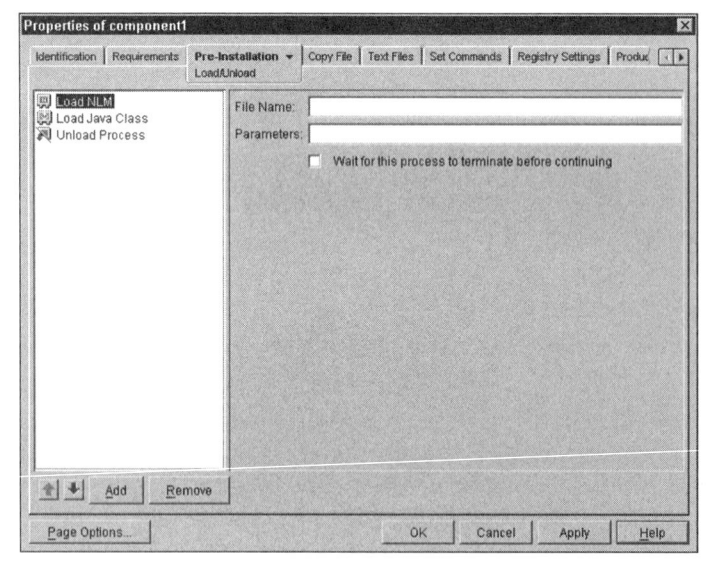

UNDERSTANDING AND CREATING SERVER SOFTWARE PACKAGES

To add an action on this page, press the Add button and select whether you wish to load an NLM, load a Java class, or unload a process. Once selected, an entry is placed in the left panel. You may edit the name of the entry by selecting the entry and typing in a new name. On the right panel, associated with each entry, you need to provide information such as filename and any parameters.

Each loading or unloading of processes occurs in the order specified on the left panel. You can rearrange the order by selecting an item in the list and pressing the up and down arrows on the page to move the item either up or down in the list.

Loading an NLM   When you select to have an NLM loaded prior to installation, you need to provide the following information in the right panel:

- **File Name** — Enter the filename to be loaded — be sure to include the full path if the NLM is not in the SYS:\SYSTEM or in the path of the server. The path can include variable names.

- **Parameters** — Enter any parameters that you want to pass to the NLM. These parameters can include variable names.

- **Wait for termination** — This is a checkbox that tells the system to wait until the NLM loads, does its work, and then unloads itself before proceeding in the installation process. If the NLM does not terminate and unload, the installation does not continue until you manually unload the NLM.

NOTE   If the software package agent tries to load an NLM that is already loaded on the server, it will fail and the entire package will be rolled back. It is recommended that you unload the NLM first in the unload parameters (the attempt to unload an NLM that is not currently loaded does not result in a failure) and then ask that it be loaded.

Loading a Java Class   When you select to load a Java process, you must also provide the following information:

- **File Name** — The filename, or traditionally referred as the class name, to load into the JVM (e.g., com.novell.application.zenworks.ted. Distributor).

- **Parameters** — This entry constitutes parameters that you want included on the command line when the process is launched (e.g., ZENTREE "Distributor_ZEN1.servers.novell"). This parameter is the parameter passed to the Java process; traditionally, these parameters follow the process name when launching the Java Virtual Machine.

- **JVM Parameters** — This entry contains the parameters to be passed to the Java virtual machine. Traditionally, these parameters are such items as the class path or other Java configuration parameters. These parameters can include variable names.
- **Wait for termination** — This flag tells the system to launch the Java class and then wait for it to run and then terminate. If the class does not self-terminate, the installation will not continue until you manually terminate the Java class.

Unloading a Process   When you choose to unload an NLM or Java process, you must also provide the following information:

- **File Name** — The class name, or NLM filename (with the .NLM extension) of the process that the system should attempt to unload. The system first attempts to unload (as if it was an NLM) the filename you specify and then the system attempts to perform a `java -kill` using the name given. If the name matches both an NLM and a Java process, both are terminated. The Java process name must match exactly the process names that appear with the `java -show` command given at the console.
- **Wait for termination** — This flag notifies the system to wait until the process is terminated before proceeding. If the process does not unload, the installation process will not continue until you manually terminate the process.

About the Script Property Page

You add a script to the policy by pressing the Add button on this property page. When you press the Add button, an entry is placed in the left window and you are allowed to edit the name of the script. Once you have named the script, you can choose on the right the type of script that you will be creating. The choices of script types are currently NCF, NETBASIC, and PERL. Once you have identified the script type, you are free to type in the script in the provided window. ZENworks for Servers 2 provides no syntax checking or validation for the script you enter.

You can add multiple scripts of any of the available types into this component. The scripts are executed in the order shown on the administration screen (from top to bottom). If you wish to reorder the running of the scripts, you must select a script name on the left pane and press the up or down arrows to move the script into a different order.

UNDERSTANDING AND CREATING SERVER SOFTWARE PACKAGES

When the ZENworks for Server 2 policy engine runs the preinstallation scripts of this component, it creates a temporary script file (in its working directory) that contains the specific script and then launches the corresponding NLM that works with the identified script, passing the NLM the name of the script to run. Consequently, netbasic.nlm and perl.nlm must already exist on the server where the script is to be run. These are normally installed with the standard NetWare 5 system. Regardless as to whether a script fails or succeeds, the engine proceeds to the next script.

Understanding the Copy File Property Page

This property page handles the placement of source files onto the server. It performs a copy of the specified file (placed into the package) onto the target server. Figure 7.5 displays a sample of this page.

FIGURE 7.5 *Copy File property page for a component of a Server Software Package*

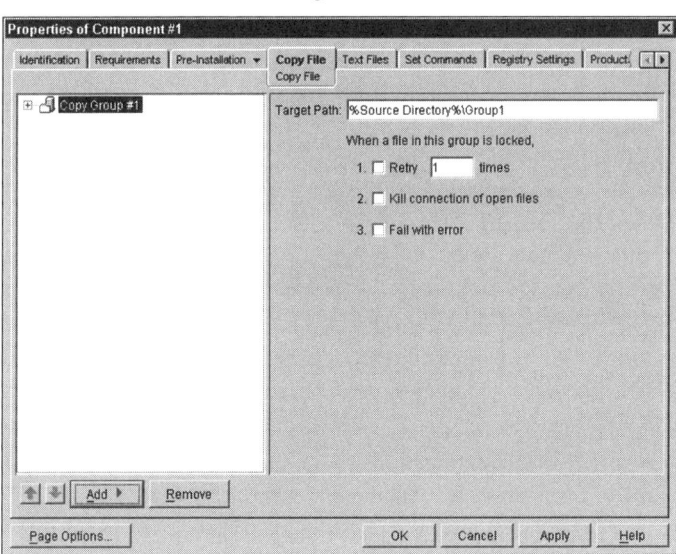

The first item to be done in the Copy File page is to define a file group. A group is a set of files that are copied onto the server into the same root directory. You may have more than one group in the software package to enable you to copy files to a different root directory. You define a new group by selecting the Add button, and the system prompts you for a group name and a target path. The target path may contain variables. Groups are processed in the order shown in the left panel. If you wish to modify the order, select a group and press the up or down arrows to rearrange the order of the groups. Folders and files cannot be reordered.

Once you have created a group, you may add files or directories under that file group in order to have these files and subdirectories created on the target server under the group target path. Select the addition of either subdirectories (folder) or files from the Add menu once your first group is created. You may also select the creation of additional groups through the Add button.

When you create each item, you have the option of naming the folder or file by editing the item name in the left panel. On the right panel you may choose options with each type to describe how you wish to have the system create or delete your files.

Identifying a Folder   A folder identifies a subdirectory under the target path. Name the folder in the left panel with a click of the mouse and then type in the name you desire. The right panel enables you to select whether this folder should be created or deleted. If it is to be created and already exists, nothing happens. If the folder is to be deleted, this folder and all contained files and subfolders are deleted from the server file system.

Identifying a File   This type identifies a file to be sent to or removed from the target server. Browsing through your file system mapped drives and selecting the file enters the filename. This represents the source path of the file (which can be different than the target path you are generating with the series of paths and folders). On the right pane, you administer the following actions associated with the designated file:

▶ **Copy mode** — This identifies the method that should be used when copying the file onto the target server from the package. The choices may be the following:

- **Copy always** — Copy the file onto the target server, either creating the file or overwriting an existing file of the same name.
- **Copy if exists** — This only copies the file if the file already exists on the server, overwriting the original target file.
- **Copy if does not exist** — This only copies the file if the file does not already exist in the specified location.
- **Copy if newer** — This only copies the file onto a target server if the file date is newer than the current file on the target server with the same name. If the file does not exist, this will *not* copy the file to the target server.

UNDERSTANDING AND CREATING SERVER SOFTWARE PACKAGES

- **Copy if newer and does not exist** — This copies the file only if it is newer than the existing file or if the file does not exist in the specified target directory.

- **Delete** — This removes the file from the server and does not copy anything from the package.

- **Attributes** — This enables you to specify the attributes that should exist on the file after it is placed on the target server. This does not modify any existing file that was not changed in the process. The possible attributes that can be set are Read Only, Archive, Hidden, and System.

Discussing the Text Files Property Page

This page enables you to enter multiple text file changes into this single package. Text files changes are edits that you want to occur to existing ASCII files on the server. You create the changes by pressing the Add button on the bottom of the screen. When you press the Add button, you are prompted to enter the name of the file (on the target server) to modify. The name should include the full path to the file to ensure that you are modifying the file you wish. You may modify more than one text file by selecting Text File from the Add button menu.

You may also make multiple changes to the same text file by selecting the text file and pressing the Add button and selecting Change. A new change is placed in the left panel with the cursor at the change name, enabling you to edit the name of the change. The changes are applied to the specified file in the order shown. Should you wish to change the order of the changes or the order of the files, select the item and move it in the list by pressing the up or down arrow.

The first to be done is to choose the change mode that corresponds to this change. You may choose either Prepend to File, Append to File, or Search File as one of your modes.

About Prepend to File

When you choose to prepend text to the file, the right side of the Administration page changes to display a large text box. You may enter any text strings that you wish in the text box and press OK to store this entry. When the change is applied, the exact strings that you typed are placed before the first lines in the existing file.

About Append to File

When you choose to append text to the file, the right side of the Administration page changes to display a large text box. You may enter any text strings that you wish in the text box and press OK to store this entry. When the change is applied, the exact strings that you typed are placed after the last lines in the existing file.

About Search File

If this change is a Search File change, you need to administer the following additional information to make the change effective:

1. Identify the search type that you will need for this change. The search type may be either Sub-String, Whole Word, Start of Line, End of Line, or Entire Line. The following describes the meaning of each of these search types:

    - **Sub-String** — Search for the search string in any of the text. The text specified may be contained anywhere in the file, even in the middle of a word. For example, if we have the substring of "day", the following text would all match with this substring: today, day, yesterday, daytime, and so forth.

    - **Whole Word** — Search for the string such that it is surrounded by white space or beginning or end of line. For example, if we have the string of "day", only the word "day" would be a match. The words today, yesterday, daytime, and so forth do not constitute a match.

    - **Start of Line** — This is a successful match if the beginning of a line (first line of file, or characters following a carriage return) starts with the string, regardless of whether the string is a whole word or not. To continue our example, if we had the string "day", this type would only match with the following lines — daytime is set, day by day, and so forth.

    - **End of Line** — This is a successful match if the end of a line (characters preceding the carriage return or end of file) contains the string, regardless of whether the string is a whole word or not. With our example, if we had the string "day", this type would only match with the following lines: the time to act is today, day by day, and so forth.

- **Entire Line** — The entire specified string must consume the entire line of text (from text following a carriage return, or beginning of the file, to the next carriage return, or end of the file) including any white space. It must be the only characters, other than the carriage returns, on the line. If our string were "day", only a line with the single word "day" on it will match.

2. Specify the search string that you're trying to match. Enter this into the Search String field.
3. Identify if you wish the search to be case sensitive by checking the checkbox to make the search only match if the case matches.
4. Change the Find all Occurrences field if you wish to only find the first occurrence of the string in the file. The default is to have this field checked, meaning that all occurrences in the file will have this policy applied to them.
5. Choose a result action that will be applied to the string once it is located in the file. The possible result actions are Delete All Lines After, Delete All Lines Before, Prepend to File if not Found, Append to File if not Found, Replace String, Replace Word, Replace Line, and Append Line. The following describes each of these choices and their resulting action:

    - **Delete All Lines After** — All lines (characters following the next carriage return) are deleted from the file. The file is basically be truncated, ending with the line that held the first matching string. Obviously, searching for all occurrences is not effectual when this is the resulting action, as a match truncates the rest of the file.
    - **Delete All Lines Before** — All lines (characters before and including the previous carriage return) are deleted from the file. The file is reset such that it begins with the line that held the first matching string. With this result action, another search continues and if another match is found, all the lines before it are deleted as well.
    - **Prepend to File if not Found** — This result action places the replacement text in the file at the very beginning of the file should the search string not be found in the file. This action only adds text, not delete or modify text.
    - **Append to File if not Found** — This result action places the replacement text at the end of the file should the specified search string not be found. This action only adds text, not delete or modify text.

- **Replace String** — This action takes the matching string and removes it from the file, placing the replacement string in the exact location of the deleted string. If the replacement string is of a different length than the search string, the surrounding characters are shifted to the left or right depending on whether less or more room is required. Basically, the new text is inserted in the location where the search string was removed.
- **Replace Word** — This result action takes the word where a substring was matched and replace the whole word (from beginning of line or space to space or end of line) with the replacement text. For example, if the substring were "day", the following words would be replaced with the replacement text: day, today, daytime, and so forth.
- **Replace Line** — This action takes the line where the match has occurred and remove the complete line from the file. The replacement text is placed in the same location where the removed line was located in the file.
- **Append Line** — This action appends the replacement string to the line that contained the match. The matching string is not removed from the file; the only change is the addition of text to the end of the line.

6. Specify the new string. In the text box that is provided, you need to supply the text that will be applied to the file based on the result action that was specified.

Discussing the Set Commands Property Page

This property page enables you to set parameters on the NetWare server as part of the installation of this package. If there is a policy that also modifies a set parameter, the next time that the policy runs it will reset the set parameter to the value defined in the policy.

To add parameters, you need to press the Add button. This activates a wizard to collect potential parameters. Because the set parameters on NetWare are dynamic and can be enhanced by various sets of NLMs, there is not a known set of set parameters. Consequently, ZENworks for Servers 2 walks you through a wizard that goes to an identified NetWare server (the server must be running ZENworks for Servers 2 policy engine) and query the server for the set of parameters. This list is then transmitted back to the wizard and used as a model for other servers in your network.

UNDERSTANDING AND CREATING SERVER SOFTWARE PACKAGES

Perform the following steps to complete the wizard and to add parameters to this component:

1. Press the Add button in the Set Parameters Policy window to activate the wizard.
2. Press the Browse button and browse the NDS tree to the server that has a representative set parameter list. Select that server. Press the Next button. This causes the wizard to query the server and retrieve all possible set parameters.
3. Select the set of parameters that you wish to have contained in the component. You can select an entire category by clicking the checkbox next to the category, or you can open the category and select individual set parameters. Once you have selected the set of parameters you wish to administer with the component, press the Finish button.
4. You will be placed back in the Set Commands property page with the list of only the categories and/or the parameters that you had selected in the wizard. To administer an individual parameter, select the parameter and press the Edit button.
5. When you press the Edit button, you are presented with a dialog box that is unique for each parameter type. From this dialog box you may administer the value of the parameter. You may also select one of the following choices: console, autoexec.ncf, or startup.ncf. These choices administer how the parameter is given to the server.

   - **Console** — The command is passed to the server console by the policy engine.
   - **Autoexec.ncf** — In addition to passing the command to the console for immediate activation, the set parameter is placed into the autoexec.ncf file so that following a reboot the server will set the parameter.
   - **Startup.ncf** — In addition to passing the command to the console for immediate activation, the set parameter is placed into the startup.ncf file so that following a restart the server will set the parameter.

6. Complete the list of parameters and press the OK button to have these items set as part of the software package.

Information About the Registry Settings Property Page

NetWare 5 introduced a registry to the server; this page enables you to modify or set registry keys into the server. This page is ignored on previous versions of NetWare. Figure 7.6 shows this page.

FIGURE 7.6 *Registry Settings property page for a component of a Server Software Package*

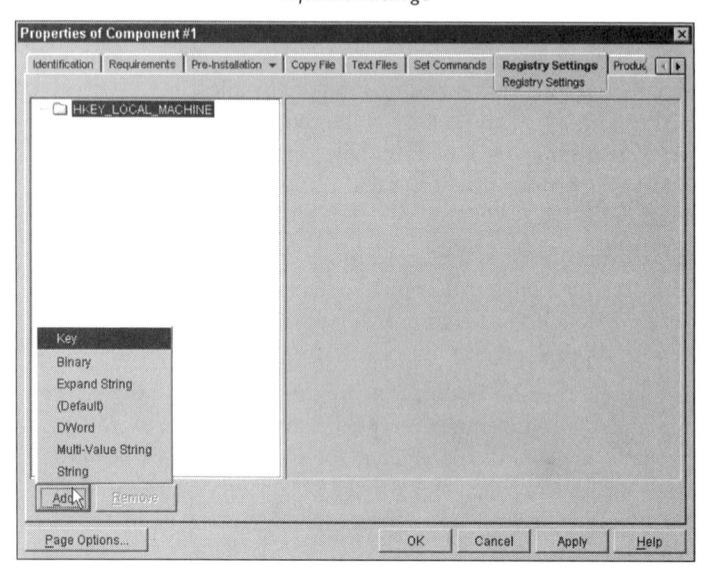

You add a key to the list by pressing the Add button and then selecting the Key menu entry. Each key may have any number of values based on the value syntax. The possible key types may be Binary, Expand String, (Default), Dword, Multi-Value String, and String.

Each type of key is presented with the value name on the left pane and the actual data value on the right pane. Depending on the type of the value, the right pane will have appropriate fields to enable you to enter the values for the registry key.

You can add multiple value or keys to this property page by continuing to press the Add button and selecting the item you desire.

About the Products.dat Property Page

See the section above on package management that discusses this property page. The same rules and modifications are available to the component.

UNDERSTANDING AND CREATING SERVER SOFTWARE PACKAGES

Simplifying the Postinstallation Load/Unload Property Page
This identifies the set of NLMs or Java processes that should be loaded or unloaded after the installation process is completed. See the section about preinstallation load/unload for more information.

Outlining Postinstallation Script Property Page
This identifies the set of scripts that should be executed after the installation process is completed. See the section about preinstallation scripts for more information.

Compiling the Software Package
Once you have completed the administration of the software package to include all of the files and changes that you desire for the installation, you must compile the package before it can be installed on the target server. The compilation process checks the rules and package for any errors, and also retrieves the files that are specified and includes them in the compressed package file. The target package file is expected to have the suffix .CPK. Obviously, because all of the files that are to be installed on the target server are contained in the compiled package, the .CPK file will be significantly larger than its .SPK counterpart. So, be prepared to consume some disk space for this process.

To compile a package, select the package under the Servers Software Packages container on the ConsoleOne main window. Press the right mouse button and select the compile menu choice. This brings up the Compile Wizard that prompts you for the output filename and places the .CPK suffix on that file, if a suffix is not specified. The wizard then compiles the .SPK file into the resulting .CPK file and places it on the disk as specified. The .CPK file can then be installed on the target server once it has been placed on the distribution server and a distribution object has been created and distributed to the target server, or you can copy the .CPK file to the target server manually.

NOTE The files defined in the .SPK are drive dependent, meaning that if you map different drives on another workstation or remap drives, these files may not be found when a compile is requested.

Installing a Server Software Package on the Target Server

Once you have created a .CPK file by compiling a defined .SPK package, you can place this .CPK file on a target server and request that the ZENworks for Servers 2 system install the package and perform the actions specified in the package.

You can get the .CPK file to your target servers a number of different ways: copy the file to the server, place the file on an external media and take it to the server, or send the .CPK file to the server with Tiered Electronic Distribution.

Sending the File with TED

Another alternative is to send your packages through the Tiered Electronic Distribution services available through ZENworks for Servers 2. You can create a distribution that contains a server software package and place this distribution into a channel. When the subscriber receives the software package through the channel, it automatically notifies the policy engine (at extraction schedule time) and begins processing the installation package. See the section titled "The Server Software Package Agent" in Chapter 6 for a more detailed description of how to do this.

Copying the File Manually

You can get the .CPK file to the server by either creating a movable media that you can then take to your target servers and mount or copying the file through the file system to a volume on the target server. Be aware that the .CPK file can be extremely large, depending on the files included in it.

Once the target server has access to the .CPK file from its local file system, you can request that ZENworks for Servers process the .CPK file by entering the following command on the ZENworks for Servers policy engine console:

```
package process <full path to .CPK file>
```

This spins off a thread that begins the unpacking and installation of the server software package onto the server.

UNDERSTANDING AND CREATING SERVER SOFTWARE PACKAGES

Updating Server Software Packages

When you modify a server software package, the .SPK file is automatically updated when you save the changes. The .CPK file, however, is not updated automatically. When you want to update the .CPK file, you need to recompile the package.

If you have set up TED to distribute your software packages, when you update the .CPK file in the same place as listed in TED in a distribution, the package will automatically be sent on the next scheduled update (because it is changed) and the changed package will be installed on the server.

CHAPTER 8

Understanding ZENworks for Servers 2 Management Services

One of the most difficult tasks network administrators have is to manage large complex networks made up of numerous servers, switches, routers, and other hardware. That task is daunting for most, and for this reason ZENworks for Servers 2 provides a powerful configuration and management engine that can be operated from a centralized location. ZENworks for Servers 2 provides administrators with several monitoring, management, and reporting tools that help them take control of their heterogeneous networks.

This chapter provides you with an overview of the ZENworks for Servers 2 management components and the console interface you will use to monitor and manage your network, as well as some strategic planning that you can do to get the most out of ZENworks for Servers 2 management services.

Understanding ZENworks for Servers Management Components

Several different components provided with ZENworks for Servers 2, each of which enable you to manage a different aspect of your network. Separately, these components are all useful tools; however, when you use them together they become an extremely powerful management engine. The first step in taking control of your network using ZENworks for Servers 2 is to understand the components that make up ZENworks for Servers 2 Management Services. The following sections cover the main components of ZENworks for Servers 2 Management Services and give you an idea of how they all fit together.

Introducing Management Site Services

The first ZENworks for Servers 2 Management Service component you need to understand is Management Site Services. Management Site Services is actually a collection of components that are used to create, monitor, and manage a management site. A management site is simply an object in NDS that represents and defines a collection of discovered network objects that together make up a group of resources and services.

Collecting network resources and services together into a single management site allows for easier and more powerful management from a centralized location. The following sections describe the components provided with ZENworks for Servers 2 that are used by Management Site Services.

UNDERSTANDING ZENWORKS FOR SERVERS 2 MANAGEMENT SERVICES

About Network Discovery

The first component of Management Site Services you need to know about is the network discovery component. Network discovery is the process of determining the topology of your network by actively probing your network, searching for services and devices that support management information bases (MIB). Once the information about the topology of your network is collected, it can be used to enable you to display, monitor, and manage your network from the management console.

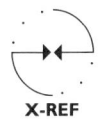

> **X-REF**
> For more information about the management console, see the section in this chapter titled, appropriately enough, "About the Management Console."

The following are the two main pieces of software that make up the network discovery component:

- **Discovery software** — A group of modules that run on a management server that searches the network discovering devices to build the network topology. This information is stored in the NETXPLOR.DAT file.

- **Consolidator software** — Software that runs on the ZENworks for Servers 2 management server. It reads data from the NETXPLOR.DAT file, which was created by the discovery software and populates the ZENworks for Servers 2 database.

Topology Mapping

Now that you understand how the ZENworks for Servers 2 database gets populated, you need to understand the best way to access the information. One of the best tools for accessing information about managed sites is topology mapping through the Atlas Manager. The Atlas Manager is made up of software that reads the ZENworks for Servers 2 database and uses it to create an atlas database as well as software that displays the network topology in an atlas on the management console. (An atlas database is a database that resides on the management server that contains the data used to create the Network Topology view.)

> **X-REF**
> For more information on the management console, see the section in this chapter titled, appropriately enough, "About the Management Console."

221

The atlas is a simple view that can be configured to give you the quickest look at your management sites. You can use this atlas of your network topology as a powerful tool to help you monitor your network for heavy usage, outages, and other problems.

About MIB Tools Administration

The next component for ZENworks for Servers 2 management site services you should know about is the MIB tools. ZENworks for Servers 2 includes tools to help you monitor and manage all SNMP devices on your network. The following are the two main MIB tools you will use to administrate SNMP devices:

- **SNMP MIB Compiler** — Parses a set of predefined SNMP MIB files written in ASN.1 and SNMP V2 format, stores the compiled files in the ZENworks for Servers 2 database, and updates trap definitions in the alarm template database. The MIB Compiler also enables you to set new SNMP alarm templates into ZENworks for Servers 2 so the SNMP alarm templates can be recognized and interpreted as alarms.

- **SNMP MIB Browser** — The MIB Browser takes the compiled MIB and displays the objects in a tree format. The MIB Browser also lets you walk the tree to view and manage the selected MIB objects.

Monitoring SNMP Services

Another component for ZENworks for Servers 2 Management Site Services you need to know about are the SNMP services that run on managed sites to provide information about connectivity and availability of resources and services within the managed group. These services notify the management console whenever the status of what they are monitoring changes. This gives network administrators fast alarms and information about what is happening on their network.

The following are SNMP services that can be monitored:

- **DNS** — Domain Name System
- **IP** — Internet Protocol
- **IPX** — Internet Packet Exchange
- **FTP** — File Transfer Protocol
- **TFTP** — Trivial File Transfer Protocol
- **SMTP** — Simple Mail Transfer Protocol
- **SNMP** — Simple Network Management Protocol
- **NNTP** — Network News Transfer Protocol

UNDERSTANDING ZENWORKS FOR SERVERS 2 MANAGEMENT SERVICES

- **HTTP** — Hypertext Transfer Protocol
- **HTTPS** — Hypertext Transfer Protocol Secure
- **NFS** — Network File System
- **Echo** — Network Echoes
- **Time Service** — Network Time Services

Discussing Database Administration

Another important component of Management Site Services is administration of the ZENworks for Servers 2 database. ZENworks for Servers 2 includes a powerful CIM-compliant database on the management server. The database acts as a repository for management site information collected from the network. That information can be displayed or formatted in various ways to provide you with specific information you need to manage your network. The information ZENworks for Servers 2 collects from your network is stored in the following three logical databases:

- **Topology database** — Contains topology, alarms, and map information.
- **Inventory database** — Contains server inventory data.
- **Server application management database** — Logs successes and failures for server policies and Tiered Electronic Distribution components.

Using Alarm Management

Another important component of Management Site Services you should be aware of is the ability to manage network alarms throughout the management site. ZENworks for Servers 2 uses alarms to monitor the state of your network and perform predefined actions when an alarm is detected. Alarms recognized by ZENworks for Servers 2 include SNMP traps, connectivity testing, and threshold profiling.

The ZENworks for Servers 2 alarm management system processes SNMP traps and proprietary alarms and then forwards the alarms to subscribing management consoles. You can configure ZENworks for Servers 2 to perform specific actions on an alarm by specifying the desired action in an alarm disposition. The following are some actions that can be automatically performed:

- Execute a program.
- Send an e-mail notification.
- Create an archive.

ZENworks for Servers 2 alarm management enables you to set specific processed alarms to be forwarded to other ZENworks for Servers 2 management servers. You can also forward unprocessed SNMP traps directly to a target address of third-party enterprise management applications.

Controlling Your Network with Role-Based Services

The role-based services component of ZENworks for Servers 2 Management Site services gives you very tight and manageable control of your network. ZENworks for Servers 2 uses role-based services, defined in NDS, to organize ZENworks for Servers 2 tasks into roles and to assign scope information to each role. Role-based services enable you to organize your network management by specifying the tasks that each user is authorized to perform.

Reporting

The final component of ZENworks for Servers 2 Management Site services you should be aware of is the ability to generate and use reports. ZENworks for Servers 2 provides reporting services for the generation of statistical reports. These reports can be displayed on the management consoles or exported to popular database and Web formats.

ZENworks for Servers 2 reports are powerful tools to understand the state of your network, resolve network problems, and plan for network growth. The following is a list of reports that can be generated by ZENworks for Servers:

- **Health reports** — General network health
- **Topology reports** — Current network configurations
- **Alarm reports** — List of active alarms
- **Server inventory reports** — Current server configurations
- **Server policies reports** — Current server policy information
- **TED (Tiered Electronic Distribution) reports** — Software distribution information

About Server Management

Now that you understand the components involved in ZENworks for Servers 2 Management Site Services, you need to understand the components specifically for server management. The ZENworks for Servers Server 2 management components enable you to monitor, configure, and control the managed servers and nodes on your network.

ZENworks for Servers 2 Server Management is made up of SNMP-based server management agents for NetWare and Windows NT servers, which provide real-time server performance data and information about server alarms and events to network management consoles.

Valuable information about your NetWare and Windows NT server can be gained by selecting one of the following views from a server or node in ConsoleOne:

- **Console view** — Provides details about the selected server or node. Enables you to display information about the internal components of the node, such as the devices, operating system, and services available.

- **Summary view** — Provides details about the server performance, such as alarms generated by the server, CPU utilization, and available disk space. Enables you to view summary information about other components, such as processors, threads, memory, and volumes.

- **Trend view** — Displays graphical representations of trend parameters, enabling you to monitor the state of a server over various periods of time. Trend data enables you to track the health status of servers and predict potential problems and be ready for upgrading your server configurations.

ZENworks for Servers 2 Server Management components also enable you to configure your NetWare servers as well as execute frequently used commands from the management console.

Analyzing Traffic

In addition to server management, ZENworks for Servers 2 includes powerful tools to help you manage and analyze LAN traffic. The traffic management component provides traffic analysis services that enable a NetWare or Windows NT server to monitor all traffic on an Ethernet, token ring, or FDDI network segment.

ZENworks for Servers traffic analysis tools can be used to understand the general health of your network, predict problem areas, and plan for future growth. The following are the tools that make up the ZENworks for Servers traffic analysis component:

- Standard and enterprise-specific RFC 1757 MIB descriptions for remote network monitoring

- Extensions added to NDS, including Remote Network Monitoring (RMON) agent configuration

- Network traffic trending and analysis tools to efficiently manage collected data

- Canned network health report templates for quick report generation
- Integration with topology maps for easy viewing
- Performance threshold configuration and profiling for tighter control
- A view of conversations on network segment and utilization for problem analysis
- Packet capture tools and view for problem analysis

Information About Remote Control

Another important component included with ZENworks for Servers 2 is remote control. The remote control component enables remote server management through the management console.

The remote control agent is installed on each NetWare or Windows NT server that you want to remotely control from the management console. The remote control agent ensures that remote control sessions are secure. This enables you to access the NetWare server console or the Windows NT server and perform maintenance operations without having to be sitting at the machine, thus saving you a considerable amount of time.

Viewing the Server Inventory

Another important component included with ZENworks for Servers 2 is the server inventory. The server inventory component allows you to quickly view the complete hardware and software inventory of all managed servers. ZENworks for Servers 2 server inventory also allows you to query the centralized database of the managed servers to quickly obtain specific information you require.

The server inventory is created by scan programs that identify each managed server by its distinguished name and the tree name and query the server for data. Once the scan data is collected, the scan program sends the scan data report to the inventory components on the inventory server. It is stored in the inventory database on the inventory server for later use.

About the Management Console

The most important component of ZENworks for Servers 2 management services you should become familiar with is the management console. The management console provides access to all the other components, providing you with a single, centralized location to manage and monitor your network from.

UNDERSTANDING ZENWORKS FOR SERVERS 2 MANAGEMENT SERVICES

ZENworks for Servers 2 provides several snap-ins to the Novell ConsoleOne management console under the ZENworks for Servers namespace. These snap-ins provide access and control to the ZENworks for Servers 2 management services. (See the next section for information of how to get the most out of your ZENworks for Servers 2 management console.)

Using the ZENworks for Servers 2 Console

Now that you understand the components that are involved with ZENworks for Servers 2 network management services, you need to get an understanding of how to access, control, and monitor them. ZENworks for Servers 2 includes several snap-ins to the ConsoleOne management tool, which expand its capabilities. This section covers how to use the ConsoleOne snap-ins to manage and monitor your network.

Navigating the ZENworks for Servers 2 Namespace

The first thing you need to understand about the ZENworks for Servers 2 console is how to navigate around the ZENworks for Servers 2 namespace. Once ZENworks for Servers 2 management services are installed, you will have new objects that can be accessed from the main Tree Browse screen in ConsoleOne.

Your network and resources are organized in the namespace as a collection of objects that are arranged in the following specific hierarchy of objects:

- **ZENworks for Servers sites object** — The ZENworks for Servers namespace container. Resides at the top of the ZENworks for Servers namespace hierarchy. Expanding this object in ConsoleOne displays a list of management sites.

- **ZENworks for Servers site** — Represents a ZENworks for Servers 2 management server. It represents an NDS object that defines a collection of discovered objects that collectively make up a group of services. Expanding the site displays an atlas for the services located there.

- **Atlas** — A container object for all objects that were created during network discovery. Expanding the atlas can show a WAN page, an Area page, and an Islands page, including segments.

- **Segments** — Network objects that are included within the selected atlas. Expanding a segment reveals a list of server and node objects.

227

- **Nodes** — Individual network entity. Expanding a node shows you a set of details that describe the node.
- **Node details** — List of system internal components in one of the following three categories: Devices, Operating System, or Services. You can drill down into the server configuration categories further to display more details about the internal components of the server such a CPUs, installed software, volumes, kernel, and adapters.

Setting ZENworks for Servers Console Options

Now that you understand the hierarchy of the ZENworks for Servers namespace in ConsoleOne and can navigate through it to find objects, you need to understand what options you have for managing those objects. From ConsoleOne, you have the ability to view objects in many different ways, set properties for the object, and perform specific actions on the object. The following sections describe the various options available from the ZENworks for Servers 2 management console.

Understanding Console Views

The first console option you should be aware of is console views. Views are basically different ways of looking at information. ZENworks for Servers 2 provides several different views designed to help you efficiently manage and monitor your network resources. The following is a list of the most common views that you will be using to manage your network:

- **Atlas** — Provides a graphical representation of the discovered network topology, the physical location of nodes, node configuration, and alarm information. This is the easiest view to use to quickly understand the status of your managed network sites.
- **Console** — Displays the objects contained in the selected container object. This is the view you should use to navigate the ZENworks for Servers 2 site. It enables you to quickly expand and shrink containers.
- **Trend** — Provides a graphical representation of current and historical trend data by hour, day, week, month, or year. You should use this view to monitor network trends, which will help you determine who is using the server, which server is used heavily, troubleshoot network problems, determine how to balance loads across multiple servers, and plan strategies for how to deploy new network resources.
- **Active Alarms** — Provides a tabular display of alarm statistics for all current alarms received from segments or devices, per management

UNDERSTANDING ZENWORKS FOR SERVERS 2 MANAGEMENT SERVICES

site. Use this view to determine any current network alerts since it is updated whenever a new alarm occurs on the network.

- **Alarm History** — Provides a tabular display of all archived alarms, including the handling status of each alarm.
- **Summary** — Provides a tabular view about the selected object's current configuration. For instance, the summary view for a server object displays information about NLMs, memory usage, adapters, network interfaces, disks and disk controllers, volumes, queues, users, connections, open files, and alarms, as well as installed software.

ZENworks for Servers 2 provides several other views for specific objects in addition to the main views listed above. For example, if you select a memory object, you can select a Disk Cache view that displays utilization for disk cache memory. Similarly, if you select a connections object, you can display an Open Files view that displays information and statistics for the connections on the server.

Setting ZENworks for Servers 2 Properties

ZENworks for Servers 2 provides property pages as well as views for its objects. The property pages enable you to modify settings for each individual object. They are accessed the same way other properties pages are in ConsoleOne, by right-clicking on them and selecting properties. ZENworks for Servers 2 provides property pages at the following levels in its hierarchy:

- **Site level** — Enables you to edit global properties, including alarm dispositions, ZENworks for Servers 2 database settings, SNMP settings, MIB pool entries, and health report profiles.
- **Server level** — Enables you to modify SNMP settings for the managed server.

Performing Actions on Managed Objects

Another option available on some managed objects in the ZENworks for Servers 2 management console is the ability to perform an action on the object. The following is a list of actions that you can perform on ZENworks for Servers 2 objects:

- Load NLMs (NetWare Loadable Modules).
- Unload an NLM.
- Mount a volume.
- Dismount a volume.

- Clear a server connection.
- Restart server.
- Shut down server.

Managing Console Views

One of the most powerful and important things you should be aware of in the ZENworks for Servers 2 management console is the ability to manage the console views. From the management console, you have different options to manage each view based on which of the following types of view it is:

- **Tabular** — Information is organized and displayed in table format. The Console, Active Alarms, and Alarm History are tabular views.
- **Graphical** — The Atlas, Trend, and Summary are graphical views. (The Summary view also contains tabular elements.)

There following sections cover the many options available for you to customize and work with the views to provide you with the most up-to-date and easiest-to-read information about your network.

Changing the Appearance of a View

One of the most useful things you should know about console views is how to modify their appearance. Modifying the appearance can help you make the view easier to read. The following sections cover how to use the ZENworks for Servers 2 console to modify the font add grid lines, and display the view title.

Changing the Display Font   You may wish to change the font in a tabular view to be a different size. For example, if item names are too long and do not fit in your columns or the columns are too wide for your screen, you may wish make the font size smaller. You may also wish to make the font larger to make it more readable.

Use the following steps to change the font used to display text on a tabular view's headings or rows:

1. Click View ⇨ Appearance. The Appearance dialog box is displayed.
2. Select either the Header Font button or the Row Font button. The Fonts dialog box is displayed.
3. Select a font from the Font Name list.
4. If you want the font to be displayed in bold or italic, check the appropriate checkbox.
5. Select the font size from the Size drop-down list.

UNDERSTANDING ZENWORKS FOR SERVERS 2 MANAGEMENT SERVICES

6. Click the OK button to close the Fonts dialog box.
7. Click the OK button to close the Appearance dialog box.
8. If you want to save the changes you've made to the view, click View ⇨ Save.

Customizing Grid Lines   Although the views displayed by ZENworks for Servers 2 do not contain grid lines, by default, you may wish to add them to make the view more readable. Use the following steps to display horizontal and/or vertical grid lines:

1. Click View ⇨ Appearance. The Appearance dialog box is displayed.
2. Select one of the following grid line styles from the Style drop-down list: No grid lines (default), Horizontal grid lines only, Vertical grid lines only, or Vertical and horizontal lines.
3. If you want to select a color for the grid lines, click the Color button.
4. Select the color you want to use for the grid lines using one of the three tab pages, then click OK to close the Color Chooser dialog box.
5. Click OK to close the Appearance dialog box.
6. If you want to save the changes you've made to the view, click View ⇨ Save.

Displaying the View Title   You may wish to display the view name in the frame of your current window in ConsoleOne to help you keep track of where you are within the ZENworks for Servers management console. To display the view title, Click View ⇨ Show View Title.

Modifying Columns in Tabular View

Another modification you may wish to make to a tabular view is to modify its columns to make it more readable or fit more data in. The following are operations you can perform on the columns in a tabular view.

Resizing a Column   To resize a column:

1. Move the mouse pointer to the margin between the columns you want to adjust.
2. When the pointer changes to a sizing arrow, drag the column to the width you want.
3. If you want to save the changes you've made, click View ⇨ Save.

Adding and Removing Columns   To add or remove columns, do the following:

1. Click View ⇨ Column Selector.
2. To add a column, select the column name from the Available Fields list and click the Add button.
3. To remove a column, select the column name from the Show These Fields in This Order list and click the Remove button.
4. Click OK.
5. If you want to save the changes you've made to the view, click View ⇨ Save.

Changing the Column Order   To change the column order follow these steps:

1. Click View ⇨ Column Selector.
2. Select the column you want to move from the Show These Fields in This Order lists and click the Move Up or Move Down button to change the location of the column.
3. Click OK.
4. If you want to save the changes you've made to the view, click View ⇨ Save.

Limiting Views with Filters

An extremely useful way to manage a tabular view is to filter the entries to limit the amount of information displayed. You can set up simple filters by selecting a single criterion or more complex filters by using several criteria and logical relationships as filters.

Use the following steps to set up a filter to limit entries in a tabular view:

1. Select View ⇨ Filter.
2. Select the column by which you want to filter alarms from the first drop-down list.
3. Select an operator from the second drop-down list. The operator defines how to constrain the column you've selected to a value — for example, equal to, not equal to, greater than, less than, greater than or equal to, less than or equal to, contain, or starts with.
4. Select a value for the logical operation set in the previous step.

5. Specify how this filter statement relates to other statements you plan to define by selecting one of the values listed below from the fourth drop-down menu.

6. Click OK when you are finished adding filter statements and the entries in the view will be filtered according to your criteria.

The following is a list of values that can be used to describe the relationships between different filters for views:

- **End** — Last statement.
- **New Row** — Adds a new line and you must define a logical relationship between the previous line and the new line.
- **And** — In the case of a filter statement, both filter statements must be met. In the case of a group of filter statements, the filter statements in both groups must be met.
- **Or** — In the case of a filter statement, at least one of the filter statements must be met. In the case of a group of filter statements, the filter statements in at least one of the groups must be met.
- **New Group** — Begins a new group and a new line that is separated from the rest by an additional drop-down list.

> **NOTE** Filters apply to the current management session only. When you exit the management console, the filters will be cleared.

Sorting Views

Another useful way to manage a tabular view is to sort the entries. Sorting the entries can be very useful to organize the data obtained from the view.

You can sort the entries based on a single column by simply double-clicking the header of the column you wish to use. Double-clicking once sorts the entries in descending order, with the most recent entries first. Double-clicking again sorts the entries in ascending order, with the oldest entries first.

You can also sort a view based on multiple columns by using the following steps:

1. Click View ⇨ Sort.
2. Select the first column you want the entries sorted by from the Sort Items By field.
3. Indicate whether you want the entries sorted in ascending or descending order.

4. Select the second column by which you want entries sorted from the Then By field and then select the ascending or descending sort order.
5. Repeat Step 4 for each subsequent column for which you want entries sorted.
6. Click OK to finish and the entries will be sorted based on your criteria.

Exporting a View

At any time, you can export a view to a more useful format. This can be useful to put the information on an internal Web site, to store it in a database, or to use it in a document. The following is a list of formats that ZENworks for Servers 2 views can be exported to by selecting File ➪ Export in ConsoleOne:

- HTML
- Comma-delimited text
- Tab-delimited text
- Blank-space-delimited text

Managing Custom Views

ZENworks for Servers 2 enables you to save and use any customizations that you may have done to views. You should customize ZENworks for Servers 2 views to meet your networks needs and organize them by using the steps in the following sections.

Saving a View At any time, you can save the changes that you have made to a view by selecting the view you wish to save and selecting View ➪ Save from the main menu. You can also save the view to a different name by selecting View ➪ Save As and entering in a descriptive name.

Deleting/Renaming Customized Views If you save several views, you may need to delete some or at least rename them to make view management more easy. Use the following steps to either delete or rename a view in ConsoleOne:

1. Click View ➪ Edit Saved Views.
2. To rename a custom view, select it from the list and click the Rename button.
3. To delete a custom view, select it from the list and click the Delete button.
4. When you are finished managing the custom views, click the Close button.

Planning Your Network Management Services

Once you understand the components that make up ZENworks for Servers 2 management services and the console used to manage them, you are ready to begin planning a strategy to configure your network to get the most out of ZENworks for Servers 2. This section covers the steps necessary to understand, plan, and configure your network to maximize the benefits of ZENworks for Servers 2 management services.

Defining Management Groups and Needs

The first step you should take in planning for network management is to define what management groups and needs exist in your network. Virtually all organizations are made up of individual groups, each of which requires its own specific information to function. ZENworks for Servers 2 is flexible enough to fit the business needs of each of the groups if you plan your management strategy correctly.

The first step in defining management groups and needs is to identify the individual groups in your organization. These groups should be organized according to management need types. Look for things such as network resources required, management needs, department location, and so forth.

Once you have identified the groups that require access to network information, you should begin to define the needs each group has. Determine specifically what information they require, how often they access it, and at what times they access it. For example, group servers that require around-the-clock monitoring for critical services into a single group and servers that are used to compile and generate monthly statistical reports into another group.

Planning Your Network Management Strategy

Once you have defined your management groups and needs, you are ready to plan a network management strategy. Your network management strategy should focus on configuring ZENworks for Servers 2 management to provide an appropriate level of monitoring for your network with a minimal impact on network performance. This may sound complicated; however, it is really only a matter of organizing the groups you created in the previous step into one of the three following categories and then configuring an appropriate polling frequency for each category:

- **Mission Critical** — Segments and network devices that need to be actively monitored to ensure high availability. Monitoring on these groups should be set at a high polling frequency.

- **Crucial** — Segments and network devices that need to be actively monitored for availability and usage, or groups that host services that require a balance between polling and network performance. Monitoring on these groups can be set from a few minutes to a few days depending on individual needs.

- **Common** — Segments and network devices that do not need to be actively monitored. Monitoring on these groups should be set to poll infrequently, or can be done manually at the administrator's request.

> **NOTE** Devices that are not polled or are polled infrequently can and should be configured to send alarms to the management server. This ensures that you are notified in the event a critical error occurs on the system; however, your network will not incur a performance hit from active polling.

Configuring Your Network

Once you have defined your network group's needs and planned your network management strategy, you should configure your network for optimal discovery and monitoring. ZENworks for Servers 2 management services rely on standard network protocols to monitor and manage devices on your network. The following sections discuss important considerations to ensure that your network channels are consistent and well configured.

Considerations for IP Addressing

ZENworks for Servers aggressively searches for IP addresses during the discovery process. The following is a list of considerations that you should check for devices you wish to be discovered and managed by IP addresses:

- The device must have a valid IP address.
- TCP/IP must be bound on the designated management console workstations.
- IP must be bound on the management server.
- A static IP address must be assigned to the management server.
- You must verify that a router's addresses are defined in either its management information base (MIB) or seed router table.

UNDERSTANDING ZENWORKS FOR SERVERS 2 MANAGEMENT SERVICES

- Routers must have static IP addresses.
- Verify that the subnet mask configurations on all IP networks are correct.

> **NOTE**
> If a subnet mask is too restrictive, you may not be able to discover all the devices in you management site. The discovery process does not support noncontiguous subnet masks, such as 255.255.0.255.

Identifying IPX Transports

Once you have verified your IP addressing, you should look for any software that needs to communicate over IPX. Once you have identified the IPX transport software, you should verify that it is configured with an IPX/SPX-compatible transport protocol.

> **NOTE**
> ZENworks for Servers 2 is fully compatible with the Novell IP compatibility mode driver.

Using IPX Software for NDS and DNS Names Resolution

Once you have verified your IPX software, you should check and set up NDS and DNS names for your network devices. ZENworks for Servers 2 uses the server name or host name instead of the IP or IPX addresses to display maps and configuration views. You should set up the most important devices with NDS and DNS names, because they are much easier to understand than network addresses. Name resolution can be in the form of local host files, NDS objects, or bindery tables.

Defining Community Names for SNMP Configuration

Once your have set up your NDS and DNS names, you need to define the community names for your SNMP configuration. SNMP agents and RMON agents, as well as SNMP-enabled devices, require a community name to be identified. You need to configure each SNMP-enabled device with a community name and trap target destination that includes the ZENworks for Servers 2 management server.

The community name secures communication channels between the manager and the agent from intruders. The names are set to "public" by default; however, you will want to change the names to something else to prevent outside intruders from accessing information and modifying your system configurations.

237

Defining Administration Roles

Once you have configured your network for ZENworks for Servers 2 management, you must define roles that will be used to administer it. You can assign administrators specific, defined roles for your organization, which enables you to delegate tasks without compromising network security.

The first step is to define the individuals who will be administering your network. Once you have that list of individuals, you should define a scope for each one based on their access needs to the network. Once you have defined administrators and their scope, they are able to log in once and have access to the specific management components that they need to perform their tasks.

The following sections discuss different types of management roles within an organization.

Understanding the ZENworks for Servers 2 Management Site

The most frequent management role you should use is the management site administrator. The ZENworks for Servers 2 management site sets boundaries for access to object data through role-based services. You create roles and tasks that utilize management functions of ZENworks for Servers in the network container space. This defines the level of access to network objects and information.

You need to develop a strategy for creating roles in a management site that reflects your management organization. Use your list of individuals and the scope of their administration needs to plan for roles that manage printers, monitor network traffic, handle alarms, and manage server systems through your network.

NDS user or group objects can be assigned to appropriate roles, thereby acquiring the permissions of the role. The following are the different levels within a role:

- **Roles** — Created for the various network management functions in your organization. This simplifies setting permissions and restrictions to management tools and network data.

- **Tasks** — Actions performed that utilize components of ZENworks for Servers management servers based on assigned responsibility.

- **Component/modules** — A specific tool that provides a network management function. (For more information about the components included with ZENworks for Servers 2 management services, see the first section in this chapter.)

UNDERSTANDING ZENWORKS FOR SERVERS 2 MANAGEMENT SERVICES

Discussing General ZENworks for Servers Roles

Once you have defined the management site roles for your network, you should look at some general roles to cover any individual and management tasks that are not yet covered.

There are several predefined roles, or you can define a role by creating an RBS role object in NDS and specifying tasks that the role can perform. The tasks are listed in properties of the RBS task objects in NDS.

The following is a list of predefined roles that ZENworks for Servers creates:

- RBS Admin role
- Segment Administrator role
- Segment Manager role
- Segment Monitor role
- Server Administrator role
- Server Manager role
- Server Monitor role
- Site Database Administrator role

The following is a list of tasks that are available to be assigned to role objects:

- Alarm Manager
- DB_ADMIN_TOOL
- MIB browser
- MIB compiler
- Node management
- Remote ping
- Traffic management
- ZfS maps

CHAPTER 9

Preparing and Using ZENworks for Servers 2 Network Discovery

Network discovery is one of the first things that must occur before you can begin managing your network using ZENworks for Servers 2. The manageable devices on the network must be found and stored in the ZENworks for Servers 2 database before they can be configured and managed through ZENworks for Servers 2. This chapter discusses the discovery process and how to set it up on your network to provide you with the best topology maps that you can use to manage your network.

Understanding Network Discovery

Network discovery is the process that ZENworks for Servers 2 uses to scan your network and discern its topology. This section discusses the specific components that are involved in network discovery, the process they use to discover your network topology, and the types of devices that are discovered.

Understanding the Discovery Components

To understand network discovery, you need to understand the discovery components that are running on the ZENworks for Servers 2 management servers. The discovery components are responsible for scanning your network for devices, collecting data, and transferring that data to NetExplorer.

NetExplorer is the main network discovery module. It is responsible for coordinating the discovery components and collecting their data, which is consolidated into a database where it can be managed and used.

The following sections discuss the main discovery components that make up network discovery: the discovery software, the consolidator software, and the Atlas Manager.

About the Discovery Software

The discovery software is software that resides on the ZENworks management server. The discovery software is responsible for actually polling the network and collecting data about devices that exist on the network. The data collected by the discovery software is stored in the SYS:\SYSTEM\NETXPLOR.DAT file.

The discovery software is comprised of the following NLMs that run on the discovery server:

- **NXPIP.NLM** — Responsible for discovering IP routers on IP networks and sending IP router information to the discovery. It communicates directly with IPCACHE and indirectly with IPGROPER, which are other discovery modules running on the server, to obtain information.

- **NXPIPX.NLM** — Responsible for discovering various NetWare systems on IPX networks and sending information about systems to NetExplorer.

- **IPGROPER.NLM** — Responsible for detecting IP host addresses and services on an IP network, including DHCP services, DNS names, HTTP, SMTP, FTP, SMTP and telnet.

- **NXPLANZ.NLM** — Responsible for communicating with traffic analysis agents for NetWare and NT to gather information about all systems communicating on their segments.

> **NOTE** ZENworks for Servers 2 discovery software uses its server and traffic management agents to obtain discovery information. You should use these agents throughout your network to improve the speed, reliability, and accuracy of the topology maps.

The server management and traffic analysis agents for NetWare use the Service Advertising Protocol (SAP) to identify themselves to other components. To enable the network discovery component to receive the SAP packets that identify manageable devices on the network, configure your routers so that they are not filtering out the needed SAP packets. Use Table 9.1 to configure your routers.

TABLE 9.1 SAP Numbers for ZENworks Management Devices

COMPONENT	SAP (DECIMAL)	SAP (HEXADECIMAL)
NetExplorer	567	237
NetWare Management Agent	635	27B
NT Management Agent	651	28B
Traffic Analysis Agent	570	23A
Print server	7	7
NetWare server	4	4

Understanding the Consolidator Software

Like the discovery software, the consolidator software resides on the ZENworks for Servers 2 management server. The consolidator takes the information that is collected by the discovery software, cleans it up, and stores it into the ZENworks for Servers 2 database for later use.

The following is a list of tasks performed by the consolidator to collect network information and store it in the ZENworks for Servers 2 database:

- Reads the NETXPLOR.DAT file
- Interprets the records in the NETXPLOR.DAT file
- Verifies that the device is not already discovered
- Queries the bridge management information base (MIB) on IP networks to discover the MAC addresses of all systems on a port
- Uses the SN3 agent to get the NDS name for network objects
- Determines if additional attributes exist in the discovered device
- Writes the consolidated information to the ZENworks database

Discussing the Atlas Manager

The atlas manager consists of components that exist both on a server and a client. These components are responsible for reading the ZENworks for Servers 2 database, creating a topology database, and enabling a user to browse and manage the network topology.

The server component runs on the ZENworks for Servers 2 management server, where it retrieves discovery information from the ZENworks for Servers 2 database. It then uses that information to create a topology database.

Once the topology database is created, the client component of the Atlas Manager can communicate with the Atlas Manager server component. The client component requests topology information from the server component to display topology maps at the client management console. When a user modifies the topology from the client management console, the client component transfers those changes to the server component. The server component then makes the appropriate changes to the topology database.

> **NOTE**
> For changes made to the network topology from the client to take effect, you must save the database.

Examining Related Components

There are other components that are not directly discovery components, but that are used during the discovery process. The following are components that NXPIP.NLM, NXPIPX.NLM and NXPLANZ.NLM use during the discovery process to obtain a full network topology:

PREPARING AND USING ZENWORKS FOR SERVERS 2 NETWORK DISCOVERY

- **Traffic analysis agent** — The traffic analysis agent discovers all devices on the segments that it is monitoring. The NXPLANZ component uses SNMP to query servers running the traffic analysis agent about the devices on their segments.
- **Server management agent** — The server management agents respond to SNMP queries from the NXPIPX component. They provide NXPIPX with usernames and addresses of the workstations that are attached or logged into them.
- **NetWare Servers** — NetWare servers have internal routing tables stored in their memory. The NXPIPX components query NetWare servers for the information in those tables.

Understanding the Discovery Process

Now that you understand the components that make up network discovery, you need to understand the process that they go through to query your network, collect data about manageable devices, and build a database.

Network discovery occurs in cycles. Each cycle is the process by which one of the discovery modules identifies every device possible, one time. The initial cycle is the first cycle that discovery makes. Although the initial cycle is enough to begin building a topology map, it usually takes several passes to complete the entire network topology.

During the initial discovery cycle, the discovery modules run sequentially; however, after the initial pass, they run independent of each other. The time it takes each module to complete a cycle varies depending on the number of new devices it discovers. When new information is discovered, the discovery modules transfer the data to the NetExplorer, which stores it in a file. Each cycle has the potential to provide the key information NetExplorer needs to identify the device and add it to the database.

The following sections discuss the discovery cycles for each of the discovery modules.

NXPIP

The first sequence in the NetExplorer discovery cycle involves the discovery of IP routers. NXPIP locates its local router using TCP/IP configuration information and then queries the router for the identity of other routers on the network. NXPIP then queries the MIBs on those routers and collects the IP addresses, interface types, and MAC addresses.

NXPIPX

The NXPIPX discovery begins after NXPIP has completed its first cycle. NXPIPX discovery begins at the management server and uses SNMP, RIP, IPX, and SPX diagnostics to discover attached IPX devices.

NXPIPX begins by examining its own server's routing table and discovers the names of other servers. It then queries each of those servers and repeats the process until no new servers are found.

NXPIPX also reads the connection table of each NetWare server to determine which NetWare clients are logged into which servers. NXPIPX sends IPX diagnostics packets to the clients to collect additional information about them. NXPIPX also discovers IPX routers in your network.

NOTE: If your clients have IPX diagnostics turned off, they will not be discovered.

NXPLANZ

NXPLANZ begins querying once NXPIPX has completed its first cycle. NXPLANZ obtains a list of all traffic analysis agents from NXPIPX and then uses SNMP to query all servers with the traffic analysis agents loaded. It reads the list of workstations that those servers have observed communicating on the network.

NOTE: At least one server per network segment should be running the traffic analysis agent in order for the discovery to be complete.

SNMP Community Name

NetExplorer uses the configured community names from NXPCON each time it attempts to access a system using SNMP. When it encounters a new system, it runs through the list of names configured in NXPCON until it receives a successful response. Once the community name is found, it is stored for later reference.

Understanding What Is Discovered

Now that you understand the process that ZENworks for Servers 2 uses to discover devices on your network, you may want to know what types of devices are being discovered. The devices that are discovered by ZENworks for Servers 2 can be categorized into either network systems or segments. The following sections discuss the devices that are discovered by ZENworks for Servers 2.

Network Systems

The first category of device that the ZENworks for Servers 2 discovery process detects is network systems. Network systems are manageable devices with addresses and/or services associated with them. Network discovery queries the network using addressing and service request to find these devices.

The following is a list of network systems that are discovered by ZENworks for Servers 2:

- **NetWare file server** — Service type 4. Discovered by NXPIPX.
- **IPX router** — Systems with more than one LAN adapter connected to different IPX networks.
- **IP router** — System that is configured as an IP router.
- **NetWare print server** — Service type 7.
- **NetWare client workstation** — Systems that respond to IPX diagnostic requests as an IPX workstation.
- **SFT III engines** — Discovered by the NXPIPX discovery module. Provides diagnostic information.
- **NetWare Management Agent** — Service type 563.
- **NetWare LANalyzer Agent** — Service type 570.
- **NetWare Management Agent for NT** — Service type 651.
- **Network printers** — Discovered if the printer generates a known service type.
- **NetWare Connect** — Service type 590.
- **NetWare communications server** — Used by NetWare for SAA management products. Service type 304.
- **Management server** — Server running discovery modules. Service type 567.
- **Other systems** — Any systems that are connected on a segment that is being monitored by the traffic analysis agent.

Network Segments

The other category of device that the ZENworks for Servers discovery process detects on your network is network segments. Network segments are the communication framework that lies underneath the network systems. The network systems use this framework to communicate with each other. Network discovery detects the different network segment topologies and stores that information in the database. The following sections discuss the different types of network segments that are discovered by ZENworks for Servers 2.

LAN and WAN Segments   ZENworks for Servers 2 discovers the typical LAN and WAN segments on your network, provided that they respond with an interface type from the MIB-II RFC 1573 specification. The following is a list of segments that are known by the ZENworks for Servers 2 database:

- ATM – ATM
- FDDI – LAN
- Ethernet – LAN
- Token ring – LAN
- X.25 – WAN
- PPP – WAN
- Frame_Relay – WAN

Source-Route Bridged Token Rings   ZENworks for Servers 2 network discovery also finds source-route bridged token ring segments. How well these segments are discovered and how they appear in your topology map depends on where traffic analysis agents are installed on each of the bridged rings.

NOTE   We suggest that you have the traffic analysis agent loaded on at least one NetWare server on each of your bridged rings to provide you with the best discovery and manageability through ZENworks for Servers.

Transparent Bridges   Network discovery is unable to fully discover transparent bridges. Therefore, because they have the same network number, it consolidates groups of transparently bridged segments into a single segment on the topology maps.

Configuration Changes   Network discovery is able to detect most changes in your network topology and relay those changes to the atlas. However, if you remove a device from the network, discovery does not detect the removed device unless it is moved to another location in the network.

Using Network Discovery

Now that you understand the ZENworks for Servers 2 network discovery process, you are ready to begin using it to build a topology database from which you can manage and configure your network.

Configuring and using discovery correctly can improve network bandwidth and make administration much easier. This section covers how to start and stop the network discovery, how to monitor its progress, and how to configure it to correctly discover your network.

Starting and Stopping Network Discovery

The first thing you should know about setting up Network Discovery is how to start it manually, as well as how to stop it. During the installation, you are prompted whether to start the autodiscovery and back-end services. If you select yes to those prompts, Network Discovery automatically launches.

To start the network discovery and load the back-end services on a server, use the following steps:

1. Start the autodiscovery process by entering the `netxplor` command at the ZENworks management server console. This command runs the netxplor.ncf file, which loads all the discovery modules.

2. Start the ZENworks for Servers database by entering the `mgmtdbs` command at the ZENworks management server console. This command runs the mgmtdbs.ncf file to load the Sybase database engine and the database.

3. Finally, start the basic services on the ZENworks management server by entering the `sloader` command at the console. This command runs the sloader.ncf file.

The discovery process runs 24-hours a day while it is loaded. The time required to run the initial discovery and build a complete database of your network varies depending on the size of your network and the load placed on your ZENworks for Servers 2 management server.

NOTE The ZENworks for Servers 2 network discovery process occurs in the background on your server. If your server is being heavily used, it takes considerably longer for the network discovery to finish. We suggest that you schedule your network discovery to occur during nonpeak hours — over a weekend, for example.

Once the management server is up and running you can start and stop the discovery process by using the following two commands and the ZENworks for Servers 2 management server console:

- **unxp** — An NCF file that unloads the discovery files and halts the discovery process.
- **netxplor** — An NCF file that reloads the discovery files, creates a new version of NETXPLOR.DAT, begins the initial discovery process, and processes the discovery data.

Checking the Status of the Initial Discovery

Once the network discovery process is running, an initial discovery is started. This can take a lengthy amount of time depending on the size of your network. Once the initial discovery is completed, your topology maps in the management console will reflect the discovered devices while discovery progresses. However, you must wait for the initial discovery to complete before the topology maps are updated.

The easiest way to determine whether the initial discovery is complete is to use the NXPCON utility on the management server to look at the status of each NetExplorer module. Each module must complete at least one full cycle to complete the initial discovery and draw a complete network map. The following is a list of modules that can be configured to run during discovery:

- NXPIP
- NXPIPX
- NXPLANZ

To view the discovery status, look at the following information displayed on the NetExplorer Console screen, shown in Figure 9.1:

- **NetExplorer Up Time** — Shows the time since the network discovery started running (in the figure, this is just shown as Up Time).
- **NetExplorer System Status** — Shows the overall status of network discovery. If the initial discovery process is still running on at least one module, the value is "Initial cycle in progress." If the initial discovery process is complete on all modules, the value is "Initial cycle complete." (In the figure, the value for this item is "1 cycle completed".)
- **Module Status** — Shows the status of each module and the number of cycles each module has completed. In the figure, note the status listed for NXPIP, NCPIPX, and NCPLANZ.

PREPARING AND USING ZENWORKS FOR SERVERS 2 NETWORK DISCOVERY

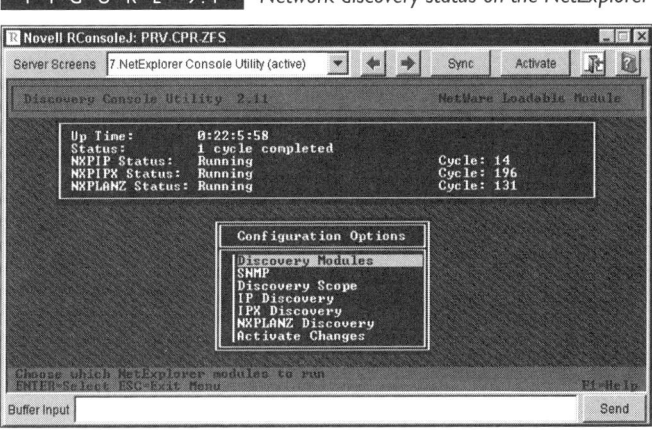

FIGURE 9.1 *Network discovery status on the NetExplorer Console screen*

The following is a list of the different statuses that each module can show and what they mean:

- **Not Loaded** — The module is not loaded. This usually means that this service is not configured for discovery.

- **Waiting to Start** — Module is loaded, but it is waiting for another module to complete a cycle before it starts.

- **Running** — Module is currently running and collecting network data.

- **Suspended** — Module is suspended because it reached the end of the schedule in which it was running.

- **Completed** — Module completed at least one discovery cycle.

- **Unknown** — NetExplorer cannot obtain the module status. This is either because the module is not loaded, but is configured to run, or because of an internal error inside the module.

Changing the Default Configuration

The ZENworks for Servers 2 network discovery software is installed with configuration defaults that are designed to work in most network environments. However, you may wish to modify the default configuration to discover more or fewer devices in your network.

To change the default network discovery configuration, you need to use the NXPCON utility on the ZENworks for Servers 2 management server. The

NXPCON utility is automatically loaded when the NetExplorer software is loaded, or you can load it manually by using the following command at the ZENworks for Servers 2 management server console prompt:

```
load nxpcon
```

The following sections describe how you can use the NXPCON utility to choose which discovery modules are loaded, how to change SNMP names, and how to modify the discovery scope to help you optimize the discovery process for your network, and how to ensure workstation discovery.

Choosing Which Modules to Load

Once the NXPCON utility is loaded, you can modify which modules are being loaded. If you choose to not load a module, the network discovery is limited to the remaining modules being loaded.

Use the following steps in the NXPCON utility to modify which modules are loaded for network discovery:

1. Select Configuration Options ⇨ NetExplorer Modules.

2. Select the module you want to modify from the Discovery Modules menu, shown in Figure 9.2, and then press the Enter key.

FIGURE 9.2 *Network discovery module setting in the NetExplorer Console screen*

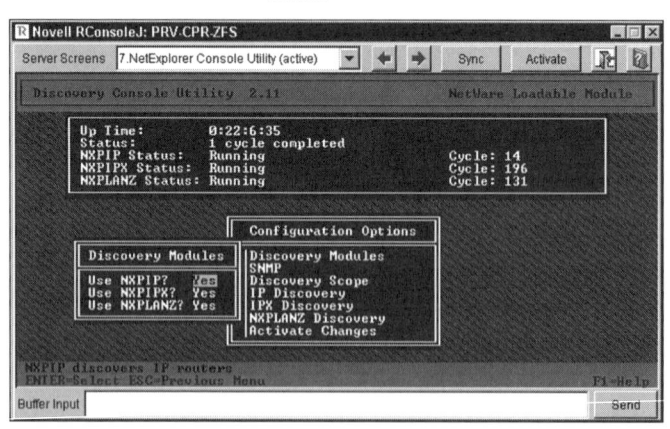

3. Select No to unload the module or Yes to load the module, and then press Enter.

4. Press the Esc key to exit the NetExplorer Modules dialog box.

PREPARING AND USING ZENWORKS FOR SERVERS 2 NETWORK DISCOVERY

5. Select Yes.
6. Unload the NetExplorer software by entering **unxp** at the ZENworks for Servers 2 management server's console prompt.
7. Reload the NetExplorer software by entering **netxplor** and the changes to network discovery are made.

Changing SNMP Community Names

Once you have selected which modules to load, you may wish to change some of the SNMP community names. ZENworks for Servers 2 automatically uses the community name of "public" by default. If your network uses SNMP names other than "public", you should reconfigure the SNMP names in NXPCON to ensure your network maintains the proper security.

To view, add, modify, or delete SNMP configuration information from within the NXPCON utility, use the following steps:

1. Select Configuration Options ➪ SNMP.
2. Select Edit Community Name List in the SNMP dialog box, shown in Figure 9.3.

FIGURE 9.3 *Network discovery SNMP options dialog box in the NetExplorer Console screen*

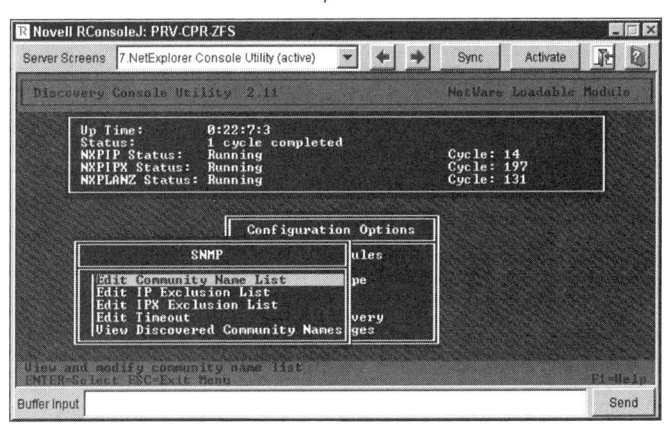

3. Select Insert to add a community name, Delete to delete the highlighted community name, or just press the Enter key to modify the highlighted community name.

253

4. Press the Esc key to exit from the SNMP dialog box.
5. Select Configuration Options ⇨ Activate Changes to update the ZENworks for Servers database.

Changing the Discovery Scope

Once you have modified your SNMP community names appropriately, you can change the scope of the network discovery. NXPCON is set to discover all IPX and IP networks by default. However, if your network is extremely large, you may wish to limit the scope of discovery for the following reasons:

- **Reduce network traffic** — Limiting the scope of discovery limits the number of discovery and management packets being sent on your network.
- **Speed up discovery** — Limiting the scope of discovery also speeds up the discovery process by skipping addresses that are not wanted.
- **Simplify manageability** — Limiting the scope of discovery limits the number of objects discovery and thereby reduces the number of objects that appear in the Atlas view. This can make it much easier to navigate the atlas.

The following two sections discuss how to use the NXPCON utility to modify the network discovery scope.

Changing the IP Discovery Scope   The NXPCON utility enables you to limit the IP discovery scope by address and subnet mask filters. Using these filters enable you to only discover certain segments or addresses.

For example, if you wished to restrict the discovery scope to your local IP network, you could set a limit to the IP address of your local network and a subnet mask that you wish to use. The mask indicates which part of the addresses needs to match for discovery to proceed on a network segment. The number 0 indicates that no match is required. If your local network IP address were 1.1.x.x, you would use the IP address of 1.1.0.0 and a mask of 255.255.0.0 to capture everything on your local network, but nothing else.

Use the following steps in NXPCON utility to limit the scope of IP discovery:

1. Select Configuration Options ⇨ Discovery Scope.
2. Select IP Discovery Scope.

PREPARING AND USING ZENWORKS FOR SERVERS 2 NETWORK DISCOVERY

3. Press the Insert key to add a new IP discovery scope entry, press the Enter key to modify the highlighted scope entry, or press the Del key to delete the highlighted scope entry.

4. Enter the address and mask for our discovery, as shown in Figure 9.4.

5. Press the Esc key and select Yes to save the changes to the configuration file.

6. Press the Esc key to exit the Discovery Scope dialog box.

7. Unload the NetExplorer software by typing **unxp** at the console prompt.

8. Reload the NetExplorer software by typing **netxplor** at the console prompt, and the changes will take effect.

FIGURE 9.4 *Network discovery IP mask dialog box in the NetExplorer Console screen*

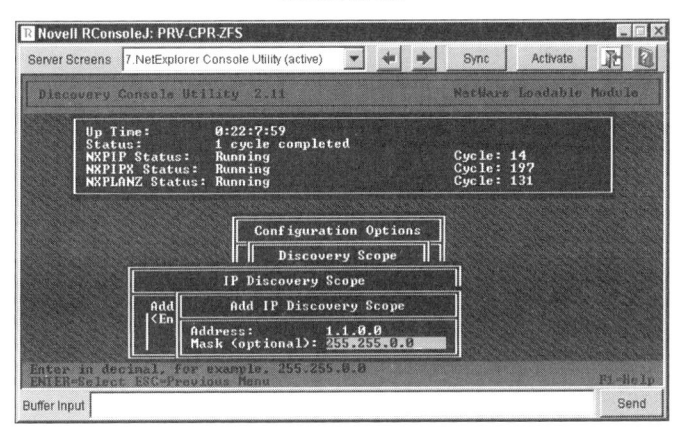

Changing the IPX Discovery Scope The NXPCON utility enables you to limit the IPX discovery scope by network number and mask filters. Using these filters enable you to only discover certain segments or addresses. A zero in the filter indicates that no match is required.

For example, if you use a specific IPX address on your servers of 1111xxxx, you could limit the scope of your IPX discovery to include only your IPX servers by using the network number of 11110000 and a mask of FFFF0000. Discovery would then only pick up IPX devices whose network number started with 1111.

255

NOVELL'S ZENWORKS FOR SERVERS 2 ADMINISTRATOR'S HANDBOOK

Use the following steps in the NXPCON utility to limit the scope of IPX discovery:

1. Select Configuration Options ⇨ Discovery Scope.
2. Select IPX Discovery Scope.
3. Press the Insert key to add a new IPX discovery scope entry, press the Enter key to modify the highlighted scope entry, or press the Del key to delete the highlighted scope entry.
4. Enter the network number and mask for your discovery, as shown in Figure 9.5.
5. Press the Esc key and select Yes to save the changes to the configuration file.
6. Press the Esc key to exit the Discovery Scope dialog box.
7. Unload the NetExplorer software by typing **unxp** at the console prompt.
8. Reload the NetExplorer software by typing **netxplor** at the console prompt and the changes will take effect.

FIGURE 9.5 *Network discovery IPX mask dialog box in the NetExplorer Console screen*

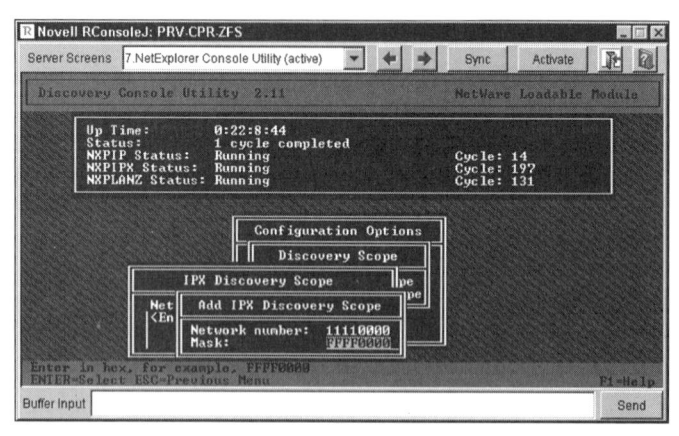

Ensuring Workstation Discovery

Once you have verified your IPX scopes in the NXPCON utility, you may wish to ensure that your IPX workstations will be discovered properly. IPX workstations are discovered with a username if the user is logged into or attached to a NetWare server that is running the management agent software. To ensure that your workstations are properly discovered, ensure that the management agent is installed on all NetWare servers that have users attached.

Checking the Results of a Network Discovery

You can check the results of the network discovery once the initial discovery is completed and after the ZENworks for Servers 2 database has been updated. You should always check your network atlas to determine whether your network topology was accurately discovered.

Your network atlas should have discovered all of the servers, desktops, switches, and routers on your network that you configured it for. For each object that is discovered the following characteristics are captured:

- **IP type** — IP router, IP host, IP service (HTTP, telnet, SMTP, DNS, FTP, and DHCP)
- **IPX type** — IPX workstation, IPX router, IPX service (file, print, any SAP service)
- **Subnet mask**
- **NetWare services**
- **NDS names and tree**

If a node is not on your network atlas, you should check the following things about the device:

- Is the device a type that NetExplorer can discover?
- Is the node in the incorrect segment? If NetExplorer is not able to get enough information about a node, it may simply have been placed in the wrong segment.
- Is NetExplorer configured to capture this type of device?

Using the Atlas

Once the initial discovery process is complete, you are able to access the data it collects through the Atlas Manager. The Atlas Manager server component reads the database created by network discovery. It then relays that information to the management console user at the client workstation.

From the client workstation, you are able to navigate through your network graphically, as shown in Figure 9.6. The following sections discuss using the atlas to view your discovered network topology.

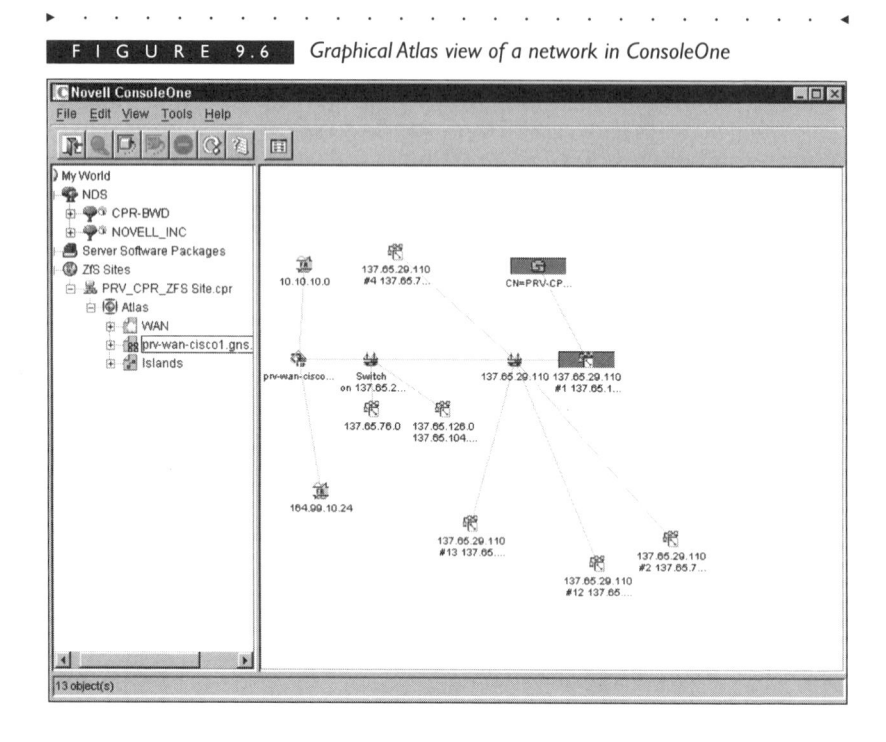

FIGURE 9.6 *Graphical Atlas view of a network in ConsoleOne*

Accessing the Atlas

You must use the ConsoleOne utility to access the ZENworks for Servers 2 network atlas. The Network Atlas view is a plug-in service to ConsoleOne that gets installed during the ZENworks for Servers 2 installation.

Use the following steps to access the atlas from within ConsoleOne:

1. Double-click the ZENworks for Servers 2 domain. Your ZENworks for Servers 2 management sites should appear.

2. Select the management site you wish to view. If the Atlas Manager is running on that management server, the atlas shows up underneath it.

3. Select the atlas.

4. Right-click the Atlas icon and select Atlas view from the pop-up menu. A screen similar to the one in Figure 9.7 should appear.

FIGURE 9.7 *Atlas view of a network in ConsoleOne*

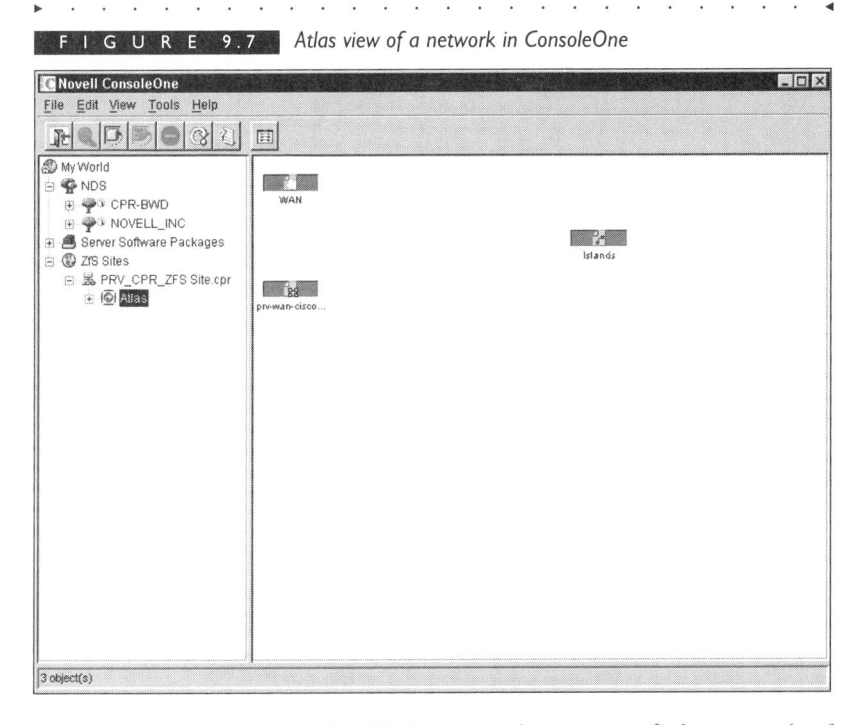

The initial Atlas screen should show you three types of objects, each of which is its own separate Atlas page. These pages represent different views for you to use to see and navigate your network topology. The following list describes the different views you see in each of the three pages:

- **WAN page** — Summarizes the entire network by showing the WAN-related network topology. There is usually only one WAN page per network.
- **Area page** — Displays the segments on your network. There can be several Area pages on your network, depending on your network configuration.
- **Island page** — Displays segments with an undetermined connectivity. During discovery, the Island page is a placeholder for network objects that are not completely discovered. Once enough information is obtained about the object, it is moved to an Area or WAN page. There is only one Island page per network.

Using the Atlas to Troubleshoot

Once the atlas is up and running, you can use it to monitor and troubleshoot your network. To use the atlas to troubleshoot your network, you must set alarms for your network devices. Once ZENworks for Servers recognizes a critical, major, or even minor alarm on a segment or node, it displays an Alarm icon above the object in the Atlas view.

Using Atlas Manager Command-Line Options

The Atlas Manager server component is a Java-based utility. There are several command-line options that enable you to modify the behavior or perform an action on the ZENworks for Servers 2 atlas database. You can configure command-line options for the Atlas Manager by modifying the Java load statement for the Atlas Manager in the following file on your ZENworks for Servers management server's management volume:

`<volume>:ZfS\MWServer\Bin\AtlasMgr.NCF`

Table 9.2 displays the available command-line options for the Atlas Manager server component:

TABLE 9.2 *Command-Line Options for the Atlas Manager*

OPTION	EFFECT ON ATLAS MANAGER
-no Notifiers	Ignores database notifications and stops notifying consoles. You should use this option to reduce overhead caused by the notifications.
-no Manager	Stops the topology updates from the database. However, changes that are made at the console (renaming, adding, or deleting objects) are still updated.
-no cmdServer	Stops the Atlas Manager server component from communicating with the client component running on the management console.
-rebuild	Deletes the existing topology database and then re-creates the map again.

CHAPTER 10

Using ZENworks for Servers 2 Traffic Analysis

ZENworks for Servers 2 includes LAN traffic analysis tools that help you monitor your LAN traffic, capture traffic data, and collect important statistics of your monitored segments and devices. You can then use the data collected through the LAN traffic tools to understand the usage and performance of your network as well as troubleshoot network issues.

The following sections discuss the different pieces of LAN traffic analysis and how to use them to monitor your managed segments, servers, and other network devices across your multitopology networks.

Understanding LAN Traffic Analysis

ZENworks for Servers 2 LAN traffic analysis is made up of several components that work together to collect, store, and display information about data packets that are being sent on your network. ZENworks for Servers provides tools that enable you to capture and decode the packets as they are sent from one node to another, giving you the ability to better analyze the traffic.

The following sections describe the ZENworks for Servers 2 LAN traffic components, how they communicate, and the functionality of their agents.

Understanding LAN Traffic Components

ZENworks for Servers 2 LAN traffic analysis system is made up of three main components: the management server, the management console, and the monitoring agent server. The following sections discuss the roles that each of the three LAN traffic analysis components play in monitoring LAN traffic on your network.

Discussing the Management Server

The management server component of ZENworks for Servers 2 LAN traffic analysis is installed on the management site server. It is comprised of an extremely scalable Sybase database that stores static information such as network names and LAN addresses of servers, routers, switches, and other nodes on you network.

The management server components include the NetExplorer, a consolidator, and the Atlas Manager (discussed in Chapter 9). These components gather information about manageable devices on the network and store that information in the management database. The management database is a Common Information Model (CIM) database that stores network data used to establish the topology of the network. ZENworks for Servers 2 extends the CIM model

USING ZENWORKS FOR SERVERS 2 TRAFFIC ANALYSIS

to provide the ability to organize the information in the database and create a topology map.

About the Management Console

The management console component of ZENworks for Servers 2 LAN traffic analysis is installed on the management client in the form of snap-ins to the ConsoleOne utility (discussed in Chapter 8). These snap-ins provide an intuitive, graphical method to access data collected by the ZENworks for Servers 2 LAN traffic analysis agents.

Exploring the Monitoring Agent Server

The final component of the ZENworks for Servers 2 LAN traffic analysis system is the monitoring agent server. The monitoring agent server is a server with network monitoring agent software installed on it. There must be one monitoring agent server per segment.

The monitoring agent server enables you to analyze a segment by searching the network and gathering information about network traffic. You can then use that information to analyze the LAN traffic on your network.

The network monitoring agents monitor network traffic and capture frames to build a database of objects in the network. Then, network monitoring agent software enables you to use the ZENworks for Servers 2 management console traffic analysis tools to maintain your network performance, monitor traffic on your network, and troubleshoot network problems.

Understanding Communication between Components

Now that you understand what components make up the ZENworks for Servers 2 LAN traffic analysis system, you need to understand how these systems communicate with each other. The management console component communicates with the management server component using Common Object Request Broker Architecture (CORBA) to obtain static and dynamic information about the managed nodes and devices on your network.

When the management console requests static information from the management server, the management server then communicates with the management database component using the Java Database Connectivity (JDBC) protocol. It gathers the requested information from the database and relays it back to the management console.

When the management console requests dynamic information from the management server, the management server communicates with the network monitoring agent using SNMP requests. It gathers the requested information dynamically and relays it back to the management console.

Understanding Agent Functionality

ZENworks for Servers 2 includes several types of monitoring agents to accommodate the various topologies and devices on your network. Network monitoring agents provide you with the functionality to remotely monitor segments and devices that are SNMP compliant. The agents collect and store statistical and trend information as well as capture real-time data from the managed nodes and devices on your network.

The following sections describe the RMON, RMON Lite, RMON Plus, RMON2, and bridge agents to help you decide which one to use based on the size and topology of your network.

RMON Agents

ZENworks for Servers 2 RMON agents use a standard monitoring specification that enables various nodes and console systems on your network to exchange network data. That network data is used to monitor, analyze, and troubleshoot your LAN from a central site.

The RMON agents are typically used to monitor Ethernet, FDDI and token ring segments. Table 10.1 describes the groups of monitoring elements that make up the RMON agent.

TABLE 10.1 RMON Agent Monitoring Groups

RMON GROUP	DESCRIPTION
Statistics	Records statistics measured by the agents for each monitored interface on the device.
History	Records periodic statistical samples from a network and stores them for later retrieval from the management console.
Alarm	Periodically takes statistical samples from parameters in the agent and compares them with previously configured thresholds. Then, if the monitored parameter crosses a threshold, an alarm event is generated.
Host	Lists the statistics associated with each host discovered on the network.
HostTopN	Prepares tables that describe the hosts that top a list ordered by one of their statistics.
Matrix	Stores statistical information for conversations between two nodes. Creates an entry in its table for each new conversation.

RMON GROUP	DESCRIPTION
Filters	Enables packets to be matched to a filtered variable. The matched packets form a data stream that may be captured or used to generate events.
Packet Capture	Enables packets to be captured after they flow through a channel.
Events	Controls the generation and notification of events from the device.

RMON Lite Agents

ZENworks for Servers 2 RMON Lite agents also use a standard monitoring specification that enables various devices on your network to exchange network data. The RMON Lite agents are typically used to monitor devices that are not dedicated for network management, such as a hub or a switch. Table 10.2 describes the groups of monitoring elements that make up the RMON Lite agents.

TABLE 10.2 RMON Lite Agent Monitoring Groups

RMON LITE GROUP	DESCRIPTION
Statistics	Lists statistics measured by the agents for each monitored interface on the device.
History	Records periodic statistical samples from a network and stores them for later retrieval from the management console.
Alarm	Periodically takes statistical samples from parameters in the agent and compares them with previously configured thresholds. Then, if the monitored parameter crosses a threshold, an alarm event is generated.
Events	Controls the generation and notification of events from the device.

RMON Plus Agents

ZENworks for Servers 2 RMON Plus agents are proprietary agents that extend the functionality of the RMON agent. They act exactly the same as the RMON agent and provide the same groups shown in Table 10-1. In addition to providing data collected from the RMON groups, they also provide data collected from the groups shown in Table 10.3.

TABLE 10.3 *RMON Plus Monitoring Groups*

RMON PLUS GROUP	DESCRIPTION
Buffer	Records the number of octets (excluding framing bits but including frame check sequence octets) in packets that are captured in the buffer.
Admin	Collects information sent to the agent, such as version number.
HostMonitor	Monitors a set of nodes for a particular host table and sets traps when a host becomes active or inactive.
DuplicateIP	Records and updates a list of packets arriving that contain duplicate IP address.
MacToIP	Stores records of the IP addresses associated with host addresses for a host mapping table.
BoardStatus	Records the status of each logical interface of the RMON or RMON Plus agent.

RMON2 Agents

ZENworks for Servers 2 RMON2 agents can be used to collect data from nodes and devices in the network and application layers of the network model, unlike the RMON, RMON Lite, and RMON Plus agents, which are used to collect data from nodes and devices in the physical and data link layers of the network model.

RMON2 agents can also determine network usage based on the protocol and application used by the nodes in your network. Table 10.4 describes the groups of monitoring elements that make up the RMON2 agent.

TABLE 10.4 *RMON2 Monitoring Groups*

RMON2 GROUP	DESCRIPTION
Protocol Directory	Creates a table of all identifiable protocols and their descriptions.
Protocol Distribution	Collects statistics for each protocol that the agent is configured to track.

RMON2 GROUP	DESCRIPTION
Address Map	Maps a network layer address to the corresponding MAC address.
Network-Layer Host	Collects statistics for each host by network layer address.
Network-Layer Matrix	Collects statistics for each network conversation between pairs of network layer addresses.
Application-Layer Host	Collects statistics on the traffic generated by each host for a specific application layer protocol. Traffic, broken down by protocols, can be recognized by the Protocol Directory group.
Application-Layer Matrix	Collects statistics on conversations between pairs of network layer addresses for a specific application layer protocol. Traffic, broken down by protocols, can be recognized by the Protocol Directory group.
User History	Enables the agent to save samples of RMON2 data for any MIB object at specific intervals.
Probe Configuration	Provides remote capability for configuring and querying agent parameters—for example, software updates, IP address changes, resets, and trap destinations.
RMON Conformance	Provides information to the management software regarding the status of support for the group.

Bridge Agents

ZENworks for Servers 2 bridge agents monitor network bridges, enabling you to collect information about switched networks. Table 10.5 describes the groups of monitoring elements that make up the bridge agents.

TABLE 10.5 *Bridge Monitoring Groups*

BRIDGE GROUP	DESCRIPTION
Base	Stores information about objects that are applicable to all types of bridges.
Spanning Tree Protocol	Stores information regarding the status of the bridge with respect to the Spanning Tree protocol.

(continued)

TABLE 10.5 Bridge Monitoring Groups (continued)

BRIDGE GROUP	DESCRIPTION
Source Route Bridging	Collects information that describes the status of the device with respect to source route bridging.
Transparent Bridging	Collects information that describes the object's state with respect to transparent bridging.
Static	Collects information that describes the object's state with respect to destination address filtering.

Setting up LAN Traffic Analysis

Now that you understand the components involved in ZENworks for Servers 2 traffic analysis, you are ready to begin setting up traffic analysis on your network. Setting up LAN traffic analysis for ZENworks for Servers 2 involves establishing normal activity for your LAN and then making the necessary configuration changes for the management console to be able to communicate with the management server.

The following sections discuss creating a baseline document of normal LAN activity to use as a measurement, selecting the preferred RMON agent, and setting the necessary SNMP parameters for the management console to access the RMON agent.

Creating a Baseline Document

The first step you should take in setting up ZENworks for Servers 2 LAN traffic analysis on your network is to create a baseline document that describes the normal activity and usage of your network. The baseline document should show the normal levels of the most common statistics segments monitored by ZENworks for Servers 2.

Once you have created the baseline document, you can use it to identify parts of your network that are experiencing problems, need to be balanced, or need to be upgraded. The following is a list of the most common network statistics that should be used to create a baseline document:

- **Bandwidth utilization** — The bandwidth utilization statistic indicates the percentage of network bandwidth used. Because the network bandwidth tends to be higher at heavy usage times your baseline document should account for those times — for example, when users are logging on in the morning.

USING ZENWORKS FOR SERVERS 2 TRAFFIC ANALYSIS

- **Packets per second** — The packets-per-second statistic indicates the raw number of packets that are being transferred on the network. This gives you the best indication of how heavy your network traffic really is.

- **Network error rates** — You should also set a baseline for network error rates. This is also based on heavy usage, so your baseline should take into account periods of the day when heavy usage would cause errors. This helps you identify times when network errors are atypical.

- **Kilobytes per second** — The kilobytes-per-second statistic indicates the raw amount of data that is being transferred on the network. This gives you the best indication of how heavy your network throughput really is.

- **Active servers** — You should keep track of the three most active servers on the network. This helps you understand where loads need to be balanced and where network upgrades must take place.

Selecting the Preferred RMON Agent

Once you have created your baseline document, you need to select which remote monitor (RMON) agent you wish to monitor each managed segment. The RMON agent is set on the RMON Agent property page for the segment in ConsoleOne.

The RMON property page displays the following information, shown in Figure 10.1, about the RMON agent:

- **Preferred** — Checked if this server is set as the preferred RMON agent server for the segment.

- **Agent Name** — Displays a list of all the servers on which the RMON agent is installed.

- **Version** — Displays the dynamically obtained version number of the RMON agent installed on this server. It is left blank if ZENworks for Servers 2 is unable to contact the server to get a version number.

- **Status** — Displays the current status of the RMON agent on the selected segment.

- **MAC Address** — Displays the MAC address of the server.

- **Interface Index** — Displays the number of interface indexes that a server can connect through its network card. Each interface corresponds to a segment.

- **Available RMON Services** — Displays the list of RMON services available from the selected agent (RMON, RMON Plus, or RMON2).

FIGURE 10.1 *RMON Agent property panel for a segment object in ConsoleOne*

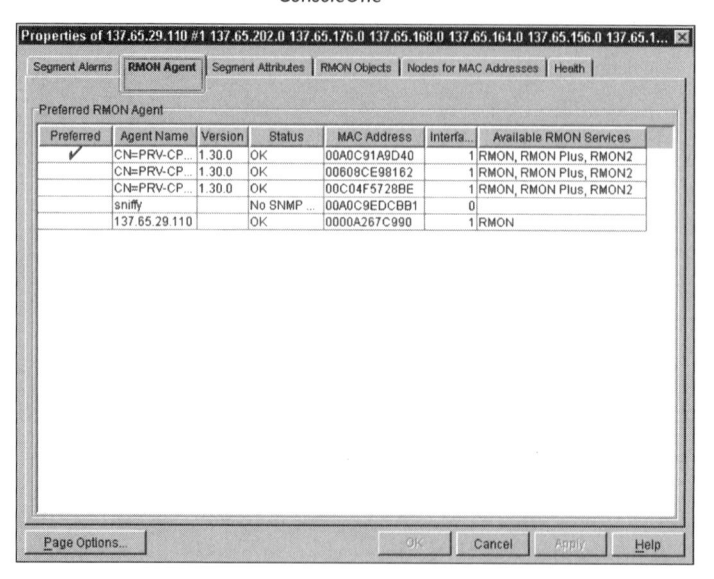

Use the following steps to set an RMON agent as the preferred agent to monitor a segment:

1. Right-click the segment object in ConsoleOne and select Properties from the pop-up menu.
2. Click the RMON Agent tab, as shown in Figure 10.1.
3. Choose a server or workstation name from the list displayed in the properties page, and then choose which server acts as the RMON agent for the segment.
4. Click the Apply button to save the settings.

Setting up SNMP Parameters

Once you have set the preferred RMON agent for each segment, you need to set up the SNMP parameters for the servers hosting your RMON agents. When you request that dynamic information be displayed at the management console, that information is obtained from the monitoring server agents using SNMP.

USING ZENWORKS FOR SERVERS 2 TRAFFIC ANALYSIS

Initially, the SNMP communication between the management servers and the management console is based on default SNMP setting; however, you may wish to modify the following settings, also shown in Figure 10.2:

FIGURE 10.2 *SNMP Settings tab for a server object in ConsoleOne*

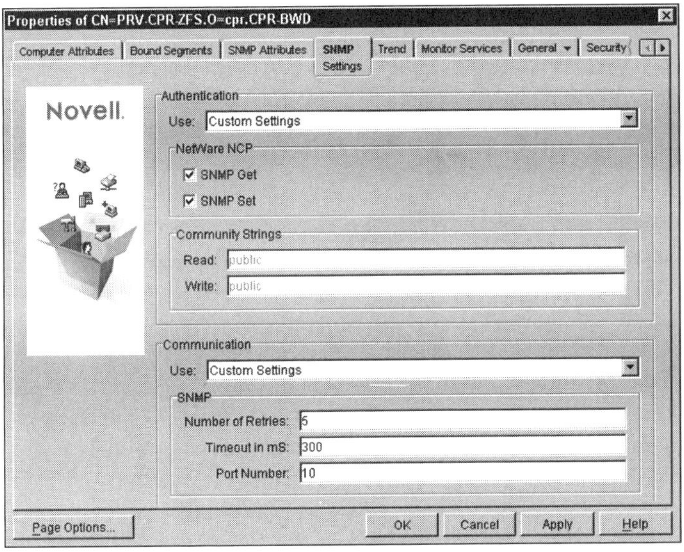

- **Secure Get (also known as SNMP get)** — Encrypts the packets sent by the monitoring agent to the management the agent.
- **Secure Set (also known as SNMP set)** — Encrypts the packets sent by the management agent to the monitoring agent.
- **Community String** — Community name of the node requesting dynamic data from the agent.
- **Number of Retries** — Number of times you wish the management server to retry connecting to the monitoring agent.
- **Timeout in mS** — Maximum duration for which the management server should wait for a response from the monitoring agent.
- **Port Number** — Port on which the management server contacts the monitoring agent.

271

Use the following steps to modify the default SNMP communication for your management servers:

1. Right-click the server object that is hosting the RMON agent for the segment and select Properties from the pop-up menu.
2. Click the SNMP Settings property panel as shown in Figure 10.2.
3. Modify the Authentication and Communication settings.
4. Click the Apply button to save your settings.

Analyzing Network Traffic

Once you have set up the RMON agents and SNMP parameters for the segments and devices you wish to analyze traffic on, you are ready to begin capturing and analyzing network traffic. ZENworks for Servers 2 enables you to monitor and collect detailed real-time statistics from nodes and segments in your network. That information is displayed back to the management console in the form of tables, graphs, and other graphical displays.

This section discusses how to use the ZENworks for Servers 2 management console to monitor and analyze traffic on segments, nodes, protocols, and switches. It also covers how to capture and analyze network packets.

Analyzing Traffic on Network Segments

The most common LAN traffic analysis you will likely be doing is on network segments. You can ensure the most cost-effective, stable, and consistent network by monitoring and managing your segments using ZENworks for Servers 2 traffic analysis.

ZENworks for Servers 2 provides several different views for analyzing network traffic on segments. The management views translate the data collected by the monitoring agent into an easy to understand graphical and textual form. The following sections discuss how to use the List Segment Statistics, Segment Dashboard, Trend Data, Alarm Statistics, and Summary views on segment to monitor and analyze their traffic.

Viewing Network Statistics for a Segment

The first segment traffic analysis view you should be familiar with is the List Segments Statistics view. This view displays a list of segments in your network as well as the following statistical information for each of them, as shown in Figure 10.3:

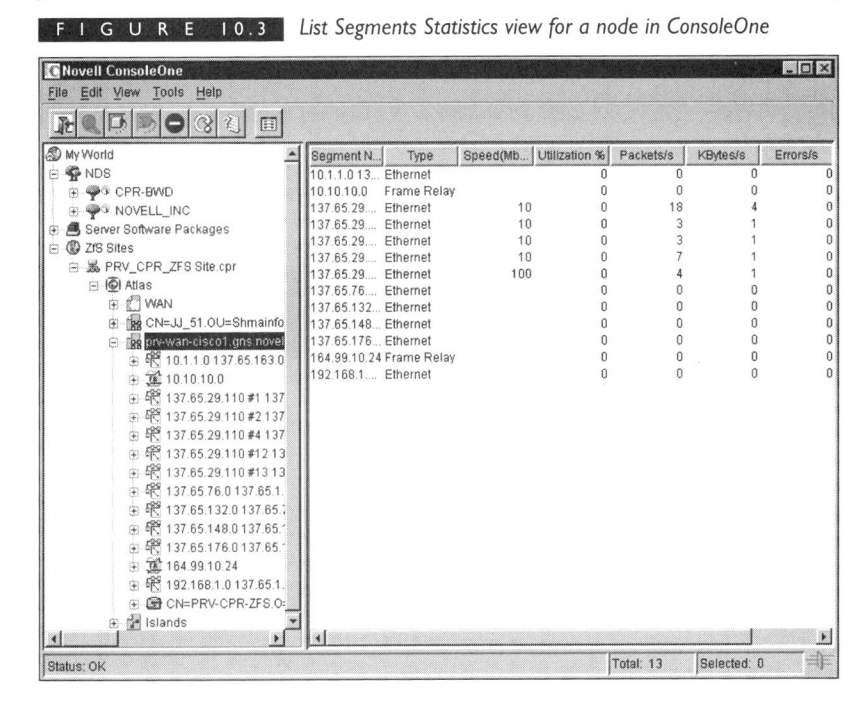

USING ZENWORKS FOR SERVERS 2 TRAFFIC ANALYSIS

FIGURE 10.3 *List Segments Statistics view for a node in ConsoleOne*

- **Segment Name** — Segment name, or address if no name is available.
- **Type** — Physical segment type (that is, Ethernet, FDDI, WAN, etc.).
- **Speed (Mbps)** — The raw speed of the segment, measured by the speed of the network interface card that attaches the RMON agent to the segment. Cable type is also used to determine the segment speed.
- **Utilization %** — Average percentage of the bandwidth currently in use by the traffic on the segment.
- **Packets/s** — Average number of packets per second currently being transmitted on the segment.
- **KBytes/s** — Average number of kilobytes per second currently being transmitted on the segment.
- **Errors/s** — Average number of errors per second the segment is currently incurring.
- **Message** — Message describing the current status of the RMON agent on the segment.

NOVELL'S ZENWORKS FOR SERVERS 2 ADMINISTRATOR'S HANDBOOK

Use the following steps from the ZENworks for Servers 2 management console to access the List Segment Statistics view:

1. Select a segment or a node from the ZENworks for Servers 2 namespace in the management console.
2. Select View ➪ List Segment from the main menu and a screen similar to the one in Figure 10.3 appears.

Determining Individual Segment Performance

The second view you should become familiar with when analyzing segment traffic is the Segment Dashboard view. The Segment Dashboard view is a graphical view that provides real-time statistical information about an individual monitored segment.

The Segment Dashboard view, shown in Figure 10.4, displays four gauges that display the following real-time statistics for that segment as well as node activity for the top nodes on the segment:

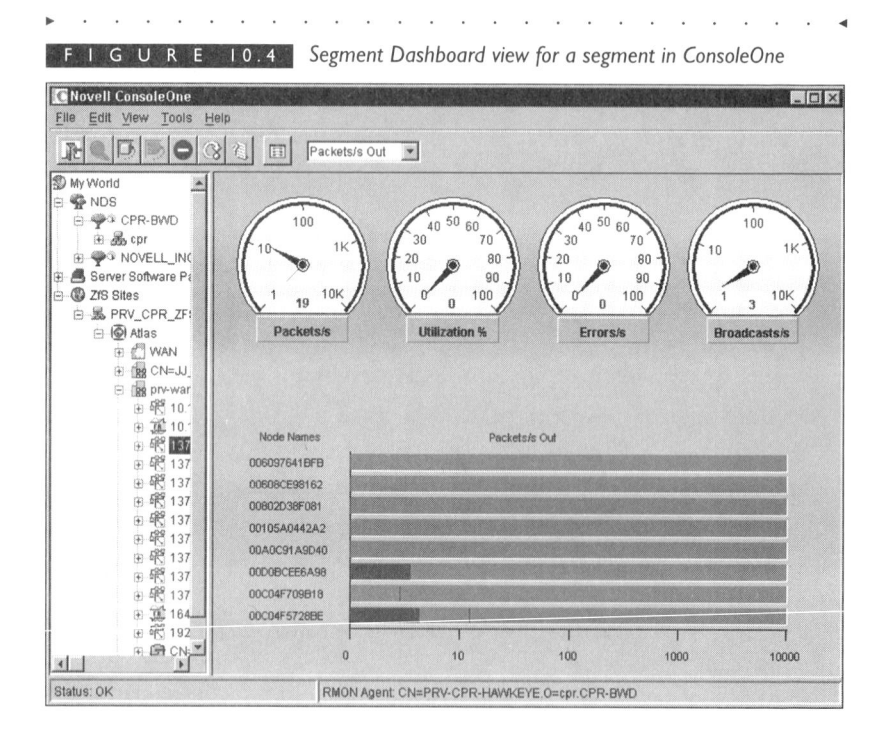

FIGURE 10.4 *Segment Dashboard view for a segment in ConsoleOne*

- **Packets/s** — The Packets gauge shows the number of packets per second that are being transmitted on the segment.
- **Utilization %** — The Utilization gauge shows the current utilization, compared to the maximum network capacity that is currently being consumed on the segment.
- **Errors/s** — The Errors gauge shows the number of errors per second the segment is currently incurring.
- **Broadcasts/s** — The Broadcasts gauge shows the number of broadcast packets per second that are currently being transmitted on the segment.

Use the following steps from the ZENworks for Servers 2 management console to access the Segment Dashboard view:

1. Select the segment you wish to monitor from the ZENworks for Servers 2 namespace in the management console.
2. Select View ⇨ Segment Dashboard from the main menu and a screen similar to the one in Figure 10.4 appears.

Analyzing Segment Trends

The next view you should be familiar with when monitoring segment traffic is the Trend Data view. You should use the Trend Data view in conjunction with the baseline document, discussed earlier in this chapter. This enables you to determine trends of traffic patterns that indicate that a segment is in trouble or needs to be updated or expanded.

Use the following steps from the ZENworks for Servers 2 management console to access the Trend Data view for a segment:

1. Select the segment you wish to monitor from the ZENworks for Servers 2 namespace in the management console.
2. Select View ⇨ Segment Trends from the main menu and a screen similar to the one in Figure 10.5 appears.

NOVELL'S ZENWORKS FOR SERVERS 2 ADMINISTRATOR'S HANDBOOK

FIGURE 10.5 *Trend Data view for a segment in ConsoleOne*

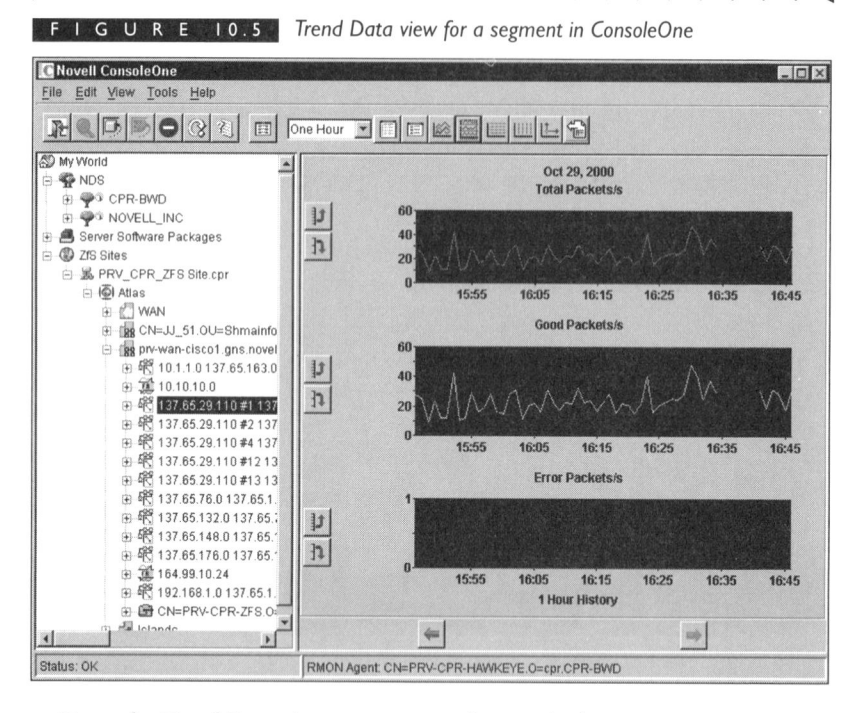

From the Trend Data view, you can configure which statistics to monitor in the Trend Data view. Use the following steps from the Trend Data view to configure the statistics that best fit your network:

1. Click the Profile button (on the right of the button bar) in the Trend Data view.
2. Select a profile from the Select Profile column in the Edit Profile window.
3. Choose which statistics you wish to view in the Select Series column. The available options depend on your network type.
4. Click the OK button and the Trend Data view should be updated with your new selections.

Viewing Alarm Statistics for a Segment

The next view you should be familiar with when monitoring segment traffic is the Alarm Statistics view. This view shows a list of all alarms for the monitored segment along with their threshold and sampling rate.

Use the following steps from the ZENworks for Servers 2 management console to access the Alarm Statistics view for a segment:

1. Right-click the segment you wish to monitor from the ZENworks for Servers 2 namespace in the management console.
2. Select Properties from the pop-up menu.
3. Select the Segment Alarms tab, as shown in Figure 10.6.

FIGURE 10.6 *Segment Alarms tab for a segment object in ConsoleOne*

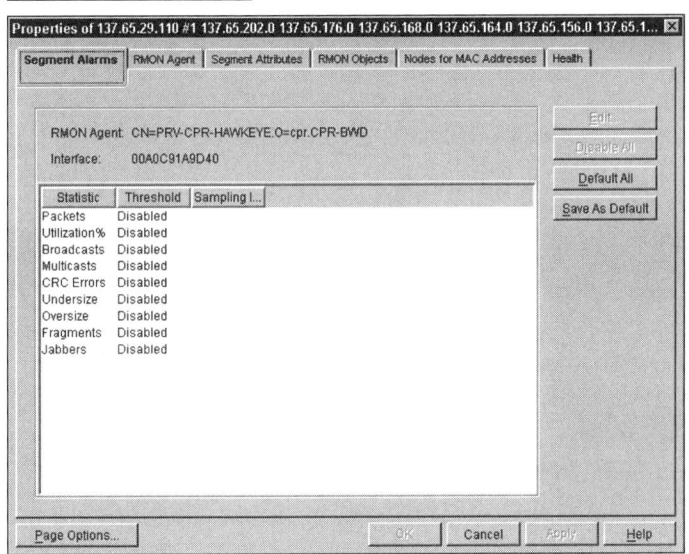

The alarms can be manually edited by highlighting the alarm and clicking the Edit button, or the Default All button can be used to set a predefined set of default values to the alarms.

Viewing a Segment Summary

The final view you should be familiar with when monitoring segment traffic is the Segment Summary view. The Segment Summary view is both a graphical and a textual view, which provides a quick summary of the managed segment. This view enables you to quickly assess the current state of the segment.

The Segment Summary view provides the following static information about the managed segment:

- **Name** — Name or address of the segment
- **Type** — Media type of the segment: Ethernet, token ring, or FDDI
- **IP Address** — IP addresses of the segment
- **IPX Address** — IPX addresses of the segment
- **Primary Agent** — Name of the preferred agent, which is monitoring nodes and traffic on the segment
- **Agent Status** — Current status of the preferred monitoring agent
- **Nodes** — Number of nodes on the segment
- **IP Nodes** — Number of nodes on the segment with IP addresses
- **IPX Nodes** — Number of nodes on the segment with IPX addresses
- **Servers** — Number of NetWare servers on the segment
- **Workstations/Others** — Number of nodes on the segment that are not NetWare Servers
- **Network Probes** — Number of monitoring agents available on the segment
- **Switches** — Number of switches on the segment
- **Routers** — Number of routers on the segment
- **Hubs** — Number of hubs on the segment

The Segment Summary view provides the following information about alarms that have occurred on the managed segment:

- **Severity** — Severity level associated with the alarm
- **From** — Network address of the device that sent the alarm to the alarm management system
- **Summary** — Summary of the event, often including the name or address of the object affected by the alarm
- **Owner** — Segment or device affected by the alarm
- **Received Time** — Date and time when the alarm management system received the alarm
- **Type** — Description of the alarm
- **Category** — Displays the category of the alarm based on the MIB

The Segment Summary view provides the following charts and gauges showing you dynamically captured information about the managed segment:

- **Utilization %** — Displays a gauge representing the current real-time usage of the network in relation to the maximum capacity

USING ZENWORKS FOR SERVERS 2 TRAFFIC ANALYSIS

- **Packets** — Displays a trend graph based on data about packets that have been transmitted on the segment
- **Protocol Distribution** — Displays a pie chart that represents the distribution of protocols on the network

Use the following steps from the ZENworks for Servers 2 management console to access the Segment Summary view for a segment:

1. Select the segment you wish to monitor from the ZENworks for Servers 2 namespace in the management console.
2. Select View ➪ Segment Summary from the main menu and a screen similar to the one in Figure 10.7 appears.

FIGURE 10.7 *Segment Summary view for a segment in ConsoleOne*

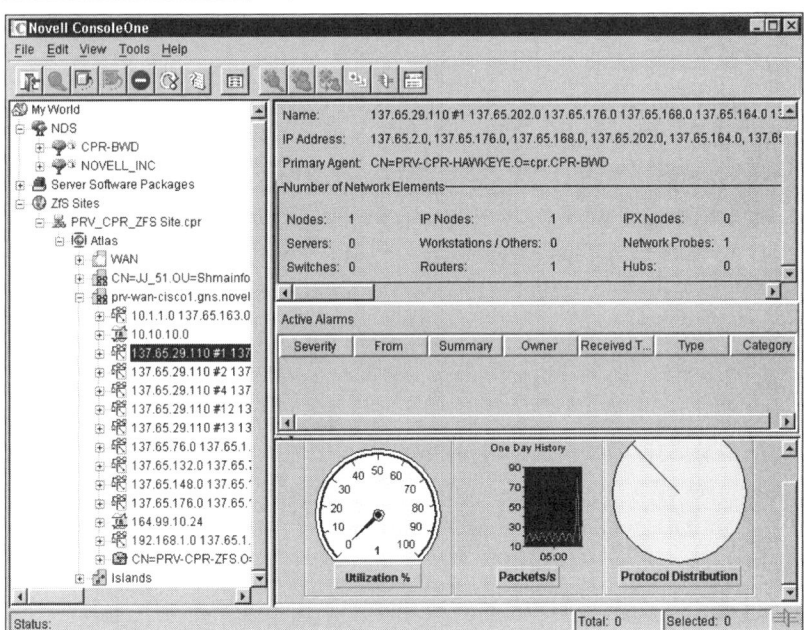

Analyzing Traffic on Nodes Connected to a Segment

ZENworks for Servers 2 also provides several views to help you monitor and analyze traffic associated with nodes connected to a monitored segment. Monitoring at the segment level gives you a good understanding about the

279

general trends and health of the entire segment. However, if you wish to analyze traffic at a more granular level, you will need to analyze traffic at the node level.

The following sections describe how to use the ZENworks for Servers management console to analyze statistics for the top 20 nodes and between two nodes, and to monitor nodes for inactivity.

Analyzing Network Statistics for the Top 20 Nodes

You should first gather information about network traffic for nodes on a segment is to view the statistics for the top 20 nodes. Viewing the statistics for the top 20 nodes give you an indication of how active the nodes on the segment are and if any nodes are exhibiting troubled behavior.

ZENworks for Servers 2 provides the Stations view to enable you to view the following statistics on the most active nodes in the segment:

- **MAC Address** — Physical address of the node
- **Node** — Name or address of the node
- **Utilization %** — Percentage of maximum network capacity consumed by packets sent from this node
- **Packets/s In** — Packets per second received by this node
- **Packets/s Out** — Packets per second sent by this node
- **Bytes/s In** — Data in bytes per second received by this node
- **Bytes/s Out** — Data in bytes per second sent by this node
- **Errors/s** — Errors per second received by this node
- **Broadcasts/s** — Broadcast packets per second received by this node
- **Multicasts/s** — Multicasts per second received by this node
- **Protocols** — Types of protocols used by this node
- **First Transmit** — Date and time this node first transmitted a packet since the traffic analysis agent was loaded
- **Last Transmit** — Date and time this node last transmitted a packet since the traffic analysis agent was loaded

Use the following steps from the ZENworks for Servers 2 management console to access the Stations view for a segment:

1. Select the segment you wish to monitor nodes on from the ZENworks for Servers 2 namespace in the management console.

2. Select View ➪ Stations from the main menu.

3. Select View ⇨ Show Top N Stations from the main menu and a screen similar to the one in Figure 10.8 appears.

4. Specify what statistic to use in determining a node's activity from the drop-down list at the top of the window.

FIGURE 10.8 *Segment Stations Summary view for a segment in ConsoleOne*

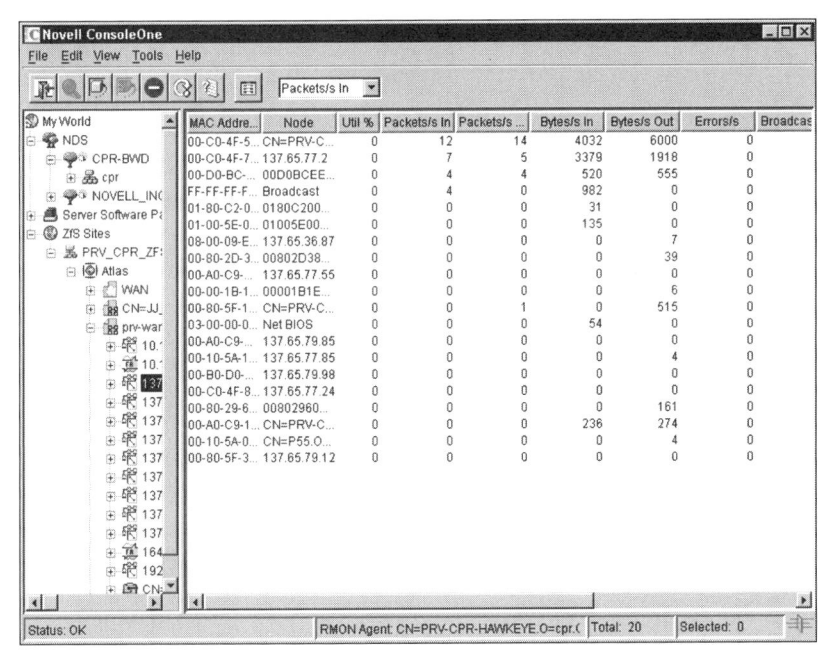

Analyzing Traffic between Nodes

The Conversations view is another useful ZENworks for Servers 2 view that allows you to view real-time data showing traffic between a specific node and one or more other nodes on the same segment. You should use this information when you need to determine communication activity between specific nodes.

For example, suppose you have a database application installed on a node on the segment and you want to see how traffic from this node behaves when the database is active as opposed to when it is shut down. You would use the Conversations view before and after activating the database and compare the data from each.

The Conversations view provides statistical data on the following characteristics of internode communication:

- **Node** — Name or address of the destination node communicating with the selected node
- **% Pkt Load** — Percentage of the total packet load being used between this node and the destination node
- **% Byte Load** — Percentage of the total byte load being used between this node and the destination node
- **Pkts/s In** — Number of packets received per second by the destination node from this node
- **Pkts/s Out** — Number of packets sent per second from the destination node to this node
- **Bytes/s In** — Number of bytes of data received per second by the destination node from this node
- **Bytes/s Out** — Number of bytes of data sent per second from the destination node to this node
- **Pkts In** — Number of packets received by the destination node from this node since the view was opened
- **Pkts Out** — Number of packets sent by the destination node to this node since the view was opened
- **KBytes In** — Number of kilobytes of data received by the destination node from this node since the view was opened
- **KBytes Out** — Number of kilobytes of data sent by the destination node to this node since the view was opened
- **Protocols** — Protocol packet types used by the destination node to communicate with this node
- **First Transmit** — Date and time that this node first transmitted on the network since the traffic analysis agent was loaded
- **Last Transmit** — Date and time that this node last transmitted on the network since the traffic analysis agent was loaded

Use the following steps from the ZENworks for Servers management console to access the Conversations view for a node:

1. Select the node you wish to monitor conversations on from the ZENworks for Servers 2 namespace in the management console.
2. Select View ➪ Conversations from the main menu and a screen similar to the one in Figure 10.9 appears.

USING ZENWORKS FOR SERVERS 2 TRAFFIC ANALYSIS

FIGURE 10.9 *Conversations view for a node in ConsoleOne*

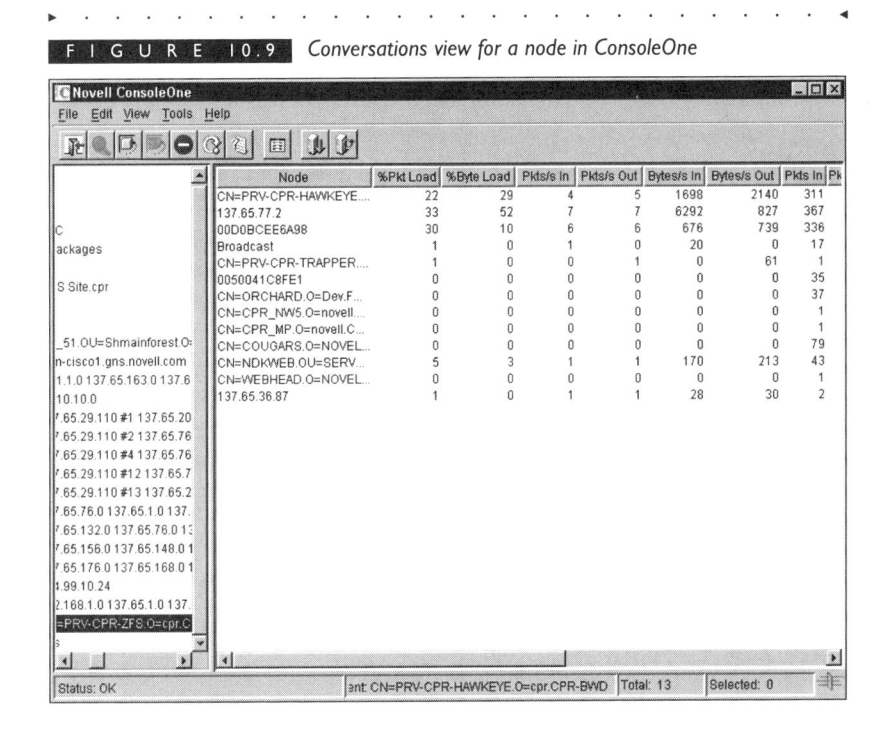

Monitoring Nodes for Inactivity

Another useful way to monitor network traffic at a node level is to monitor nodes for inactivity. ZENworks for Servers 2 enables you to monitor nodes to determine if they become inactive and alert you if they do. This does not impact network traffic because the traffic analysis agent does not poll the node to obtain status.

Use the following steps from the ZENworks for Servers 2 management console to set it to monitor inactivity of a node:

1. Right-click the node you wish to monitor for inactivity from the ZENworks for Servers 2 namespace in the management console.

2. Select Monitor Nodes for Inactivity ⇨ Add from the pop-up menu to enable monitoring of the node.

Once you have selected the nodes that you wish to monitor, you can view the following information about them from the Monitor Nodes for Inactivity view:

283

- **Name** — Name of the node being monitored
- **MAC Address** — Physical address of the node
- **Status** — Current status of the node (updated every 60 seconds by default)

Use the following steps from the ZENworks for Servers 2 management console to access the Monitor Nodes for Inactivity view:

1. Select the segment you wish to see a list of nodes monitored for inactivity for from the ZENworks for Servers 2 namespace in the management console.
2. Select View ⇨ Monitor Nodes for Inactivity from the main menu.

Capturing Packets from the Network

ZENworks for Servers 2 makes it possible for you to be even more detailed than LAN traffic analysis at a node level by enabling you to capture specific sequences of packets from the network. As nodes communicate on a segment, they send packet sequences to each other, which are captured by the RMON agents in a local buffer and can be accessed by the management console.

Packet captures provide much more detail to LAN traffic analysis because they provide information about request and replies that nodes are making on the network. This can be useful in troubleshooting interserver or client-to-server communication issues.

The following sections describe how to use the ZENworks for Servers 2 management console to set up a filter and capture packets from the network.

Setting up a Capture Filter

The first step in capturing packets from a segment is to set up a filter to limit the number of packets captured. Without a filter, there would be far too many packets captured, making it extremely difficult to use the capture. Filtering enables you to capture only the packets that are needed.

For example, if you are troubleshooting a client-to-server communication issue on an IP application, you would only want to capture IP packets between the client node and the server node.

Use the following steps from the ZENworks for Servers 2 management console to define a capture filter:

1. Select a node or a segment from the ZENworks for Servers 2 namespace in ConsoleOne.

2. Select File ⇨ Actions ⇨ Capture Packets from the main menu and the Packet Capture Setup window, shown in Figure 10.10, appears.
3. Type in a descriptive name for the buffer in the Name text box. This typically should describe the purpose of the capture.
4. Select the source and destination nodes from drop-down lists in the Stations box. You can use Any for either the source or destination, or both to include all nodes. If it is possible, use specific nodes to reduce the size of the capture.
5. Select the direction of traffic flow between nodes. You can select only source to destination, only destination to source, or both directions. This can help limit the capture greatly if you only need one direction.
6. Add protocols to filter on by selecting the protocol in the Selected protocols list and clicking the Add button. If you do not add protocols to filter on, all protocols are captured.
7. Specify what kind of packets to capture. See Table 10-6 for a list of available statistics by topology.
8. Specify whether you wish to overwrite the buffer or stop the capture when the buffer is full. Overwriting the buffer means that the oldest packets are overwritten with the newest ones. If you specify to overwrite, you must manually stop the capture.
9. Specify the buffer size. This depends on what you need to capture and for how long. If you are capturing all packets from all nodes, you need a very large buffer; however, if you only need to capture packets from one node to another one, the default buffer of 32K is probably enough. Keep in mind that there must be enough free memory at the RMON server to create the buffer.
10. Specify the packet slice size. The Slice Size field specifies the maximum number of bytes of each packet, starting from the packet header, to store in the buffer. This also depends on what you need out of the capture. For header information, you only need 150 bytes or so. However, if you need data out of the packet itself, you should select the entire packet. This parameter determines the number of packets that a buffer can hold.
11. Click the OK button and the filter will be set.

FIGURE 10.10 *Packet Capture Setup window for filtering packet captures in ConsoleOne*

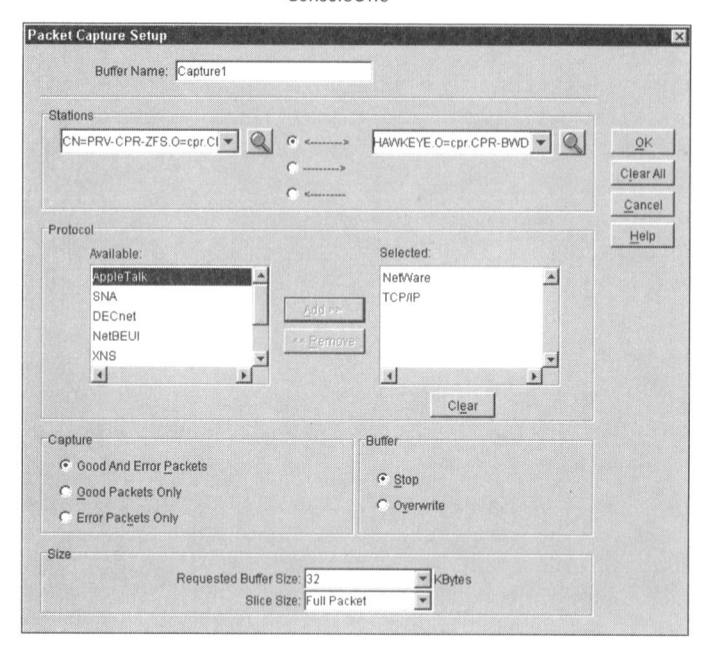

TABLE 10.6 *Available Statistics to Filter on Based on Segment Type*

SEGMENT TYPE	AVAILABLE STATISTICS	DEFAULT STATISTICS
Ethernet	Only good packets, only error packets, both good and error packets	Both good and error packets
FDDI ring	All packets, LLC packets, MAC packets, SMT packets	All packets
Token ring	All packets, non-MAC packets, MAC packets	All packets

Starting a Packet Capture

Once you have set the filter, you are ready to start the capture. Once you click the OK button from the Packet Capture Filter window, a Capture Status

USING ZENWORKS FOR SERVERS 2 TRAFFIC ANALYSIS

window similar to the one in Figure 10.11 appears. The Capture Status window displays the following information about the capture:

FIGURE 10.11 *Packet Capture Status window for packet captures in ConsoleOne*

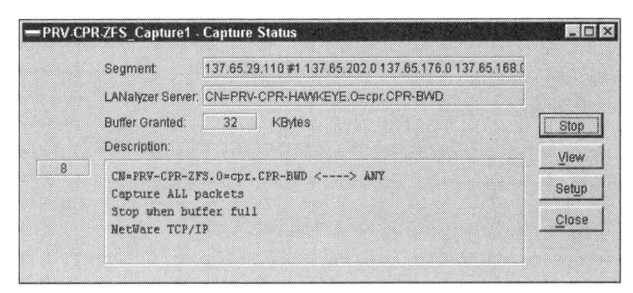

- **Segment** — Name or address of the segment on which the packet capture is occurring
- **LANalyzer Server** — Name or address of the server running the RMON agent that is collecting the captured packets
- **Buffer Granted** — Size of the buffer used for the capture
- **Description** — Description of the filter settings for the capture
- **Count** — Incrementing count, shown as 8 in Figure 10.11, for every packet that is captured

From the Capture Status window, click the Start button to start the capture. If you are trying to capture a specific sequence, you should start the capture and then perform the sequence — for example, opening a database file or starting an application.

When you have captured enough packets, you can click the Stop button to stop the capture, or you can simply wait until the buffer fills up if you specified to stop the capture when the buffer was full.

Analyzing Captured Packets

Once you have set up a capture filter and captured the sequence of packets, you are ready to begin analyzing them from the management console. The packet captures reside on the server hosting the RMON agent; however, ZENworks for Servers retrieves the packet data from the RMON agent individually as you view each packet.

The following sections discuss how to use the ZENworks for Servers 2 management console to view captured packets.

Viewing Captured Packets

ZENworks for Servers provides an extremely useful Trace Display view to help you view and decode packet data. The Trace Display view, shown in Figure 10.12, provides summary information about the captured packets (top), a decoded view of the selected packet (middle), and a hexadecimal view of the packet (bottom).

FIGURE 10.12 *Trace Display view for packet captures in ConsoleOne*

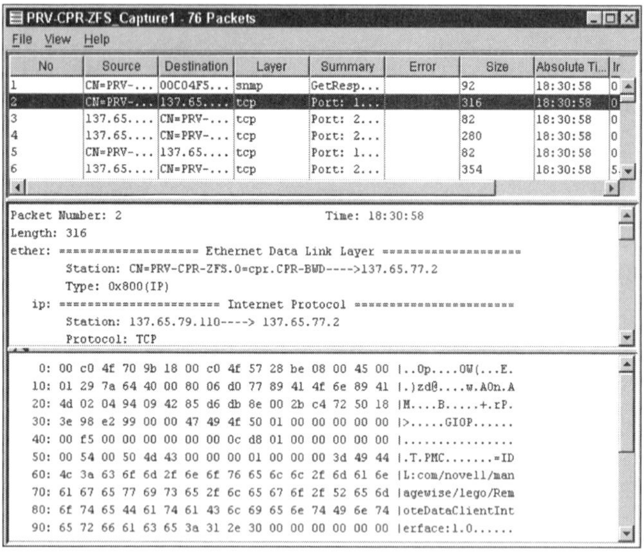

You can open the Trace Display view by clicking the View button on the Capture Status window or by Selecting Tools ➪ View Packet File from the main menu in ConsoleOne.

The following sections discuss the three different sections of the Trace Display view.

Captured Packet Summary The summary pane in the Trace Display view displays a list of captured packets. This provides you with an overview of the communications between source and destination nodes. You can highlight a packet in this pane to display the decoded and hexadecimal packet data in the panes below.

The summary pane provides the following statistical information about the captured packets:

- **No.** — Numbers the packets in the order in which they were received at the RMON agent
- **Source** — Name or MAC address of the node from which the packet was sent
- **Destination** — Name or MAC address to which the packet was sent
- **Layer** — Abbreviation of the highest protocol layer in the packet — for example, "ncp" for NetWare Core Protocol or "ether" for Ethernet
- **Summary** — Displays a brief description of the contents of the highest protocol layer
- **Error** — Shows the error type, if any, that occurred in the packet
- **Size** — Displays the number of bytes contained in the packet
- **Absolute Time** — Displays the hardware clock time when the packet arrived
- **Interpacket Time** — Displays the time that elapsed from the end of the preceding packet to the end of the current packet
- **Relative Time** — Displays the time that elapsed since the arrival of the oldest packet still in the buffer

Decoded Packet Data The decode pane in the Trace Display view displays detailed information about the contents of the selected packet. The packet data is decoded and displayed according to defined protocol fields. This is an extremely useful tool because it tells you information such as the station that sent the packet, protocol, NCP request information, reply results, and so forth. You typically use this field to understand packet sequences and why they failed.

Hexadecimal Packet Data The hexadecimal pane in the Trace Display view displays the raw packet data in hexadecimal format. The column on the left is the hexadecimal offset from the packet header. The second column is the raw hexadecimal data of the packet. The column on the right is the ASCII form of the hexadecimal data.

You will likely only use the hexadecimal display if you know exactly what you are looking for. For example, if you know the structure of the data that is being sent from a client application to a server, you would be able to manually decode the hexadecimal data.

The text column of the hexadecimal display, however, is often useful because it shows textual data in the packet. For example, file pathnames will show up in the ASCII column.

Filtering the Display for Captured Packets

ZENworks for Servers 2 also enables you to filter out packets even after you are viewing the packet trace. This is extremely useful in situations where once you begin viewing a packet trace, you narrow down the problem to a specific node or even a specific request.

For example, suppose your original capture captured packets going to and from a server, but you only need to see the packets going to that server from a specific node. You could filter on only those packets that are going to the specific node you are troubleshooting.

Another example would be if you knew the structure of the exact packet type you wished to view. You could filter on a value, such as a key sequence, at a specific offset and only see those packets that matched.

Use the following steps to set a display filter for captured packets from the Capture Trace view in ConsoleOne:

1. Select View ⇨ Filter from the main menu and the Display Filter dialog box, shown in Figure 10.13, appears.
2. Modify the stations setting to narrow down to specific stations.
3. Modify the packet direction, if possible, to packets going one way.
4. Add or remove protocols from the selected protocols list.
5. Set the hexadecimal Offset and the From fields if you are looking for packets containing specific data.
6. Specify the data value and type to search for at the specified offset.
7. Click the OK button and your capture display filters on the criteria you have specified.

NOTE If your packet capture is large, you may have to wait a considerable time for the ZENworks for Servers 2 management console to be transferred enough of each packet to filter on. This takes up considerable bandwidth. We recommend that you use the capture filter setting to narrow down your captures first.

FIGURE 10.13 *Trace Display Filter dialog box for packet captures in ConsoleOne*

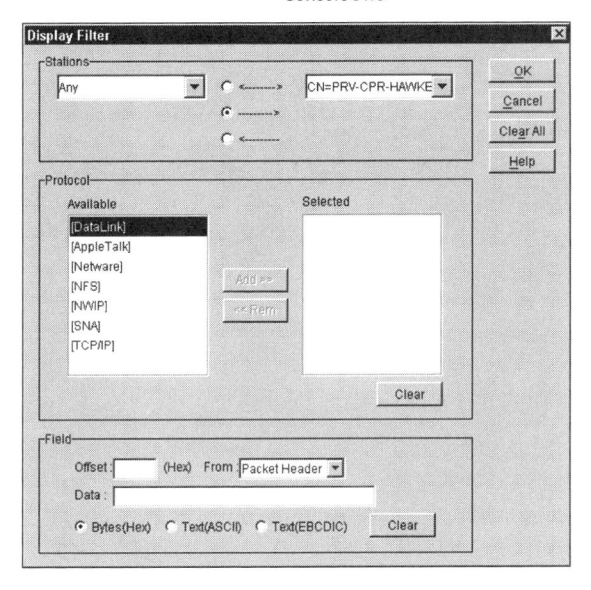

Highlighting Protocol Fields and Hex Bytes

One of the most valuable features of the Trace Display view is its ability to match data in the decoded pane with the hexadecimal values in the hexadecimal pane. It does this by highlighting the data areas that you select, either in the decode pane or the hexadecimal pane, in both panes. The following is a list of examples of how you can use the highlighting tool:

- Highlight a protocol layer in the decode pane and view the hexadecimal bytes in the Hex view.
- Click a specific field in the decode pane and view the hexadecimal value associated with it.
- Click a hexadecimal byte in the hexadecimal pane and see which protocol field is associated with it in the decode pane.
- Click ASCII text in the hexadecimal pane and see the hexadecimal values and the specific decode field associated with it.

> **NOTE** You can save a trace file to a *.tr1 file format so that you can send it to someone else to look at, too, by selecting File ▷ Save.

Analyzing Protocol Traffic

The ZENworks for Servers 2 traffic analysis agent also allows you to monitor statistics of traffic generated by protocols in your network. The following sections discuss how to display protocols used on a network as well as determining distribution of protocols on a segment.

Displaying Protocols Used on a Network

The RMON2 agent object in the NDS tree provides a Protocol Directory property page to view a list of supported and custom protocols used in the network. This is a hierarchical list with the protocols used in the data link layer at the top level.

Use the following steps from within ConsoleOne to display the protocols used on your network:

1. Select the node object running the RMON2 agent from the ZENworks for Servers namespace.
2. Expand the view by clicking the plus sign next to it.
3. Expand the view for the services object.
4. Right-click the RMON2 object under Services and select Properties from the pop-up menu.
5. Select the Protocol Directory tab.

From the Protocol Directory tab, you can also add custom protocols to the supported protocol tree by clicking the Add button. You can also click the Remove button to remove a protocol from being monitored in the tree.

Determining Segment Distribution of Protocols

ZENworks for Servers 2 also enables you to view the distribution of protocols on a segment. This gives the following statistics of the protocol communications in the network layer, transport layer, and application layer that are occurring on your network:

- **Protocol Name** — The name of the protocol
- **Packets/s** — The average number of packets per second that are being sent using this protocol
- **Bytes/s** — The average number of bytes of data per second that are being sent using this protocol
- **Packet Rate %** — The percentage of packets transmitted using this protocol, relative to the total percentage of packets transmitted
- **Byte Rate %** — The percentage of bytes of data transmitted using this protocol, relative to the total bytes of data being transmitted

USING ZENWORKS FOR SERVERS 2 TRAFFIC ANALYSIS

Use the following steps from within the ZENworks for Servers namespace in ConsoleOne to view the distribution of protocols in a segment:

1. Select the managed segment you wish to view protocols on.
2. Select View ⇨ Protocol Distribution from the main menu and a window similar to the one in Figure 10.14 appears.

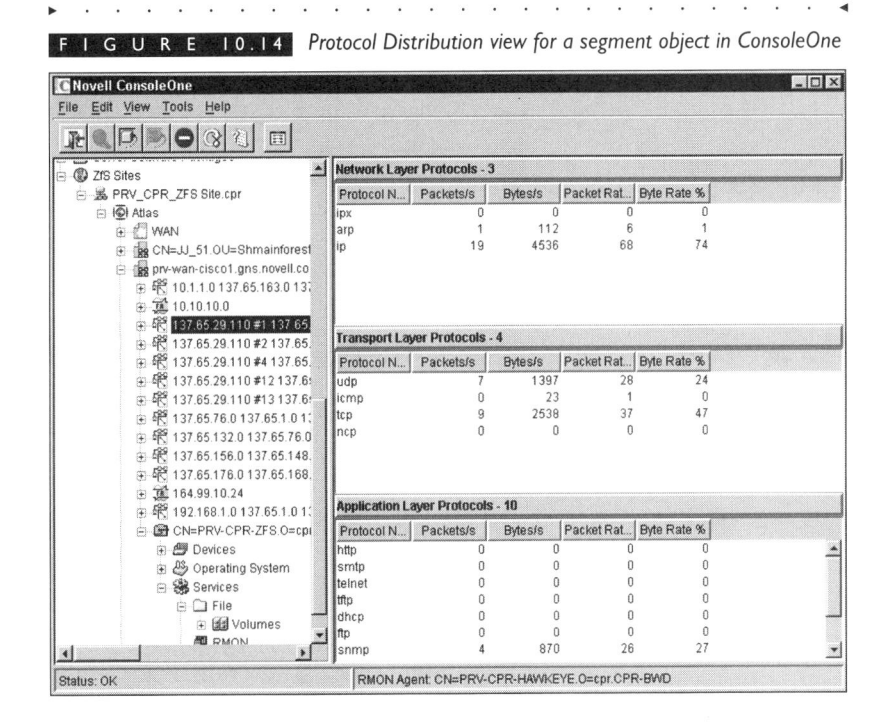

FIGURE 10.14 *Protocol Distribution view for a segment object in ConsoleOne*

Analyzing Switch Traffic

The ZENworks for Servers 2 traffic analysis agent also enables you to monitor statistics of traffic generated on switches in your network. This helps you determine the load on workstation and workgroup switches in your network, enabling you to plan for future upgrades.

ZENworks for Servers monitors ports and nodes connected to those ports by using an RMON agent, external RMON agent, or a bridge agent. The following sections discuss how to use these agents to display statistics for ports on the switches on your network as well as viewing the summarized information for a specific switch.

293

Viewing Port Statistics for a Switch

You can view port statistics of a switch using the ZENworks for Servers Unified Port Traffic view. This view obtains statistical information about every port in your network. It then displays a list of nodes connected to ports on the switch and statistics for each port.

Use the following steps from within the ZENworks for Servers namespace in ConsoleOne to display the Unified Port Traffic view:

1. Select the managed switch on which to view port statistics.
2. Expand the view by clicking the plus sign next to the switch.
3. Expand the view by clicking the plus sign next to services under the switch.
4. Select Switch/Bridge under services.
5. Select View ⇨ Port Traffic from the main menu to bring up the Unified Port Traffic view.

Viewing Switch Summary Data

ZENworks for Servers also provides a summary view of switch data that provides brief information about the switch. This gives you a quick look at the current status, usage, and alarms generated on the switch.

The following statistical information is provided in the switch summary view:

- **Vendor** — Name of the manufacturer of the switch
- **Switch Type** — Type of switch: transparent or source route
- **Number of Ports Active** — Number of ports currently active on the switch
- **Forwarding Table Overflow Count** — Number of times the forwarding table has exceeded its capacity
- **Up Time** — Time since the switch was last rebooted
- **Number of Ports Present** — Number of ports that actually exist on the switch
- **Number of MAC Addresses Learned** — Number of MAC addresses dynamically discovered by the switch

Use the following steps from within the ZENworks for Servers 2 namespace in ConsoleOne to display the Unified Port Traffic view:

1. Select the managed switch for which to view the summary.
2. Click View ⇨ Switch Summary from the main menu to bring up the Switch Summary view.

USING ZENWORKS FOR SERVERS 2 TRAFFIC ANALYSIS

Setting Up ZENworks for Servers 2 Traffic Analysis Agents

ZENworks for Servers 2 provides traffic analysis agents and RMON agents for both NetWare and Windows NT to enable you to monitor heterogeneous LANs. These agents collect information about activity on your network and relay that information back to the management agent, which in turn sends it to the management console for viewing.

The following sections describe how to set up and use the traffic analysis agents for both NetWare and Windows NT.

Setting up the Traffic Analysis Agents for NetWare

You should take some time to set up the traffic analysis agents on the NetWare servers they are installed on. This involves setting the SNMP parameters, modifying the LANZ.NCF file, and restarting the agents. The following sections describe how to set up the traffic analysis agents on NetWare servers.

Configuring NetWare SNMP Parameters

The fist step in setting up ZENworks for Servers traffic analysis agents on NetWare servers is to configure the SNMP parameters. This involves setting the appropriate read, write, and error-handling options for your agent server.

Use the following steps to configure the SNMP parameters on NetWare 4.x or 5.x server (for NetWare 3.x, use the TCPCON utility):

1. At the traffic analysis agent server, load the INETCFG utility.

2. From the Internetworking Configuration screen in the INETCFG utility, select Manage Configuration ⇨ Configure SNMP Parameters.

3. From Monitor Community Handling options, select Specified Community May Read, and then enter **public** for the community name.

4. From Control Community Handling options, select Specified Community May Write, and then enter **public** for the community name.

5. From Trap Handling options, select Send Traps with Specified Community, and then enter **public** for the community name.

6. Press ESC to exit from the SNMP Parameters screen and save changes.

7. Press ESC again to exit from the Internetworking Configuration screen and restart the server. These are not changes that the Reinitialize System command make. In order for these changes to take place, you have to unload and reload SNMP, and that is done by restarting the server.

Modifying the LANZ.NCF File

The LANZ.NCF file is a script used to launch the traffic analysis agent on NetWare servers. You can modify the LANZ.NCF file to customize agent loading. Use a text editor to modify the commands in Table 10-7 to customize your LANZ.NCF file.

TABLE 10.7 *LANZ.NCF File Commands for the Traffic Analysis Agents*

COMMAND	DESCRIPTION
LOAD LANZSU DEBUG=1	Enables the LANZ control screen. Add the DEBUG=1 option to turn on the LANZ control screen, which reports significant events for traffic analysis agent on NetWare.
#LOAD LANZFCB	Disables packet capturing to prevent someone from observing secure traffic to and from the server. Comment out the load line for LANZFCB by putting a # sign in front of the statement to disable packet capturing.
LOAD LANZSM DUPIP=0	Disables generation of duplicate IP address alarms to prevent alarm generation in a DHCP environment. Add the DUPIP=0 option to disable duplicate IP address alarms.
LOAD LANZDI LEVEL=1	Sets packet flow control to yield to other server operations when traffic is high. This reduces the impact of traffic analysis on the server. Add the LEVEL=1 option to enable flow control.
LOAD LANZMEM BOUND=####	Sets the upper limit of available memory to increase the memory that the traffic analysis agents will take. Add the BOUND=#### option to set the amount of memory (####) traffic analysis will use before returning an out-of-memory error.
LOADLANZMEM BOUND=3072 AGE=###	Sets the amount of time the traffic analysis agent will hold data in memory. Add the age to specify the amount of time, measured in hours, that traffic analysis data will be left in memory before it is purged.

COMMAND	DESCRIPTION
LOAD LANZSM TOPN=#	Sorts the number of concurrent sort computations per network adapter. Add the TOPN=# to set the number, between 2 and 10, of sort computations.
LOAD LANZCTL TRAPREG=1	Enables alarms to be sent automatically to the management console. Add the TRAPREG=1 option to tell the traffic analysis agent to automatically send SNMP alarms to management consoles.
LOAD LANZTR POLL=#	Enables/disables polling of source routed bridges on token ring networks. Add the POLL=# option, where #=0 for off or #=1 for on, to turn polling of source routed bridges on or off.

Starting/Stopping the Agent

The ZENworks for Servers 2 LAN traffic agents for NetWare are comprised of several modules. The following two script files are included with ZENworks for Servers 2 and should be used to start and stop the LAN traffic agents:

- **LANZ.NCF** — Script file that loads the LAN traffic agent NLMs
- **ULANZ.NCF** — Script file that unloads the LAN traffic agent NLMs

Using the NetWare LANZCON Utility

The LANZCON utility provided with ZENworks for Servers 2 enables you to configure and view the traffic analysis agents. The LANZCON utility is an NLM that is installed into the SYS:LANZ directory on the servers that the traffic analysis agents were installed to.

Load the LANZCON utility on your NetWare server with the traffic analysis agents running to view and configure the following items:

- **Network Adapter Information** — Types of items that are currently being monitored by the adapter. You can also enable or disable an adapter from monitoring the network.
- **Agent Status** — Status of the selected agent and items related to the agent monitoring the segment.
- **Statistics Information** — Packet and event statistics for the selected network adapter.

- **History Information** — Provides sampling information collected at intervals for the networks that are being monitored by this agent — for example, data source, buckets requested, and buckets granted.
- **Hosts Information** — Statistics about specific host or nodes on the monitored network.
- **Matrix Information** — Consists of three tables that record information about conversations between pairs of nodes on the monitored segment.

Setting up the Traffic Analysis Agents for NT

Once you have set up the traffic analysis agent on your NetWare servers, you should take some time to set up the traffic analysis agents on your Windows NT servers as well. Once again, this involves setting the SNMP parameters and then restarting the agents. The following sections describe how to set up the traffic analysis agents on Windows NT servers.

Configuring NT SNMP Parameters

The first step in setting up ZENworks for Servers traffic analysis agents on NT servers is to configure the SNMP parameters. This involves setting the appropriate read, write, and error-handling options for your agent server.

Use the following steps to configure the SNMP parameters on your Windows NT servers:

1. From the Control Panel, double-click Network.
2. Select the Services tab.
3. Select SNMP Services and click the Properties button.
4. Click the Traps tab.
5. From the Accepted Community Names box, click the Add button.
6. Enter **public** in the Service Configuration dialog box.
7. Click the Add button.
8. Enter the DNS names or IP addresses of workstations or servers that should receive traps.
9. Click the Add button.
10. Click the Security Tab.
11. From the Accepted Community Names, click the Add button.
12. Enter **public** in the Service Configuration Dialog box.

USING ZENWORKS FOR SERVERS 2 TRAFFIC ANALYSIS

13. Set the appropriate rights.
14. Click the Add button.
15. Select Accept SNMP Packets from Any Host.
16. Click the OK button to return to the Network window.

NOTE If SNMP is not already installed on the NT Server, after you install it from the NT Server CD, you have to reboot and get some SNMP errors. To correct this, reapply the NT support pack (whichever one you were on or newer).

Starting/Stopping the SNMP Service

Whenever you make changes to the settings for the SNMP service, you should stop and restart the agent. Use the following steps to stop and restart the traffic analysis agent on a Windows NT server:

1. From the Control Panel, double-click Services.
2. Select SNMP Services.
3. Click the Stop Button.
4. Once the agent is stopped, click the Start button.

Using the NT LANZCON Utility

The Windows NT LANZCON utility provided with ZENworks for Servers 2 enables you to configure and view the traffic analysis agents. The Windows NT LANZCON utility is an executable that is installed on the desktop of Windows NT servers that the traffic analysis agents were installed to.

Load the LANZCON utility on your Windows NT server with the traffic analysis agents running to view and configure the following items:

- **Configure LANalyzer Agent** — Takes the place of editing the LANZ.NCF file on NetWare servers by letting you enable or disable packet capture and enable/disable station monitoring, and set memory bounds and age (how long to retain packet data before it is too old), concurrent sorting, and duplicate IP address alarms.

- **Network Adapter** — Displays a list of network adapters discovered by the agent. You can enable or disable a network adapter from monitoring the network.

- **Agent Log** — Displays a list of significant events and errors that occurred during a session.

- **Agent Status** — Displays the current status and description of all agents that are installed on the server.
- **RMON Tables** — Displays the statistics, history control, history data, host control, host entry, host topN control, host topN entry, matrix control, matrix SD entry, filter, channel, and buffer RMON tables for the network adapter. Also displays the alarm, event, and log RMON tables.
- **SNMP Traps** — Displays a list of traps that occurred on the managed segment, including the received time and a summary of the trap.

NOTE The ZENworks for Servers traffic analysis agent does not have to be installed on every NetWare and NT server. You only need it installed on one server (NT or NetWare) per segment that you want to monitor. This also helps with the discovery process.

CHAPTER 11

Understanding and Using ZENworks for Servers 2 Server and Alarm Management

One of the most powerful features of ZENworks for Servers 2 is its ability to make network management much more controlled and easy. ZENworks for Servers 2 adds a powerful alarm management system and a service monitoring system to help you more easily monitor, manage, and control problems on your network.

The ZENworks for Servers 2 alarm management system employs a series of trap and alarm handlers to manage and store information about important events that are occurring on your network. You can then use tools provided by the ZENworks for Servers 2 management console to understand, manage, and resolve those events.

The ZENworks for Servers 2 service monitoring system employs utilities and views from the management console to help you actively test and understand the connectivity between the management console and the monitored services. This feature helps you detect, locate, and understand service and network outages much faster.

The following sections describe the components and utilities that make up the ZENworks for Servers 2 alarm management system and the ZENworks for Servers 2 monitoring services system. They also discuss how to configure and use the services to best detect, diagnose, and resolve network issues.

Understanding Alarm Management Components

The ZENworks for Servers 2 alarm management system is comprised of several components, each of which has a specific responsibility to either send, receive, transfer, handle, store, or view network alarms. ZENworks for Servers 2 uses these components to alert you when conditions or events occur on the network that require an action on your part to resolve.

The following sections discuss the different components that ZENworks for Servers 2 uses to monitor and manage alarms on your network.

About the SNMP Trap Receiver

The SNMP trap receiver is an agent that actively receives SNMP traps from managed servers with SNMP agents loaded on them. Once the SNMP trap receiver gets an alarm, it is this agent's responsibility to pass the alarm to the SNMP trap injector component and the SNMP trap forwarder component.

Discussing the SNMP Trap Forwarder

The SNMP trap forwarder checks traps passed from the SNMP trap receiver against the Alarm Manager database to determine whether the trap has an SNMP trap-forwarding disposition. If the Alarm Manager database has a forwarding disposition for the trap, the SNMP trap forwarder forwards the trap based on the criteria specified by the disposition. If there is no forwarding disposition, the SNMP trap forwarder simply ignores the trap.

Understanding the SNMP Trap Injector

The SNMP trap injector is responsible for converting the SNMP traps into manageable alarms. Once the trap is converted into an alarm, the SNMP trap injector then passes the alarm to the alarm injector.

About the Alarm Injector

The alarm injector is responsible for collecting alarms from the SNMP trap injector as well as other applications that can transfer alarms to the ZENworks for Servers 2 management system. Once it receives an alarm, it then passes it to the inbound processor.

Discussing the Three Types of Alarm Processors

The alarm processors are responsible for processing network and server alarms that are added to them by the alarm injector. The following are the three types of alarm processors and their functions:

- **Inbound processor** — The inbound processor receives alarms from the alarm injector and applies a predefined alarm template to them. The alarm template is based on SNMP traps and other proprietary definitions based on specific criteria from the ZENworks for Servers 2 alarm management system. Once the inbound processor has applied the template to the alarm, it transfers it to the archive processor.

- **Archive processor** — The archive processor takes alarms from the inbound processor, adds them to a log, and then stores data about them in the Alarm Manager database. Once the alarm data is stored, the archive processor passes the alarm to the outbound processor.

- **Outbound processor** — The outbound processor accepts alarms from the archive processor and then dispatches them to the subscription server and the disposition server.

Understanding the Alarm Manager Database

Now that you understand how traps are picked up and converted to alarms and then handled by the processors, you need to understand the Alarm Manager database. The Alarm Manager database is responsible for storing information about processed alarms as well as alarm templates and dispositions. The following sections discuss the different types of alarm information stored in the database.

Introducing Processed Alarms

The biggest responsibility of the Alarm Manager database is to store data about alarms that have been handled by the alarm processors. This is the data that you are able to view at the ZENworks for Servers 2 management console via the alarm query server, using the alarm reporting discussed later.

Information About Alarm Templates

Another key type of alarm information that is stored in the Alarm Manager database are the templates used by the inbound processor to format the alarm so that it can be properly handled by the ZENworks for Servers 2 alarm management system.

For example, many SNMP traps do not have an object ID associated with them. However, an object ID is required by the ZENworks for Servers 2 alarm management system to process the alarm. Therefore, a template is applied to the alarm at processing, which associates an object ID to the device or node that triggered the alarm.

About Alarm Dispositions

The Alarm Manager database also stores any configured alarm dispositions. Alarm dispositions enable you to configure, prior to the alarm occurring, an automated method of handling the alarm. The alarm dispositions enable you to launch applications, send an e-mail alert, and send console alerts in the form of messages or beeps, forwarding the SNMP traps to other ZENworks for Servers management systems or even to other non-ZENworks for Servers 2 management systems.

Information About Database Archivers

Now that you understand what information is stored in the Alarm Manager database, you need to understand what components are responsible for putting it there. The following is a list of alarm database archivers and their responsibilities:

USING ZENWORKS SERVER AND ALARM MANAGEMENT

- **Alarm archiver** — The alarm archiver stores the actual data and statistics about alarms that have occurred on the network. You can configure the alarm archiver to store whatever alarms you wish to manage. The default for the alarm archiver is to store all alarms.
- **Disposition archiver** — The disposition archiver receives alarm disposition information from the ZENworks for Servers 2 management console and saves it to the Alarm Manager database to be used by the SNMP trap forwarder.
- **Template archiver** — The template archiver stores changes made to alarm templates by the MIB compiler in the database. ZENworks for Servers includes basic templates for all SNMP traps and proprietary alarms; however, you can reconfigure them using the MIB compiler.

Discussing Alarm Viewers

The final component involved in the ZENworks for Servers 2 alarm management system is the alarm viewers. The alarm viewers are simply different views available at the ZENworks for Servers 2 management console.

The ZENworks for Servers 2 management console uses alarm queries to the Alarm Manager database to provide you with views on currently active alarms as well as historically archived alarms. You should become familiar with how to view alarm information. The different alarm views are discussed more fully in the next section.

Managing ZENworks for Servers 2 Alarms

Now that you understand the components that make up the ZENworks for Servers 2 alarm management system, you need to know how to begin managing alarms on your network. Alarm management is a process of enabling alarms, then monitoring for alarm conditions, handling the alarm situations, and then deleting the alarm.

The following sections describe how to use the ZENworks for Servers 2 management console to enable alarms, disable alarms, understand alarm indicators, work with alarm views, manage alarms, perform actions on the alarms, and then remove alarms from the system.

Enabling and Disabling Alarms

The first task you have to be familiar with when managing the ZENworks for Servers 2 alarm management system is how to enable and disable alarms. Alarm thresholds are associated with each managed server and segment. When an alarm threshold is exceeded, an alarm is generated.

Although server threshold alarms are enabled by default, segment threshold alarms are not. You need to use the ZENworks for Servers 2 management console to enable and configure the threshold alarms for your network.

Use the following steps in the management console to enable and disable the alarms for your managed servers and segments to best match your needs:

1. Select the server or segment object you wish to enable or disable alarms on.
2. Right-click the object and select Properties from the pop-up menu.
3. Select the Segment Alarms property tab, shown in Figure 11.1.

FIGURE 11.1 Segment Alarms property tab for a segment object in ConsoleOne

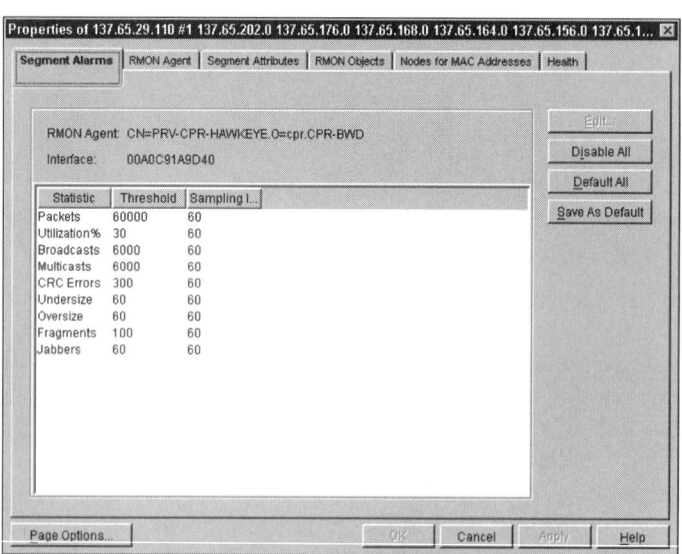

4. Select the alarm you wish to modify.
5. Click the Edit button and an Edit Alarm dialog box appears.

USING ZENWORKS SERVER AND ALARM MANAGEMENT

6. Select Enable to enable the alarm or Disable to disable the alarm.
7. If you are enabling an alarm, set the threshold value.
8. If you are enabling an alarm, you should also set the amount of time in the Sampling Interval field by which the threshold value must be exceeded in order to generate the alarm.
9. Click OK to save your alarm setting and return to the Segment Alarms property tab.

Understanding Alarm Indicators

Once you have enabled, disabled, and configured the alarm thresholds for the managed servers and segments on you network, ZENworks for Servers 2 starts tracking, storing, and relaying network alarms as they occur. At this point, you need to become familiar with the different alarm indicators so that you can recognize and respond to the alarms as they occur.

The following sections discuss the different indicators that you can watch for when alarms are triggered on your network.

About Alarm Icons Anchored to the Affected Object

Alarms that are triggered with a critical, major, or minor severity are displayed in the ZENworks for Servers 2 management console in both the Atlas and Console views. When an alarm is triggered on a segment or server that is being managed by the ZENworks for Servers 2 alarm management system, an Alarm icon is anchored to the object. Therefore, as you browse through the ZENworks for Servers namespace, watch out for Alarm icons.

Discussing the Ticker Tape Message on the Status Bar

You can also configure the ZENworks for Servers 2 alarm management system to display alarm messages on the status bar of the management console. This option is on by default. If this option is on, as the alarm management system recognizes an alarm it displays a descriptive message on the status bar that an alarm has been triggered. This is another thing that you should keep an eye out for. The messages let you know which object is affected so that you can quickly find the problem and resolve it.

Information about the Audible Beep

The final alarm indicator is an audible beep that is sent to the management console. The alarm management system can be configured to force an audible beep on the management console when an alarm occurs. This is very useful if you are not actively browsing or looking for alarms. If you hear a beep on the management console, look for the Alarm icon on your server or segment objects and investigate the alarm.

Working with Alarm Views

Now that you understand the alarm indicators that you should look and listen for, you need to understand how to use the views provided with ZENworks for Servers to monitor and manage alarms. The ZENworks for Servers management console gives you access to both active and historical data about alarms that are occurring or have occurred on your network.

You can define access restrictions to alarm data and management functions through ZENworks for Servers 2 role-based services. You can also modify the presentation of the alarm data displayed in the views by sorting and filtering on specific data elements.

The following sections discuss the different alarm views provided with ZENworks for Servers 2 and how to use them to monitor and manage alarms.

Monitoring Active Alarms

Active alarms are typically the most important type of alarm that you will encounter. Active alarms indicate that a problem is currently happening on either a monitored segment or a server. The ZENworks for Servers 2 Active Alarm view, shown in Figure 11.2, displays alarm statistics for all current alarms for the managed site.

The ZENworks for Servers 2 Active Alarm view displays the following statistics for alarms that are currently affecting your network:

- **Severity** — Displays an Alarm icon that is color coded to indicate the level of alarm severity: Red = Critical, Magenta = Major, Yellow = Minor, Blue = Informational and White = Unknown.

- **From** — Specifies the network address of the device that sent the alarm to the alarm management system.

- **Summary** — Displays a summary of the alarm event, including names, addresses, and other information about the alarm.

- **Owner** — Specifies the person or group that is responsible for handling the alarm. SYSTEM is specified until an owner is set.

- **Received Time** — Displays the date and time when the alarm management system received the alarm.

USING ZENWORKS SERVER AND ALARM MANAGEMENT

- **Type** — Specifies the generic type description of the alarm.
- **Category** — Specifies the category of the trap-type object identified from its MIB association.

For each of the alarms, the ZENworks for Servers 2 Active Alarm view displays the following alarm-specific data for the selected alarm, shown in Figure 11.2:

FIGURE 11.2 *Active Alarms view for a ZENworks for Servers site management object in ConsoleOne*

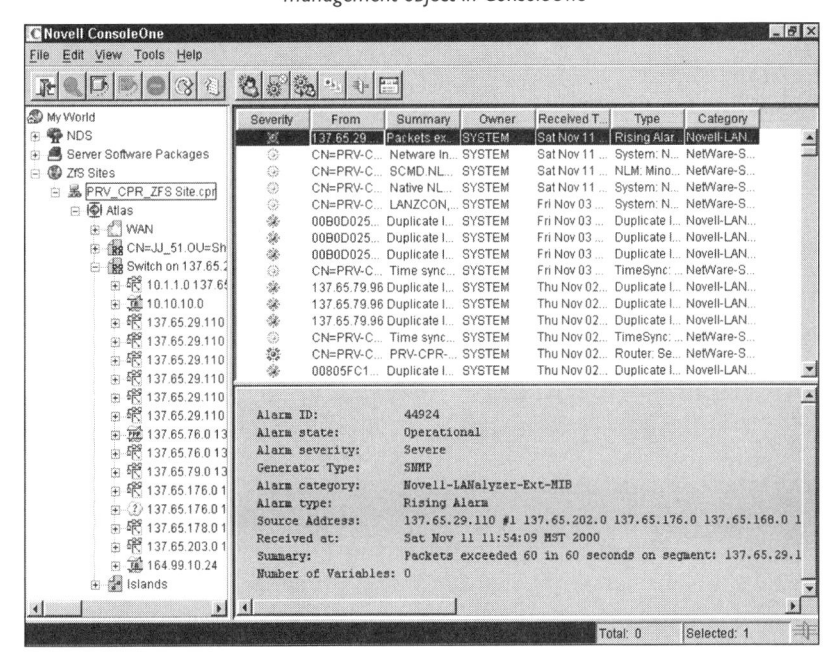

- **Alarm ID** — Displays the object ID of the alarm in the Alarm Manager database.
- **Alarm State** — Displays the current status of the alarm. This tells you if the alarm is currently operational or not.
- **Alarm Severity** — Displays the severity of the alarm: Severe, Major, Minor, Informational, or Unknown.

- **Generator Type** — Displays the type of agent that activated the alarm.
- **Alarm Category** — Displays the category of the trap-type object identified from its MIB association.
- **Alarm Type** — Displays the generic type description of the alarm.
- **Source Address** — Displays the address of the device that triggered the alarm.
- **Received At** — Displays the time at which the alarm management system received the alarm from the agent.
- **Summary** — Gives a descriptive summary of the alarm. This is one of the most useful statistics because the descriptions include node names and specific data about the nature of the alarm.
- **Number of Variables** — Lists the number of variables associated with the alarm.

Use the following steps from within the ZENworks for Servers 2 management console to access the Active Alarm view:

1. Select the ZENworks for Servers 2 site object.
2. Select View ➪ Active Alarms from the main menu in ConsoleOne and the Active Alarm view, shown in Figure 11.2, is displayed.

Displaying Alarm History

In addition to the currently active alarms, ZENworks for Servers 2 also enables you to view data about all archived alarms that have occurred on the network. The Alarm History view is very similar to the Active Alarm view. However, the Alarm History view includes a Handled status field, shown in Figure 11.3, in addition to the same information about the alarms.

Use the following steps from within the ZENworks for Servers management console to access the Alarm History view:

1. Select the ZENworks for Servers site object.
2. Select View ➪ Alarms History from the main menu in ConsoleOne and the Alarm History view, shown in Figure 11.3, is displayed.

Sorting Alarms

Once you have brought up either the Active Alarm or the Alarm History view on the management console, you can change the look of the view by sorting the alarms according to a specific criterion. This enables you to tailor the view to meet the needs of the problem you are trying to resolve or a report that you need to prepare.

USING ZENWORKS SERVER AND ALARM MANAGEMENT

FIGURE 11.3 *Alarm History view for a ZENworks for Servers site management object in ConsoleOne*

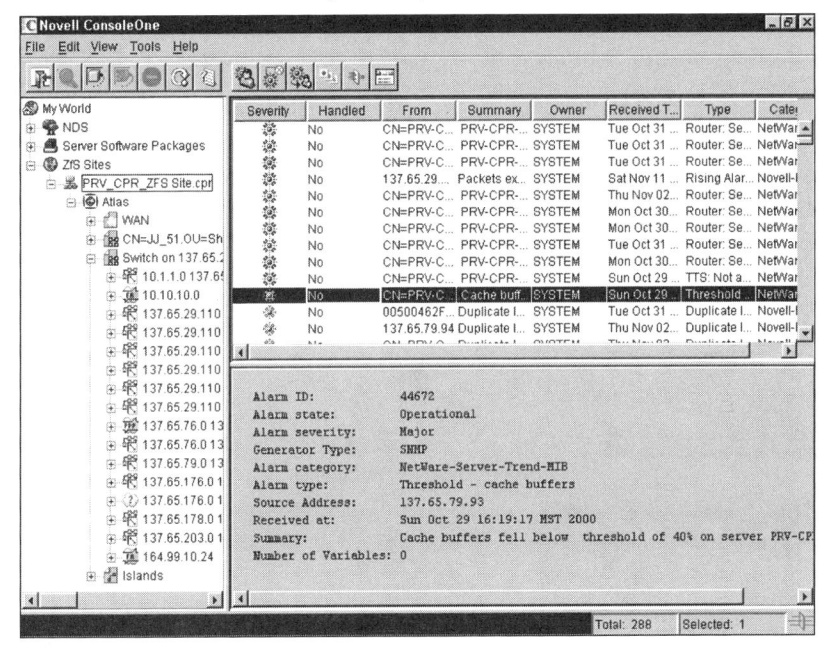

The following are the most common criteria you may wish to sort alarms on and examples of when to use them:

- **Received Time** — Received time is the default sort order. This enables you to see the alarms in the chronological order that they occurred. This is the most useful view in understanding the initial status of the network and when problems started occurring.

- **From** — Sorting using From enables you to focus on the specific server or node that triggered the alarm. This is most useful when you are troubleshooting a server or router issue.

- **Severity** — Sorting according to the severity enables you to focus on a specific level of error. Typically, you sort according to severity when you only want to see the most severe errors that are occurring and resolve them first.

- **Category** — Sorting by category enables you to focus on specific trap types identified in the MIB. This enables you to focus on a specific alarm. Use this if you are troubleshooting or monitoring a specific router or server issue where you know the specific SNMP trap you are looking for.

- **Type** — Sorting by type can also be very useful to troubleshoot some specific issues. For example, if you were watching for disk space problems, you may sort by type, and all the volume out of disk space alarms would be together.

Use the following steps from within the ZENworks for Servers management console to sort the Active Alarm or the Alarm History view:

1. Open up the alarm view you wish to sort.
2. Select View ➪ Settings ➪ Sort from the main menu in ConsoleOne.
3. From the Alarm Sorting dialog box, shown in Figure 11.4, select the criteria by which you want the alarms to be sorted.

FIGURE 11.4 *Alarm Sorting dialog box for a ZENworks for Servers 2 site management object in ConsoleOne*

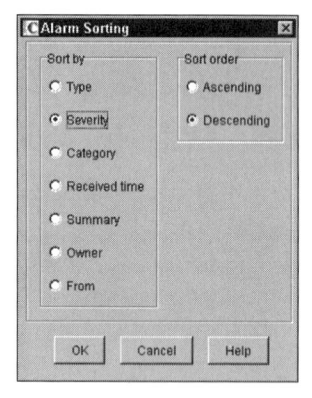

4. Select the sort order: Ascending or Descending.
5. Click OK to save your setting and the alarm view should be sorted according to your selections.

Filtering Alarms

ZENworks for Servers 2 also enables you to filter on alarms according to specific criteria once you have brought up either the Active Alarm or the Alarm History view on the management console. This enables you even greater control to customize the view to meet more specific needs of the problems you are trying to resolve or reports that you need to prepare.

Table 11.1 shows the available criteria and options that you may wish to use to filter alarms in the Active Alarm or Alarm History view.

TABLE 11.1 *Criteria Available to Filter Alarm Views on*

CRITERIA	OPERATORS	VALUES
Severity	=(equals), !=(does not equal), > or <	SEVERE, MAJOR, MINOR, INFORMATIONAL
Generator type	=(equals) or !=(does not equal)	Only SNMP (unless you have additional alarm generator types on you network)
Alarm category	=(equals) or !=(does not equal)	Any one of the alarms categories available in the MIB—that is, Antivirus-MIB, LANDesk-Alarm-MIB, NetWare-Server-Alarm-MIB, and so on.
Alarm type	=(equals) or !=(does not equal)	Any one of the alarm types provided on the alarm system—that is, Threshold – cache buffers, System:Trap NLM Loaded, and so on.
Source address	=(equals) or !=(does not equal)	IP address of source to filter on. This enables you to filter on a specific device.
From	=(equals), !=(does not equal), contains, starts with, or ends with	Full distinguished name of a ZENworks for Servers 2 management site server. This lets you filter on a single site if you are using site forwarding.

(continued)

TABLE 11.1 *Criteria Available to Filter Alarm Views on (continued)*

CRITERIA	OPERATORS	VALUES
Alarm owner	=(equals), !=(does not equal), contains, starts with, or ends with	Full distinguished name of a user or group that is responsible for alarms. This could be used to view the alarms that you are currently responsible for.
Alarm summary	=(equals), !=(does not equal), contains, starts with or ends with	Any text string that may equal, start, end, or be contained in the alarm summary string. For example, if you were looking at lost connection issues, you could filter on "Lost Connection" and use the contains operator.

Use the following steps from within the ZENworks for Servers management console to filter the Active Alarm or the Alarm History view:

1. Bring up the view that you wish to filter.
2. Select View ➪ Settings ➪ Filter from the main menu in ConsoleOne and the Alarm Filter dialog box, shown in Figure 11.5, is displayed.

FIGURE 11.5 *Alarm Filter dialog box for a ZENworks for Servers 2 site management object in ConsoleOne*

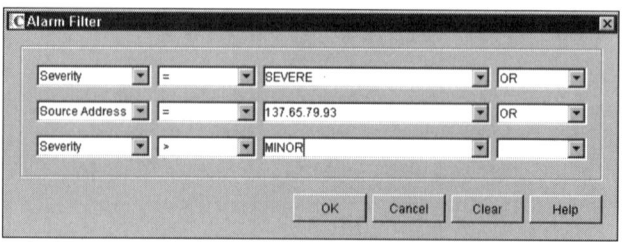

3. Select the criteria by which you wish the alarm management system to filter alarms from the drop-down list on the left.
4. Select an appropriate operator, from Table 11.1, to use from the next drop-down list.

USING ZENWORKS SERVER AND ALARM MANAGEMENT

5. Select an appropriate value from the third drop-down list, or specify a value if one is not provided.
6. Specify how this specific filter relates to other statements you wish to define. You can use the AND, OR, new row, delete row, and new group relationship criteria. This enables you to add multiple filters and groups of filters to the alarm view, as shown in Figure 11.5.
7. If you defined relationship criteria in Step 6, repeat Steps 3 through 6.
8. When you are finished specifying filters, click the OK button. The filter will be saved and the view should be adjusted according to your criteria.

Managing Alarms

Now that you understand how to detect and view network alarms from the ZENworks for Servers 2 management console, you need to understand how to manage them on large networks. This is especially important if numerous administrators are managing different aspects of the management site.

ZENworks for Servers 2 adds options to the alarm to enable you to assign, own, and handle alarms. This feature helps you keep track of who is responsible for what issues and which issues have been resolved.

Once you select an alarm from the Active Alarm or the Alarm History view, you can manage the alarm by selecting one of the following options for it from the View menu in ConsoleOne:

- **Assign** — The assign option enables you to specify a person or group that is responsible for handling an alarm. When this option is set, other administrators know that they do not need to respond to it.

- **Own** — When you select Own from the View menu of an alarm in ConsoleOne, the owner that is filed changes to the NDS name you are logged in as. This lets other administrators know that you are handling this alarm. Therefore, they do not need to act on the alarm and they have a person to contact for estimated resolutions and so forth.

- **Handle** — Once an alarm has been handled by someone, you can select Handled and the alarm is removed from the Active Alarm view. This removes the alarm from active issues that need resolving, enabling administrators to focus on current problems. However, the alarm still shows up on the Alarm History view.

Setting Alarm Actions

One of the most powerful features of the ZENworks for Servers alarm management system is its ability to perform actions automatically to help you manage alarms as they are triggered. You can use the ZENworks for Servers 2 management console to configure an alarm to automatically trigger an action when it occurs.

Alarm actions are configured through alarm dispositions. Use the following steps to access the Alarm Disposition page, shown in Figure 11.6, to configure alarm actions in ConsoleOne:

1. Select the ZENworks for Servers 2 site management object you wish to configure alarm dispositions on.

2. Select the Alarm Disposition tab, shown in Figure 11.6.

FIGURE 11.6 *Alarm Disposition tab for a ZENworks for Servers 2 site management object in ConsoleOne*

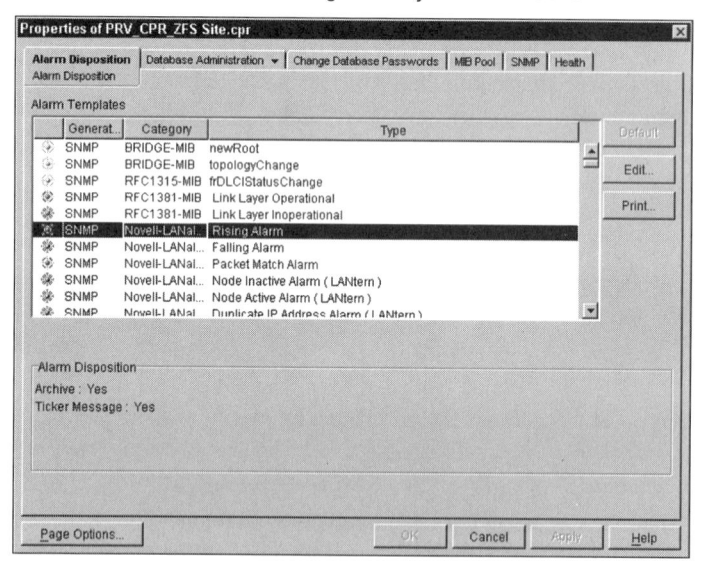

3. Select the alarm you wish to configure from the list.

4. Click the Edit button to bring up the Edit Alarm Disposition dialog box.

The following sections discuss the actions to be performed when an alarm is triggered, and that are available from the Edit Alarm Disposition dialog box.

USING ZENWORKS SERVER AND ALARM MANAGEMENT

Sending E-mail Notification

The first available option from the Alarm Disposition dialog box is the ability to send an e-mail notification to a user or group. It is very useful to be notified when critical alarms occur on the network.

Network administrators use this feature for various kinds of notification. Some have their SMTP mail server configured to page them with the notification e-mail when it is received.

Use the following steps to configure an e-mail notification action for an alarm from the Edit Alarm Disposition dialog box in ConsoleOne:

1. Select the SMTP Mail Notification tab, shown in Figure 11.7.

FIGURE 11.7 *SMTP Mail Notification tab of an alarm disposition for a site management object in ConsoleOne*

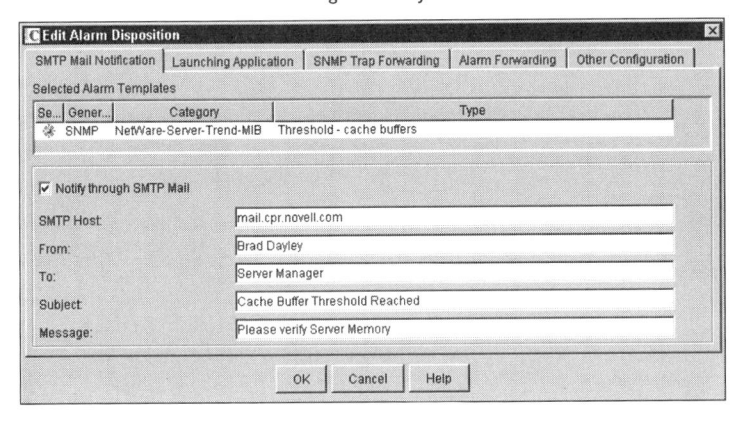

2. Select the Notify through SMTP Mail option.

3. Specify the IP address of the SMTP host server that handles incoming and outgoing e-mail in the SMTP Host text box.

4. Specify the mail ID you wish to use in the From text box. This is usually important for any additional automation on the back end.

5. Specify the mail IDs of the users or groups you wish to notify when the alarm is triggered in the To text box.

6. Specify the subject line you wish to appear on the mail message that is sent, in the Subject text box. This is also often important for additional automation on the back end. You can also add variables to the subject line by specifying a % sign in front of them. Use Table 11.2 to specify any variables that might be useful in the e-mail Subject line.

7. Specify the text message you wish to appear in the body of the e-mail that is sent, in the Message text box. This should include a description of what the alarm means. You can also add variables to the subject line by specifying a % sign in front of them. Use Table 11.2 to specify any variables that might be useful in the e-mail body.
8. Click the OK button to save your settings and return to the Alarm Dispositions tab.

TABLE 11.2 *Available Variables for Use in the Subject and Message Options for SMTP Mail Notifications*

VARIABLES	NAME	DESCRIPTION
a	Alarm ID	Identification number of the alarm as it is stored in the database
c	Affected Class	Class of the device that sent the alarm
o	Affected Object Number	Identification number, from the database, of the node that generated the alarm
s	Alarm Summary String	Message describing the alarm (same message that is displayed in the status bar ticker tape message)
T	Alarm Type String	Description of the alarm (same as the description in the Alarm Type element of the Alarm summary window)
V	Severity Number	Alarm severity level: 1 = Critical 2 = Major 3 = Minor 4 = Informational

Launching an Application

The next option available from the Alarm Dispositions dialog box is the ability to launch an application. This option enables you to specify an NLM to be launched when an alarm is triggered on a server.

USING ZENWORKS SERVER AND ALARM MANAGEMENT

For example, if your network utilization is too high, you could launch an NLM that shuts down noncritical applications that normally consume high amounts of network bandwidth.

Use the following steps to configure, from the Edit Alarm Disposition dialog box in ConsoleOne, an external program to be launched when an alarm is triggered:

1. Select the Launching Application tab, shown in Figure 11.8.

FIGURE 11.8 *Launching Application tab of an alarm disposition for a site management object in ConsoleOne*

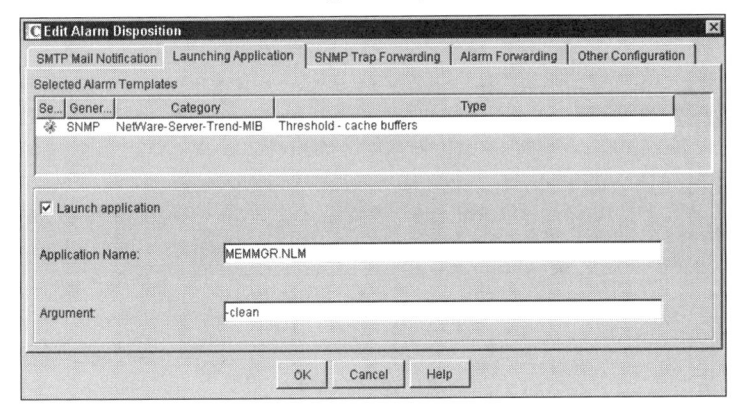

2. Select the "Launch application" option.
3. Specify the application path and filename in the Application Name text box.
4. Specify any additional arguments in the Argument text box. You can use variables listed in Table 11.2 as parameters by preceding them with the % sign.
5. Click the OK button to save your settings and return to the Alarm Dispositions tab.

NOTE The Application Name field cannot exceed 126 characters in total length. The Argument field cannot exceed 119 characters in total length. The combined total of the Application Name and the Argument fields cannot exceed 139 characters in total length.

Forwarding the SNMP Trap

The next option available from the Alarm Dispositions dialog box is the ability to forward the SNMP trap to another management system. This option enables you to specify the IP address of another management station or server to forward the SNMP trap to.

For example, if you had another SNMP management system, in addition to ZENworks for Servers 2, and wished that system to receive the trap as well, you could send an SNMP trap to that management system, too.

Use the following steps to configure an IP address, from the Edit Alarm Disposition dialog box in ConsoleOne, to which the SNMP trap should be forwarded:

1. Select the SNMP Trap Forwarding tab, shown in Figure 11.9.

FIGURE 11.9 *SMTP Trap Forwarding tab of an alarm disposition for a site management object in ConsoleOne*

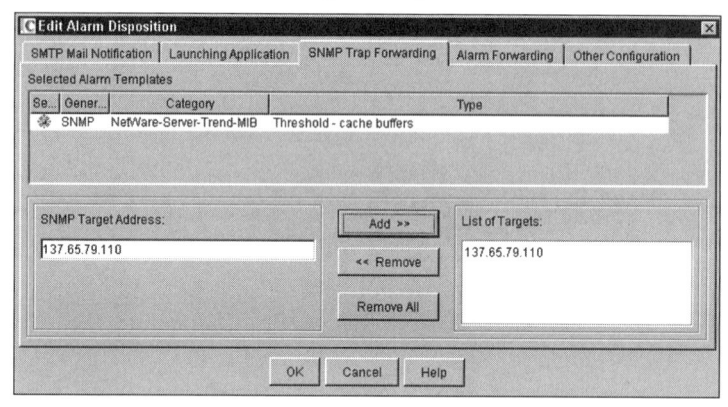

2. Enter the IP address of the server to which you want to forward the SNMP traps in the SNMP Target Address field.
3. Click the Add button to add it to the list of targets.
4. Click the OK button to save your settings and return to the Alarm Dispositions tab.

Forwarding the Alarm

The next option available from the Alarm Dispositions dialog box is the ability to forward the alarm to another ZENworks for Servers 2 management

USING ZENWORKS SERVER AND ALARM MANAGEMENT

site. This option enables you to specify a ZENworks for Servers management site name and host name to forward the alarm to.

Use the following steps to configure another ZENworks for Servers management site, from the Edit Alarm Disposition dialog box in ConsoleOne, to which the alarm should be forwarded:

1. Select the Alarm Forwarding tab, shown in Figure 11.10.

FIGURE 11.10 *Alarm Forwarding tab of an alarm disposition for a site management object in ConsoleOne*

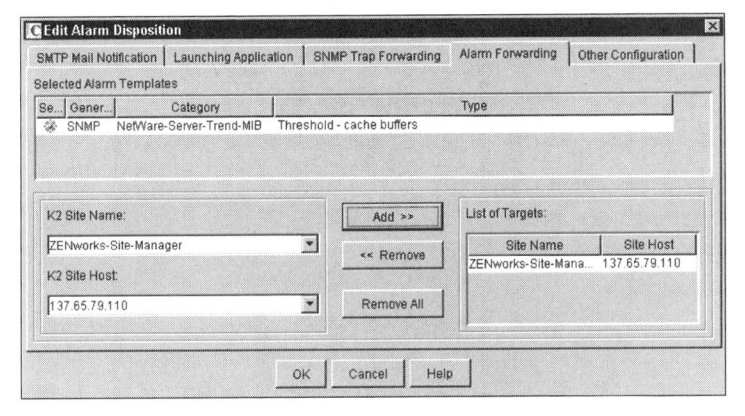

2. Enter the ZENworks for Servers 2 management site name to which you want to forward the alarm in the Site Name field.
3. Enter the ZENworks for Servers 2 site host name in the Site Host field.
4. Click the Add button to add it to the list of targets.
5. Click the OK button to save your settings and return to the Alarm Dispositions tab.

Additional Alarm Disposition Actions

The final options panel available from the Edit Alarm Dispositions dialog box is the Other Configuration tab, shown in Figure 11.11. This tab enables you to configure the following actions to be performed when an alarm is triggered:

- **Archive** — Stores the statistical data for the alarm instance in the Alarm Manager database on the management server. If you wish to see the alarm in the Alarm History view, you need to select this option. It is on by default.

- **Beep on Console** — Sends an audible beep to the ZENworks for Servers 2 management console to notify the administrator that an alarm has been triggered.
- **Show on Ticker Bar** — Displays a message of the alarm on the status bar of the ZENworks for Servers management console to silently notify the administrator of the most recent alarm.

Use the following steps to configure additional options for the alarm from the Edit Alarm Disposition dialog box in ConsoleOne:

1. Select the Other Configuration tab (see Figure 11.11).

FIGURE 11.11 SMTP Mail Notification tab of an alarm disposition for a site management object in ConsoleOne

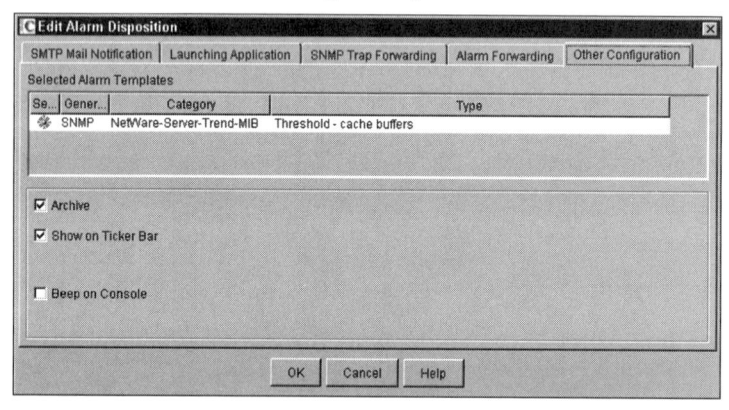

2. Set the Archive option if you wish to save the alarm to the Alarm Manager database.
3. Set the Show on Ticker Bar option if you wish a message to be displayed in the status bar of the management console.
4. Set the Beep on Console option if you wish the alarm to send an audible beep to the management console.
5. Click the OK button to save your settings and return to the Alarm Dispositions tab.

Deleting Alarms

The final task you need to be familiar with when managing ZENworks for Servers 2 alarms is how to remove them once you are completely finished with them. The alarms take up space in the Alarm Manager database until they are removed. If you do not consistently keep the alarms cleaned out of the database, the database can begin to take up an excessive amount of disk space.

The following sections discuss how to manually and automatically remove unwanted alarms from the Alarm Manager database.

Deleting Alarms from the Management Console

You can manually delete alarms from the Alarm Manager database by simply deleting them from the ZENworks for Servers 2 management console. This is the best way to delete an individual alarm. However, if you have numerous alarms that have occurred, this process could be too time-consuming. If you have numerous alarms, instead use the automatic alarm deletion method described in the next section.

Use the following steps to manually delete an alarm from the Alarm Manager database from the management console:

1. Navigate to the server or segment object the alarm occurred on.
2. Open the Alarm History view to display the alarms.
3. Select the alarm you wish to delete.
4. Select View ⇨ Delete from the main menu and the alarm is deleted from the database.

Automating Alarm Deletion

The best way to handle the deletion of alarms is to automate the process by configuring the purge utility to delete the alarms for you. The purge utility is a Java application that runs on the server where the Alarm Manager database is stored.

The purge utility is controlled by a configuration file, AMPURGE.PROPERTY, which defines the criteria for selecting alarms to be purged as well as when to start purging alarms. The first step in using the purge utility to automatically delete alarms is to configure the criteria listed in Table 11.3, according to how long you need the alarms and when to start purging.

TABLE 11.3 *Criteria for Purging Alarms Listed in the AMPURGE.PROPERTY File*

CRITERIA SETTING	DESCRIPTION
SeverityInformationalPurgeWait	Specifies the number of days to wait before informational alarms are purged. The default is 7.
SeverityMinorPurgeWait	Specifies the number of days to wait before minor alarms are purged. The default is 7.
SeverityMajorPurgeWait	Specifies the number of days to wait before major alarms are purged. The default is 7.
SeverityCriticalPurgeWait	Specifies the number of days to wait before critical alarms are purged. The default is 7.
SeverityUnknownPurgeWait	Specifies the number of days to wait before unknown alarms are purged. The default is 7.
PurgeStartTime	Specifies the start time hour to begin the daily purge process. Valid values are from 0 (midnight) to 23 (11 P.M.).
AlarmPurgeService	Specifies whether or not to automatically run the purge process on a daily basis. You can specify either Yes (enable) or No (disable). Omitting this setting also disables it.

Once you have configured the criteria for purging alarms, you have two options. The first option is to wait for the start time that you specified the purge to begin. The second option is to manually start the purge process.

You may wish to manually start the purge process because you turned off the automatic run by setting AlarmPurgeService to No, or because the database has grown too rapidly because of a network problem and you need to free up disk space.

Use the following command from the console of the server where the Alarm Manager database is stored to start the automatic purge process manually:

```
java com.novell.managewise.am.db.purge.AutoPurgeManager -s
-d <properties_file_directory>
```

The properties_file_directory parameter should be replaced with the directory location where the AMPURGE.PROPERTY file is located.

> **NOTE** The purge process is highly memory and CPU intensive. Therefore, you should only run the purge during off hours or when it is extremely needed — for example, at night, on weekends, or if the server runs out of disk space.

Using ZENworks for Servers 2 Monitoring Services

ZENworks for Servers 2 provides monitoring services, in addition to the alarm management services, to monitor devices on the network. The ZENworks for Servers 2 alarm management system relies on agents either on the device or on the management server to capture events, turn them into alarms, and relay them to the management console.

The ZENworks for Servers 2 monitoring services does the opposite. It enables the management console to check the status of network devices from the point of view of the console itself. This enables you to be immediately notified if connectivity between the console and critical nodes is interrupted.

You should use the monitoring service as another option to monitor the status of the critical services on your network. The following sections describe how to define and configure target services you wish to monitor.

Monitoring Services on Target Nodes

ZENworks for Servers 2 uses a ping method to monitor service status on target nodes. A ping packet is sent from a remote server to the target node. The remote server then waits for a specific interval. If a reply is received back from the target node before the interval elapses, the status of the server is up. If a reply is not received back from the target node before the interval elapses, the status of the server is down.

The following sections describe the different utilities and views that ZENworks for Servers 2 provides from the management console to monitor servers on one or more target nodes.

Testing a Single Target Node

ZENworks for Servers provides the ping test as a quick method for you to monitor the status of specific node. You should use the ping test if you suspect a problem with a specific node in the network.

The ping test provides you with the status — up or down — of communication from the management console to the node as well as the round-trip delay for the ping to be received back.

Use the following steps to perform a ping test on a particular node from the management console:

1. Select the node you wish to monitor.
2. Select File ➪ Actions ➪ Ping from the main menu and the Ping dialog box, shown in Figure 11.12, is displayed.

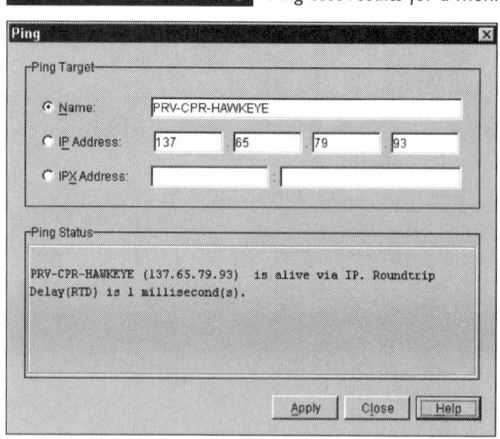

FIGURE 11.12 *Ping test results for a monitored server object in ConsoleOne*

3. The IP address should be already displayed for you, if it is the default. However, you can also specify a name or IPX address as well at this point, and click the Apply button.
4. View the status in the Ping Status area. The status continues to be updated at a configured interval.

Monitoring Services on Several Nodes

ZENworks for Servers 2 also enables you to monitor the services of several target nodes, from the management console, through the use of a connectivity

USING ZENWORKS SERVER AND ALARM MANAGEMENT

test utility and Polling view. Each of these options displays the following statistics that are dynamically updated:

- **Target** — The name or address of the node for which connectivity to services are being tested.
- **Service** — The service that is being monitored on the target node.
- **Port** — The port number of the service on the target node.
- **Status** — The status, up or down, for the service. Up means that a ping packet is sent to the service and a reply is returned; it doesn't necessarily mean that the service is operating normally.
- **Roundtrip Delay** — Time interval, in milliseconds, from when the remote ping server sends a ping to the target service and a reply is received back from the target.
- **Packets Sent** — Number of packets that were sent from the remote ping server to the target node.
- **Packets Received** — Number of packets received by the remote ping server that were sent from the target node.
- **Packets Lost** — Number of ping packets and percentage of total packets that were lost during the connectivity testing.
- **Interval** — Time, in seconds, the remote ping server waits after sending one ping packet before sending the next.
- **Timeout** — Time, in milliseconds, the remote ping server waits for a reply from the target node before declaring the service in a down state.

The Polling view displays connectivity statistics for all configured services on the managed segment. This view can give you a quick understanding of the current status of a segment, which can be extremely useful when trying to understand problems such as network outages or LAN overusage. To view the Polling view for a segment, select the desired segment in ConsoleOne and then select View ➪ Polling from the main menu.

The connectivity test utility displays statistics for services from a selective group of nodes. You can tailor the Connectivity view to more closely meet your needs by adding only the most important nodes. Typically, you will want to use the Connectivity view when you are troubleshooting issues on a selective group of servers.

NOVELL'S ZENWORKS FOR SERVERS 2 ADMINISTRATOR'S HANDBOOK

Use the following steps to start the Connectivity view from the management console:

1. Select the segment that contains the nodes you wish to monitor services on.
2. Select the nodes you wish to monitor services on in the right pane of the console.
3. Select File ➪ Action ➪ Connectivity Test from the main menu and a screen similar to the one in Figure 11.13 appears.
4. Click the Add button, located in the button bar in Figure 11.13, to add additional services (discussed in the next section) to the view.

FIGURE 11.13 *Connectivity test results for a monitored segment object in ConsoleOne*

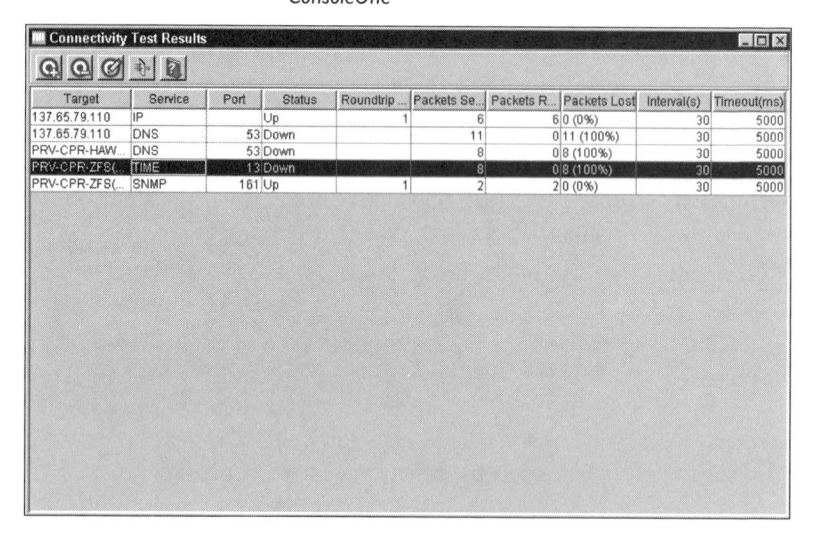

Target	Service	Port	Status	Roundtrip...	Packets Se...	Packets R...	Packets Lost	Interval(s)	Timeout(ms)
137.65.79.110	IP		Up	1	6	6	0 (0%)	30	5000
137.65.79.110	DNS	53	Down		11	0	11 (100%)	30	5000
PRV-CPR-HAW...	DNS	53	Down		8	0	8 (100%)	30	5000
PRV-CPR-ZFS(...	TIME	13	Down		8	0	8 (100%)	30	5000
PRV-CPR-ZFS(...	SNMP	161	Up	1	2	2	0 (0%)	30	5000

Adding Services to the Connectivity Test

Once you have the connectivity test utility running, you can add new services to be monitored. This can be useful as you are monitoring connectivity issues on a node because it enables you check additional services on the monitored node to see if all or only some services are affected.

ZENworks for Servers 2 enables you to monitor the following services on monitored nodes from the management console:

USING ZENWORKS SERVER AND ALARM MANAGEMENT

- **IP** — Internet Protocol
- **IPX** — Internet Packet Exchange
- **DNS** — Domain Name System
- **ECHO** — Echo Protocol
- **FTP** — File Transfer Protocol
- **TFTP** — Trivial File Transfer Protocol
- **HTTP** — Hypertext Transfer Protocol
- **HTTPS** — Hypertext Transfer Protocol Secure
- **SNMP** — Simple Network Management Protocol
- **SMTP** — Simple Mail Transfer Protocol
- **TIME** — Time Services
- **WUSER** — Windows User
- **NNTP** — Network News Transfer Protocol
- **NFS** — Network File System

Use the following steps, from the connectivity test utility, to add services to the Connectivity Test window:

1. Select the target node you wish to monitor another service from — or, if you wish to add a server from a node not already listed, select any node.

2. Click the Add button and the Add Ping Targets dialog box, shown in Figure 11.14, appears.

FIGURE 11.14 *Add Ping Targets dialog box for the connectivity test on a monitored segment object in ConsoleOne*

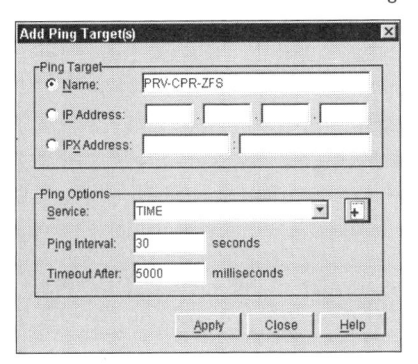

329

3. If you are adding a service from a node not already listed, enter the name, IP address, or IPX address in the Ping Target field.
4. Select the service from the drop-down menu, or click the Plus button next to the Service field and specify a new service and port number.
5. Specify the interval at which you wish to ping the service in the Ping Interval field.
6. Specify the amount of time you wish to wait for a ping reply before determining that the service is down, in the Timeout After field.
7. Click the Close button to add the service to the monitor list and close the Add Ping Targets dialog box, or click the Apply button to add the service to the list but keep the dialog box open to add additional services.

Setting up Monitoring Services on Monitored Nodes

You must configure monitoring services on each node you wish to monitor from the Polling view in the management console. The connectivity test utility simply uses a list of targets to test; however, the Polling view must read the node object contained within it and check for nodes with monitoring services enabled on them before they can be added to the view.

Use the following steps from the management console to configure and enable monitoring services on nodes you wish to monitor:

1. Select the segment you wish to monitor nodes on.
2. Select a node located in the selected segment that you wish to configure monitor services for.
3. Right-click the node and select Properties from the pop-up menu.
4. Select the Monitor Services tab, as shown in Figure 11.15.
5. Select the IP or IPX address you wish to use for the node. If the node is connected to multiple segments, make certain that you use the address for the segment you wish to monitor.
6. Select the services that you wish to monitor on the node and click the Add button, or you can also click the Add Service button to specify a new service name and port number.
7. Set the polling interval to ping the server in the Interval field.
8. Set the amount of time to wait for a reply from the service before declaring it down in the Timeout After field.

9. Specify whether or not to send an alarm if the state changes either from up to down or down to up.
10. Click the Apply button to save the changes.

FIGURE 11.15 *Monitor Services tab of managed server node object in ConsoleOne*

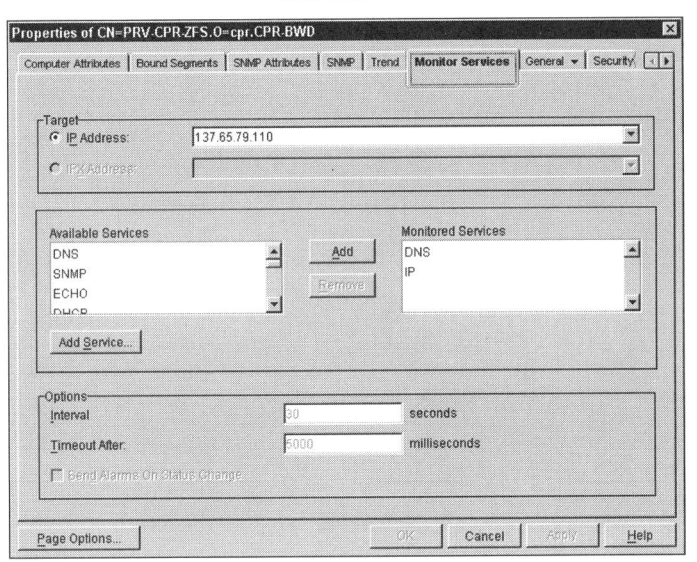

CHAPTER 12

Using ZENworks for Servers 2 Server Management

NOVELL'S ZENWORKS FOR SERVERS 2 ADMINISTRATOR'S HANDBOOK

One of the most difficult tasks enterprise network administrators must face is how to manage the numerous servers on their network. ZENworks for Servers 2 includes powerful tools and services that will help you manage your network servers. This chapter discusses the utilities, agents, and databases that enable you to monitor, maintain, and control your servers.

Using ZENworks for Servers 2 SMNP Agents to Manage Servers

ZENworks for Servers 2 has several management agents that enable you to configure, monitor, and manage servers from a single console interface. This section discusses the SNMP agents for server management, how to plan and prepare your network for optimal server management, and details several tasks that ZENworks for Servers 2 handles that will enable you to more effectively manage servers.

Understanding SNMP-Based Server Management

One of the biggest advantages in using ZENworks for Servers 2 to manage your servers is that its server management agents support the industry standard Simple Network Management Protocol (SNMP). These ZENworks for Servers 2 server management agents also support the UDP/IP, IPX, and NCP implementations for packet sending. Therefore, any SNMP console or manager can request information from them.

The ZENworks for Servers 2 server management agents run on both NetWare and Windows NT servers in your network. These agents continuously monitor the servers and collect dynamic data in response to requests from the management console.

ZENworks for Servers 2 uses several different management servers to manage servers. The following is a list of the different types of agents ZENworks for Servers 2 use to communicate with servers:

- **Monitoring** — The server monitoring agents provide instant information about the current state of the monitored elements of the server, including CPU utilization, memory size, available cache buffers, connected users, volumes, disks, disk space usage per user, network adapters, available print queues, current print jobs, and NLMs loaded on the server.

USING ZENWORKS FOR SERVERS 2 SERVER MANAGEMENT

- **Trending** — The server trend agents provide historical data about various server objects and can be displayed in a graphical diagram on the ZENworks for Servers 2 management console. The trend data is stored on the managed server, which eliminates the need for extra LAN traffic to poll the SNMP Agent Manager.
- **Alarm notification** — The server alarm notification agents monitor for predefined alarms or events and then notify the ZENworks for Servers 2 management system (or any SNMP management console). Currently, ZENworks for Servers 2 agents monitor more than 580 different types of alarms or events . Any Windows NT system, security, or application event will be converted to an SNMP trap and sent to the management system as well.
- **Configuration Management** — The server configuration management agents for NetWare servers enable you to remotely view and modify the NetWare server's configuration from the management console. The configuration management agent enables you to modify 187 SET parameters on the NetWare server to tune performance.

> **NOTE**
> The ZENworks for Servers 2 SNMP agents must be installed on every server you wish to manage.

Discussing the ZENworks for Servers 2 Management Views

The ZENworks for Servers 2 management agents provide information to the administrator's management console through the use of server management views. You can access the following three main types of server management views by selecting a server or network node from the ZENworks for Servers namespace in ConsoleOne. The three types of views are as follows:

- **Console view** — Provides details about the selected server or node. You can also drill down into the server configuration to display information about the internal component of the server — for example, operating system version, installed devices, and memory.
- **Summary view** — Provides details about the server's current performance — for example, alarms generated by the server, CPU utilization, and available disk space. Once again, you can drill down into the server configuration and view summary information about its components — for example, processor, running threads, memory, and NetWare volumes.

335

- **Trend view** — Provides a graphical representation of the trend parameters set up for the server. This enables you to monitor the trends of server's state over specific periods of time. Then, using this trend data, you can track the general health status of the server and predict potential problems and needs for growth.

Planning Server Management

Now that you understand the ZENworks for Servers 2 management agents and the console interface used to monitor the state of your server, you need to do a little planning to get the most out of the data that ZENworks for Servers 2 provides you.

This section discusses how to use the data you obtain from the ZENworks for Servers 2 console views to create a baseline document. We then discuss how to use that baseline document to monitor, troubleshoot, and optimize your servers.

Creating a Server Baseline Document

You should create a baseline document that defines the normal activity and usage of your network servers. This is later used to identify atypical performance or problems on your servers.

You can create a baseline document either from data out of the Trend view or from a server health report (see the information on health reports in Chapter 13). The following elements are vital elements for every baseline document:

- **CPU utilization** — The CPU utilization statistic indicates how busy the processor is on the server. High CPU utilization greatly impacts the performance of the server. The utilization of the CPU rises and falls with user and network activity throughout each day. For example, CPU utilization is usually high first thing in the morning when all of the users are logging into the server and reading e-mail, or on Friday when large weekend reports are being run. You should create a daily, weekly, and monthly graph for your baseline document, if necessary, to map out a CPU utilization pattern that should be expected.

- **Cache buffers** — Cache buffers represent the amount of server memory usable for processes. The availability of cache buffers greatly impact the performance of the server. Once again, the available cache buffers rise and fall during the day based on users and application usage — you should typically have between 65 to 70 percent of your cache buffers available to applications. Create a daily graph for your baseline document showing the typical trend of cache buffers on your server.

- **File reads and writes** — The file reads and writes by the server should also be graphed into a baseline document. This helps you determine if a server is performing a high or low number of file I/O.
- **Volume utilization** — You should also create a graph showing typical volume usage as users create and delete files. This is useful in determining when you must add storage space to a volume.
- **Running software** — Another useful parameter to add to a baseline document is the software running on the server. This helps you in network planning and troubleshooting software issues.

Using a Server Baseline Document

Once you have created a baseline document you should keep it available and up-to-date. The following sections describe situations that you can use to create an accurate and up-to-date baseline document.

Setting Alarm Thresholds   The most useful function of a baseline document is its ability to help you understand what thresholds to set for servers monitored by management agents. You can use the baseline document statistics to set alarm threshold values that alert you when normal server usage is being surpassed — for example, the server starts running out of memory or disk space.

Tracking Server Utilization   Another useful function of a baseline document is to help you track server utilization. You can use the current and past data evaluate the usage trends of the server and understand needed configuration changes. For example, you can use the baseline document to predict a volume running out of disk space, available cache buffers insufficient for running software, and so forth.

Server Troubleshooting   The final function of a baseline document is to aid you in troubleshooting your servers. Using the typical data in the baseline document, you can recognize atypical behavior of your servers, which will help you isolate the problem.

For example, say a server is running out of memory. You compare the baseline document to the current state of the server and notice that the only difference is that a new application is running on the server. The first step in troubleshooting would be to remove the application.

Displaying Server Configuration Information

Using the ZENworks for Servers 2 namespace in ConsoleOne, you can display and view critical configuration information about your servers. You can then use this information to manage and control the servers on your managed network.

The following is a list of the configuration information components and information that you can retrieve about your managed servers through the ZENworks for Servers namespace:

- **Processors** — Processor number, type, speed, bus, and utilization
- **LAN adapters** — Driver name, adapter number, MAC address and usage
- **Disk adapters** — Drive number and type
- **Storage devices** — Drive number, vendor name, partition types, size, ID, redirection information, and fault tolerance
- **OS kernel threads** — Thread name, parent NLM, execution time, state, stack size, and affinity
- **OS kernel interrupts** — Interrupt name, number, number of occurrences, execution time, type, processor, service routines, and spurious interrupts
- **OS kernel memory** — Memory type, size, maximum size, and usage
- **OS kernel address spaces** — Space name, number of NLMs loaded, mapped pages, restarted bits, memory, and block usage
- **Network interfaces** — Protocol name, board name, board number, packets out, packets in, address, and descriptions
- **Network connections** — Connection number, username, client address, state, privileges, connection time, bytes read/written, NCP requests, open files, and locked files
- **Users** — Username, disk usage, last login time, account and password status, real name, and bad logins
- **Installed software** — Application name, type, and date installed
- **NLMs** — Filename, version, release date, memory usage, description, copyright, and resource tag information
- **File services** — Volume name, segment number, segment index, logical ID, physical ID, size, fault tolerance, and disk name
- **RMON services** — Agent name and version, IP and/or IPX address, number of interfaces, current status, agent type, resources, owners, and indexes

USING ZENWORKS FOR SERVERS 2 SERVER MANAGEMENT

Use the following steps to access the server configuration from within the ZENworks for Servers 2 namespace in ConsoleOne:

1. Locate the server object you wish to display configuration information about.

2. Click the "+" sign next to the server object to expand the view. The view should expand to reveal the configuration devices, operating system, and services configuration data groups.

3. Click the "+" sign next to each of the data groups and data elements to reveal data about each configuration component, as shown in Figure 12.1.

FIGURE 12.1 Server configuration groups and components located in the ZENworks for Servers namespace in ConsoleOne

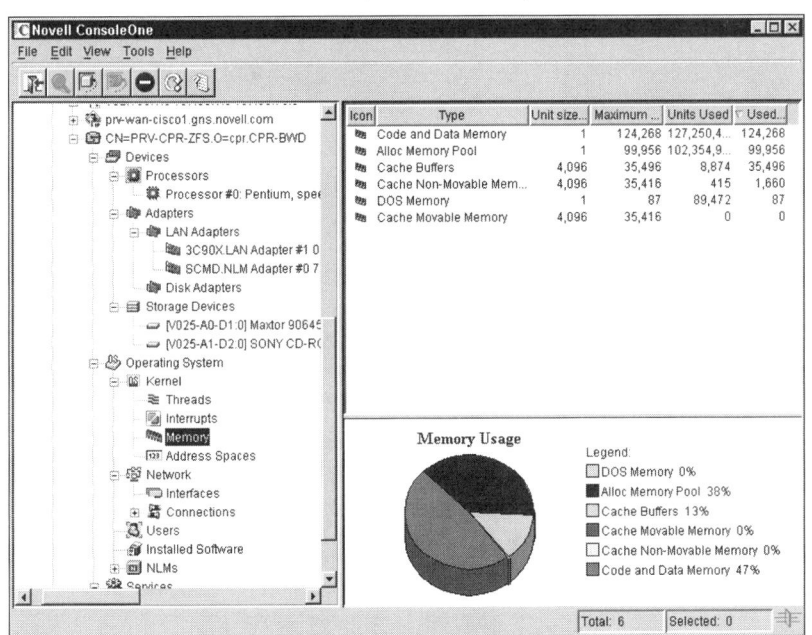

Showing Server Summary Data

Displaying the configuration data for each individual component gives you a lot of extremely detailed and useful information. However, at times you may wish only to take a quick look at a server's configuration information. For this reason ZENworks for Servers 2 also enables you to display a quick summary view of the most vital information about the managed server.

ZENworks for Servers 2 uses a series of SNMP GET requests to the ZENworks for Servers management agents to create a quick collection of summary data. That summary data is dynamically updated by ZENworks for Servers 2 as it continuously polls the server.

To access the summary information about a server, right-click the server object and then select Views ⇨ Summary from the pop-up menu. A screen similar to the one in Figure 12.2 is displayed showing the following information about the managed server:

FIGURE 12.2 *Server summary of a NetWare server, located in the ZENworks for Servers namespace in ConsoleOne*

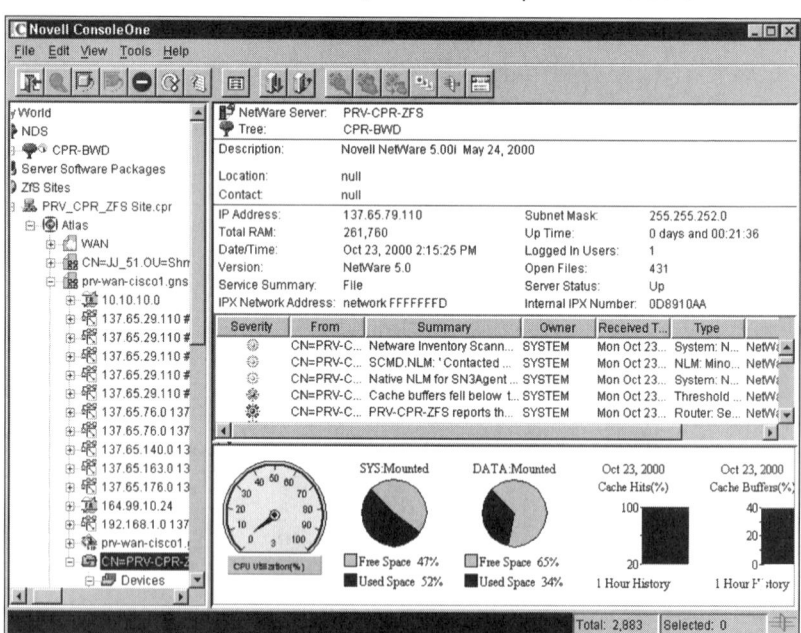

- **Server Type** — Tells you whether it is a NetWare server or an NT server.
- **Server Name** — Lets you know which server you are viewing the summary for.

- **Server Tree** — Useful when troubleshooting NDS issues.
- **Description** — Tells you the server type, version, and revisions. This is useful in determining if a support pack has been applied to the server.
- **Location** — If a Location field is set up for the server in the management database, that location shows up here. This is essential if you have a WAN with numerous servers located in several different buildings, cities, or countries.
- **Contact** — Useful for finding the person responsible for the server, because most enterprise networks are partitioned and administered by several different people.
- **IP Address** — Gives you the IP address and subnet mask for the server.
- **IPX Address** — Gives you the IPX address and network number for the server.
- **Total RAM** — Indicates total RAM installed, which is useful in troubleshooting server problems.
- **Up Time** — The uptime of the server is very useful for things such as knowing when the server was last serviced, if the server has been recently downed, or if the server has experience critical problems and reset itself.
- **Date/Time** — The current time that the server thinks it is. This is helpful if you are having any issues involving time synchronization in NDS.
- **Service Summary** — Lists the services that are currently available on the server. This can be helpful if you are browsing servers to find a candidate to take on extra services.
- **Logged in Users** — Gives you the number of users currently logged into the server.
- **Open Files** — Gives you the number of files that are currently open on the server.
- **Server Status** — If for any reason the server cannot be contacted, the most recent summary data is collected and the server shows up as being down.
- **Managed Events** — All events that are monitored by ZENworks for Servers that occur on the server are listed here. This can be extremely useful in understanding the current state of a server, because alarms are also listed here.
- **CPU Utilization** — Displays a speedometer of the current percentage of utilization of the server's CPU.

- **Volume Data** — Displays the mount status and free and used space on the server's volumes.
- **Cache Activity** — Displays a graph showing the history of the server's cache memory in terms of cache hits and percentage of free cache buffers.

> **NOTE** ZENworks for Servers 2 also enables you to display similar summary data for processors, LAN adapters, disk adapters, storage devices, threads, interrupts, memory, address spaces, interfaces, connections, users, installed software, NLMs, and volumes.

Viewing Trend Data

Another important aspect of your servers that ZENworks for Servers 2 enables you to view and monitor is trend data. ZENworks for Servers 2 is continuously gathering data about the trends in CPU usage, memory usage, and network traffic from the managed server as it is operating.

You can view the trend data from the management console in terms of current data or historically by day, week, month, or year. That trend data can be extremely useful in troubleshooting network and server issues as well as understanding the current workload on the server.

You should monitor the trend data to help with making decisions on setting trend alarm thresholds, determining peak usage of the server, balancing server loads, and allocating new resources. To view the trend data from the management console, simply right-click the server you wish to monitor and select Views ⇨ Trend from the pop-up menu, and a screen similar to the one in Figure 12.3 should be displayed.

ZENworks for Servers 2 enables you to customize the Trend Data view to give you the maximum use of the data. The following sections describe how to customize the Trend Data view by displaying the legend, modifying time spans, displaying grid lines, stacking/unstacking graphs, and modifying the Trend view profile.

Displaying the Legend

You must display a legend to understand the Trend Data view shown in Figure 12.3 and use it to understand the current status of the server. The legend is simply a window that relates the trend data parameters used in the Trend view with its color of line shown on the graph. Viewing the legend will help you understand what trends are being displayed on the server so that the graph makes sense.

USING ZENWORKS FOR SERVERS 2 SERVER MANAGEMENT

FIGURE 12.3 *Trend Data view of a NetWare server, located in the ZENworks for Servers 2 namespace in ConsoleOne*

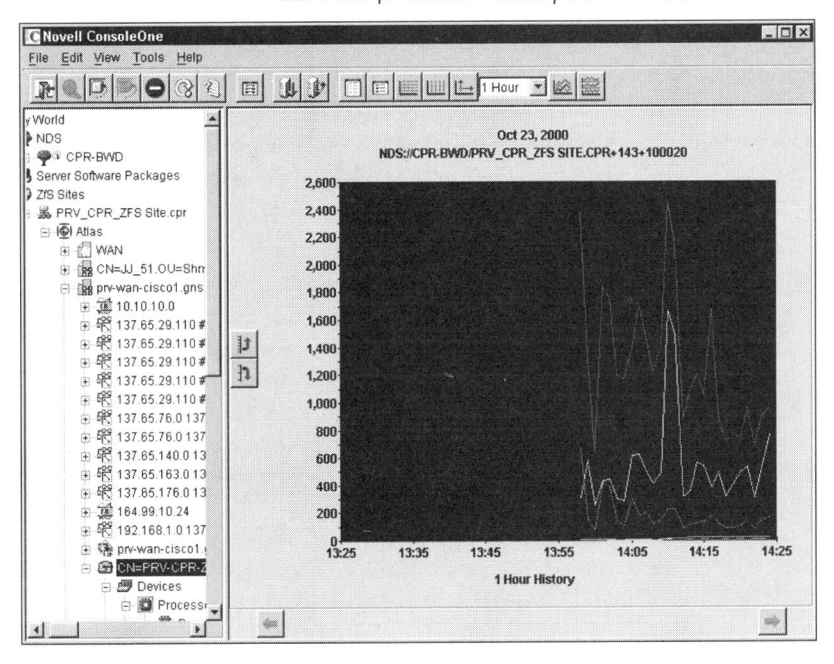

To view the Trend view legend, simply click the Legend icon in the Trend view toolbar, shown in Figure 12.3, and a pane similar to the one in Figure 12.4 appears.

FIGURE 12.4 *Legend window for the Trend Data view in ConsoleOne*

Modifying Time Spans

Once you have viewed the legend and understand what parameters the graph is showing you, modify the time spans for the trend data to give you the

343

best understanding of how the server is doing. You can modify the time span by clicking the down arrow in the toolbar of the Trend Data view and selecting one of the following time spans:

- **1 Hour**—Use the one-hour time span to show you what the current status of the server is. For example at 9 A.M. you may want to view the 1-hour span to see how the server is doing during the morning login.

- **1 Day**—Use the one-day time span to see how the server did over the past 24 hours. This can be useful to see how the server performed over a workday, or overnight while reports and backups were running.

- **1 Week**—Use the one-week time span to monitor your servers week to week. This is the most commonly used time span to judge overall usage and performance of a server.

- **1 Month**—Use the one-month time span to monitor the long-term performance of your server. This can be helpful in determining increased workload trends.

- **1 Year**—Use the one-year time span to compare the usage of your servers over the past year. This can help you determine where more servers are needed or where you can reallocate users.

Displaying Grid Lines

Another task you can perform in the Trend Data view is to display horizontal and vertical grid lines. The grid lines make the graphs easier to read. You can turn the horizontal grid lines on and off by clicking the Horizontal Grid button in the Trend Data view toolbar. Conversely, you can turn the vertical grid lines on and off by clicking the Vertical Grid button in the Trend Data view toolbar.

Stacking and Unstacking Graphs

One of the most useful ways to customize your Trend Data view is to stack and unstack the graphs. Stacking the graphs means that they are all overlaid on top of each other on a single graph with several lines for all parameters. Unstacking the graphs makes several different graphs, each with its own line for a single parameter, as shown in Figure 12.5. (Figure 12.3 shows what a graph would look like stacked.)

USING ZENWORKS FOR SERVERS 2 SERVER MANAGEMENT

FIGURE 12.5 *Unstacked Trend Data view of a NetWare server, located in the ZENworks for Servers 2 namespace in ConsoleOne*

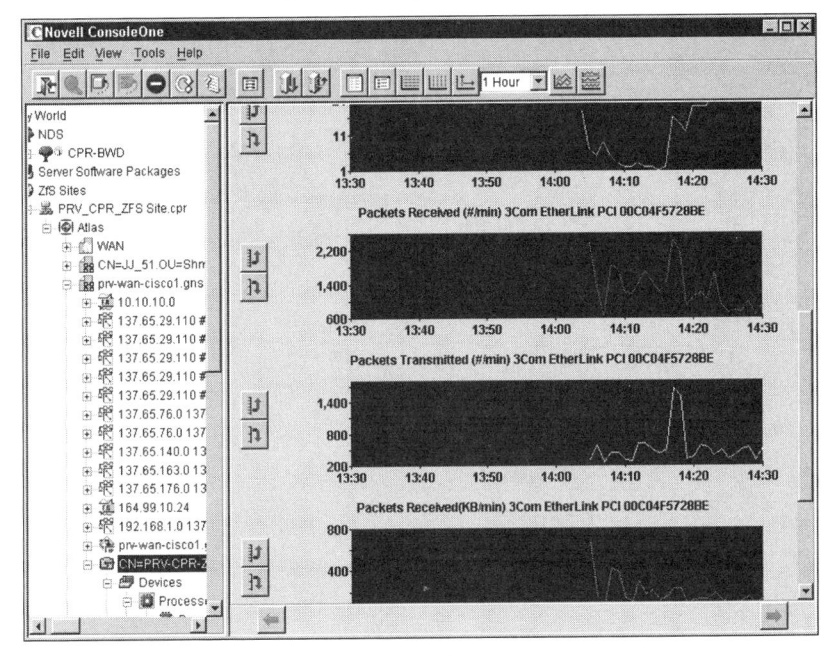

To stack the graphs on top of each other, simply click the Stack Chart button on the Trend Data view toolbar. To unstack the graphs, simply click the Strip Chart button on the Trend Data view toolbar.

Modifying the Trend View Profile

The biggest way to modify the Trend Data view is to modify the Trend view profile. The Trend view profile is basically the set of parameters that are displayed on the Trend view graph. You should modify the Trend view profile to best fit your servers and your environment.

Use the following steps to modify the Trend view profile:

1. Click the Profile button in the Trend Data view toolbar. A window similar to the one in Figure 12.6 appears.

345

FIGURE 12.6 Trend view Profile Settings window for the Trend Data view in ConsoleOne

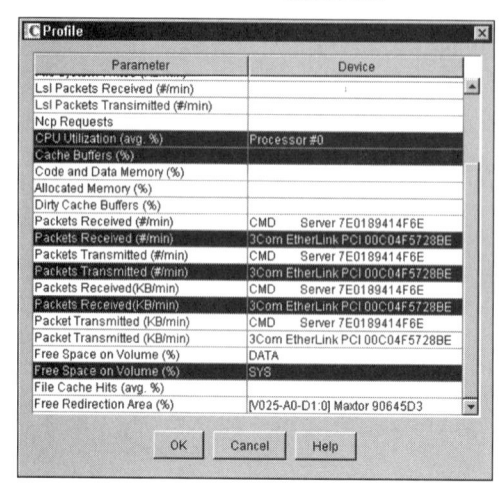

2. Edit the profile by clicking the parameters to either select or deselect them. Use the Shift+click and Ctrl+click methods to select multiple parameters.

3. Click OK to apply the setting and the Trend Data view should be updated.

Managing Trend Samplings

Now that you understand how to view the trend data, you need to know how to manage the way that the data is collected. ZENworks for Servers 2 enables you to modify the trend data sampling rates and thresholds used to collect the data. The following sections discuss how to use the management console to customize trend sampling to fit your network.

Modifying Trend Samplings and Intervals

The first step in managing trend sampling is to set the sampling and interval rates for trend parameters. Setting the sampling rate effectively determines the duration for which data from a particular parameter is collected by specifying the number of samples to take. Setting the interval rate determines how often data is collected from a particular parameter.

Use the following steps to set the sampling and intervals for trend data parameters:

1. Right-click the server object and select Properties from the pop-up menu.
2. Select the Trend tab, as shown in Figure 12.7.

FIGURE 12.7 *Trend tab for a managed server object in ConsoleOne*

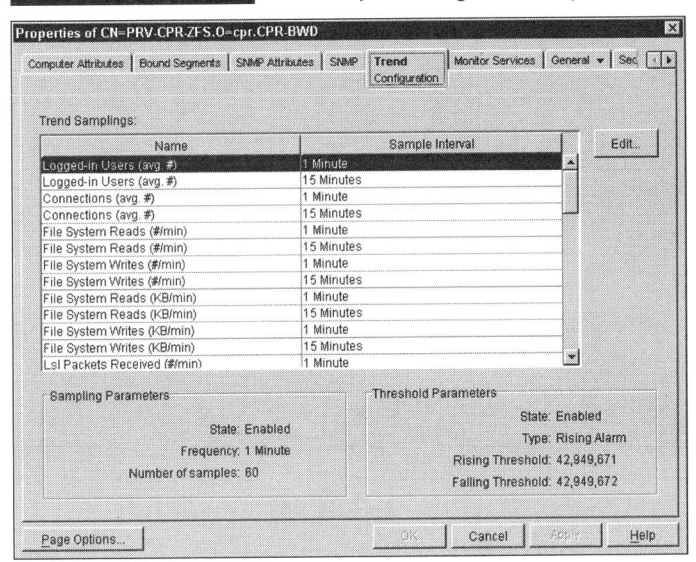

Properties of CN=PRV-CPR-ZFS.O=cpr.CPR-BWD

Tabs: Computer Attributes | Bound Segments | SNMP Attributes | SNMP | **Trend Configuration** | Monitor Services | General ▼ | Sec

Trend Samplings:

Name	Sample Interval
Logged-in Users (avg. #)	1 Minute
Logged-in Users (avg. #)	15 Minutes
Connections (avg. #)	1 Minute
Connections (avg. #)	15 Minutes
File System Reads (#/min)	1 Minute
File System Reads (#/min)	15 Minutes
File System Writes (#/min)	1 Minute
File System Writes (#/min)	15 Minutes
File System Reads (KB/min)	1 Minute
File System Reads (KB/min)	15 Minutes
File System Writes (KB/min)	1 Minute
File System Writes (KB/min)	15 Minutes
LsI Packets Received (#/min)	1 Minute

Edit...

Sampling Parameters:
State: Enabled
Frequency: 1 Minute
Number of samples: 60

Threshold Parameters:
State: Enabled
Type: Rising Alarm
Rising Threshold: 42,949,671
Falling Threshold: 42,949,672

Page Options... | OK | Cancel | Apply | Help

3. Select the trend parameter you wish to modify and click the Edit button. An Edit Trend dialog box is displayed.
4. From the State drop-down list in the Edit Trend dialog box, shown in Figure 12.8, select Enabled to enable trend sampling for the parameter.
5. Modify the time interval by selecting a value from the Frequency drop-down list. Values are from five minutes to one day.
6. Specify the duration of time for which to collect samples by entering a value in the "Number of samples" field.
7. Click the OK button and the parameter will be modified.

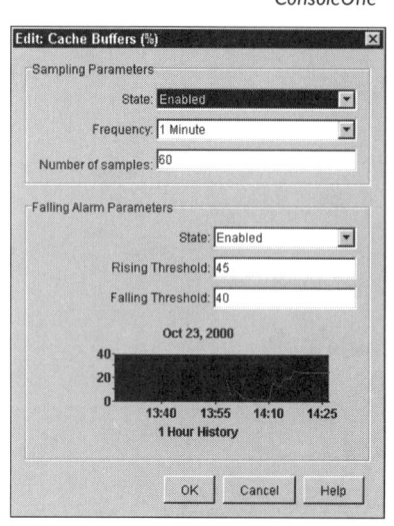

FIGURE 12.8 *Edit Trend dialog box for trend data parameters in ConsoleOne*

Modifying Threshold Alarm Settings

Once you have set the sampling and interval rates for the trend data parameter, you need to set the threshold alarm settings for the parameter as well. Modifying the threshold alarm settings for a particular parameter controls the range at which the parameter can operate before triggering an alarm. It also controls the scope of the graph in the Trend Data view.

Use the following steps to modify the threshold alarm setting for a trend data parameter:

1. Right-click the server object and select Properties from the pop-up menu.
2. Select the Trend tab, as shown in Figure 12.7.
3. Select the trend parameter you wish to modify and click the Edit button. An Edit Trend dialog box is displayed.
4. From the Edit Trend dialog box, shown in Figure 12.8, select Enable in the Alarm section to enable trend sampling for the parameter.
5. Set the Rising Threshold to a value that reflects a safe amount for the parameter.

6. Set the Falling Threshold to a value that reflects an unhealthy state for the parameter.
7. Click the OK button and the parameter will be modified.

> **NOTE** An alarm is sent the first time the rising threshold is surpassed, and if the parameter never dips back below the falling threshold, an alarm will not be re-sent if the rising threshold is surpassed again. In other words, for an alarm to be sent again after it has already been sent once, it has to dip down below the falling threshold and then surpass the rising threshold again.

Configuring Server Parameters

Another server management innovation that ZENworks for Servers 2 provides is the ability to modify server parameters without being at the server itself or having a remote management session open to it. ZENworks for Servers 2 enables you to modify the managed server's NDS object to make changes to its parameters.

Use the following steps to modify server parameters from within ConsoleOne:

1. Select the server object in the ZENworks for Servers 2 namespace.
2. Right-click the server object and select Properties from the pop-up menu.
3. Select the Set Parameters tab.
4. Click the down arrow and select the category of set parameters you wish to change from the pull-down list, shown in Figure 12.9.
5. Select the specific parameter you wish to modify and click the Edit button.
6. From the Edit Parameters dialog box, shown in Figure 12.10, enter the new value for the parameter into the field (the field type will change based on the parameter selected).
7. Indicate when you wish the change to occur by selecting one of the following times: "Now, until reboot" (the change disappears after the server is rebooted), "Only after reboot" (the change does not take effect until the server is rebooted), or "Now, and after reboot" (the change is made immediately and permanently).
8. Click the OK button and the change to the parameter will be made according to the criteria you selected.

> **NOTE** This is a way to manually change set parameters on a server-by-server basis. If you want to do this on more than one server at a time throughout your network, you would use the Server Policy Package – Set Parameters policy in the policies piece of ZENworks for Servers.

FIGURE 12.9 Set Parameters tab for server objects in the ZENworks for Servers namespace in ConsoleOne

FIGURE 12.10 Edit Parameters dialog box for server set parameters in ConsoleOne

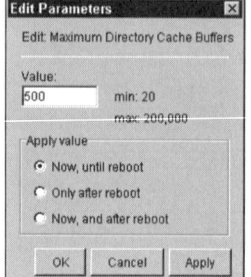

USING ZENWORKS FOR SERVERS 2 SERVER MANAGEMENT

Executing Server Commands

Another server management innovation that ZENworks for Servers 2 provides is the ability to execute server commands without being at the server itself or having a remote management session open to it.

Earlier in this chapter we discussed how to navigate the server object portion of the ZENworks for Servers 2 namespace to view configuration data. You can also use the server level of the ZENworks for Servers 2 namespace to execute server commands at the server level or below.

ZENworks for Servers 2 enables you to execute the following server commands from the ZENworks for Servers 2 namespace area in ConsoleOne:

- **Loading and unloading NLMs** — You can load or unload an NLM by right-clicking the NLM object in the ZENworks for Servers 2 namespace and selecting Load or Unload from the Command menu.

- **Mounting and dismounting volumes** — You can mount or dismount a volume by right-clicking the volume object in the ZENworks for Servers 2 namespace and selecting Mount or Dismount from the Command menu.

- **Clearing a server connection** — You can clear a server connection by right-clicking the connection in the ZENworks for Servers namespace (Server ⇨ Operating System ⇨ Network ⇨ Connections) and selecting Clear Connection from the Command menu.

- **Restarting a server** — You can restart a server by right-clicking the server object in the ZENworks for Servers namespace and selecting Restart Server from the Command menu.

- **Shutting down a server:** You can shut down a server by right-clicking the server object in the ZENworks for Servers namespace and selecting Down Server from the Command menu.

Managing Remote Servers

Managing servers remotely has become an industry standard as companies have increased the number of servers, which require large data centers. ZENworks for Servers 2 greatly enhances the ability to remotely manage servers through the addition of applications that enable you to remotely take control of the server. The following sections describe how to use the ZENworks for Servers 2 management console to remotely manage a server.

Managing Remote NetWare Servers

ZENworks for Servers 2 adds the ability to use the RCONSOLEJ utility provided with NetWare 5.x to remotely manage a server from the management console. This enables you to manage NetWare servers based on your role in the organization and tasks assigned to you.

You can use ZENworks for Servers 2 remote management capability to perform the following role-based remote management tasks on a managed NetWare Server:

- **Console commands** — Remotely execute console commands just as if you were at the server. For example, you may wish to execute a command to start or stop an NDS trace.

- **Scan directories** — Scan directories looking for installed software, data files, or file locations.

- **Edit text files** — Edit text files on both NetWare and DOS partitions to modify scripts or other files.

- **Transfer files** — Send files to the server to update an application or data. You cannot transfer files from a server due to security reasons.

- **Install or upgrade** — Perform an install or upgrade. For example, you can remotely install the latest NetWare support pack to the server.

Use the following steps to begin a remote management session with a NetWare server from the ZENworks for Servers 2 management console on an IP-only server:

1. Load the RCONSOLEJ agent (RCONAG6.NLM) on the NetWare Server.
2. Right-click the server object in ConsoleOne and select Remote Console from the pop-up menu.
3. Enter the RCONSOLEJ agent password.
4. Enter the TCP port number on which the agent will listen for requests from RCONSOLEJ. (The default value is 2034.)
5. Click the Connect button and an RCONSOLEJ session similar to the one shown in Figure 12.11 loads.

USING ZENWORKS FOR SERVERS 2 SERVER MANAGEMENT

FIGURE 12.11 *RCONSOLEJ remote management session launched from ConsoleOne*

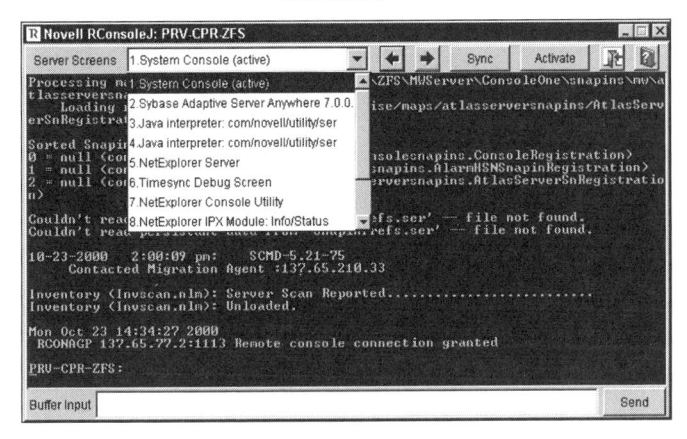

Use the following steps to begin a remote management session with a NetWare server from the ZENworks for Servers 2 management console on an IPX-only server:

1. Load the RCONSOLEJ agent (RCONAG6.NLM) on the NetWare Server.
2. Right-click the server object in ConsoleOne and select Remote Console from the pop-up menu.
3. Enter the RCONSOLEJ agent password.
4. Enter the TCP port number on which the agent will listen for requests from RCONSOLEJ. (The default value is 2034.)
5. Enter the IP address of the proxy server or choose a proxy server in the Proxy Server options section of the RCONSOLEJ window. The server acting as a proxy server for the RCONSOLEJ session needs to be running both IP and IPX so it can communicate with both the workstation and the IPX server.
6. Enter the SPX port number on which the agent will listen for requests from the proxy server.
7. Click the Connect button and an RCONSOLEJ session similar to the one shown in Figure 12.11 loads.

353

Managing Remote NT Servers

ZENworks for Servers 2 adds the ability to remotely manage a Windows NT server from the management console. This enables you to manage Windows NT servers based on your role in the organization and tasks assigned to you.

You can use ZENworks for Servers 2 remote management capability to perform the following role-based remote management tasks on a managed Windows NT Server:

- **Remote control** — Enables you to remotely take control of a Windows NT server to resolve any software-related problems and perform any administrative tasks.

- **Remote view** — Enables you to remotely view the desktop of the Windows NT server. This enables you to monitor activity on the NT server and see when actions are performed.

Use the following steps to begin a remote management session with a Windows NT server from the ZENworks for Servers management console:

1. Verify that the remote management agent installed with the ZENworks for Servers 2 install is running the on the Windows NT server you wish to manage.

2. Right-click the server object from within ConsoleOne.

3. Click Remote Operation ⇨ Control to open a remote control session, or Remote Operation ⇨ View to open a remote view session.

4. Enter the password for the ZENworks for Servers 2 Remote management agent and the remote management session should be activated.

> **NOTE**
> During a remote management session, the user of the Windows NT server receives an audible signal indicating that they are being accessed. Every five seconds the user receives a visible signal displaying the name of the user accessing the remote server. These setting can be changed by selecting Edit Security Parameters from the Remote Management icon's pop-up menu in the task bar of the remote server.

Optimizing Server Management

Now that you understand how ZENworks for Servers 2 uses trend data and alarm thresholds to help you manage your servers, you need to know how to optimize the data that ZENworks for Servers 2 gathers for you. When a managed server is first started, agents for trend data, alarm thresholds, and alarm

USING ZENWORKS FOR SERVERS 2 SERVER MANAGEMENT

management are loaded and begin collecting data. The best way to optimize server management is to control the initial settings that are loaded on your servers.

The following sections describe how to modify the configuration files that initialize the server management agents to give you tight control over the information collected and presented at the management console.

Setting Initial Trend Values

The first configuration file you should know how to modify is the trend initialization file. This file sets the initial trends for monitoring a device. Each time a new managed device is discovered on the server, a trend file is created for it.

The trend initialization file is named NTREND.INI on a NetWare server and N_NTREND.INI on a Windows NT server. The following sections describe how to use a text editor to modify the initial trend file shown in Figure 12.12.

FIGURE 12.12 *Trend initialization file for a NetWare server*

```
# ntrend.ini - Notepad
File  Edit  Search  Help
#
# Having two thresholds prevents multiple traps being generated for what
# is essentially a single event.  This is ilustrated diagramatically below.
#
#      Alarm         Alarm       Alarm          Alarm
#        v             v           v              v
#        .             .           .
# |-----.-.-.------.----|-.-----------.-.------ Rising Threshold
# |         .       .   |      .     .
# |              .      |         .    .
# |--.------------.-----|----.-.---.-.--------.--- Falling Threshold
# | .                   |       .       .
# |.                    |
# |--------------------  |---------------------
#      Rising Alarm           Falling Alarm
#
# Edit the following table to change the initial values for each
# trend and Threshold.
#
#------------------------------------------------------------------
#                   | Sample  |    Trend      |     Threshold       |
# Parameter         | Interval| Buckets Enbl  | Rising Falling Enbl Type |
#------------------------------------------------------------------
NUMBER_LOGGED_IN_USERS    5       60   1        100    90   1  rising
NUMBER_LOGGED_IN_USERS    7     8928   1         90    81   1  rising

NUMBER_CONNECTIONS        5       60   1          0     0   0  rising
NUMBER_CONNECTIONS        7     8928   1          0     0   0  rising

FILE_READS                5       60   1          0     0   0  rising
FILE_READS                7     8928   1          0     0   0  rising
```

Setting the Sample Interval The first column in the trend initialization file is the parameter name, and the second is the sample interval. The sample interval indicates the frequency that samples of the specified parameter are collected in terms of a time interval between five seconds and one day.

You should evaluate each parameter to determine how often it should be sampled. If you sample too often, you run the risk of poor performance. However, if you do not sample often enough, you run the risk of incomplete or inaccurate information.

Use the codes listed in Table 12.1 to set the sample interval for each trend data parameter.

TABLE 12.1 *Sample Interval Codes for Trend Initialization*

TREND INITIALIZATION CODE	SAMPLE INTERVAL RATE
1	5 seconds
2	10 seconds
3	15 seconds
4	30 seconds
5	1 minute
6	5 minutes
7	15 minutes
8	30 minutes
9	1 hour
10	4 hours
11	8 hours
12	1 day

Setting the Trend Buckets Once you have set the sample interval for the trend data parameters, you need to set the number of trend buckets in the third column. Setting the number of trend buckets determine the duration of time for which samples will be collected for the parameter.

For example, if you wish to review the number of users logged into a server for one day and you set the sample interval to be 30 minutes, you need to specify 48 trend buckets. Each bucket contains one sample taken at a 30-minute interval.

After a particular time duration is exceeded for a file, the oldest trend buckets are emptied and replaced with the most recent samples. Therefore, once the duration has been reached, you will always have samples for that amount of time from the present backward.

Enabling and Disabling Trend Files The fourth column in the trend initialization file is the Enable Trend Data option. This value can be set to either 0 or 1. Specifying 1 enables the gathering of trend data for this parameter. Specifying 0 disables the gathering of trend data for the parameter.

Setting Initial Threshold Values

Once you have set up the initial trend values, you need to specify the threshold values for alarm generation. Alarm thresholds control the values at which alarms are generated.

Two values are associated with these thresholds: a rising limit and a falling limit. For rising thresholds, the rising limit is the value at which an alarm is generated for the parameter. The falling limit, for rising thresholds, is the value at which the alarm is reset. They work conversely for falling thresholds. This way, an alarm is only generated when a server goes from a good condition to a bad condition — not if it simply stays in a bad state.

For example, if you have set a falling threshold on cache buffers and set a falling limit of 30 percent and a rising limit of 50 percent, the server would send out an alarm if cache buffers got below 30%. If the cache buffers then wavered between 25 and 35 percent, only the one alarm would be sent. However, if the servers' cache buffers climbed back up to 60 percent and then back down to 30 percent, a second alarm would be sent.

Setting Rising and Falling Thresholds The fifth and sixth columns in the trend initialization file are the rising and falling limits, respectively. They represent a value that indicates a problem for the trend parameter and a value that indicates the trend parameter is out of trouble.

You need to evaluate each parameter to determine the appropriate threshold limits and specify them in their columns. You also need to specify which type of threshold the parameter has by putting "rising" or "falling" in the Type column of the trend initialization file.

Enabling and Disabling Threshold Traps Once you have specified the limits you can enable or disable the threshold trap by specifying 0 or 1 in the seventh column. Specifying 0 disables alarm generation for the parameter. Specifying 1 enables alarm generation for the parameter.

Configuring Alarm Generation

The next configuration file you should know how to modify is the trap configuration file, which controls alarm generation. The trap configuration file consists of keywords with associated information about alarm generation.

The trap configuration file is located in the following locations on the managed servers:

- **NetWare** — SYS:\ETC\NWTRAP.CFG
- **Windows NT** — \MW\INI\NTTRAP.INI

The following sections describe how to modify the trap configuration file, shown in Figure 12.13, to modify the types of alarms forwarded to management consoles, community strings used for sending SNMP traps, traps to be disabled, and specific alarms that you wish to prevent from being forwarded.

FIGURE 12.13 *Trap configuration file, NWTRAP.CFG, for a NetWare server*

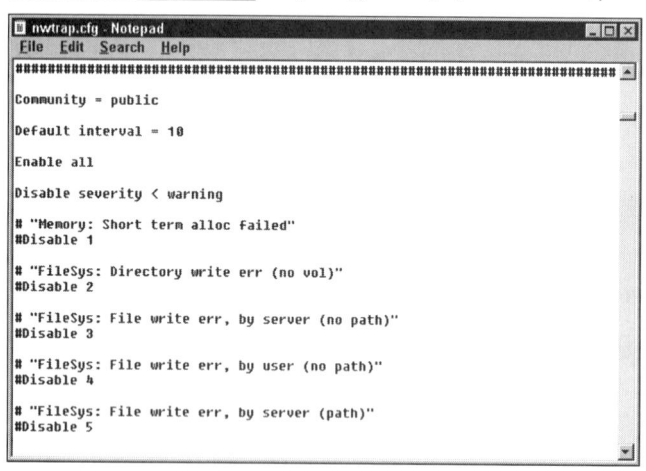

```
Community = public
Default interval = 10
Enable all
Disable severity < warning

# "Memory: Short term alloc failed"
#Disable 1

# "FileSys: Directory write err (no vol)"
#Disable 2

# "FileSys: File write err, by server (no path)"
#Disable 3

# "FileSys: File write err, by user (no path)"
#Disable 4

# "FileSys: File write err, by server (path)"
#Disable 5
```

Setting the Community String The first thing you can set in a trap configuration file is the community string. The community string is used to generate traps and is restricted to 32 characters. The default community string is public.

Setting the Time Interval Once you have set the community string, you need to specify the time interval that alarm generation will wait before issuing the next alarm. This is to prevent the network and management console from being inundated with identical alarms. The time interval can be any value between 0 and 232.

USING ZENWORKS FOR SERVERS 2 SERVER MANAGEMENT

For example, if you wished to set the amount of time between alarms for traps 5, 10, and 100 to 20 seconds, you would use the following command in the trap configuration file:

```
5 10 100 INTERVAL = 20
```

Configuring Alarm Security Levels   Once you have specified the time interval for alarms, you should set the severity levels for alarm generation. Each SNMP alarm has a severity level associated with it. You can specify at what severity level to generate alarms so that only those alarms are actually sent to the management console.

You can use the ENABLE and DISABLE commands, with a severity level code or number, in the alarm configuration file to control which severity levels to pass through. Table 12.2 shows the severity levels for alarm generation and the associated codes for the configuration file.

The following are examples of specifying severity levels in the configuration file:

```
ENABLE SEVERITY >= MINOR
DISABLE SEVERITY <= WARN
```

TABLE 12.2   *Severity Levels and Codes for Alarms*

NETWARE SEVERITY	SNMP SEVERITY	ZFS SEVERITY	SEVERITY CODE
0 - Informational	Informational	Informational	INFORM
1 - Warning	Minor	Minor	WARN
2 - Recoverable	Major	Major	MINOR
3 - Critical	Critical	Critical	MAJOR
4 - Fatal	Fatal	Critical	CRITICAL
5 - Operation Aborted	Fatal	Critical	CRITICAL
Unrecoverable	Fatal	Critical	CRITICAL

Defining Alarm Recipients

The final configuration file you should know how to modify to optimize server management is the TRAPTARG.CFG file. The TRAPTARG.CFG file is used to send traps to third-party management consoles. It defines recipients of SNMP traps that are detected on the server.

If you plan to use third-party management consoles or utilities to monitor SNMP traps, you need to add their IP address or IPX address to the TRAPTARG.CFG file for alarms to be sent to them.

Use the following steps to modify the TRAPTARG.CFG file:

1. Open the file in a text editor.
2. Add the IPX network number and MAC address of any management consoles to the IPX section of the TRAPTARG.CFG file — for example, FFFF1111:00001B123456.
3. Add the IP address or logical name, if you have DNS configured, of any management consoles to the UDP section of the TRAPTARG.CFG file — for example, 111.111.5.2. If DNS is configured in your network, you can use the logical name.
4. Save the file.
5. Unload and reload NWTRAP.NLM on the agent server.

Using ZENworks for Servers 2 Server Inventory

Another important component of ZENworks for Servers 2 server management is the server inventory. ZENworks for Servers 2 uses inventory scan programs to scan and store hardware and software inventory of your managed servers.

The following sections describe the inventory components and discuss how to scan server inventory and customize software scanning.

Understanding the Inventory Server Components

The ZENworks for Servers 2 server inventory component is made up three subcomponents, each of which is responsible for either gathering data, storing data, or managing data. The following sections describe the inventory gatherer, inventory storer, and inventory manager database pieces of the ZENworks for Servers 2 server inventory component.

Inventory Gatherer

The inventory gatherer is responsible for collecting information from the scan programs and relaying it to the inventory storer. The data that the gatherer collects is stored in temporary files on the server.

The following is a list of pieces that make up the inventory gatherer and storer:

- **ZENINV.NLM** — Executable application that runs on the server.
- **GATHERER.NCF** — Script file that launches the inventory gatherer on the server.
- **STORER.NCF** — Script file that launches the inventory storer on the server.
- **STR_DIR** — Command-line option that specifies the location where temporary files should be stored. The default location is SYS:SYSTEM\STRFILES.
- **SYS:ETC\ZENINV.LOG** — Logs information and errors that occur in the gathering process.

Inventory Storer

The inventory storer is responsible for sending the information collected by the inventory gatherer to the inventory database. The inventory storer reads the files located in the STR_DIR directory and creates them as objects inside the inventory database. Once the objects are created, the temporary files are deleted. The files it reads and then deletes have an .STR extension.

Inventory Manager Database

The ZENworks for Servers inventory database is a centralized CIM-compliant Sybase database that is located on the management server in the \ZFS\DB directory on the volume you chose to install it to. For more information on the inventory database, see Appendix B.

Scanning Inventory of Servers

The ZENworks for Servers 2 inventory scan program scans managed servers' hardware and software, enabling you to collect inventory data on both NetWare and Windows NT servers. The following sections describe how to use the ZENworks for Servers 2 scanning software on NetWare and NT servers.

Inventory Scanning on NetWare

The NetWare scan program collects data from NetWare 4.x and later servers. After it has collected the inventory data from the server, it sends that information back to the inventory gatherer. Then the inventory storer grabs the .STR files that are created and injects the information into the database. Inventory scanning on NetWare servers is made up of the following components:

- **INVSCAN.NLM** — Scanning application that runs on a NetWare server and searches for hardware and software.
- **INVSCAN.INI** — Contains setting for the INVSCAN.NLM applications that are set at load time. See Table 12.3 for a description of the settings.
- **SCANNER.NCF** — Script that launches the scanner on the NetWare server.

TABLE 12.3 Settings in INVSCAN.NII for INVSCAN.NLM

SETTING	DESCRIPTION
inv_server=<server_name>	Indicates which server is the inventory server.
file=<location_of_software_description_file>	Identifies the path to the software description file (SWAPPL.INI). The default location is SYS:\ETC.
protocols=<IP_or_IPX>	Determines the protocol that INVSCAN.NLM uses to communicate with the inventory server.

Inventory Scanning on Windows NT

The Windows NT scan program collects data from Windows NT 3.5 and later servers. After it has collected the inventory data from the server, it sends that information back to the inventory gatherer. Then the inventory storer grabs the .STR files that are created and injects the information into the database. Inventory scanning on NT servers is made up of the following components:

- **NTSCAN32.EXE** — Windows application that runs on the NT server and searches for hardware and software.

USING ZENWORKS FOR SERVERS 2 SERVER MANAGEMENT

- **NTSCAN32.INI** — Contains setting for the NTSCAN32.EXE applications that are set at runtime. See Table 12.4 for a description of the settings.

- **ZENworks for Servers 2 Inventory Service** — Service that is set up at startup time on the Windows NT server that launches the scan program.

TABLE 12.4 *Settings in NTSCAN32.INI for NTSCAN32.EXE*

SETTING	DESCRIPTION
InvServer=<server_name>	Indicates which server is the inventory server
InvPath=<location_of_NTSCAN.EXE>	Indicates the directory where NTSCANE.EXE is installed to

Customizing Software Application Scanning

ZENworks for Servers 2 provides a tremendous amount of control in determining what software is scanned on your managed servers. The following sections describe how to use the Software Scan Editor to perform the following tasks:

- Modifying the details of the application listed in the Software Scan Editor
- Specifying applications that you wish to scan
- Modifying the list of file scan extensions that the scan program will scan on managed servers
- Deleting applications from being scanned

Understanding the Software Description File

One of the most useful ways to customize software scanning is to modify the software description file. The software description file is a file that contains details of the software list specified by the software scan editor. The filename is SWAPPL.INI and it is usually located in the SYS:\ETC directory.

The following is a list of components that make up the software description file, shown in Figure 12.14:

FIGURE 12.14 *Software description file, SWAPPL.INI, for a NetWare Server*

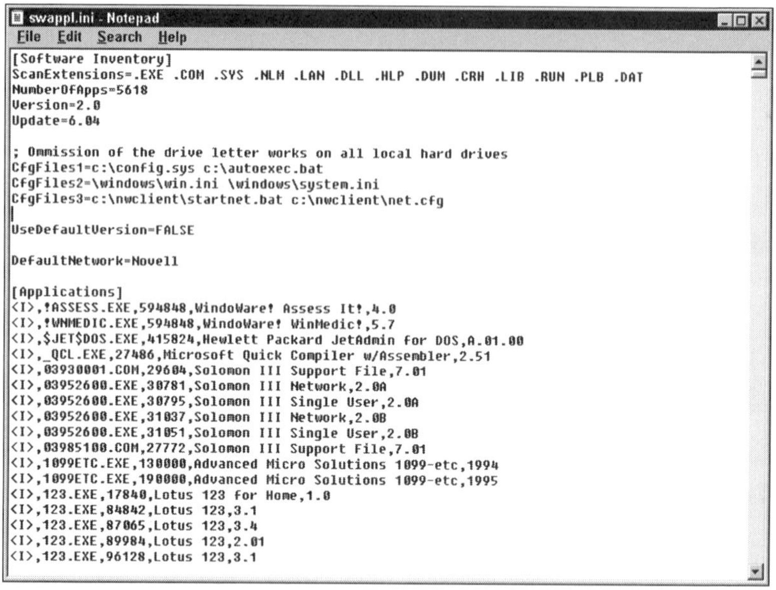

```
swappl.ini - Notepad
File Edit Search Help
[Software Inventory]
ScanExtensions=.EXE .COM .SYS .NLM .LAN .DLL .HLP .DUM .CRH .LIB .RUN .PLB .DAT
NumberOfApps=5618
Version=2.0
Update=6.04

; Ommission of the drive letter works on all local hard drives
CfgFiles1=c:\config.sys c:\autoexec.bat
CfgFiles2=\windows\win.ini \windows\system.ini
CfgFiles3=c:\nwclient\startnet.bat c:\nwclient\net.cfg

UseDefaultVersion=FALSE

DefaultNetwork=Novell

[Applications]
<I>,!ASSESS.EXE,594848,WindoWare! Assess It!,4.0
<I>,!WNMEDIC.EXE,594848,WindoWare! WinMedic!,5.7
<I>,$JET$DOS.EXE,415824,Hewlett Packard JetAdmin for DOS,A.01.00
<I>,_QCL.EXE,27486,Microsoft Quick Compiler w/Assembler,2.51
<I>,03930001.COM,29604,Solomon III Support File,7.01
<I>,03952600.EXE,30781,Solomon III Network,2.0A
<I>,03952600.EXE,30795,Solomon III Single User,2.0A
<I>,03952600.EXE,31037,Solomon III Network,2.0B
<I>,03952600.EXE,31051,Solomon III Single User,2.0B
<I>,03985100.COM,27772,Solomon III Support File,7.01
<I>,1099ETC.EXE,130000,Advanced Micro Solutions 1099-etc,1994
<I>,1099ETC.EXE,190000,Advanced Micro Solutions 1099-etc,1995
<I>,123.EXE,17840,Lotus 123 for Home,1.0
<I>,123.EXE,84842,Lotus 123,3.1
<I>,123.EXE,87065,Lotus 123,3.4
<I>,123.EXE,89984,Lotus 123,2.01
<I>,123.EXE,96128,Lotus 123,3.1
```

- **Scanextensions** — List of extensions that specifies the type of files that will be scanned looking for installed software.
- **NumberofApps** — Displays the number of applications listed in the file.
- **Version** — Version number of the SWAPPL.INI file.
- **Update** — Update number of the SWAPPL.INI file.
- **CfgFiles#** — Lists the configuration files that the scan program will scan looking for installed software. The # sign represents a number of multiple entries, such as CfgFiles1, CfgFiles2, and CfgFiles3.
- **Applications** — Lists the details of the application, including ScanMethod(<I>), filename with extension, file size in bytes, application name, and application version.

Adding Applications for Scanning

One of the most common tasks that you need to perform in the Software Scan Editor, shown in Figure 12.15, is adding new applications that need to be scanned for. You will need to do this if you add new applications to your network that are not already in the software scan editor.

FIGURE 12.15 *Software Scan Editor window for a server object in ConsoleOne*

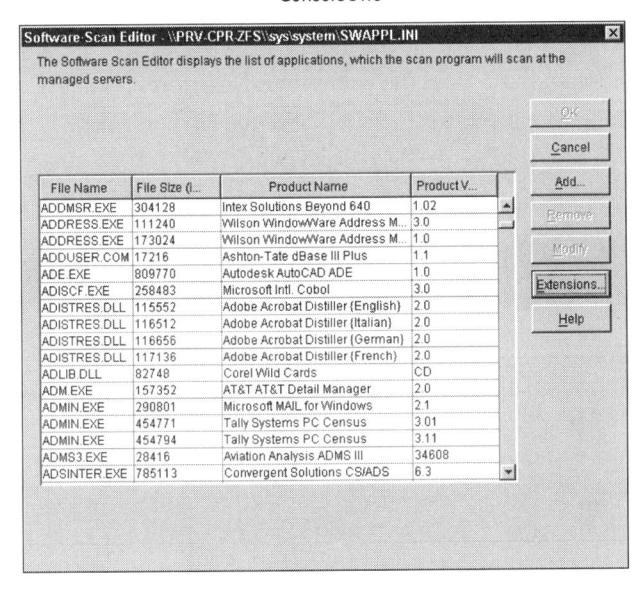

Use the following steps from within ConsoleOne to add a new application for scanning:

1. Right-click the managed server objects and select Actions ➪ Software Scan Editor from the pop-up menu.
2. Click the Add button and the Add Application dialog box appears.
3. Specify the application name, filename, file size, and product version in the fields provided.
4. Click the OK button to close the Add Application dialog box.
5. Click the OK button to close the Software Scan Editor dialog box and the changes are made to the SWAPPL.INI file.

Editing File Extensions for Scanning

The second most common task you will perform in the Software Scan Editor, next to adding new applications, is to edit the list of file extensions used for software scanning. You may wish to add new extensions, such as CGI, to the file extension list to scan for additional applications. A maximum of 12 extensions can be specified for scanning.

Use the following steps from within ConsoleOne to specify new file extensions for scanning software on managed servers:

1. Right-click the managed server objects and select Actions ⇨ Software Scan Editor from the pop-up menu.
2. Click the Extensions button and the Extensions dialog box appears.
3. Type the extensions that you wish to scan for in the field provided.
4. Click the OK button to close the Extensions dialog box.
5. Click the OK button to close the Software Scan Editor dialog box and the changes are made to the SWAPPL.INI file.

Removing an Application from Scanning

ZENworks for Servers 2 also enables you to remove applications from the Software Scan Editor list. You may wish to do this if an application is no longer being used on your network. Removing unwanted applications from scanning makes the scanning process run faster and take fewer resources.

Use the following steps, from within ConsoleOne to remove an application from being scanned for on managed servers:

1. Right-click the managed server objects and select Actions ⇨ Software Scan Editor from the pop-up menu.
2. Select the application you wish to remove.
3. Click the Remove button and the application will be removed from the list.
4. Click the OK button to close the Software Scan Editor dialog box and the changes are made to the SWAPPL.INI file.

NOTE You can also manually modify the SWAPPL.INI file with a text editor if you type the new entries in with the proper syntax.

CHAPTER 13

Making the Most of ZENworks for Servers 2 Reporting

One of the most powerful tools included with ZENworks for Servers is its extensive reporting engine. ZENworks for Servers has the ability to generate reports for you that show you everything from your server inventory to network health. Using ZENworks for Servers reporting can be a useful tool in helping you understand the condition of your network and plan for future additions.

The following sections describe understanding, creating, and using server inventory reports, topology reports, network health reports, and TED reports to quickly understand and administer your network.

Reading ZENworks for Servers Reports

The first step in making the most out of ZENworks for Servers reports is to understand what types of reports are available and what information can be obtained from them. ZENworks for Servers provides inventory reports that enable you to create lists of hardware and services available on your network to use for tracking and planning your network resources. You can use topology reports, generated by ZENworks, to understand the layout and design of your network, enabling you to plan for future growth. ZENworks for Servers also includes health reports that you can use to understand the overall health of your network and quickly diagnose issues. Reports on TED distribution are also provided to enable you to understand the current status of your distribution to determine progress and any errors that might have occurred.

This section describes the four different groups of ZENworks for Servers 2 reports and discusses the information found in them.

Understanding Server Inventory Reports

ZENworks for Servers enables you to create inventory reports of hardware and software that are located on your managed servers. These reports can be very useful to you if you need to know what hardware or software is on a particular machine.

For example, let's say you wish to install new server software that requires a server with a minimum of 256MB of RAM and a processor speed of at least 500 MHz. You can use ZENworks for Servers 2 to generate a report of all NetWare servers that are possible candidates for the software.

The following sections describe the two different types of inventory reports that can be generated by ZENworks for Servers: simple inventory lists and comprehensive inventory lists.

MAKING THE MOST OF ZENWORKS FOR SERVERS 2 REPORTING

Simple Inventory List Reports

The most common report you will likely use is the simple inventory list report. The simple inventory list report enables you to selectively create reports on every aspect of you server by selecting specific criteria that must be matched.

Simple inventory list reports are usually generated very quickly, so the information you need will be almost instantaneously available. You may wish to run several different inventory list reports, shown in Table 13.1, depending on what information you need.

TABLE 13.1 *Available Server Inventory List Reports*

REPORT NAME	INFORMATION PROVIDED
Server Scan Time Listing	Date and time of the last inventory scan on each server. Useful to know how up-to-date the report is.
Server Operating System Listing	List of all servers with the specified OS Version and OS. Essential if you plan to upgrade your servers.
Server BIOS Listing	List of all servers with BIOS release date and the total number of such servers. Essential if your manufacturer releases a BIOS update.
Server Processor Family Listing	List of all servers with a specific processor family. Useful for software upgrades.
Server Processor Speed Greater than Listing	List of all servers whose processor speed is greater than or equal to a specific value.
Server Processor Speed Less than Listing	List of all servers with a processor speed lesser than or equal to a specific value.
Server Memory More than Listing	List of all servers with memory greater than or equal to a specified MB value.
Server Memory Less than Listing	List of all servers with memory less than or equal to a specified MB value.
Server Video Adapter Listing	List of all servers with a specific video adapter.
Server Network Adapter Listing	List of all servers with a specific network interface card.

(continued)

TABLE 13.1 *Available Server Inventory List Reports (continued)*

REPORT NAME	INFORMATION PROVIDED
Server Software Listing by Software	List of all servers with software installed on them. Listed in order by software.
Server Software Listing by Software	List of all servers with software installed on them. Listed in order by server.
Software Summary Listing	List of the number of servers with a particular software and version installed on them.

Comprehensive Inventory Reports

The other type of inventory report that you will use is the comprehensive inventory reports. The comprehensive inventory reports combine several aspects of server inventory into each report. They take considerably longer to generate; however, they are more specific and inclusive.

You will typically use one of the comprehensive inventory reports listed in Table 13.2 to help you with business and network planning.

TABLE 13.2 *Available Comprehensive Inventory Reports*

REPORT NAME	INFORMATION PROVIDED
General Server Inventory report	Includes system description, OS description, BIOS, video type, video display details, network interface card type, hard disk information, IP address, and MAC address for each server.
Hardware Inventory report	Includes conventional memory, extended memory size, processor type and speed, hard disk information, video type, and modem information for each server.
Asset Management report	Includes computer description, OS description, and BIOS information for each server.
Networking Information report	Includes OS description, network interface card type, IP address, MAC address, and network drive mappings for each server.

MAKING THE MOST OF ZENWORKS FOR SERVERS 2 REPORTING

Analyzing Topology Reports

ZENworks for Servers can also deliver reports on your network topology. These topology reports provide information about the specific topology of selected ZENworks for Servers management sites or segments.

Two basic types of topology reports can be generated by ZENworks for Servers. The first is a site-level report, which provides details about the discovered devices on each segment included in the ZENworks for Servers management site. The second type of report is the segment-level topology report, which enables you to narrow the report down to a specific segment in the ZENworks for Servers management site.

NOTE Whenever possible, generate a segment-level topology report instead of a site-level topology report. A site level will take considerably longer to generate.

The following five predefined topology reports can be generated by ZENworks for Servers:

- Computer Systems by Segment report
- NCP Servers report
- Routers report
- Segment report
- Segment Topology report

The following sections describe each of the five different topology reports and the different information contained in them.

Computer Systems by Segment Report

The first type of topology report we discuss is the Computer Systems by Segment report. This report can be done at a segment level to only get the systems in that segment; however, it is typically used as a comprehensive report to obtain a list of systems at the management site level.

The Computer Systems by Segment report lists the following information about each computer system and group them by segment:

- **System name** — Use descriptive names for your systems to make these reports more useful.
- **MAC address** — Physical address.
- **IP address** — Useful to match to captured packets and trend data.
- **IPX address** — Useful to match to captured packets and trend data.
- **Services** — Manageable services for the computer system.

- **MIB services** — Manageable MIB services for the device.
- **Community string** — SNMP community names associated with this computer system.

NCP Servers Report

When running the NCP Servers report, ZENworks for Servers 2 will query the management site or segment (depending on where the report was run from) and return the following information for each NetWare server:

- **Server name** — Use descriptive names for your servers to make these reports more useful.
- **MAC address** — Physical address.
- **IP address** — Useful to match to captured packets and trend data.
- **IPX address** — Useful to match to captured packets and trend data.
- **Labels** — Other names by which the server is known.
- **MIB servers** — Manageable MIB services for the device.
- **Services** — Manageable services for the computer system.
- **Community strings** — SNMP community names associated with the server.

Router Report

When running the Router report, ZENworks for Servers will query the management site or segment (depending on where the report was run from) and return the following information for each router discovered:

- **IPX address** — Useful to match to captured packets and trend data.
- **IP address** — Useful to match to captured packets and trend data.
- **MAC address** — Physical address.

Segment Report

When running the Segment report on a management site, ZENworks for Servers will query the management site and list the number of computer systems on all segments. If this report is run at the segment level, it will only list the systems on the selected segment. The following information will be shown for each computer system listed:

- **IPX address** — Useful to match to captured packets and trend data.
- **IP address** — Useful to match to captured packets and trend data.

Segment Topology Report

The Segment Topology report provides network information about routers and bridges in a ZENworks for Servers management or segment (depending on where the report is run from).

The following information is shown for each router listed in the report:

- **Router name** — Use descriptive names for your routers to make these reports more useful.
- **MAC address** — Physical address.
- **IP address** — Useful to match to captured packets and trend data.
- **IPX address** — Useful to match to captured packets and trend data.
- **MIB services** — Manageable MIB services for the device.
- **Community strings** — SNMP community names associated with the router.

The following information is shown for each router listed in the report:

- **Bridge name** — Use descriptive names for your bridges to make these reports more useful.
- **Bridge type** — Type of bridge device.
- **IP address** — Useful to match to captured packets and trend data.
- **Number of ports** — Number of ports on bridge. Useful when planning network growth.
- **Port number (attached address)** — Useful when troubleshooting software and network problems.

Understanding Network Health Reports

The next group of reports that ZENworks for Servers is able to generate is a network health profile. Network health reports provide information about the overall health of a specified ZENworks for Servers management site or managed network segment.

ZENworks for Servers uses a predefined health profile to generate health reports. These health profiles define the trend parameters, shown in the following tables, that are used to calculate the overall health of the segment or site. Table 13.3 lists trend parameters that are used to calculate the health of managed servers.

TABLE 13.3 Trend Parameters for Managed Servers

TREND PARAMETER	AVAILABLE PROFILES
AVERAGE_CONNECTIONS	NetWare server, Windows server
AVERAGE_DISK_TRANSFER	Windows server
AVERAGE_FAILED_LOGONS	Windows server
AVERAGE_LOGGED_IN_USERS	NetWare server, Windows server
FILE_READ_KBYTES	NetWare server, Windows server
FILE_READS	NetWare server, Windows server
FILE_WRITE_KBYTES	NetWare server, Windows server
FILE_WRITES	NetWare server, Windows server
LSL_IN_PACKETS	NetWare server
LSL_OUT_PACKETS	NetWare server
NETWORK_IN_KBYTES	Windows server
NETWORK_OUT_KBYTES	Windows server
NETWORK_TOTAL_KBYTES	Windows server
NCP_REQUESTS	NetWare server
NO_ECB_COUNT	NetWare server
OS_PACKETS_RECEIVE_BUFFER	NetWare server
PERCENT_ALLOCATED_MEMORY	NetWare server
PERCENT_CACHE_BUFFERS	NetWare server
PERCENT_CACHE_HIT_RATE	NetWare server, Windows server
PERCENT_CODE_AND_DATA_MEMORY	NetWare server
PERCENT_CPU_UTILIZATION	NetWare server, Windows server
PERCENT_DIRTY_PACKET_RECEIVE_BUFFERS	NetWare server
PERCENT_DISK_FREE_REDIRECTION_AREA	NetWare server
PERCENT_LOGICAL_DISK_FREE_SPACE	Windows server

MAKING THE MOST OF ZENWORKS FOR SERVERS 2 REPORTING

TREND PARAMETER	AVAILABLE PROFILES
PERCENT_MEMORY_AVAILABLE	Windows server
PERCENT_VOLUME_FREE_SPACE	NetWare server
PHYSICAL_INTERFACE_IN_KBYTE	NetWare server, Windows server
PHYSICAL_INTERFACE_IN_PACKETS	NetWare server, Windows server
PHYSICAL_INTERFACE_OUT_KBYTE	NetWare server, Windows server
PHYSICAL_INTERFACE_OUT_PACKETS	NetWare server, Windows server
QUEUE_AVERAGE_LENGTH	Windows server
QUEUE_AVERAGE_NEXT_JOB_WAIT_TIME	NetWare server
QUEUE_AVERAGE_NUBMER_READY_ITEMS	Windows server
QUEUE_AVERAGE_NUBMER_READY_JOBS	NetWare server
QUEUE_AVERAGE_NUMBER_READY_KBYTES	NetWare server, Windows server
SERVER_PROCESSES	NetWare server

Table 13.4 lists trend parameters that are used to calculate the health of managed networks.

TABLE 13.4 *Trend Parameters for Managed Networks*

TREND PARAMETER	AVAILABLE PROFILE
ABORT_DELIMETERS	Token ring
AC_ERRORS	Token ring
BEACONS	FDDI
BEACON_EVENTS	Token ring
BROADCASTS	Ethernet, token ring, FDDI
BURST_ERRORS	Token ting
CLAIM_TOKENS	Token ring, FDDI
CRC_ERRORS	Ethernet, FDDI

(continued)

TABLE 13.4 *Trend Parameters for Managed Networks (continued)*

TREND PARAMETER	AVAILABLE PROFILE
DATA_ OCTETS	Token ring
DATA_PACKETS	Token ring
ECHO_PACKETS	FDDI
ELASTICITY_BUFFER_ERRORS	FDDI
ERROR_PACKETS	Ethernet, FDDI
FRAGMENTS	Ethernet
FRAME_COPIED_ERRORS	Token ring
FRAME_NOT_COPIED_COUNT	FDDI
FREQUENCY_ERRORS	Token ring
GOOD_PACKETS	Ethernet
INTERNAL_ERRORS	Token ring
JABBERS	Ethernet
LINE_ERRORS	Token ring
LOST_FRAME_ERRORS	Token ring, FDDI
MAC_ OCTETS	Token ring, FDDI
MAC_PACKETS	Token ring, FDDI
MULTICASTS	Ethernet, token ring, FDDI
OVERSIZED_ERRORS	Ethernet, FDDI
PERCENT_UTILIZATION	Ethernet, token ring, FDDI
RECEIVE_CONGESTIONS	Token ring
RING_POLL_FAILURES	Token ring
RING_PURGES	Token ring
RING_WRAPS	FDDI
SMT_OCTETS	FDDI
SMT_PACKETS	Ethernet
TOKEN_ERRORS	Token ring

MAKING THE MOST OF ZENWORKS FOR SERVERS 2 REPORTING

TREND PARAMETER	AVAILABLE PROFILE
TOTAL_ERRORS	Token ring
TOTAL_OCTETS	Ethernet, FDDI
TOTAL_PACKETS	Ethernet, FDDI
UNDERSIZED_ERRORS	Ethernet, FDDI
UNICASTS	Ethernet, token ring, FDDI

The following segments describe the five predefined health profiles provided with ZENworks for Servers.

NetWare Server Profile

The first type of health profile used by ZENworks for Servers to generate health reports is the NetWare server profile. The NetWare server profile is used to monitor and understand the basic health of your NetWare servers. It provides graphs and data about the following types of trend parameters, listed in Table, 13,3, which are used to calculate the overall health of NetWare servers on the managed site or segment:

- **Cache buffers** — Enables you to see the amount of free memory on the server. Low memory is one of the most common symptoms of a sick server.

- **Cache hits** — Enables you to see memory usage to troubleshoot overaggressive applications.

- **CPU utilization** — Enables you to see how hard the server processor is being worked. High utilization for extended periods can lead to server health problems. Watching the server's utilization can help you strategically plan for network growth in overused areas.

- **Volume free space** — Enables you to monitor available disk space on each volume. Low disk space, especially on the SYS volume, often causes server and application problems.

Microsoft Windows Profile

ZENworks for Servers 2 uses the Microsoft Windows profile to generate reports that monitor the basic health of your Microsoft Windows servers. It provides graphs and data about the following types trend parameters, listed in Table, 13.3, which are used to calculate the overall health of Microsoft Windows servers on the managed site or segment:

- **Available memory** — Enables you to see the amount of free memory on the Windows server. Low memory is one of the most common symptoms of a sick server.
- **Cache hits** — Enables you to see memory usage to troubleshoot overaggressive Windows applications.
- **CPU utilization** — Enables you to see how hard the Windows server processor is being worked. High utilization for extended periods can lead to server health problems. Watching the Microsoft Windows server's utilization can help you strategically plan for network growth in overused areas.
- **Disk free space** — Enables you to monitor available disk space on each disk. Low disk space, especially on the Windows drive, will often cause Windows server and application problems. A health report is generated for this parameter, but no trend graph.

Ethernet Network Profile

The Ethernet network profile is used to monitor and understand the basic health of your network. It provides graphs and data about the following types of trend parameters, listed in Table, 13.4, which are used to calculate the overall health of your Ethernet network on the managed site or segment:

- **Total errors** — Enables you to see the number of network errors occurring on your managed site or segment. This helps you troubleshoot problem networks.
- **Network utilization** — Enables you to see the current usage of your Ethernet networks. This can help you understand which segments are being overused and help you plan for future expansion.
- **Total packets** — Enables you to monitor the packets being sent on your managed Ethernet networks. A health report is generated for this parameter, but no trend graph.
- **Good packets** — Enables you to see the good packets that are being sent on your managed Ethernet networks. Combined with the total packets, this can help you troubleshoot network problems and overusage. A health report is generated for this parameter, but no trend graph.

Token Ring Network Profile

The token ring network profile is used to monitor and understand the basic health of your token ring network. It provides graphs and data about the

MAKING THE MOST OF ZENWORKS FOR SERVERS 2 REPORTING

following types of trend parameters, listed in Table, 13.4, which are used to calculate the overall health of your token ring network on the managed site or segment:

- **Total errors** — Enables you to see the number of token ring network errors occurring on your managed site or segment. This helps you troubleshoot problems on your token ring networks.

- **Network utilization** — Enables you to see the current usage of your token ring networks. This can help you understand which segments are being overused and help you plan for future expansion.

FDDI Network Profile

Lastly, the FDDI network profile is used to monitor and understand the basic health of your FDDI network. It provides graphs and data about the following types of trend parameters, listed in Table, 13.4, which are used to calculate the overall health of your FDDI network on the managed site or segment:

- **Total errors** — Enables you to see the number of FDDI network errors occurring on your managed site or segment. This helps you troubleshoot problems on your FDDI networks.

- **Network utilization** — Enables you to see the current usage of your FDDI networks. This can help you understand which segments are being overused and help you plan for future expansion.

- **Total packets** — Enables you to monitor the total packets being sent on your managed FDDI networks. A health report is generated for this parameter, but no trend graph.

Appreciating Tiered Electronic Distribution Reports

Tiered Electronic Distribution (TED) is an extremely valuable tool for delivering data server to server across the network. For this reason ZENworks for Servers includes several reports that enable you to view the status and history of data distribution through the TED system.

The following sections discuss the different types of TED reports that you can run from the ZENworks for Servers management console.

379

Detailed Reports

ZENworks for Servers enables you to create detailed reports for data distribution at both the distribution and subscriber levels. These reports can be used to understand distribution processes that have occurred and that are occurring on your network.

The detailed reports contain the following statistical information about data distributions on the TED distributors and subscribers:

- **Stage** — This describes the current stage of the distribution, either in extract or receive stage.
- **Status** — Successful or not successful on the receiving of or extraction of the distribution.
- **Date/time** — The date and time the distribution was received on the subscriber.
- **Acting process** — The agent that is to extract the distribution.
- **Channel** — The name of the channel that contained the distribution.
- **Error description** — Description of the error associated with the distribution, traditionally at the subscriber side.

History Reports

ZENworks for Servers also create revision history reports. These reports help you understand the revisions of data distributions that have occurred on your network. For example, each time you distribute a new version of software on your network using TED, it would have a new revision. Therefore, you can track successful and unsuccessful distributions of the software.

There are two Revision History reports. The first report is for normal distribution. The second report is for failed distributions. The Revision History reports contain the following statistical information about data distributions on the TED distributors:

- **Version** — Revision number of the distribution package.
- **Creation date/time** — The date and time that the distributor created the distribution package.
- **Size of distribution** — The size of the distribution file that contains the compressed combination of files for the particular revision (only on regular report).
- **Distribution error** — Description of the error that the distribution experienced (only on failure report).

MAKING THE MOST OF ZENWORKS FOR SERVERS 2 REPORTING

Using ZENworks for Servers Reports

Now that you understand the types of reports that ZENworks for Servers can generate and the trend profiles that it uses to calculate health, you need to understand how you use the ZENworks for Servers console to create, view, and manage those reports. The following sections discuss how to use the three types of ZENworks for Servers health reports to monitor and maintain your network health.

Generating Server Inventory Reports

The first type of ZENworks for Servers health report that we will discuss is the Server Inventory report. The Server Inventory report enables you to create inventory reports of hardware and software that are located on your managed servers, as discussed earlier in this chapter. The following sections describe how to create, customize, print, and export the Server Inventory reports.

Creating and Viewing Inventory Reports

The first task you should know to use Server Inventory reports is how to generate them. Use the following steps to generate and view the inventory report from within ConsoleOne:

1. Select an object in the NDS or Atlas namespace.
2. Select Tools ⇨ Server Inventory Reports from the main menu.
3. Select the report category from the Reports window, which is shown in Figure 13.1.
4. Specify any additional options you wish to use as filters when generating the report. Each report will have different options available to filter the report and reduce the number of entries.
5. Click the Run Selected Report button and a report similar to the one in Figure 13.2 is displayed.

Once the report has been generated it will be displayed in a window similar to the one in Figure 13.2. You can now view the information ZENworks for Servers collected. Notice that the report in Figure 13.2 is a server software listing — listed are the server name, the software title, version (if available) and the number of servers with this software installed. The left and right arrow buttons enable you to navigate from page to page in a multipage report.

381

FIGURE 13.1 Server Inventory reports list in ConsoleOne

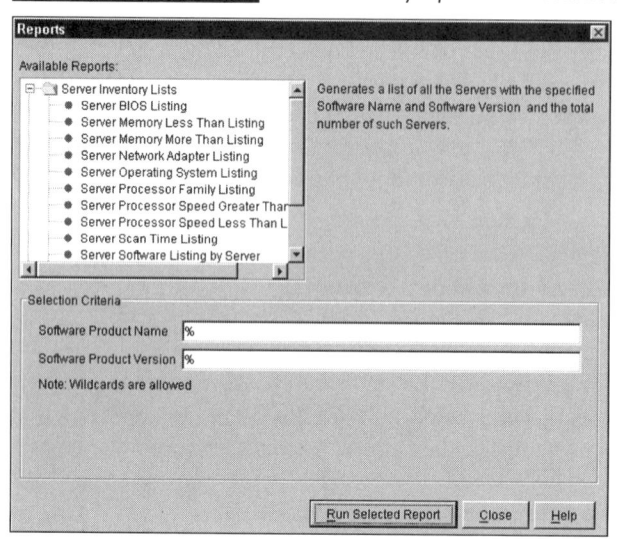

FIGURE 13.2 Server Software Inventory reports in ConsoleOne

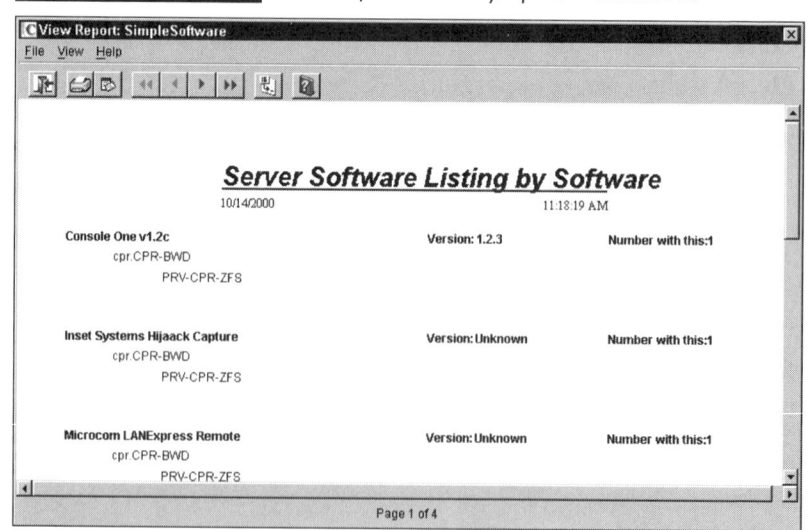

Filtering Inventory Reports

ZENworks for Servers enables you to customize the provided reports by filtering certain parameters. This is vital in large managed sites since it enables you to reduce the number of entries returned in the report. If wildcards are allowed, the report will show filter options and state that wildcard characters are allowed, as shown for the Software List report in Figure 13.1.

Table 13.5 lists several character filters you can use to narrow down your report.

TABLE 13.5 *Character Filters*

CHARACTER	PURPOSE
*	Selects all items for the criteria (* will pick up all, PRV-* will pick up all objects that begin with "PRV-", that is, PRV-SERV1, PRV-HOST2, etc.).
?	Uses all items that match the rest of the criteria (PRV-APP? will pick up PRV-APP1, PRV-APP2, but not PRV-HOST2).
%	Is the SQL equivalent of the * character.
_	Is the SQL equivalent of the ? character.
Specific name	Filters on a specific name for the criteria (PRV-APP1 will only pick up objects with that name for the criteria).

Printing Inventory Reports

Once you have generated the report you may wish to make a hard copy for later reference. To print the report, simply click the Printer button shown in Figure 13.2. The printer dialog box comes up, enabling you to print the report.

Exporting Inventory Reports

Once the report is generated you also have the option to export the report to a file. Exporting the report can be extremely useful if you wish to publish the report in a presentation, on the Web, or import it into another database.

To export a report select File ⇨ Export report from the menu when you have the report up, then select one of the following types of files that you wish ZENworks for Servers to export report to as shown in Figure 13.3:

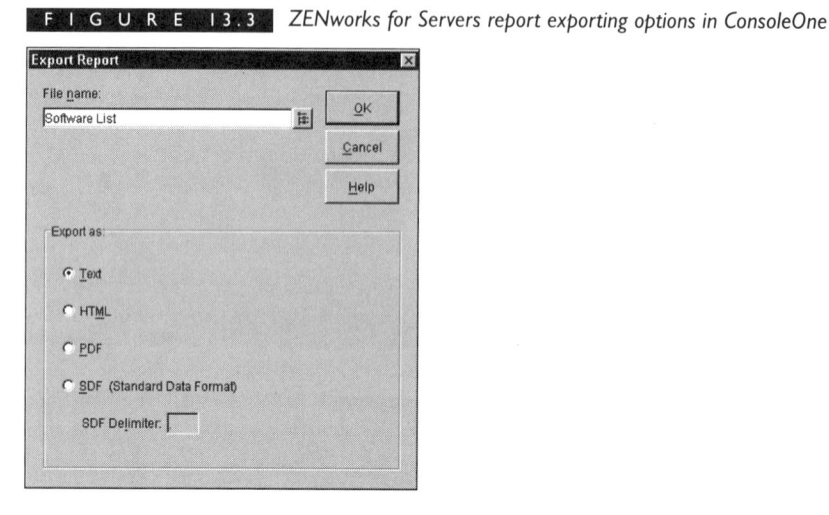

FIGURE 13.3 ZENworks for Servers report exporting options in ConsoleOne

- **Text** — Exports the report to a simple text file that could be imported into a word processor for a status report.
- **HTML** — Exports the report directly to a HTML format. This could be extremely useful to publish server status directly to an internal Web site automatically.
- **PDF** — Export the report to an Adobe Acrobat format. This can be useful when preparing a presentation or publishing it on the Web.
- **SDF** — Exports the report to a Standard Delimited Format (SDF). This is useful to import the report into another database for tracking purposes. You must specify a common delimiter such as a comma, a space, or a tab.

Creating Topology Reports

ZENworks for Servers also enables you to generate topology reports that help you understand the status and infrastructure of your network. You can generate two types of reports, one based at a managed site level and the other based at a segment level. The segment level reports provide information about managed devices on the selected segment only.

MAKING THE MOST OF ZENWORKS FOR SERVERS 2 REPORTING

Use the following steps to generate and view one of the types of topology reports from within ConsoleOne:

1. Select a ZENworks for Servers managed site or managed segment.
2. Select Tools ➪ Reports from the main menu.
3. Select the topology report category from the Reports window, shown in Figure 13.4.

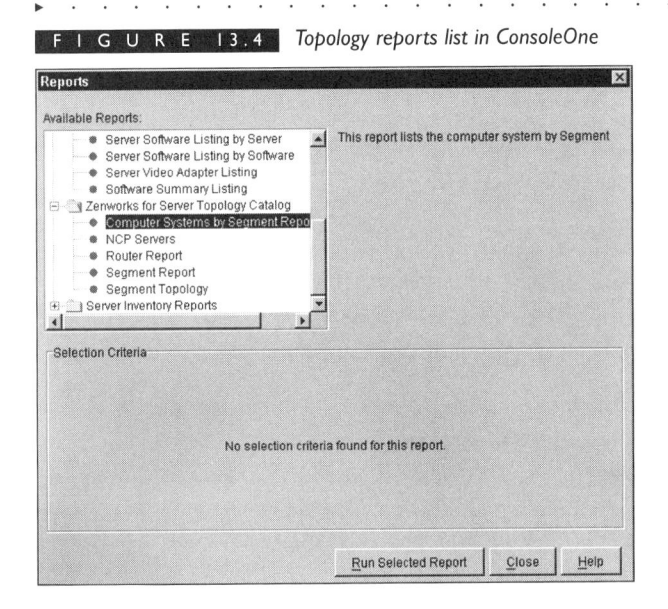

FIGURE 13.4 *Topology reports list in ConsoleOne*

4. Click the Run Selected Report button and a report similar to the one in Figure 13.5 is displayed.

Once the topology report has been generated it will be displayed in a Report window similar to the one in Figure 13.5. You can now view the information collected by ZENworks for Servers, such as network names, addresses, and severs. The left and right arrow buttons enable you to navigate from page to page in a multipage report. You also have the same options to export and print the report as you do with inventory reports (discussed in the previous section).

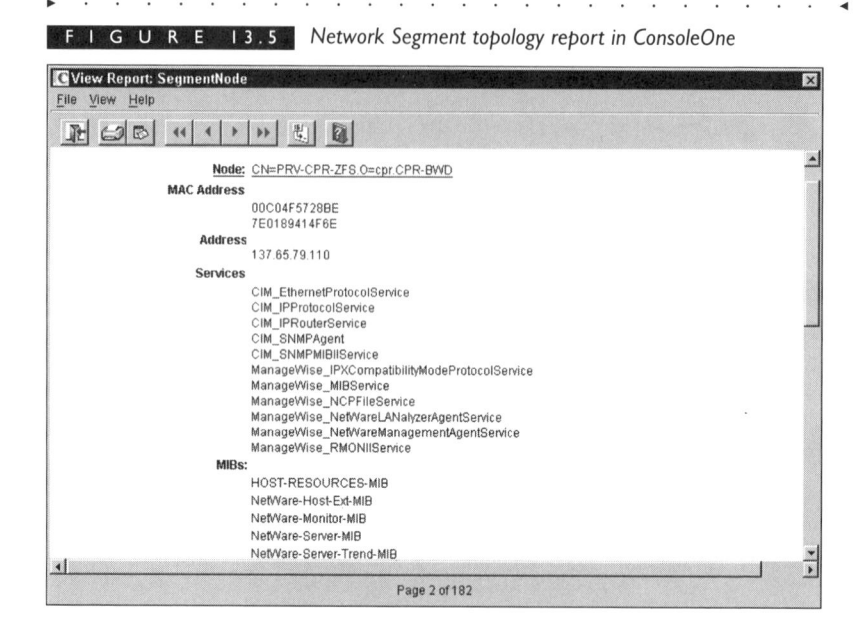

FIGURE 13.5 Network Segment topology report in ConsoleOne

Generating Network Health Reports

The final type of ZENworks for Servers report is the Network and Server Management health report. You should become very familiar with this report. Earlier in this chapter we discussed the five standard profiles that are used by ZENworks for Servers to generate health reports:

- Netware server profile
- Microsoft server profile
- Ethernet server profile
- Token ring network profile
- FDDI network profile

The following sections discuss using those five basic profiles as well as customizing profiles of your own to schedule, run, and view health reports.

Customizing Health Profiles

The first task you should be familiar with when working with network health reports is how to customize one of the existing health profiles that you use to generate a health report. Customizing an existing health profile means modifying the trend parameters, discussed earlier in the chapter, to more accurately reflect the health of the monitored devices.

Use the following steps to customize one of the existing health profiles from within ConsoleOne:

1. Right-click the ZENworks for Servers managed site object and select Properties from the pull-down menu.
2. Select the Health Profiles tab.
3. Select the health profile you wish to customize and click the Edit button, as shown in Figure 13.6. If you do not want to edit one, but want to create a new one, click the New button (discussed in the next section).

FIGURE 13.6 *Available health profiles in the Health Profiles tab for a managed site object in ConsoleOne*

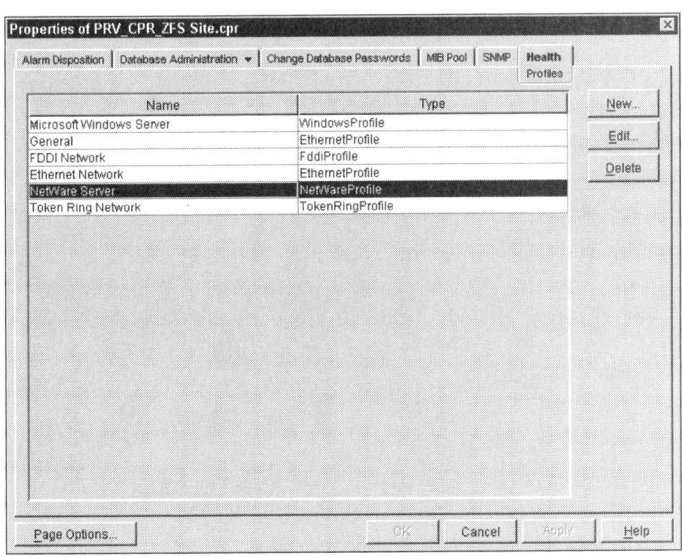

Name	Type
Microsoft Windows Server	WindowsProfile
General	EthernetProfile
FDDI Network	FddiProfile
Ethernet Network	EthernetProfile
NetWare Server	NetWareProfile
Token Ring Network	TokenRingProfile

4. From the Edit profile box, shown in Figure 13.7, you can modify the directory location to which reports generated by this profile should be published by typing a network path in the Publish Directory box.

FIGURE 13.7 Health trend parameters in the Edit Profile dialog box in ConsoleOne

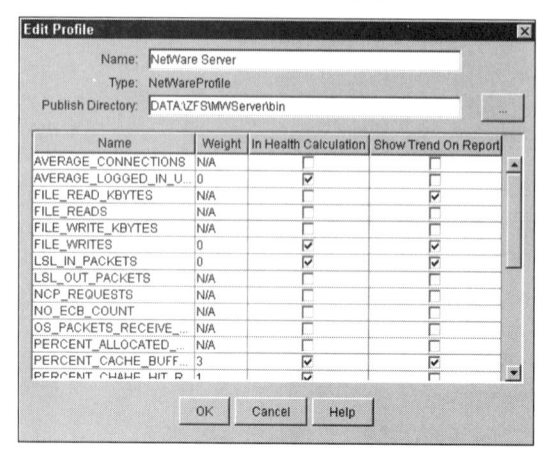

   5. Next, modify the trend parameters (listed earlier in Tables 13.3 and 13.4) that are used to calculate health by either checking or unchecking the In Health Calculation box next to them. This adds or removes the parameter from a list used to calculate the health of the device or segment.
   6. Then, modify the rank of importance of each of the checked trend parameters by specifying a value in the Weight field. You may enter any whole number in the Weight field. ZENworks for Servers uses the number you specify to determine how important the parameter is in calculating the overall health of the device or segment. Larger numbers mean more weight is given to the trend parameter when calculating health of the device.
   7. Finally, modify the trend parameters you wish to see rendered graphically in the health report. Data from the parameters that are checked will be calculated and graphically represented on the health report.
   8. Click the OK button to save your changes.

Adding New Health Profiles

The next task you should be familiar with when working with network health reports is how to add a new health profile that can you use to generate a health report. Adding a new health profile means defining the location of the report, the type of report, the trend parameters, and the weights to parameters that are used to generate a health report of the monitored device.

Use the following steps to add a new health profile from within ConsoleOne:

1. Right-click the ZENworks for Servers managed site object and select Properties from the pull-down menu.
2. Select the Health Profiles tab.
3. Select the health profile you wish to customize and click the New button, as shown in Figure 13.6.
4. From the New Profile dialog box, shown in Figure 13.8, type in the name of the new profile.
5. Next, select the type of device or segment to which the profile applies from the drop-down list, shown in Figure 13.8.

FIGURE 13.8 *Drop-down list of health profile types shown in the New Profile dialog box in ConsoleOne*

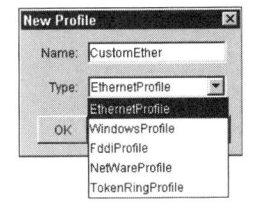

6. Click the OK button and the Edit Profile dialog box is displayed.
7. From the Edit Profile box, shown in Figure 13.9, you can modify the directory location to which reports generated by this profile should be published, by typing a network path in the Publish Directory box.
8. Next, select the trend parameters, listed earlier in Tables 13.3 and 13.4, that are used to calculate health by either checking or unchecking the In Health Calculation box next to them. This adds or removes the parameter from a list used to calculate the health of the device or segment.
9. Enter the rank of importance of each of the checked trend parameters by specifying a value in the Weight field. You may enter any whole number in the Weight field. ZENworks for Servers uses the number you specify to determine how important the parameter is in calculating the overall health of the device or segment. Larger numbers mean more weight is given to the trend parameter when calculating health of the device.

NOVELL'S ZENWORKS FOR SERVERS 2 ADMINISTRATOR'S HANDBOOK

10. Finally, select which of the trend parameters you wish to see rendered graphically in the health report. Data from the parameters that are checked will be calculated and graphically represented on the health report.

11. Click the OK button to save your changes.

FIGURE 13.9 *Edit Profile dialog box showing the health trend parameters and location for the new health profile in ConsoleOne*

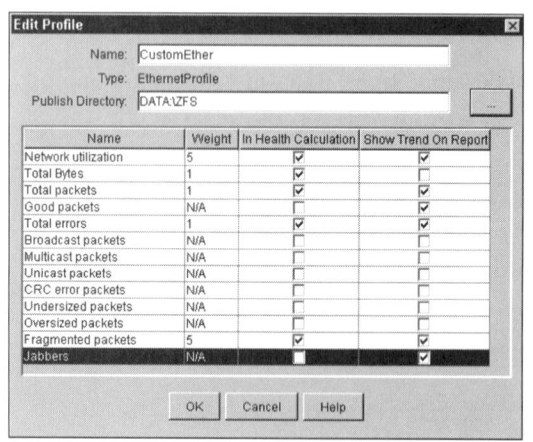

Creating and Scheduling Health Reports

Once you have created and customized the health profiles for your managed network devices and segments, you need to know how to create and schedule a health report to run. You must tell ZENworks for Servers which devices you wish a health report to be run on, what type of report to run, and when to run it.

Use the following steps in ConsoleOne to create and schedule a health report:

1. Right-click the ZENworks for Servers managed site object or a container object in the ZENworks for Servers namespace and select Properties from the drop-down menu.

2. Select the Health Reports tab, shown in Figure 13.10.

MAKING THE MOST OF ZENWORKS FOR SERVERS 2 REPORTING

FIGURE 13.10 *Drop-down list of health profile types shown in the New Profile dialog box in ConsoleOne*

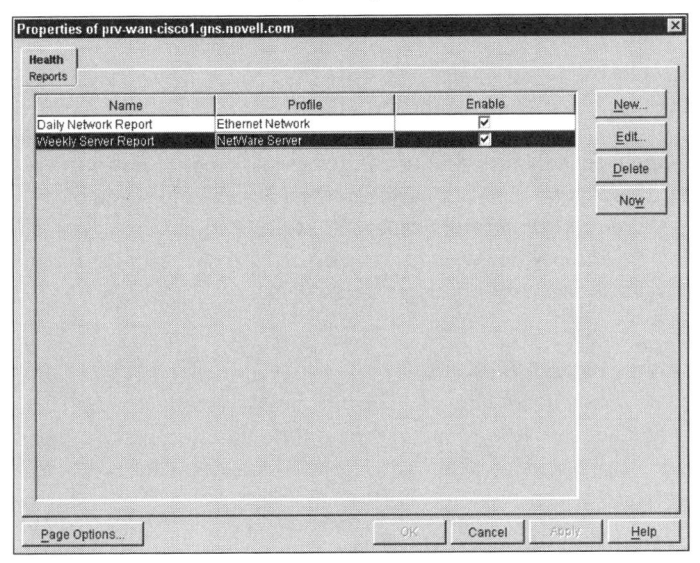

3. Click the New button and the Edit Report dialog box is displayed.
4. From the Edit Report dialog box, shown in Figure 13.11, enter the name you wish to call the report.

FIGURE 13.11 *Edit Profile dialog box showing the health trend parameters and location for the new health profile in ConsoleOne*

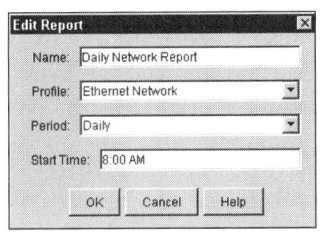

5. Next, select the profile that you wish ZENworks for Servers to use when generating the health report by selecting one of the available types from the Profile drop-down list.

391

6. Next, set the frequency that you wish to run by selecting Daily, Weekly, or Monthly from the Period drop-down list.
7. Then, set the time that you wish the health report to be generated by entering the appropriate values in the Start Time field.
8. Click the OK button and the report will be generated using the date and time that you entered for the report.

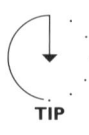

> **TIP**
> You should schedule reports to run at optimal times to balance data gathering and network performance. For example, some of the segment reports tend to be somewhat network intensive; therefore, you may not wish to run then at 9 a.m., when all users are logging in and network usage is at its peak.

Force Running Health Reports

Now that you understand how to schedule health reports to run, you should also be familiar with how to force them to run. Although health reports are scheduled to run on a daily, weekly, or monthly basis at predefined times, you may also need to run them at unscheduled times.

For example, you may wish to force a report to run if you are troubleshooting a network problem, or need to know the current health of a segment of servers before upgrading them.

Use the following steps in ConsoleOne to force a health report to run:

1. Right-click the ZENworks for Serves managed site object or a managed container object and select Properties from the pop-up menu.
2. Select the Health Reports tab, shown earlier in Figure 13.10.
3. Sect the report you want to force generation on.
4. Click the Now button and the report is saved to the publish directory specified in the health profile for the report.

Viewing Health Reports

Now that you understand how to schedule a health report or force one to run, you need to know how to actually view it. After the health report is created by ZENworks for Servers, it will be automatically published to a directory specified by its controlling profile.

Also located in the published directory is an HTML document, named INDEX.HTM, that is associated with the health report. The INDEX.HTM file is an HTML document that contains a Java application that provides access to all the reports that are stored in the directory.

Use the following steps to view a health report once it has been generated by ZENworks for Servers:

1. From your console workstation, browse to the directory where the health reports for the associated profile are stored.
2. Open the INDEX.HTM file located in the directory specified in the controlling profile. The left column of INDEX.HTM lists the report hierarchy based on profiles and your network topology.
3. Click the plus sign next to the health profile that is associated with the health report you wish to view. The profile object expands to display a list of container objects.
4. Click the plus sign next to the container object associated with the health report you wish to view. The container object should expand and display a list of report names that are associated with it.
5. Click the plus sign next to the report you want to view. The report object expands to display a list of instances of that particular report. For example, a report that is scheduled to run daily would have one instance for each day the report was run. The report's name is generated by using the date and time at which the report was run. For example, a report that was generated on October 11, 2000 at 5:05:00 mountain daylight time would have a name of 2000.10.11_05.05.00_MDT.
6. Click the plus sign next to the report name to display a list of individual report pages. The number of report pages depends on which profile you selected and which managed device or segment the report was generated for.
7. Click the individual report page to display the health report in the right frame, as shown in Figure 13.12. The top of the report displays statistical information about the segment or device and provides an overall calculation of health. The trend parameters specified in the report's health profile are listed with trend data. Below the statistical information are trend graphs depicting health based on the trend data selections in the health profile.
8. Click the Print button at the bottom of the left frame to print the report if you need a hard copy.

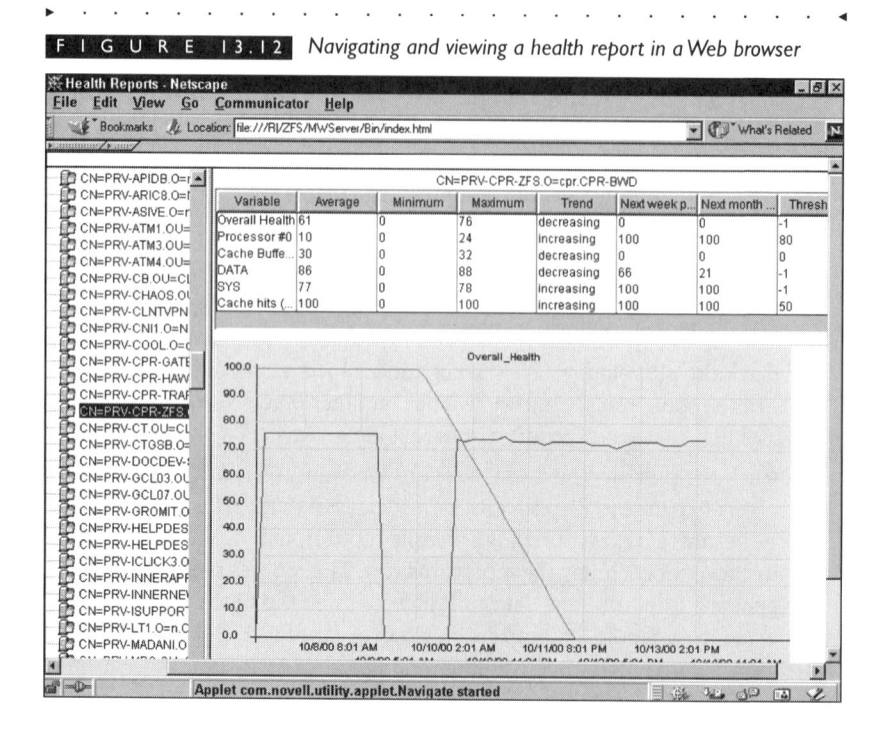

NOVELL'S ZENWORKS FOR SERVERS 2 ADMINISTRATOR'S HANDBOOK

F I G U R E   13.12   *Navigating and viewing a health report in a Web browser*

> **NOTE** The Java application in the INDEX.HTM file for health reports requires that the Java 1.1.2 plug-in for your Web browser be installed prior to viewing the report. If you do not have the plug-in, you will not be able to view the report. Also, if there has not been a report fully generated in that directory yet, the Java application will fail to initialize.

Using Tiered Electronic Distribution Reports

ZENworks for Servers also enables you to generate TED reports that help you understand the status and history of software and data distributions on your network. The following sections describe how to use the management console to create detailed and history reports of TED distributions.

Creating a Distribution Detail Report

This report describes the information that has occurred on the distributor and subscriber to handle the distribution.

Use the following steps from the management console to create a Distribution Detail report:
1. Select the ZENworks for Servers database object.
2. Select Reports from the right–mouse click menu.
3. Select the Distribution Detail report from the available reports list.
4. Check the Latest box if you simply want the latest version of the report; otherwise, specify a from and to date in the Date Range field.
5. Click the Run Selected Report button to generate the report.

Creating a Subscriber Detail Report

This report gives detailed status information on the various subscribers that receive information from a particular distributor's perspective.

Use the following steps from the management console to create a Distribution Detail report:
1. Choose the ZENworks for Servers database object.
2. Select Reports from the right–mouse click menu.
3. Pick the Subscriber Detail report from the available reports list.
4. Specify the distribution object in NDS using the Browse button.
5. Select a version number to use as a criterion for generating the report.
6. Specify a distribution stage to use as a criterion for generating the report.
7. Choose a distribution status to use as a criterion for generating the report. For example, you could specify only completed or failed distributions.
8. Click the Run Selected Report button to generate the report.

Creating a Subscriber Distribution Detail Report

The Subscriber Distribution Detail report describes the distribution information based on information from the subscriber involved in the distribution. This report is similar to the Distribution Detail report that you are given from the database object.

Use the following steps from the management console to create a Distribution Detail report, similar to the one shown in Figure 13.13:

FIGURE 13.13 *Subscriber Distribution Detail report in ConsoleOne*

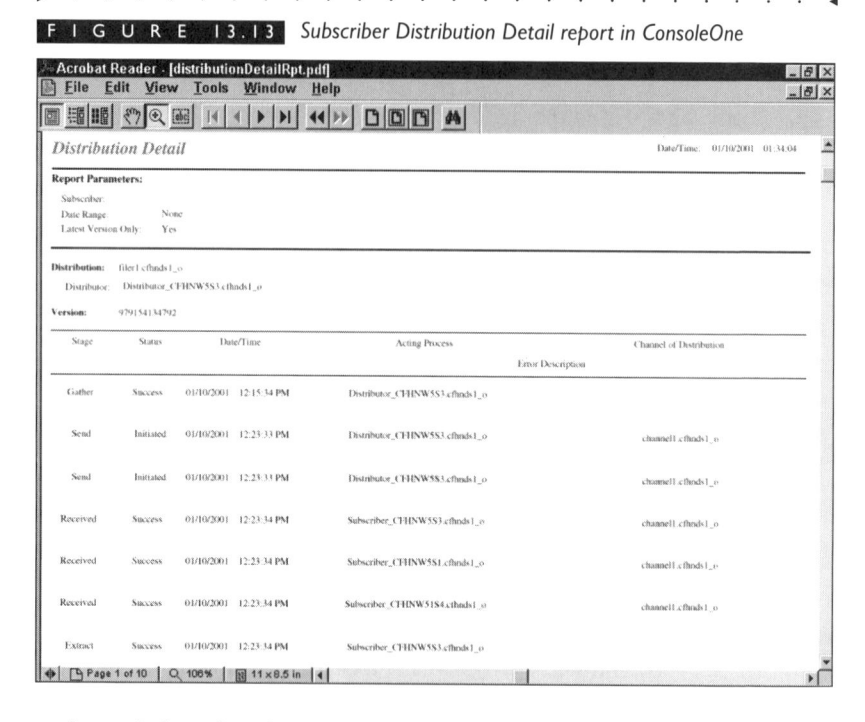

1. Pick the subscriber object.
2. Select Reports from the right–mouse click menu.
3. Select the Distribution Detail report from the available reports list.
4. Specify the subscriber object in NDS using the Browse button.
5. Check the Latest box if you simply want the latest version of the report; otherwise, specify a from and to date in the Date Range field.
6. Click the Run Selected Report button to generate the report.

Creating a Revision History Report

This report displays a history of the various distribution package's versions.

Use the following steps from the management console to create a Distribution Detail report:

1. Choose the ZENworks for Servers database object.
2. Select Reports from the right–mouse click menu.

3. Pick the Revision History report from the available reports list.
4. Specify the distribution object in NDS using the Browse button.
5. Click the Run Selected Report button to generate the report.

Creating a Revision History Report for Failures

This report displays a list of the distributions that had failed during creation of the distribution. This creation occurs on the distributor and deals with the file types.

Use the following steps from the management console to create a Distribution Detail report:

1. Select the ZENworks for Servers database object.
2. Select Reports from the right–mouse click menu.
3. Select the Revision History Failure report from the available reports list.
4. Specify the distribution object in NDS using the Browse button.
5. Click the Run Selected Report button to generate the report.

CHAPTER 14

Troubleshooting ZENworks for Servers 2

ZENworks for Servers 2 is an extremely powerful tool that saves network administrators much needed time. However, because of the complexity of network environments, problems can occur that prevent ZENworks for Servers 2 from doing its job. This chapter covers how to troubleshoot and diagnose many of these problems.

Troubleshooting Policy and Distribution Services

It's important that you know how to troubleshoot policy and distribution services. Common types of issues that you will need to troubleshoot are covered in the next few sections.

Reviewing Server and Agent Object Associations

Make sure that the server is associated with the policies that you expect. You can determine the policies that the server is using by going to the server object and choosing the ZENworks tab and then looking at the Effective Policies page. On this page you can press the Effective Policies button and ConsoleOne then displays all of the policies that are associated either directly or indirectly with the server.

To see the effective policies for the TED objects, you can go to the TED object and look on the General tab pages. This page displays the effective policy DN.

> **TIP**
> Make certain to look for potential problems with a Container Policy Package if you are only using the container to associate the NDS or eDirectory server object. If you are not sure, it is a good idea to associate the NDS or eDirectory server object directly (as a troubleshooting step, not as an implementation design).

You can also check the policies that the agents are using by entering the `policy list` command on the ZENworks for Servers 2 (ZFS agent that ZFS.NCF loads) console. This displays the effective policies that the agent on that server is using. Additionally, you can enter `policy status` to display the order that is being used, as specified in the Container Policy. By doing these tasks you can track down which policy the agents are using.

Distributor Hangs if License not Installed

The distributor software on the server may hang if the NLS license for the policy and distribution services is not installed into NDS or eDirectory.

You need to ensure that the license is properly installed in NDS or eDirectory and that a ZENworks for Servers 2 License Location policy is created and associated with the distributor and ZFS 2 servers in the tree. The license is installed as part of the installation process (see Chapter 2) and the location policy is created as part of the policy system (see Chapter 5). You only need one license object in your tree if you don't have any WAN links, but if you have WAN links, install one at each site for all ZFS servers and distributors.

Subscriber May Timeout with Patching

The connection timeout for the subscriber (administered in the General Property page of the subscriber object) determines how long the subscriber waits to receive a package from the distributor. When sending a distribution with patching turned on, the distributor connects with the subscriber and figures out the details of the path and then builds the patch on the distributor server. The building of the patch may take longer than the administered connection timeout of the subscriber, causing the subscriber to timeout waiting for the distributor (while it is still building the patch). The distributor then notices that the subscriber has timed out the connection and stops building the patch, putting the distribution back into its queue for the next distribution cycle. This may continue to happen because each time the patch is building the subscriber times out, causing the distribution to never be sent to the subscriber.

The current default timeout for the subscriber and distributor is 3,600 seconds. You may need to increase this in the property pages of the distributor and subscriber (see Chapter 6).

Distributor Only Sends to Concurrent Connections

The system may only distribute to the number of maximum concurrent distributions in the distributor object. So, for example, if the maximum connections were set to 10, only the first 10 subscribers that are receiving distributions directly from the distributor will receive the distributions.

Set the number of maximum concurrent distributions in the Distributor object to the value of 0. The zero value signals the distributor to have no limit.

Alternatively, you may use a combination of parent subscribers to make sure that the distributor never attempts to distribute to more subscribers than set in the maximum concurrent distributions. Remember that the number of subscribers receiving from the distributor is the list of subscribers in each channel where a distribution is placed. However, if a subscriber were pulling a distribution from a parent subscriber, it would not make a connection to the distributor and would not take up a connection number on that object. It would take up a connection to the parent subscriber object.

Distributor Building Corrupt Path Files

When multiple subscribers require the same patch file from a single distributor, the distributor attempts to build a patch file for each of the subscribers at the same time. Because the simultaneous builds are trying to create the same file, the patch file can become corrupt and, when sent to the subscriber, it may not accept the file because it detects "corrupt stream errors."

Set up a parent subscriber and have the distributor send the patch to the parent, and have the parent distribute the patch. Because the patch is already calculated before sending it to the parent, the problem is eliminated.

ZENworks for Servers 2 Policy Engine and Distributor State Cannot Find Database

The policy engine and the distributor may report that there was no database specified, or specified incorrectly, when you have installed a ZENworks for Servers 2 database on the network.

The problem is that both of these agents look for a Database Location Policy in a Service Location Package to find where the database is located. If this policy is not defined and associated with the agent objects or the server, the agents will not find the database. See Chapter 5 for more information on this specific policy.

Software Package Distribution Files Are Received But Not Extracted

The extraction of software distribution files is dependent on the subscriber server running the ZENworks for Servers 2 policy engine. This policy engine must be started before the subscriber is started on the server.

Make sure that on the subscriber server the ZFS.NCF file is executed before the SUB.NCF file. Once this is corrected, the subscriber should automatically extract the distribution.

Error-Extending Schema in a NetWare 4.x Tree

If you install ZENworks for Servers 2 onto a NetWare 4.x tree (that is, the master replica of the tree is located on a NetWare 4.x server), you may get a −10 error and the schema extensions for ZENworks for Servers 2 will not be applied to the tree.

This happens because the Management and Monitoring Services portion of ZENworks for Servers 2 assumes that the base schema on the server matches the NetWare 5 system and the NetWare 4.x is missing some schema that is standard on NetWare 5. You can install the Policy and Distribution Services independently to a NetWare 4.x tree without any problems. You can make sure that the master replica for your tree is on a NetWare 5 server, even if NetWare 4 servers are in your network. This should enable the schema to be extended.

If you do not have the tree on a NetWare 5 server and you still want to install the Policy and Distribution Services, perform the following steps to get the schema properly extended and then install the policy system:

1. Log into the desired tree as Administrator, who has full privileges.
2. Open a DOS box on the workstation and place the ZENworks for Servers 2 program CD into the CD drive (we'll assume drive E).
3. Make sure you have a mapped drive to the SYS:\public directory (we'll assume Z).
4. Execute the command z:\ndssch.exe E:\ZfS\TedPol\sfiles\schema\SAS.sch. This executes the schema extensions described in the SAS.sch file.
5. Execute the command z:\ndssch.exe E:\ZfS\TedPol\sfiles\schema\DMPolicy.sch.
6. Execute the command z:\ndssch.exe E:\ZfS\TedPol\sfiles\schema\DMPackage.sch.
7. Execute the command z:\ndssch.exe E:\ZfS\TedPol\sfiles\schema\DMSearch.sch.
8. Execute the command z:\ndssch.exe E:\ZfS\TedPol\sfiles\schema\ZENConsl.sch.
9. Execute the command z:\ndssch.exe E:\ZfS\TedPol\sfiles\schema\ZENLoc.sch.
10. Execute the command z:\ndssch.exe E:\ZfS\TedPol\sfiles\schema\ZFSPol.sch.
11. Execute the command z:\ndssch.exe E:\ZfS\TedPol\sfiles\schema\ZENDb.sch.
12. Execute the command z:\ndssch.exe E:\ZfS\TedPol\sfiles\schema\ZENTed2.sch.
13. Execute the command z:\ndssch.exe E:\ZfS\TedPol\sfiles\schema\ZENRWC.sch.
14. Execute the command z:\ndssch.exe E:\ZfS\TedPol\sfiles\schema\nalted.sch.
15. Now run through the normal install to install the Policy and Distribution Services system.

Extraction Fails on Subscriber Because Files Not Found

When the subscriber performs an extraction on a distribution that is done with the File Agent, each new distribution is only a delta from the previous distribution. In order to perform the extraction, both the delta and the previous version of the distribution must be accessible to the agent.

When the maximum number of revisions is reached, the File Agent builds a new "baseline" of the distribution that includes a complete copy of all of the files. In some cases, when the deltas are large enough and the distribution is rebuilt frequently, the new baseline may arrive when the subscriber is still processing the previous delta.

The new baseline, when it arrives, deletes all previous delta files on the subscriber upon extraction. If a previous delta distribution of the same package is still being processed, the previous delta file will be gone because the baseline extraction has removed the files. This causes the subscriber to fail the delta extraction because the file was not found.

You need to either set the maximum revisions so far out that you avoid this problem for a while or you need to space the sending and extraction of the distribution apart sufficiently so that the subscriber has time to perform the extraction before the next distribution is sent.

Installing ZFS Agent Without Appropriate Java on NetWare

If you choose via the install process (Policy and Distribution Services) to only install the ZENworks for Servers 2 policy engine, the install does not install all of the required Java libraries needed for the engine to perform properly.

If you install the subscriber or the distributor to the target server, the install copies these files.

You need to manually copy the following files from the ZENworks for Servers companion CD to the specified directory.

Copy the following files to the SYS:\JAVA\NJCLv2\BIN directory on the server where the policy engine is to run:

JNCPv2.NLM

PFTDLBS.NLM

Copy the following files to the SYS:\JAVA\NJCLv2\LIB directory on the target server:

NJCLv2.JAR

JNSE.JAR

Installing JVM Twice Causes Loading Problems

If you install the Java Virtual Machine (JVM) twice on the server, after you have installed the ZENworks for Servers 2 distribution and policy agents, you may get an overflow error reported. This occurs because the Java install places the loading commands in the AUTOEXEC.NCF file at the end of the file after the attempted load of the ZFS agents.

If you need to install the JVM after you have installed the ZFS agents onto the server, you need to manually modify the AUTOEXEC.NCF file on the server. You need to make sure that the search paths specified for finding the Java components (placed in the AUTOEXEC.NCF file by the JVM install) occur before the loading of the ZFS agents (ZFS.NCF, DIST.NC, and SUB.NCF).

Make sure the following lines occur (traditionally after a `mount all` statement) before the loading of the ZFS Agents:

```
SEARCH ADD SYS:\JAVA\BIN
SEARCH ADD SYS:\JAVA\NWGFX
```

RWC Port Remains Open after Exit

Currently, when the Remote Web Console (RWC) terminates, the port that the RWC has been using will be left open, and therefore unusable. As the console terminates, it activates Java system calls to close the port. Due to timing and functionality set in the JVM, the system will not completely close the port for approximately one minute after termination.

Reports Print in Portrait Mode

Reports from the system only print in portrait mode. This occurs only in some environments. You can export the report to PDF format and then use your PDF system to change the output to be in landscape mode.

Troubleshooting Traffic Analysis

The ZENworks for Servers traffic analysis system can be an extremely useful tool when debugging LAN-related issues. However, there is a possibility for problems with the traffic analysis system itself. The following sections discuss steps to take if you are experiencing problems with the traffic analysis system.

Verifying That LAN Traffic Agents Are Loaded on Devices

The first step you should take is to check the servers and other devices that have LAN traffic analysis agents on them. Make certain that the agents are loaded (NetWare servers) or started (Windows NT servers) properly.

Verifying RMON Agent Settings

Once you have verified that the traffic analysis agents are loaded properly, you should check the RMON agent's settings for the device in ConsoleOne. You should verify that the RMON agent is enabled for the nodes you are trying to analyze. You should also verify that you have the correct preferred agent set. (See Chapter 10 for more information about setting up the RMON agent.)

Verifying Settings in the LANZ.NCF File

Once you have verified the RMON agent, you should verify that the settings in the LANZ.NCF files for your NetWare servers are correct. You can also enable the LANZ control screen that can help you understand the current state the agents. (See Chapter 10 for more information about setting up the LANZ.NCF File.)

Verifying Settings in the LANZCON Utility

Once you have verified the settings in the LANZ.NCF files for your NetWare servers, you should verify that the settings in the LANZCON utility for your Windows NT servers are correct. (See Chapter 10 for more information about setting up the LANZ.NCF File.)

Additional Debugging Tips

The following sections discuss some possible problems in the traffic analysis system and agents and how to resolve them.

Unable to Load NE3200.LAN Driver after Installing ZENworks for Servers

Installing the traffic analysis agent on NetWare updates the NE3200.LAN driver with the NE3200P.LAN. Therefore, the driver cannot be found. You should modify the files that load the driver to correct the driver name.

LANalyzer Error – Ethernet Adapter <address> Is Not Monitored Because the Driver Does Not Support Promiscuous Mode

A promiscuous mode driver receives all packets and errors on the network. This is required for the ZENworks for Servers 2 traffic analysis agents. The driver currently loaded does not support promiscuous mode; therefore, you need to update your driver for the traffic analysis agents to work.

No SNMP Response

No SNMP service is currently started on the Windows NT server, or the agent is not configured to receive SNMP requests. Start the SNMP server on the NT server and verify that the IP address of the selected host is included in the trap destination address list. This could also be caused if you have some community string settings wrong or SNMP parameters set wrong on the servers.

RMON Tables Are Not Listed

Adapter monitoring is not enabled in the LANZCON utility or the RMON tables have been deleted. You should enable adapter monitoring in the LANZCON utility.

False Duplicate IP Address Alarm Generated in DHCP

The DHCPRELEASE packet from the client has not reached the server, resulting in a false duplicate IP address. Use the LANZCON utility to disable the generation of duplicate IP address alarms.

No Response Message on Management Console

The most common cause is that adapter monitoring is not enabled. Use the LANZCON utility in Windows NT or the LANZ configuration utility in NetWare to enable adapter monitoring.

MIB-2 Not Found

MIB-2 refers to the information base that the RMON agents are located in. You should reload the agent on the device.

No Statistics Are Reported

The monitoring agent is not running on the segment, the interface cannot be monitored because the driver is not supported or is disabled, or the statistics entry has been deleted. You should enable monitoring on the agent, update the driver to a promiscuous mode driver, and/or reload the agent.

This Segment Does Not Have an RMON Agent Connected to It

The segment does not have a supported topology, the RMON agent is not configured or installed correctly, or insufficient memory is on the management server to run the RMON agent. You should first verify that your topology is supported. Second, you should install or configure the RMON agent. Verify that the server has plenty of memory. Then unload and reload the RMON agent.

Interface Not Found

The management console is not able to find the interface on the server to contact the monitoring agent.

The LAN adapter may not be loaded on the server. You should load the LAN driver for the adapter on the server.

The network card for the server was removed and replaced with a new one. Simply wait until NetExplorer discovers the new card and removes the old one.

You installed or reinstalled a new server on the network, but used an IP or IPX address that has been previously assigned. Change the address and run NetExplorer.

Management Server Is Not Responding

The server is down, out of memory, or has a communication problem. If you're experiencing this sort of problem, first verify that the server is up and running. Next verify that the server has plenty of memory. Then check the connectivity status of all services to the management server using the connectivity test utility.

Troubleshooting Alarm Management

The ZENworks for Servers 2 alarm management system can be an extremely useful tool when debugging LAN and server-related issues through the use of a number of alarm events. However, if a problem exists in the alarm management system itself, you may not be notified. The following sections discuss steps to take if you are experiencing problems with the alarm management system.

TROUBLESHOOTING ZENWORKS FOR SERVERS 2

Verifying That SNMP Agents Are Loaded on Devices

The first step when troubleshooting the alarm management system is to verify that the SNMP agents are loaded on the servers. The agents are responsible for capturing events as they occur. If the agent is not loaded, then events will not be captured. Therefore, you should check your servers and any other devices, such as a bridge, that may have SNMP agents loaded. (For more information on SNMP agents, see Chapter 11.)

Verifying Status of Alarm Manager Database

The next step you should take is to check the status of the Alarm Manager database on your NetWare management server. To do this, first make certain that the database is loaded. Next, make sure that the server itself is not having problems and that there are no error messages relating to the database. (For more information on the Alarm Manager, see Chapter 11.)

Verifying SNMP Connectivity Between Management Console and SNMP Devices

Once you have verified that the Alarm Manager database is up, you need to verify connectivity to the devices. Use the connectivity test utility, discussed in Chapter 11, to test the SNMP connectivity between the management console and all devices that you are not receiving alarms from.

Verifying Alarm Thresholds

Once you have verified that the SNMP service on the devices in question can communicate with the management console, you should verify the alarm thresholds for the alarms that you are not receiving. If the alarm threshold is too great, or too little for falling thresholds, it may never be reached and trigger the alarm. (See Chapter 11 for more information on alarm thresholds.)

Receiving and Using Unknown Alarms

If you are receiving the alarm, but it shows up as an unknown alarm, there is no alarm template available in the MIB pool. It is likely that the alarm is being triggered by a third-party device or software. If you need to use an alarm that is showing up as unknown, you should obtain an MIB from the device or software vendor and add it to the MIB pool.

Troubleshooting Server Management

Most issues involving inability to use the ZENworks for Servers 2 server management servers are results of traffic analysis agent or alarm management issues. The first step you should take when troubleshooting issues involving server management components is to test the traffic analysis and alarm systems. The following sections discuss some additional things you can do to troubleshoot server management problems.

Verifying Connectivity between the Management Console and Server

One of the first things you should do when you are having trouble accessing the server management components is to verify that the management console can actually connect to the server itself. You should use the ping or connectivity tests, discussed in Chapter 11, to verify that the console can communicate over IP or IPX to the server in question.

Verifying Remote Management Agent Is Loaded on the Server

Another thing you should do when troubleshooting server management issues is to check and see if the remote management agent, discussed in Chapter 12, is properly loaded and running on the server.

Verifying Port Number for RCONSOLEJ

You may also wish to verify that the port number and password you are using for the RCONSOLEJ utility match the settings on the server you are attempting to remotely manage.

Troubleshooting NetWare Errors

When troubleshooting ZENworks for Servers you should always be aware of any NetWare error messages that are occurring. ZENworks for Servers 2 is heavily tied into the NetWare operating system, NDS, and file system. Therefore, any error occurring in NetWare possibly affects ZENworks for Servers as well.

410

NetWare Server File System Errors

When ZENworks for Servers is having problems distributing on the server, you should always look for errors in the NetWare or NT file system. These errors often help you narrow down the problem to a specific cause and resolution.

Table 14.1 lists common file system errors.

TABLE 14.1 *Common File System Errors*

CODE	TEXT	DESCRIPTION
0x8901	INSUFFICIENT SPACE	The station does not have sufficient disk space. Make certain that the minimum free disk space requirements are set up for the application object being used.
0x8980	FILE IN USE	An attempt was made to open or create a file that is already open. Set the shareable attribute if you wish multiple users to access the file at the same time.
0x8983	DISK IO ERROR	A hard disk I/O error occurred on a NetWare volume. Typically, a bad sector has been encountered and could not be migrated to the hot fix area. Replace the drive.
0x8999	DIR FULL	An attempt was made to write to a volume without available directory space. Make certain that you are not exceeding the maximum number of directory entries for the volume.
0x899C	INSUFFICIENT RIGHTS INVALID PATH	An attempt was made to access a path with invalid rights to the path or with an invalid path name. Make certain that the user has appropriate rights to the path and that the path name is correct.
0x89A8	ACCESS DENIED	Access has been denied. Make certain that the user has appropriate rights to the file.
0x89BF	NAME SPACE INVALID	An invalid namespace was used. Make sure the correct namespaces are loaded on the volume being used.

Troubleshooting NDS Errors

Another area you should always review when troubleshooting ZENworks for Servers is the NDS error messages. ZENworks for Servers 2 uses NDS not only for normal authentication and access, but also as a service for controlling ZENworks for Servers objects.

NDS errors can be categorized as follows.

NDS Operating System Error Codes

Some NDS background processes require the functionality provided by the NetWare operating system. These processes, such as communication and transaction servers, can return operating system–specific error codes to NDS. These error codes are then passed on to the NDS background process that initiated a request. In NetWare 4.x, versions of NDS can also generate operating system error codes.

Usually, operating system error codes that are generated by NDS have a negative numerical representation, while normal operating system error codes have a positive numerical representation. The numerical range for operating system error codes generated by NDS is –1 through –255; inversely, the numerical range for operating system error codes is 1 through 255.

> **NOTE** NDS returns the positive numerical error code rather than the negative error code normally used by NDS to return to application to prevent any incompatibility. Therefore, any occurrence of an error code within the range of 1 through 255 or –1 through –255 should be treated as the same error.

NDS Client Error Codes

The next class of NDS error codes is the client error codes. Some NDS background processes require the functionality provided by other NDS servers. Use of these functions, such as bindery services, requires that an NDS server act as an NDS client to the server providing the functionality. Therefore, these functions often result in client-specific error codes being returned to the NDS background processes and operations.

NDS client error codes are generated by the NDS client that is built into NDS. The NDS client error codes fall in the range of codes numbered –301 through –399.

NDS Agent Error Codes

Another class of NDS error codes is the NDS agent error codes. NDS agent error codes represent errors that originated in the NDS agent software in the server that are returned through NDS. These codes are numbered –601 through –799 (or FDA7 through F9FE).

> **NOTE** Temporary errors are normal, because the NDS database is designed as a loosely consistent database. You should not be alarmed if NDS error conditions exist temporarily. However, some errors might persist until the error condition is resolved.

Other NDS Error Codes

Some NDS background processes require the functionality provided by other NLM programs, such as timesync.nlm or unicode.nlm. If any of these modules encounter an error, it can be passed on to the ds.nlm. Unicode.nlm and other errors in this category range from –400 through –599.

Tools for Troubleshooting NDS Errors

To effectively troubleshoot NDS errors that affect ZENworks for Servers 2, you should be familiar with the tools available to troubleshoot NDS problems. The following tools are provided to monitor and repair error conditions with NDS.

The NDS Manager Utility   The NDS Manager utility provides partitioning and replication services for the NDS database on a NetWare server. It also provides repair capabilities for repairing the database from a client workstation, which alleviates the network administrator's total dependence on working from the server console.

The DSREPAIR Utility   The DSREPAIR utility enables you to work from the server console to monitor and repair problems with the NDS database on a single-server basis. It does not correct problems on other servers from a single, centralized location. It must be run on each server that you want to correct NDS database errors on.

The DSTRACE Utility   The DSTRACE utility enables you to work from the server console to diagnose NDS errors. These errors might appear when you are manipulating NDS objects with the administration utilities. NDS errors also show up on the DSTRACE screen.

Table 14.2 lists common NDS errors.

TABLE 14.2 *Common NDS Errors*

CODE	TEXT	DESCRIPTION
−601 FDA7	NO SUCH ENTRY	The specified NDS object could not be found on the NDS server that is responding to a request.
−603 FDA5	NO SUCH ATTRIBUTE	The requested attribute could not be found. In NDS, if an attribute does not contain a value, the attribute does not exist for the specific object.
−625 FD8F	TRANSPORT FAILURE	The source server is unable to communicate with the target server. This error is almost always LAN related.
−626 FD8E	ALL REFERRALS FAILED	The object could not be found; however, it is still possible that the object does exist. It is likely that the server could not communicate with another server that is holding a copy of the object.
−634 FD86	NO REFERRALS	The source server has no objects that match the request and has no referrals on which to search for the object. This is not a serious error, but just a response. This error usually resolves itself.

APPENDIX A

Understanding NDS Changes for ZENworks for Servers 2

When ZENworks for Servers 2 is installed on your network, it makes several extensions to your current NDS schema. These extensions enable new ZENworks for Servers 2 objects to be created and data linking those objects to existing objects to occur.

This appendix identifies the new objects that have been introduced to your tree and changes to existing base objects when ZENworks for Servers 2 was installed.

Identifying New Objects for ZENworks for Servers 2

Table A.1 lists the significant new objects introduced into NDS for ZENworks for Servers 2. Additionally, it describes all significant objects — not just objects that have been introduced since ZENworks for Servers 1.

TABLE A.1 List of New Objects Added to the Tree for ZENworks for Servers 2

OBJECT	DESCRIPTION
MW: Account object	This holds the account information for users that are included in the role-based services. This information holds database accounts and passwords.
	This object is administered as part of the role-based for management and monitoring services. See Chapter 8 for more information.
MW: Domain object	This contains information about the Management and Monitor Services database that holds the data and topology information for the system. This object is set up as part of the install process.
	This object is administered as part of Management and Monitoring Services. See Chapter 8 for more information.

UNDERSTANDING NDS CHANGES FOR ZENWORKS FOR SERVERS 2

OBJECT	DESCRIPTION
MW: Scope	This is part of the role-based services and provides the range of devices that a user may manage in the system.
	This object is administered as part of the role-based for management and monitoring services. See Chapter 8 for more information.
MW: Service object	This keeps the passwords and rights that are needed by the Management and Monitoring Services agents to connect to NDS. This object is set up as part of the install process.
NT Server object	This object is introduced to apply associations into the NT servers that are running NDS.
RBS: External Scope	This object holds a key that is to be given as data to a service outside of NDS, with the expectation of limiting the set of objects in external databases that a user may manage.
RBS: Module	This is a role-based services object that defines a function or set of functions that a user may execute as part of his or her role.
RBS: Role	This object identifies a role that the user may have in order to perform tasks.
RBS: Task	This is a role-based services object that identifies a single function that the user may execute as part of the role. A task may be contained in several modules or roles.
RWC Server object	This object contains the configuration information for the Remote Web Console that can be used with the ZENworks for Servers Policies and Distribution management. The object is associated with the server where the RWC service runs — traditionally, its name includes the name of the server.

(continued)

TABLE A.1 List of New Objects Added to the Tree for ZENworks for Servers 2 (continued)

OBJECT	DESCRIPTION
SAS: Service	This object holds the rights and passwords associated with a service that may be running on the server. The agents on the server that require access to NDS log into the directory using this service object. This object may already exist, but it will be extended if it does.
Scheduled Down policy	This policy enables you to specify a schedule that should bring the NetWare server down periodically.
	This policy is administered as part of the Server Policy Package. See Chapter 5 for more information.
Scheduled Unload/Load policy	This policy enables you to schedule when NLMs or Java processes may be executed or unloaded on the NetWare server. This can be useful to schedule when a backup or other NLM should periodically run.
	This policy is administered as part of the Server Policy Package. See Chapter 5 for more information.
Search policy	This policy will tell the server agents the order to enforce any policies found in the tree. The default order is object, group, then container, and to search all the way up to the root of the tree. With this policy you can change the order and stop the agent from searching up the tree at a container or partition level.
	This policy is part of the Container Policy Package and is associated with containers, which will impact any server or service in that container or subcontainer. See Chapter 5 for more details.

UNDERSTANDING NDS CHANGES FOR ZENWORKS FOR SERVERS 2

OBJECT	DESCRIPTION
Server Downing policy	This policy enables you to specify the behavior of the NetWare server when a down command is requested.
	This policy is administered as part of the Server Policy Package. See Chapter 5 for more information.
Server Group	A new group is introduced that enables you to group a set of servers together. This is useful if you wish to associate policies with the set of servers in the group when they may not be grouped in the same container.
Server Script policy	This policy enables you to specify a script that should be executed periodically on the server. The script may be an NCF, PERL, or NETBASIC script.
	This policy is administered as part of the Server Policy Package. See Chapter 5 for more information.
Server Set Parameters policy	This policy enables you to specify the value of NetWare set parameters that should be set on the server. Each time the policy schedule is activated the parameter will be set to the specified values, even if someone has modified the value on the console command line.
	This policy is administered as part of the Server Policy Package. See Chapter 5 for more information.
Site Distribution object	This object is used as part of the distribution of ZENworks for Desktops 2 application objects over the TED network. This object will tell the remote location which user to give access to the application and the particulars on the launching of the application. See Chapter 6 for more details.

(continued)

TABLE A.1 List of New Objects Added to the Tree for ZENworks for Servers 2 (continued)

OBJECT	DESCRIPTION
SNMP Community Strings	This policy enables you to specify in the policy the community strings that the associated NetWare SNMP agents should use for access to their information.
	This policy is administered as part of the Server Policy Package. See Chapter 5 for more information.
SNMP Trap Target policy	This policy enables you to give the IP addresses for the servers that will receive SNMP traps and alarms from the NetWare SNMP agents on the system. All associated NetWare servers that are running SNMP agents use the specified host addresses.
	This policy is administered as part of the Server Policy Package. See Chapter 5 for more information.
TED Channel object	This object contains the set of subscribers and external subscribers that should receive the distributions that are placed in the channel. See Chapter 6 for more details.
TED Distribution object	This object represents the set of files or server software packages (and possible actions) that should be sent to a subscriber. These objects are placed into a channel and all subscribers in the channel are given the distribution. Each distribution is associated with a distributor who is responsible for the transmission. See Chapter 6 for more details.
TED Distributor object	This object holds configuration information for the distributor agent that is running on the server. Each server that is running the distributor agent must have its own distributor object. See Chapter 6 for more details.
TED External Subscriber object	This object holds the IP address of a subscriber that does not have a server object or subscriber object in the tree. See Chapter 6 for more details.

UNDERSTANDING NDS CHANGES FOR ZENWORKS FOR SERVERS 2

OBJECT	DESCRIPTION
TED Subscriber object	This object holds configuration information for the subscriber agent that is running on the server. Each server that is running the subscriber agent must have its own subscriber object in some tree. See Chapter 6 for more details.
Text File Change policy	This policy allows enables you to make text searches, changes, and updates to text files on your server. This policy is administered as part of the Server Policy Package. See Chapter 5 for more information.
Tiered Electronic Distribution policy	This policy specifies the variables and other configuration information that can be generally applied to TED agents that are associated with this policy. This policy is administered as part of the Service Location Policy Package. See Chapter 5 for more information.
ZENworks Database object	This object refers to the Sybase or Oracle database in the system that is used to hold the inventory and event information from the ZENworks system. This is the same object for ZENworks for Desktops and ZENworks for Servers 2. The object just would be extended so you can configure both databases within the one object. This database is located via a Service Location Policy effective for the agents that will contact the database.
ZENworks for Servers Database Location policy	This policy informs the Policy and Distribution Services agents where to locate the Sybase database that should hold the event information. This policy is administered as part of the Service Location Policy Package. See Chapter 5 for more information.

(continued)

NOVELL'S ZENWORKS FOR SERVERS 2 ADMINISTRATOR'S HANDBOOK

TABLE A.1 List of New Objects Added to the Tree for ZENworks for Servers 2 (continued)

OBJECT	DESCRIPTION
ZENworks for Servers License Location policy	This policy informs the Policy and Distribution Services agents where to locate the license that activates the service. Without this license, the agents will not function. This policy does not need to be configured if the license object resides in the same container as the server. It will search there first.
	This policy is administered as part of the Service Location Policy Package. See Chapter 5 for more information.
ZENworks for Servers policy	This policy provides configuration information to the ZENworks for Servers policy engine that runs on the associated NetWare server.
	This policy is administered as part of the Server Policy Package. See Chapter 5 for more information.

Modified Objects for ZENworks for Servers 2

Table A.2 shows the significant objects that will be modified to contain additional attributes following the installation of ZENworks for Servers 2. It is assumed by ZENworks for Servers 2 that these objects already exist in NDS. If not, then an error occurs at install time.

TABLE A.2 List of Modified Objects in the Tree for ZENworks for Servers 2

OBJECT	DESCRIPTION
Country	This object is modified to enable a ZENworks policy package to be associated with the object.
Group	This object is modified to enable a ZENworks policy package to be associated with the object. This object is also modified to hold an MW:Account object, RBS:Assigned Roles, and RBS: Owned Roles, to correlate the users to their role-based services accounts.

UNDERSTANDING NDS CHANGES FOR ZENWORKS FOR SERVERS 2

OBJECT	DESCRIPTION
Locality	This object is modified to enable a ZENworks policy package to be associated with the object.
NCP Server	This object is modified to optionally contain a reference to a SAS object that is used by the services to log into NDS.
Organization	This object is modified to enable a ZENworks policy package to be associated with the object. This object is also modified to hold an MW:Account object, RBS:Assigned Roles, and RBS: Owned Roles, to correlate the users to their role-based services accounts.
Organizational Unit	This object is modified to enable a ZENworks policy package to be associated with the object. This object is also modified to hold an MW:Account object, RBS:Assigned Roles, and RBS: Owned Roles, to correlate the users to their role-based services accounts.
Server	This object is modified to enable a ZENworks policy package to be associated with the object.
User	This object is modified to hold an MW:Account object, RBS:Assigned Roles, and RBS: Owned Roles, to correlate the users to their role-based services accounts.

APPENDIX B

ZENworks for Servers 2 Database Schemas

NOVELL'S ZENWORKS FOR SERVERS 2 ADMINISTRATOR'S HANDBOOK

ZENworks for Servers 2 comes with several views incorporated into the management console to retrieve information from the various databases. However, those views may not always give you the information you need exactly in the format you want it in. You can access the ZENworks for Servers 2 databases directly by creating your own queries and views; however, to do so you must be very familiar with the Common Information Model (CIM) and have a solid understanding of Relational Database Based Managed Systems (RDBMS). Be aware that if you modify the Sybase database directly, it will not be supported if there are problems.

Accessing the ZENworks for Servers 2 databases can be a powerful tool for you to expand the capabilities of ZENworks for Servers 2 in helping you manage you network. This appendix contains tables that define the schema and associations for tables in the various ZENworks for Servers 2 databases. Also included in this appendix are sample queries that will give you a jump-start at accessing the databases.

Understanding the Inventory Database Schema

The first thing you must understand when accessing the ZENworks for Servers inventory database is what is available and how is it available. Tables B.1 and Table B.2 help you understand the schema structure for inventory classes, class associations, association attributes, and class attributes of inventory objects.

TABLE B.1 Tables Used by the ZENworks for Servers 2 Inventory Database

CIM CLASS NAME	DETAILS OF INFORMATION STORED
InventoryScanner	Details of inventory scan that was executed on the server. This includes the scan date and the name of the inventory server to which the scan was sent.
MWDesktopMonitor	Monitor details of the servers such as type, resolution, etc.
EnvironmentVariableSetting	Servers's environment variables name and the value set. Only for Windows NT servers.
BIOS	Hardware BIOS information of the machine like release date, ID bytes, copyright string, model, etc.

426

ZENWORKS FOR SERVERS 2 DATABASE SCHEMAS

CIM CLASS NAME	DETAILS OF INFORMATION STORED
ConfigurationFile	Information about the configuration files on the machine. This includes autoexec.bat, config.sys, win.ini, system.ini, and so on. Attributes used are name and contents to store the name of the configuration file and the contents in it, respectively. Stored only for Windows NT servers.
MWKeyboard	Server's keyboard details such as number of keys, number of function keys, type, subtype, typematic rate, and delay.
Bus	Type of bus used in the system, which includes bus type (for example, PCI), version, and so on.
SerialPort	Same as port class; also stores serial port information such as COM1, COM2.
ParallelPort	Same as port class; also stores parallel port information such as LPT1, LPT2.
VideoAdapter	Installed video adapter information such as type, chipset, DACType.
MWDiskDrive	Installed disks information such as disk type (floppy disk/hard disk/tape/CD-ROM), cylinders, sectors, tracks, and partitions.
MWLocalFileSystem	Local file system on the Winsdows NT server such as C:, D: and so forth. The attributes used are SectorsPerTrack, FileSystemType (FAT, NTFS and so on), VolumeSerialNumber.
LogicalDisk	This class stores information about the volumes mounted on the NetWare server.
MWRemoteFileSystem	Mapped drives on the server, such as the name of the mapped drive, and the directory path. Stored only on Windows NT server.
NTService	Name and status (running, stopped) of the services running on NT servers.
MWPointingDevice	Attached mouse on the system, which includes number of buttons, port, IRQ.

(continued)

TABLE B.1 *Tables Used by the ZENworks for Servers 2 Inventory Database (continued)*

CIM CLASS NAME	DETAILS OF INFORMATION STORED
MWOperatingSystem	Installed operating system on the system, which includes OS type, version. Stored only for Windows NT server.
NetWareOperatingSystem	Stored only for NetWare servers. This class has attributes specific to NetWare operating system.
MWProcessor	Processor details like current clock speed, family, stepping, and so forth.
ComponentID	A separate class created to store the name and details of the instrumented DMI components. These details include identifying number, install date, name, and vendor. Stored only on Windows NT server.
EthernetProtocolEndPoint	MAC address of the server.
IPProtocolEndPoint	IP address of the server.
IPXProtocolEndpoint	IPX address of the server.
WsUser	Username logged in to the server. Stored only on Windows NT server.
CDROMDrive	Installed CD-ROM drive information on the server such as name, description, mapped drive, manufacturer, product ID.
DnsName	DNS name of the server.
NetworkAdapter	NIC type and name of the card installed on the server. This is stored in the Description field.
IPNetwork	Subnet mask.
Product	Installed software details such as name, description, and version.
POTSModem	Contains the name, description, serial port connected on, and so forth, of the attached modem device.

ZENWORKS FOR SERVERS 2 DATABASE SCHEMAS

TABLE B.2 Associations and Attributions of the ZENworks for Servers Inventory Database

LOOKUP CLASS	TARGET CLASS	ASSOCIATION CLASS	ATTRIBUTE1	ATTRIBUTE2
MWProcessor	UnitaryComputerSystem	SystemDevice	PartComponent	GroupComponent
MWDesktopMonitor	UnitaryComputerSystem	SystemDevice	PartComponent	GroupComponent
DesktopMonitor	UnitaryComputerSystem	SystemDevice	PartComponent	GroupComponent
ParallelPort	UnitaryComputerSystem	SystemDevice	PartComponent	GroupComponent
SerialPort	UnitaryComputerSystem	SystemDevice	PartComponent	GroupComponent
ConfigurationFile	MWLocalFileSystem	FileStorage	PartComponent	GroupComponent
MWSCSIController	UnitaryComputerSystem	SystemDevice	PartComponent	GroupComponent
MWKeyboard	UnitaryComputerSystem	SystemDevice	PartComponent	GroupComponent
MWPointingDevice	UnitaryComputerSystem	SystemDevice	PartComponent	GroupComponent
Bus	UnitaryComputerSystem	SystemDevice	PartComponent	GroupComponent
MWDiskDrive	UnitaryComputerSystem	SystemDevice	PartComponent	GroupComponent
CDROMDrive	UnitaryComputerSystem	SystemDevice	PartComponent	GroupComponent
Server	UnitaryComputerSystem	SystemComponent	PartComponent	GroupComponent
BIOS	UnitaryComputerSystem	InstalledBIOS	PartComponent	GroupComponent
MonitorResolution	MWDesktopMonitor	MonitorSetting	Setting	Element
NTService	UnitaryComputerSystem	HostedService	Dependent	Antecedent

(continued)

TABLE B.2 Associations and Attributions of the ZENworks for Servers Inventory Database (continued)

LOOKUP CLASS	TARGET CLASS	ASSOCIATION CLASS	ATTRIBUTE1	ATTRIBUTE2
OperatingSystem	UnitaryComputerSystem	InstalledOS	PartComponent	GroupComponent
OperatingSystemSetting	MWOperatingSystem	OSElementSetting	Setting	Element
DOSOperatingSystem	UnitaryComputerSystem	InstalledOS	PartComponent	GroupComponent
DOSStyleMemorySetting	UnitaryComputerSystem	InstalledOS	PartComponent	GroupComponent
ExtendedMemorySetting	DOSOperatingSystem	DOSMemoryElementSetting	Setting	Element
ExpandedMemorySetting	DOSOperatingSystem	DOSMemoryElementSetting	Setting	Element
MWOperatingSystem	UnitaryComputerSystem	InstalledOS	PartComponent	GroupComponent
NetwareOperatingSystem	UnitaryComputerSystem	InstalledOS	PartComponent	GroupComponent
MWPhysicalMemory	UnitaryComputerSystem	SystemPhysicaldevice	PartComponent	GroupComponent
Memory	UnitaryComputerSystem	ComputerSystemMemory	PartComponent	GroupComponent
MWLocalFileSystem	UnitaryComputerSystem	HostedFileSystem	PartComponent	GroupComponent
MWRemoteFileSystem	UnitaryComputerSystem	HostedFileSystem	PartComponent	GroupComponent
MWDisketteDrive	UnitaryComputerSystem	SystemDevice	PartComponent	GroupComponent
CDROMDrive	UnitaryComputerSystem	SystemDevice	PartComponent	GroupComponent
IPProtocolEndpoint	UnitaryComputerSystem	HostedAccessPoint	Dependent	Antecedent
IPXProtocolEndpoint	UnitaryComputerSystem	HostedAccessPoint	Dependent	Antecedent

ZENWORKS FOR SERVERS 2 DATABASE SCHEMAS

LOOKUP CLASS	TARGET CLASS	ASSOCIATION CLASS	ATTRIBUTE1	ATTRIBUTE2
EthernetProtocolEndpoint	UnitaryComputerSystem	HostedAccessPoint	Dependent	Antecedent
DNSName	UnitaryComputerSystem	Designates	Designation	Host
EnvironmentVariableSetting	MWOperatingSystem	Environment	SettingElementSetting	Element
Product	UnitaryComputerSystem	InstalledProduct	Product	ComputerSystem
InventoryScanner	UnitaryComputerSystem	InstalledProduct	Product	ComputerSystem
ComponentID	UnitaryComputerSystem	ComponentSystem	PartComponent	GroupComponent
MWPCVideoController	UnitaryComputerSystem	SystemDevice	PartComponent	GroupComponent
VideoAdapter	UnitaryComputerSystem	SystemDevice	PartComponent	GroupComponent
MWCacheMemory	UnitaryComputerSystem	ComputerSystemMemory	PartComponent	GroupComponent
PhysicalComponent	UnitaryComputerSystem	SystemPhysicalDevice	PartComponent	GroupComponent
WsUser	UnitaryComputerSystem	WsUsedBy	WsUser	Computer
NetworkAdapter	UnitaryComputerSystem	SystemDevice	PartComponent	GroupComponent
IPNetwork	ipprotocolendpoint	InIPNetwork	GroupComponent	PartComponent

You should keep the following points about Table B.2 in mind:

- Lookup class is our class for which we need the inventory attributes — say, Product.
- The Target class is the class that it is associated to. This class is UnitaryComputerSystem for direct associations.
- Association class is the class that is used to associate the Lookup class with the Target class.
- Association Attribute1 points to the Lookup class.
- Association Attribute2 points to the Target class.

For example, if you are interested in getting all the software products installed on a given server, the following query should be formed using Table B.2:

```
SELECT  Product.name, Product.version FROM Product,
UnitaryComputerSystem, InstalledProduct WHERE
Product.id$=InstalledProduct.Product AND
UnitaryComputerSystem.id$=InstalledProduct.ComputerSystem
AND UnitaryComputerSystem.id$ = (SELECT id$ FROM
UnitaryComputerSystem WHERE Name=?)
```

By replacing ? with the name of the server, the query gives you the name and version of the products installed on the server.

In the same way, you can build different queries to get other inventory information. Follow this format:

```
SELECT <LookupClass>.* FROM <LookupClass>, <TargetClass>,
<AssociationClass>
WHERE<LookupClass>.id$=<AssociationClass>.<Attribute1> AND
<TargetClass>.id$=<AssociationClass>.<Attribute2> AND
UnitaryComputerSystem.id$ = (SELECT id$ FROM
UnitaryComputerSystem WHERE Name=?)
```

About the TED Database Schema

Table B.3 describes the tables used by ZENworks for Servers 2 for TED objects in the NDS database. These include distribution, subscriber, and channel objects. The ID field is the primary key for each table.

Table B.4 describes the tables used by ZENworks for Servers 2 for Policy and Software packages. The * denotes the primary key for each table.

TABLE B.3 Tables Used by ZENworks for Servers for TED Entries in the Database

TABLE	FIELDS	DESCRIPTION
TAB_NODE	ID, NAME, TYPE, NETWORK_ADDRESS, SERVER_NAME	Contains one record for each distributor, subscriber, and external subscriber in the tree.
TAB_CHANNEL	ID, NAME	Contains one record for each channel object in the tree.
TAB_DISTRIBUTION	ID, NAME, DISTRIBUTOR_ID	Contains one record for each Distribution object in the tree. It is linked to the TAB_NODE table. The DISTRIBUTOR_ID field has a many-to-one relationship with the ID field in the TAB_NODE table.
TAB_DIST_VERSION	ID, DISTRIBUTION_ID, VERSION, SIZE, TIMESTAMP, DIRECT ROUTING, PATCHING, LATEST_VERSION	Contains one record for each version of the distribution. Each version is linked to the TAB_DISTRIBUTION table. The DISTRIBUTION_ID field has a many-to-one relationship with the ID field in the TAB_DISTRUBTION table.

(continued)

TABLE B.3 Tables Used by ZENworks for Servers for TED Entries in the Database (continued)

TABLE	FIELDS	DESCRIPTION
TAB_DIST_ACTION	ID, DIST_VERSION_ID, NODE_ID, TIMESTAMP, STAGE, STATUS, STATUS_TIMESTAMP, REASON_TEXT, CHANNEL_DIST_ID	Contains multiple records for each distribution version for Gathered, Sent, Received, and Extracted. It is linked to many other tables. The DIST_VERSION_ID has a many-to-one relationship with the ID field in the TAB_DIST_VERSION table. The NODE_ID has a many-to-one relationship with the ID field in the TAB_NODE table. The CHANNEL_DIST_ID has a many-to-one relationship with the ID field in the TAB_CHANNEL_DISTRIBUTION table.
TAB_CHANNEL_	ID, CHANNEL_ID, DISTRIBUTION_ID, DISTRIBUTION TIMESTAMP	Contains one record for each distribution/channel combination. If one distribution was sent in two channels, there are two records for that distribution, each with a different value for CHANNEL_ID. The CHANNEL_ID field has a many-to-one relationship with the ID field in the TAB_CHANNEL table. The DISTRIBUTION_ID field has a many-to-one relationship with the ID field in the TAB_DISTRIBUTION table.

TABLE B.4 Tables Used by ZENworks for Servers for Policy Entries in the Database

TABLE	FIELDS	DESCRIPTION
SERVERS	SERVERID*, SERVERNAME, SERVERDN, REVERSEDN, OSNAME, OSVERSION, TREENAME	Contains one record for each server running the ZENworks for Servers policy/package agent.
SERVERIP	SERVERIPKEY*, SERVERID, IPADDRESS	Contains one record for each server running the ZENworks for Servers policy/package agent.
PACKAGES	PACKAGEGUID*, PACKAGENAME, PACKAGEDESC, PACKAGEVERSION, BUILDDATE	Contains one record for each version of a software package that the ZENworks for Servers agent has attempted to process.
POLICIES	POLICYID*, POLICYDN, POLICYPACKAGE, POLICYCLASS, POLICYTREENAME	Contains one record for each policy or policy package combination.
POLICYACTION	POLICYACTIONKEY*, POLICYID, SERVERID, CREATIONDATAE, DESCRIPTION, CODE, ACTIONCODE	Contains one record for each action performed.
PACKAGEACTION	PACKAGEACTIONID* PACKAGEGUID, SERVERID, CREATIONDATE, DESCRIPTION, CODE, ACTIONCODE, STARTEDPACKAGEACTIONID	Contains one record for each action taken on a software package.
SOFTWARE COMPONENTACTION	OFTWARECOMPONENTACTIONKEY*, SPACKAGEACTIONID, NAME, CREATIONDATE, DESCRIPTION	Contains one record for each software component.

Using the MIB Browser

ZENworks for Servers 2 provides an extremely useful tool to help you navigate and manage the SNMP-manageable nodes in the management database. The following sections discuss this tool (MIBs), how to start the MIB browser, and how to use it to view the management database.

Understanding MIBs

An MIB is a text file that contains specifically formatted data that describes the management information on a particular class of an SNMP-manageable device. Each SNMP-manageable device has a specific standard it adheres to. The MIB file is simply a definition of that standard.

ZENworks for Servers 2 compiles most of the MIBs that you need to manage your network. However, you can use the MIB Compiler to add or remove files from the MIB pool. You may want to compile an MIB from Cisco, for example, so you can manage and receive SNMP traps from those types of devices in the ZENworks for Servers console. Use the following steps from the management console to compile the MIBs:

1. Select ZENworks for Servers management site object.
2. Right-click the object and select Properties from the pop-up menu.
3. Click the Add/Remove button.
4. Select the MIBs that you wish to remove and click the Remove button.
5. Click the Add button and navigate to the .MIB files you wish to add.
6. Click the Compile button to compile the files with the .MIB extension and add them to the database.
7. Click the Close button to return.

Starting the MIB Browser

The MIB browser enables you to select object that you wish to display and then queries the node to obtain the data objects. It then periodically pools the node to update the information. Once it has obtained the data object from the node, it enables you to walk through a tree of data object in the MIB Tree Browser pane and displays the data about the object in the pane below.

Use the following steps from the management console to access the MIB browser:

ZENWORKS FOR SERVERS 2 DATABASE SCHEMAS

1. Select an SNMP-manageable node in the ZENworks for Servers namespace.
2. Select File ⇨ Action ⇨ MIB Browser from the main menu to bring up the MIB Browser window, shown in Figure B.1.
3. Click the + sign next to container objects in the MIB Tree Browser pane to expand them and walk through the MIB objects.

   View the description of the object in the following pane.

FIGURE B.1 *MIB browser of an SNMP-manageable server object in ConsoleOne*

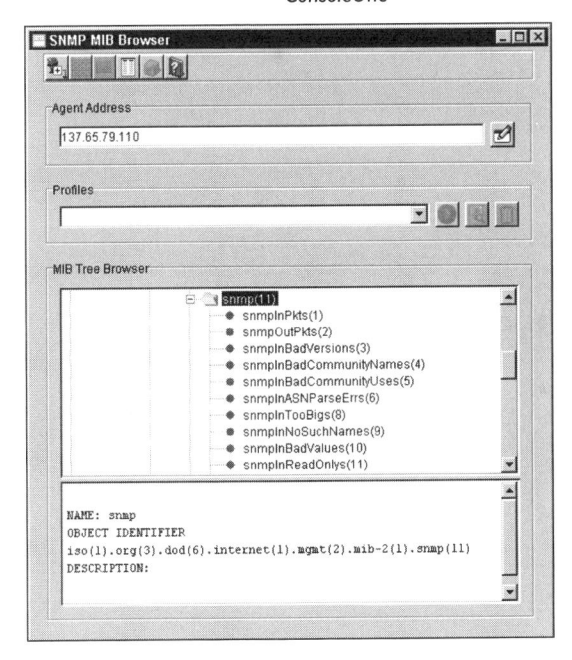

Viewing Tables of Scalar Objects

You can view tables of the scalar objects in the MIB and their dynamically updated values from the MIB browser. This enables you to see how the object data is being updated in the database.

Use the following steps from the MIB browser to view a table of scalar objects that you wish to monitor:

1. Navigate through the MIB tree until you find the scalar object(s) that you wish to monitor. If you wish to monitor more than one object, you must select the container object; otherwise, select the scalar object itself.
2. Click the "Display data as scalar table" button (fourth from left) shown in Figure B.1.
3. From the Scalar Table view, shown in Figure B.2, select any object you do not wish to monitor and click the Remove button to narrow your view down.
4. Save the settings profile so that the next time you browse through the tree you can select the same Scalar view.
5. Close the Scalar Table view window when you are finished.

FIGURE B.2 *Scalar Table view of scalar objects from the MIB browser in ConsoleOne*

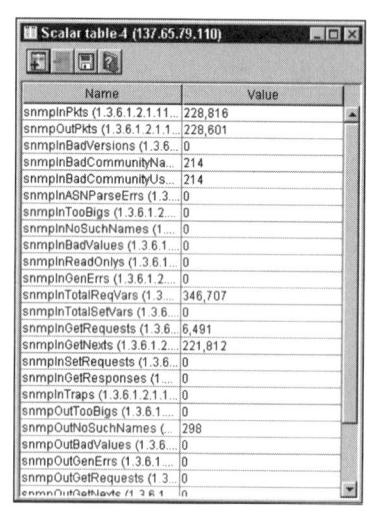

Name	Value
snmpInPkts (1.3.6.1.2.1.11...	228,816
snmpOutPkts (1.3.6.1.2.1.1...	228,601
snmpInBadVersions (1.3.6...	0
snmpInBadCommunityNa...	214
snmpInBadCommunityUs...	214
snmpInASNParseErrs (1.3...	0
snmpInTooBigs (1.3.6.1.2...	0
snmpInNoSuchNames (1...	0
snmpInBadValues (1.3.6.1...	0
snmpInReadOnlys (1.3.6.1...	0
snmpInGenErrs (1.3.6.1.2...	0
snmpInTotalReqVars (1.3...	346,707
snmpInTotalSetVars (1.3.6...	0
snmpInGetRequests (1.3.6...	6,491
snmpInGetNexts (1.3.6.1.2...	221,812
snmpInSetRequests (1.3.6...	0
snmpInGetResponses (1...	0
snmpInTraps (1.3.6.1.2.1.1...	0
snmpOutTooBigs (1.3.6.1...	0
snmpOutNoSuchNames (...	298
snmpOutBadValues (1.3.6...	0
snmpOutGenErrs (1.3.6.1...	0
snmpOutGetRequests (1.3...	0
snmpOutGetNexts (1.3.6.1...	0

APPENDIX C

ZENworks for Servers 2 Console Commands

There are several ZENworks for Servers 2 and Tiered Electronic Distribution processes that are running on the server and provide independent consoles. This appendix discusses each of these consoles and the commands that you can execute on them.

ZENworks for Servers Policy Engine

The ZENworks for Servers policy engine runs on the NetWare server and provides enforcement of server policies and also installs server software packages. The commands listed in Table C.1 are available from the ZENworks for Servers 2 console. The console is labeled as "Java Interpreter: ZENworks_for_Servers" in the screens list.

TABLE C.1 List of Console Commands for ZENworks for Servers Console

COMMAND	DESCRIPTION
cls	Clears the screen and places the prompt at the top of the screen.
down !	Downs the server, ignoring any downing policy that may be in effect.
down cancel	Cancels the current down process. If the server is still sending out messages and so forth from the down policy, the down is cancelled, the logins are re-enabled, and so forth to bring the server back to its previous state. Any previously dropped connections will, obviously, be lost.
down reset	Downs the server by performing a reset of the server. If a downing policy is administered it is enforced.
down restart	Downs the server and restarts the hardware, bringing the system back up. If a downing policy is administered, it is enforced.
down server	Downs the server and does not bring the server back up, enforcing the downing policy if one is administered.

ZENWORKS FOR SERVERS 2 CONSOLE COMMANDS

COMMAND	DESCRIPTION
`down status`	Reports whether the server is in the process of handling a down request. It tells you, for example, how many minutes before the down actually occurs.
`events fire <eventid>`	Fires an event as if the event actually happened in the server. The `eventid` is the exact string that is displayed on the events list. It is not a number, but the name of the class handling the event.
`events list`	Lists all of the events that the ZENworks for Servers 2 system is monitoring and the Java process that is watching for the event.
`events status`	This command is nonfunctional.
`exit`	Terminates the policy engine and unloads the processes. Any other enforcer or other Java processes related to ZENworks for Servers 2 policy management will continue.
`exitall`	Terminates the policy engine and all other Java processes. This command unloads `JAVA.NLM`, resulting in every Java process (even Java processes that are not related to ZFS) being terminated.
`help`	Provides help on the ZENworks for Servers 2 console commands. You may also enter **help <command>** to get more specific help on individual commands.
`listplugins`	Lists the plug-ins that are in the system.
`package list`	Lists the current set of installed software packages and the dates that they were installed. An asterisk by the item means that package can be uninstalled by requesting a rollback.
`package process <file>`	Processes the specified .CPK (software package) file and installs it onto the server.
`package rollback`	Uninstalls the last package installed (shown with an asterisk in the package list).

(continued)

TABLE C.1 List of Console Commands for ZENworks for Servers Console (continued)

COMMAND	DESCRIPTION
`policy enforce [all] [#]`	Causes a policy to be enforced, or executed, on the server even if the schedule has not fired. You may specify "all" if you wish all effective policies to be reapplied, or give a policy number (from the `policy list` command) for the policy to reapply.
`policy eventbased`	Displays the policies that are effective on this server that are activated by an event on the server.
`policy list`	Lists the current effective policies. Also displays a policy number with each effective policy. This number is used in the `policy enforce` command.
`policy plugins`	Displays the current plug-ins that are in the policy engine. There is a policy plug-in, called an enforcer, for each policy that can be associated with the server. These enforcers are responsible to make the policy effective when launched by the scheduler. This also lists the event handler that watches events that occur on the server (for example, down server) that may be monitored by the engine because a policy may affect behavior.
`policy refresh`	Causes the policy engine to refresh its configuration and policy information by going to NDS and getting all policies and re-caching them internally and rescheduling any scheduled policies.
`policy refreshonly`	Retrieves from NDS all of the effective policies associated with this server and refreshes them into the server's cache of the policies. This does not refresh or reschedule any scheduled policy.
`policy rescheduleonly`	Retrieves from NDS all of the scheduled effective policies associated with this server and refreshes them into the server's cache of the policies and reschedules them.

ZENWORKS FOR SERVERS 2 CONSOLE COMMANDS

COMMAND	DESCRIPTION
policy schedules	Displays the policy schedules that are to be fired on this server.
policy status	Displays information about the configuration of the policy engine. This information includes: tree, engine state, search policy name, policy top container, refresh seconds (time between reads of NDS for new or updated policies), search level, search order, and search type. Search order and type are a set of single-digit values that represent an order from left to right. Search order values are: 0 = object, 1 = group, 2 = container. Search type values are: 0 = root, 1 = container, 2 = partition, 3 = specified container.
prompt [new prompt]	Displays the current prompt, if none is given on the command line. If a new string prompt is given, the new prompt is set as the prompt for the console. No quotes are required for the parameter. The system automatically tacks on the > character after the prompt.
refresh	Manually requests that the server refresh its configuration policy. This does not read all policies — only the ZENworks for Servers Policy associated with this server. Use the policy refresh command to read all other policies.
setfilelevel [#]	Sets the level number for the messages to be sent to the log file. If no level number is entered, the current level is displayed. This does not change the messages that are sent to the console.
showschedule	Displays the current scheduled actions and the Java classes (plug-in) that will handle the action when the schedule fires.
showvars	Lists the current variables that are defined on the system. This gives the keys and their values.

(continued)

TABLE C.1 List of Console Commands for ZENworks for Servers Console (continued)

COMMAND	DESCRIPTION
status	Displays status information on the policy engine, including: base path, number of plug-ins loaded, number of events registered, number of scheduled items, and the current console message level.
time	Displays the current date and time of the server.
version	Displays the current version of the ZENworks for Servers 2 Policy Manager.

The commands listed in Table C.2 are the debug commands that are available with the policy engine. These commands are not supported by Novell, Inc. and may not be fully functional. These commands are valid even if debug is not turned on in the console.

TABLE C.2 List of Debug Console Commands for ZENworks for Servers 2 Console

COMMAND	DESCRIPTION
addtables	Adds tables to the Sybase database for logging policy messages and events.
debug	Instructs user to use the debugon command to turn on help for debug commands.
debugoff	Turns off help for debug commands.
debugon	Turns on help for debug commands.
deltables	Deletes the log tables that were created in the Sybase database for logging policy messages and events. All of the data that are in the tables will be lost.
echo <command> <console>	Sends the given command to the specified ZENworks for Server 2 console, such as distributor or subscriber. For example, echo help distributor causes the distributor console to execute the help command.

ZENWORKS FOR SERVERS 2 CONSOLE COMMANDS

COMMAND	DESCRIPTION
`load <module name>`	Loads the specified Java class module into the Java engine.
`logconsoleoutputoff`	Turns off sending all characters displayed on the console to the log file.
`logconsoleoutputon`	Turns on sending all characters displayed on the console to the log file.
`off`	Performs a clear screen, just like `cls`.
`q`	Quits the policy engine. This is the same as `exit`.
`resolve [ip address|dns name]`	Resolves a given IP address or DNS name. This returns the IP address and the DNS name known to the system.
`send <message>`	Performs a broadcast of the message to all connected users.
`setconsolelevel [#]`	Sets the level of messages to display on the policy engine console. The level is the same as the `setfilelevel` command. The default level is 4, but can be specified in the ZFS policy. The level is reset back to the level specified on any refresh, or restart of the policy engine.
`showstates`	Displays the various Java components (in policy engine threads) that are currently active and the state they are in, such as downing in five minutes and so forth.
`spc <dn><plugin><cmd><string>`	Executes a "server procedure call" to the specified server DN. The call causes the plug-in specified to be loaded and the command with the given string parameters to be launched. This can be used to launch an enforcer on a remote server.
`threads`	Lists the current threads that the policy engine is managing.

445

TED Distributor

The ZENworks for Servers TED distributor engine runs on the NetWare server and provides processing of distributions to subscribers. The commands listed in Table C.3 are available from the Distributor console. The console is labeled as Distributor in the screens list.

TABLE C.3 *List of Console Commands for the TED Distributor Console*

COMMAND	DESCRIPTION
`agent -k [agent_id]`	Terminates any agent (thread) that the distributor is using to build a distribution. The `-k` option alone kills all agents, which will be restarted at the next scheduled event (the next time the distribution schedule fires). The optional `agent_id` can be specified to kill exactly one agent. To look up an agent_id, use the `threads` command.
`channel [-s] [-d][-n DN]`	Displays configuration information and actions for channels that this distributor is participating in. The following options are available: `-s` = shows information about each channel that there is a distribution from this distributor. `-d` = sends the distributions. `-n DN` = only performs the actions for the given channel DN. For example, `channel -d` sends every distribution from this distributor in every channel, but `channel -d -n chan1.novell` only sends the distributions from this distributor that are in the `chan1.novell channel`. Note: Enclose the `DN` parameter in double quotes ("") if the DN contains special characters or white space.
`cls`	Clears the screen and place the prompt at the top of the screen.

ZENWORKS FOR SERVERS 2 CONSOLE COMMANDS

COMMAND	DESCRIPTION
`config [-s [ip]] [-d file]`	Displays all of the configuration information for the distributor, or for the given IP address. The given IP address is expected to be a subscriber or parent subscriber. The `-d file` option enables you to place this configuration information into the specified file. You should only specify the name of the file, as the location cannot be specified. The file will always be written to the working directory for the distributor.
`distribution [-s][-b][-n DN]`	Displays information about any distributions that this distributor is responsible to handle. The options are as follows: `-s` = shows information about each distribution. `-b` = builds the distributions. `-n DN` = only performs the actions for the given channel DN. For example, `distribution -b` causes the distributor to build every distribution, but `distribution -b -n virusupdate.novell` causes the distributor to only build the `virusupdate.novell` distribution. Note: Enclose the `DN` parameter in double quotes ("") if the DN contains special characters or white space.
`exit`	Terminates the distributor process on the server.
`help`	Displays help on the commands.
`prompt [new prompt]`	Displays the current prompt, if none is given on the command line. If a new prompt is given, the new prompt is set as the prompt for the console. No quotes are required for the parameter. The system automatically tacks on the > character after the prompt.
`refresh`	Manually requests that the distributor refresh all configuration information. This includes looking at the distributor's distributions and scheduling any distributions. Note: All distributions and channels with the Run Immediately schedule type start immediately upon refreshing the distributor.

(continued)

TABLE C.3 *List of Console Commands for the TED Distributor Console (continued)*

COMMAND	DESCRIPTION
route <subscriberDN>	Displays the IP address(es) of the subscriber(s) that participate in passing distributions from this distributor to the subscriber or external subscriber specified. This command enables you to verify that this distributor is implementing your routing hierarchy in the manner you intended. Note: Enclose the subscriberDN in double quotes ("") if the DN contains special characters or white space.
schedule	Shows the currently scheduled actions (waiting to be fired). This includes building distributions, sending channels, and refreshing configuration information from NDS.
setfilelevel <#>	Sets the level of messages that should be logged to the log file. This level is specified in the distributor object in NDS, or the TED policy effective for the distributor object. Any changes you make to this level with console commands are reset to the value specified in NDS upon the next distributor refresh.
time	Displays the current date and time.
version	Displays the current version of the distributor.
wo [-s [ip]] [-k ip][-d file] [-dead]	Displays work order information. When a channel is to be sent to a subscriber, the scheduler places a work order into the distributor's queue. This can be used to see and manipulate these work orders. The following options are available: -s = shows all outgoing work orders from this distributor or only those work orders going from this distributor to the specified IP address (subscriber or parent subscriber). -k = kills all work orders from this distributor to the specified IP address (subscriber or parent subscriber). Work orders to the specified subscriber will resume at the next scheduled event (the next time a channel is to be distributed to that subscriber).

ZENWORKS FOR SERVERS 2 CONSOLE COMMANDS

COMMAND	DESCRIPTION
	`-d file` = dumps the information into a specified file. This file will always be written in the working directory for the distributor.
	`-dead` = shows work orders that seem to be dead.

The commands listed in Table C.4 are the debug commands that are available with the distributor. These commands are not supported by Novell, Inc. and may not be fully functional. These commands are valid even if debug is not turned on in the console.

TABLE C.4 List of Debug Console Commands for TED Distributor Console

COMMAND	DESCRIPTION
`debugoff`	Turns off help for the debug commands.
`debugon`	Turns on help for the debug commands.
`logconsoleoutputoff`	Stops sending the output sent to the console also to the log file.
`logconsoleoutputon`	Turns on sending all of the characters to the log file as well as the console.
`off`	Performs a `cls` command.
`setconsolelevel [#]`	Sets the level of messages to display on the distributor console. The level is similar to the level set with the `setfilelevel` command. This level is specified in the distributor object, or in a TED policy effective for the distributor object. Any changes you make to this level with console commands are reset to the level specified in NDS upon the next distributor refresh.
`threads`	Lists the current threads that the policy engine is managing.

NOVELL'S ZENWORKS FOR SERVERS 2 ADMINISTRATOR'S HANDBOOK

TED Subscriber

The ZENworks for Servers 2 TED subscriber engine runs on a NetWare or NT/2000 server and provides processing of distributions from distributors. The commands listed in Table C-5 are available from the subscriber console. The subscriber console is labeled as Subscriber on the screens list in NetWare. On Windows NT/2000 machines, the subscriber console runs in a window that looks similar to a command prompt.

TABLE C.5 List of Console Commands for TED Subscriber Console

COMMAND	DESCRIPTION
agent -k [agent_id]	Terminates any extraction agent (thread) that the subscriber is using to extract a distribution. The -k option alone kills all agents, which will be restarted at the next scheduled event. The optional agent_id can be specified to kill exactly one agent. To look up an agent_id, use the threads command.
certs [-s] [-u][-l]	Displays the known certificates that the subscriber has for the distributors from which it will accept distributions. The following options are available: -s = shows all known certificates from distributors. -u = unloads all certificates. -l = loads all certificates from the security directory.
cls	Clears the screen and places the prompt at the top of the screen.
config [-s [ip]] [-d file]	Displays all of the configuration information for the subscriber, or for the given IP address. The given IP address is expected to be a subordinate subscriber or external subscriber. The -d file option allows you to place this configuration information into the specified file. You should only specify the name for the file, as the location cannot be changed. The file will always be saved in the working directory for the subscriber. On Windows NT/2000 subscribers, you can specify the location for the file, but not on NetWare subscribers.
exit	Terminates the subscriber process.

ZENWORKS FOR SERVERS 2 CONSOLE COMMANDS

COMMAND	DESCRIPTION
extract [-s [tree,dn]] [-x tree,dn] [-r tree,dn]	Extracts the specified distribution, running the agent to process the distribution. This also forwards the distribution to other subscribers if this is a parent subscriber. The options are as follows: -s = shows all received distributions and their status. If the tree and DN are specified, only the status for the specified distribution is displayed. -x = extracts the specified distribution. -r = resets the distribution status to be available for extraction. Note: Enclose the parameters (that is, tree,dn) in double quotes ("") and do not put a space after the comma (,) unless a leading space is part of the DN name. For example type extract -x "zentree,virusdist.novell" to extract the virusdist.novell distribution from the zentree.
prompt [new prompt]	Displays the current prompt, if none is given on the command line. If a new prompt is given, the new prompt is set as the prompt for the console. No quotes are required for the parameter. The system automatically tacks on the > character after the prompt.
schedule	Shows the currently scheduled actions (waiting to be fired). This includes when the subscriber is scheduled to extract distributions and any messages that are scheduled to be sent to a distributor.
setfilelevel <#>	Sets the level of messages that should be logged to the log file. This level is specified in the subscriber object in NDS, or the TED policy effective for the subscriber object. Any changes you make to this level with console commands will be reset to the value specified in NDS upon the next reception of a distribution.
time	Displays the current date and time.
version	Displays the current version of the subscriber.

(continued)

TABLE C.5 List of Console Commands for TED Subscriber Console (continued)

COMMAND	DESCRIPTION
wo [-s [ip]] [-k ip][-d file] [-dead]	Displays work order information. When there is something for the distributor to do, such as build a distribution and so forth, the scheduler places a work order into the distributor's queue. This can be used to see and manipulate these work orders. The following options are available: -s = shows all outgoing work orders from this subscriber or from this subscriber to the specified IP address (subordinate subscriber or external subscriber). -k = kills all work orders from this subscriber to the specified IP address (subordinate subscriber or external subscriber). Work orders to the specified subscriber resume at the next scheduled event (the next time a channel is to be distributed to that subscriber). -d file = dumps the information into a specified file. -dead = shows work orders that seem to be dead. This file is always written in the working directory for the subscriber.

The commands listed in Table C.6 are the debug commands that are available with the subscriber. These commands are not supported by Novell, Inc. and may not be fully functional. These commands are valid even if debug is not turned on in the console.

TABLE C.6 List of debug console commands for TED Subscriber Console

COMMAND	DESCRIPTION
debugoff	Turns off help for the debug commands.
debugon	Turns on help for the debug commands.
logconsoleoutputoff	Stops the sending of output to the log file (although it will be sent to the console file).
logconsoleoutputon	Turns on the sending all of the characters to the log file, as well as to the console.

ZENWORKS FOR SERVERS 2 CONSOLE COMMANDS

COMMAND	DESCRIPTION
off	Performs a cls command.
setconsolelevel [#]	Sets the level of messages to display on the subscriber console. The level is similar to the level set with the setfilelevel command. This level is specified in the subscriber object, or in a TED policy effective for the subscriber object. Any changes you make to this level with console commands are reset to the level specified in NDS upon the next reception of a distribution.
threads	Lists the current threads that the policy engine is managing.

APPENDIX D

ZENworks for Servers 2 Resources

This appendix describes several resources that are available to assist you to discover and implement ZENworks for Servers 2.

Novell Support and Online Documentation

Novell has set up a Web site that is the home for ZENworks products, www.novell.com/products/zenworks. You can find Novell's online documentation and announcements for updates to the product on this site.

Additionally, from this page you can follow the links to support.novell.com/products, where you can find any patches and fixes that may be released for the product. You can find ZENworks products under the NetWare Products categories.

ZENworks Cool Solutions

There are many more uses for ZENworks for Servers 2 than can ever be described in a book like this. There are many customers who use ZENworks for Servers 2 every day and get very creative in using the system.

Novell has set up a location on the Internet, www.novell.com/coolsolutions/zenworks, where customers can go and ask questions of the actual ZENworks for Servers 2 engineers and see what solutions other customers have done with ZENworks for Servers 2. This is also the destination site for users of ZENworks for Desktop and ZENworks Cool Solutions.

The site changes often and features articles from real customers and insiders on how to make ZENworks for Servers 2 work in your network. It also includes a list of frequently asked questions and their answers, and articles from other deployment specialists who are in the trenches. You can often find a white paper at the Cool Solutions site that will have the information you need for your issues.

Occasionally, the site also posts software that is not supported by Novell, but is provided by some internal Novell engineers, Novell consultants, or customers. These tools can help you deploy and manage ZENworks for Servers 2.

Once, on the ZENworks Cool Solutions site, the Webmaster organized a live "Ask the Experts" session with several ZENworks for Desktops engineers, where customers could ask their questions online and get real-time answers. We even have seen some job postings for companies that are looking for ZENmasters to come and implement ZENworks in their environments.

Novell Consulting Services

Novell Consulting Services has many good engineers who are familiar with ZENworks for Servers and how it can help Novell customers in their environments. They can assist you, beyond support, in getting ZENworks for Servers 2 to do exactly what you want for your network. Novell Consulting Services can help you with field consulting and with any custom developments you may need, tailoring ZENworks for Servers 2 to your organization's needs.

APPENDIX E

ZENworks for Servers 2 Support Packs

The ZENworks for Servers 2 product team is planning on supplying support packs for this product in order to fix software problems that were shipped in the product. At the time of the publication of this book, the team was preparing a support pack 1 for ZENworks for Servers 2. This appendix discusses the problems and changes that are expected to be in support pack 1. This appendix may not contain or describe all of the fixes that will ultimately be in the support pack.

You can download the ZENworks for Servers 2 support packs from the ZENworks for Servers 2 home page, located at `support.novell.com/products`. From there, you can find the ZENworks for Servers 2 product and any additional information, TIDs, or patches and files.

Support Pack 1

We expect the following items to be modified in support pack 1 for ZENworks for Servers 2 in early 2001.

Problem:

The system only distributes to the number of maximum concurrent distributions in the distributor object. So, for example, if the maximum connections were set to 10, only the first 10 subscribers that are receiving distributions directly from the distributor receive the distributions.

Current Solution:

Set the number of maximum concurrent distributions in the Distributor object to the value of **0**. The zero value signals the distributor to have no limit.

Alternatively, you may use a combination of parent subscribers to make sure that the distributor never attempts to distribute to more subscribers than set in the maximum concurrent distributions. Remember that the number of subscribers receiving from the distributor is the list of subscribers in each channel where a distribution is placed.

Resolution:

The system cycles properly through all subscribers.

Problem:

The port broker process has built-in safeguards to help in denial-of-service attacks on the TED system. If the port broker receives over 100 requests per second, it shuts down for 60 minutes, after which it starts accepting requests again. This can appear in your system if you have a distributor that is servicing a large number of subscribers (say 300, or any number greater than 100) and all of the subscribers attempt to reply to the distributor at the same time. This causes the distributor to accept the first 100 subscriber messages before the port broker times out because it is receiving more than 100 replies in the second. The remaining subscriber messages (200) never get through to the distributor.

Current Solution:
None

Resolution:

New command-line arguments are allowed on the port broker. These arguments enable you to set the timeout and request rates for the port broker to time out. The expected command-line arguments are as follows: timeout=<number of milliseconds>; request_rate=<count per second>. Also, the default timeout is changed to 15 minutes.

For example, the following command line added to the port broker NCF file would tell the port broker to time out for 5 minutes when it receives 200 or more requests per second:

```
timeout=300000 request_rate=200
```

Problem:

When multiple subscribers require the same patch file from a single distributor, the distributor attempts to build a patch file for each of the subscribers at the same time. Because the simultaneous builds are trying to create the same file, the patch file can become corrupt, and when sent to the subscriber, they may not accept the file because it detects "corrupt stream errors."

Current Solution:

Set up a parent subscriber and have the distributor send the patch to the parent, and have the parent distribute the patch. Because the patch is already calculated before being sent to the parent, the problem is eliminated.

Resolution:

The system detects if the patch file is being created when a second request for the same patch file is activated. The subsequent request for the same patch file is rescheduled until the patch file from the first request is completed.

Problem:

If you choose via the install process (Policy and Distribution Services) to only install the ZENworks for servers policy engine, the install does not install all of the required Java libraries needed for the engine to install properly.

If you install the subscriber or the distributor to the target server, the install copies these files.

Current Solution:

You need to install at least one TED agent or manually copy the following files from the ZENworks for Servers Companion CD to the specified directory:

Copy the following files to the SYS:\JAVA\NJCLv2\BIN directory on the server where the policy engine is to run:

JNCPv2.NLM

PFTDLBS.NLM

Copy the following files to the SYS:\JAVA\NJCLv2\LIB directory on the target server:

NJCLv2.JAR

JNSE.JAR

Resolution:

A complete Install Wizard for the support pack does not occur, so this issue is not fixed.

Problem:

The NAL agent does not match and use the volumes listed in the site object if they do not match the case on the target server.

Current Solution:

None

Resolution:
The agent is no longer case sensitive to the volume names.

Problem:
When the distributor launches, it connects to NDS to authenticate. Once it has done so, it looks for the license that activates the TED system. It does so by searching the effective service location policy package that contains a ZENworks license location policy that points to the ZENworks for Servers license object in NDS. If this license is not found, on some systems the distributor causes the server to abend.

Current Solution:
Make sure that the licenses are properly installed via the ZENworks for Servers 2 installation process and that the license location policy is activated and effective for the distributor. (See Chapter 5 for more details.)

Resolution:
The distributor does not make calls that may abend the server.

Problem:
In a clustering environment, the distributor may not be able to connect to NDS in order to retrieve its configuration information and all of the information concerning channels and distributions.

Current Solution:
None

Resolution:
The distributor has been updated to properly reference NDS in a cluster environment.

Problem:
Sometimes the distributor cannot begin functioning unless it can locate and use the root partition of the NDS tree. This is primarily associated with its need to walk the tree to look for policies.

Current Solution:

Ensure that at least one replica of the root partition is accessible from the servers that are running distributors.

Resolution:

Support pack 1 does not have any changes. The distributor will continue to require access to a replica of the root partition. This replica does not need to exist on the machine running the distributor, but at least one replica of the root partition must be available to the distributor.

Index

A

accessing
   atlas, 258–259
   List Segment Statistics view, 274
   Segment Dashboard view, 275
   Trend Data view, 275
Actions command (File menu), 285
active alarm views, 228
Add Application dialog box, 365
Add Ping Targets dialog box, 329
adding
   applications for scanning, 364–365
   columns, 232
   components to Server Software Packages, 202–203
   objects as trustee, 57
   rules to Server Software Packages, 197
   scripts to policies, 96–97
Agent property page of TED distribution objects, 161–162
alarm management services, 4
   for Management Site Services, 223–224
Alarm Manager, 34
alarms
   actions, setting, 316
   Alarm Filter dialog box, 314
   alarm injector, 303
   Alarm Sorting dialog box, 312
   applications, launching, 318–319
   archive, 321
   audible beeps, 307–308
   beep on console, 322
   database archives, 304–305
   deleting, 323–324
   disabling, 306–307
   dispositions, 304
   e-mail notifications, 317–318
   enabling, 306–307
   filtering, 312–315
   forwarding, 320–321
   history, disabling, 310
   history views, 229
   indicators, 307
   managing, 315
   monitoring active, 308–310
   processed, 304
   processors, types of, 303
   purge process, 324–325
   reports for, 224
   show on Ticker Bar, 322
   SNMP trap receivers, 302
   sorting, 310–312
   templates, 304
   troubleshooting, 408–409
   viewers, 305
Appearance command (View menu), 230–231
application TED site distribution object, 42
applications
   adding for scanning, 364–365
   removing from scanning, 366
archive alarm processors, 303
asset management inventory reports, 370
Assigned Rights button, 56

Association pages
　Container Policy Package, 56
　Service Location Policy Package, 63
atlas
　accessing, 258–259
　Area page, 259
　island page, 259
　troubleshooting networks with, 260
　WAN page, 259
Atlas Manager, 244, 257–258
　command-line options, 260
atlas views, 228
autodiscovery, 35

B

bridges
　monitoring groups, 267–268
　transparent, 248
Broadcast Message pages, Server Down Process Policies, 92
buttons
　Assigned Rights, 56
　Effective Rights, 60
　Horizontal Grid, 344
　Reset, 62
　Run Selected, 381
　Vertical Grid, 344

C

capture packets
　capture filter, setting up, 284–285
　decoded packet data, 289
　filtering display for, 290
　hexadecimal packet data, 289–290
　highlighting tools, 291
　overview, 284
　starting, 286–287
　stopping, 287
　summary pane, 288–289
　viewing, 288
Capture Packets command (File menu), 285
channel objects, 177
　distributions property page, 178
　Schedule property page, 178
　Settings property page, 178
　subscriber property page, 178
channels
　creating, 27
　defined, 27
　schedules, 126
Channels property page
　of external subscriber objects, 157
　of subscriber objects, 149–150
　of TED distribution objects, 160–161
Column Selector command (View menu), 232
columns
　adding, 232
　changing order of, 232
　removing, 232
　resizing, 231
command-line options for Atlas Manager, 260
commands
　Actions, Software Scan Editor, 365
　console, list of, 440–444
　console for TED distributor, 446–448
　debug console, list of, 444–445
　File menu, Actions, 285
　File menu, Connectivity Test, 328
　File menu, Export, 234, 383
　File menu, Ping, 326
　File menu, Save, 291
　New (Policy Package), 54, 63

INDEX

for TED distributor, 449
for TED subscriber console, 450–453
Tools menu, Reports, 385
Tools menu, Server Inventory Reports, 381
View menu, Alarms History, 310
View menu, Appearance, 230–231
View menu, Column Selector, 232
View menu, Conversations, 282
View menu, Edit Saved Views, 234
View menu, Filter, 232, 290
View menu, List Segment, 274
View menu, Monitor Nodes, 284
View menu, Protocol Distribution, 293
View menu, Pulling, 327
View menu, Save As, 234
View menu, Segment Dashboard, 275
View menu, Segment Summary, 279
View menu, Segment Trends, 275
View menu, Show Top Stations, 281
View menu, Show View Title, 231
View menu, Sort, 233
View menu, Stations, 280
View menu, Summary, 340
View menu, Switch Summary, 294
Common Object Request Broker Architecture. *See* CORBA
community names, changing, 253–254
compiling
  MIBs, 436
  Server Software Packages, 215
Computer Systems by Segment reports, 371–372
Conditions page of Server Down Process Policies, 94–96
configuring
  NetWare SNMP parameters, 295
  server parameters, 349–350
  TED systems, 123

TED systems, distributor validation, 124–125
TED systems, hierarchy routing construction, 124
TED systems, scheduler interactions, 125–127
Connectivity Test (File menu), 328
console views. *See* views
ConsoleOne
  installing, 17
  overview, 5
  snap-ins, 39
Consolidator software, 221, 243–244
container package objects, 42
Container Policy Package
  Associations page, 56
  creating, 54–55
  Effective Rights page, 58
  Inherited Rights Filters page, 57–58
  NDS Rights property page, 56
  Other Property page, 58–60
  policy page, 55–56
  Rights to Files and Folders Property page, 60
  Trustees of This Object page, 56–57
Conversations command (View menu), 282
Cool Solutions Web site, 456
Copy File Property page of Server Software Packages, 207–208
copying files/folders, 208–209
CORBA (Common Object Request Broker Architecture), 263
.CPK files, 189
creating
  baseline documents, 268–269
  channels, 27
  Container Policy Package, 54–55
  distribution detail report, 394–395

(continued)

467

creating *(continued)*
  distributions, manual, 165–166
  health reports, 390–391
  inventory reports, 381
  NetWare Set Parameters Policies,
    83–85
  revision history report for failures, 397
  revision history reports, 396–397
  Server Policy Package, 63
  Server Scripts Policies, 96–97
  Server Software Packages, 194–195
  Service Location Policy Package,
    60–61
  .SPK files, 190
  subscriber detail reports, 395
  subscriber distribution detail reports,
    395–396
  Text File Changes policies, 102–103
  topology reports, 384–385
cumulative policies versus plural
  policies, 53–54

D

database administration components,
  223
Database Location Policy, 80–81
database objects, 42
deleting
  alarms, 323–324
  views, 234
detailed reports, 380
dialog boxes
  Add Application, 365
  Add Ping Targets, 329
  Alarm Filter, 314
  Alarm Sorting, 312
  Display Filter, 291
  Edit Alarm, 306
  Edit Alarm Disposition, 316
  Edit Parameters, 350
  Edit Profile, 388
  Edit Report, 391
  Edit Trend, 347–348
  Extensions, 366
  NetExplorer Modules, 252
  Network discovery IP mask, 255
  New Profile, 389
  SNMP, 253
digital certificates, 115
disabling
  alarm history, 310
  alarms, 306–307
  trend files, 357
discovery. *See* network discovery
discovery software, 221, 242–243
Display Filter dialog box, 291
disposition alarm archivers, 305
distribution reports, creating, 394–395
distribution services, activating in tree,
  49–50
distributions
  creating manual, 165–166
  importing, 166–167
Distributions property page of distributor objects, 133
distributor objects
  Distributions property page, 133
  Effective Rights page, 141
  Inherited Rights Filter page, 140–141
  Messaging property page, 130–132
  NDS Rights property page, 138
  Other property page, 142–143
  Routing Hierarchy property page,
    133–135
  Schedule property page, 135–138
  Settings property page, 129–130
  Trustees of This Object page,
    138–140
distributors
  defining configuration information
    for, 28
  function of, 40
  limits of, 123

INDEX

schedules, 125–126
validating, 124–125
Down Procedure page of Server Down Process Policies, 88–89

E

e-mail, 76–77
Edit Alarm dialog box, 306
Edit Alarm Disposition dialog box, 316
Edit Parameters dialog box, 350
Edit Profile dialog box, 388
Edit Report dialog box, 391
Edit Saved Views command (View menu), 234
Edit Trend dialog box, 347–348
editing
 file extensions for scanning, 365–366
 search orders, 69
 time spans, 343–344
 Trend Data view profiles, 345–346
Effective Rights button, 60
Effective Rights page
 Container Policy Package, 58
 of distributor objects, 141
enabling
 alarms, 306–307
 trend files, 357
Export command (File menu), 234, 383
exporting
 inventory reports, 383–384
 views, 234
Extensions dialog box, 366
external subscriber objects
 Channels property page, 157
 defined, 155
 General property page, 157
 Network Address property page, 157–158
Extract Schedule property page of subscriber objects, 150–153

F

FDDI network profiles, 379
File agents, 174–176
File menu commands
 Actions, 285
 Connectivity Test, 328
 Export, 234, 383
 Ping, 326
 Save, 291
files
 appending text to, 210
 copying, 208–209
 extensions, editing for scanning, 365–366
 identifying, 208–209
 searching, 210–212
Filter command (View menu), 232, 290
filtering
 alarms, 312–315
 inventory reports, 383
filters, limiting views with, 232–233
folders
 copying, 208–209
 identifying, 208
forwarding alarms, 320–321
FTP agents, 171–172

G

General property pages
 of external subscriber objects, 157
 Server Policy Package, 64–65
 of TED distribution objects, 159–160
general server inventory reports, 370
graphical views, 230
graphs
 grid lines, 344
 stacking, 344–345
 unstacking, 344–345
grid lines, viewing, 344

469

H

hardware inventory reports, 370
health reports, 224
   creating, 390–391
   defined, 373
   Ethernet network profiles, 378
   FDDI network profiles, 379
   force running, 392
   Microsoft Windows profiles, 377–378
   NetWare server profiles, 377
   profiles, adding new, 388–390
   profiles, customizing, 386–388
   scheduling, 392
   token ring network profiles, 378–379
   trend parameters, 374–377
   viewing, 392–393
highlighting tool, 291
history reports, 380
Horizontal Grid button, 344
HTTP agents, 170–171

I

Identification property page of Server Software Packages, 196, 203
importing distributions, 166–167
inbound alarm processors, 303
Inherited Rights Filters page
   Container Policy Package, 57–58
   of distributor objects, 140–141
installing
   ConsoleOne, 17
   JVM (Java Virtual Machine), 15, 405
   Remote Web Console, 179
   Server Software Packages on target servers, 216
installing ZENworks for Server 2
   completion of, 29–30
   distributions services, 14–16, 25–29
   management services, 11–14
   monitoring services, 11–14
   policy services, 14–16, 25–29
   server components, 16–19
   site management Console snap-ins, 25
   site management services and agents, 20–24
   site management services licenses, 25
   from workstations, 10–11
inventory. *See also* server inventory
   comprehensive, 370
   general server, 370
   management of, 36
   topology, 371
inventory reports. *See also* reports
   asset management, 370
   creating, 381
   exporting, 383–384
   filtering, 383
   hardware, 370
   health, 373–377
   health, profiles, 377–379
   networking information, 370
   printing, 383
   simple list of, 369–370
   troubleshooting, 405
   viewing, 381
IP addressing considerations, 236–237
IPX transports, 237

INDEX

J

Java Class
  loading, 205–206
  unloading, 206
Java Virtual Machine. *See* JVM
JDBC (Java Database Connectivity), 263
JVM (Java Virtual Machine)
  installing, 15
  installing, troubleshooting, 405

L

LAN traffic analysis
  baseline documents, creating, 268–269
  bridge agent monitoring groups, 267–268
  LANZCON utility, 297–298
  LANZ.NCF file commands, 296–297
  management console components, 263
  manager server components, 262
  monitoring agent servers, 263
  NetWare SNMP parameters, 295
  RMON agent property panel, 269–270
  RMON agents, 264–265
  RMON lite agent monitoring groups, 265
  RMON plus agent monitoring groups, 265–266
  RMON2 agent monitoring groups, 266–267
  SNMP parameters, setting up, 270–272
  troubleshooting, 405
launching alarm applications, 318–319
license paths, 21

List Segment command (View menu), 274
loading
  Java Class, 205–206
  NLM, 205
log files
  errors within, 30
  message files, 76
logins, disabling before downing, 89

M

management and monitoring services feature
  inventory management, 36
  management site services, 34–35
  remote management, 36
  server management, 35–36
  starting up, 47–48
management console
  hardware requirements, 13
  LAN traffic components, 263
  overview, 226–227
  software requirements, 13
management servers
  defined, 11
  hardware requirements, 11
  software requirements, 12
Management Site Services
  alarm management, 223–224
  database administration components, 223
  MIB tools, 222
  network discovery components, 221
  overview, 220
  reporting components, 224
  role-based services, 224
  SNMP services, 222
  topology mapping, 221–222

471

ManageWise
    migrating from ZENworks for Servers 2, 30–31
    and ZENworks relationship, 5–6
MD5 message digests, 115
Messaging property page
    configuration parameters, 76
    of distributor objects, 130–132
    message levels, 75–76
    of subscriber objects, 147–149
    TED (Tiered Electronic Distribution) Policies, 75–77
MIB browser
    compiling, 436
    starting, 436–437
MIB tools
    function of, 35
    SNMP MIB Browser, 222
    SNMP MIB Compiler, 222
migrating
    from ManageWise 2 to Zenworks for Servers 2, 30–31
    from ZENworks for Servers 1.0, 31–32
Monitor Nodes command (View menu), 284
monitoring
    LAN traffic agent servers, 263
    nodes activity, 283–284
    services on monitored nodes, 330–331
    services on target nodes, 325
    services on target nodes, multiple, 326–328
    services on target nodes, single, 326
    SNMP services, 222–223
MW account objects, 43
MW domain objects, 43
MW scope objects, 43
MW service objects, 43

N

NAL application distribution agents, 168–169
namespaces, 227–228
    and server management, 338
NCP Servers report, 371–372
NCPIPX discovery cycle, 246
NDS objects
    channel, 114
    distribution, 113
    external subscriber, 113
    installation connections, 15
    subscriber, 113
NDS Rights property pages
    Container Policy Package, 56
    of distributor objects, 138
NetExplorer Modules dialog box, 252
NetWare
    Policies property page of Server Policy Package, 65–66
    Set Parameters Policies, creating, 83–85
    SNMP parameters, configuring, 295
    target services, 14
    versions, 198
Network Address property page of external subscriber objects, 157–158
network discovery
    Atlas Manager, 244
    community names, changing, 253–254
    Consolidator software, 243–244
    default configuration, changing, 251–252
    discovery software, 242–243
    LAN segments, 248
    modules, loading, 252–253

INDEX

NCPIPX, 246
Network discovery IP mask dialog box, 255
network segments, 247
network systems, 247
NXPIP, 245
NXPLANZ, 246
overview, 242
related components, 244–245
results of, reviewing, 257
scope of, limiting, 254
SNMP community name, 246
starting, 249–250
status, viewing, 250–251
stopping, 249–250
WAN segments, 248
workstations, 256–257
network segments. *See* segments
networking information inventory reports, 370
networks
   administration roles, 238–239
   configuring, 236–237
   IPX transports, 237
   management groups, defining, 235
   management strategies, 235–236
   systems, list of, 247
   troubleshooting, 260
New commands, Policy Package, 54, 63
New Profile dialog box, 389
NLM
   loading, 205
   unloading, 206
nodes
   activity of, monitoring, 283–284
   analyzing traffic between, 281–282
   analyzing traffic on, 279–280
   Conversations view, 282–283
   network statistics of, 280–281

Novell Consulting Services, 457
Novell eDirectory, 2
Novell Web site, 456
NT server objects, 43
NXPIP discovery cycle, 245
NXPLANZ discovery cycle, 246

O

objects
   adding as trustee, 57
   application TED site distribution, 42
   container package, 42
   database, 42
   MW account, 43
   MW domain, 43
   MW scope, 43
   MW service, 43
   NT server, 43
   policy, 43
   Policy packages, 46
   RBS module, 43
   RBS role, 44
   RBS task, 44
   Remote Web Console, 44
   SAS service, 44
   Server group, 44
   server package, 44
   service location package, 44
   TED channel, 44
   TED distribution, 44
   TED external subscriber, 45
   TED subscriber, 45
Ordered Unload page of Server Down Process Policies, 90–91
Other Property page of Container Policy Package, 58–60
outbound alarm processors, 303

P

packet capture. *See* capture packets
Ping command (File menu), 326
platform-specific policies, 52–53
plural policies versus cumulative policies, 53–54
policies
    adding scripts to, 96–97
    cumulative, 53–54
    platform-specific, 52–53
    plural, 53–54
Policy and Distribution Services
    Remote Web Console, 38
    server packages, 37
    server policies, 37
    starting up, 48–50
policy objects, 43
Policy Package command (New menu), 54, 63
policy packages, 46
policy pages
    Container Package, 55–56
    Server Policy Package, 64
    Service Location Policy Package, 62
portal services, 5
Preinstallation Load/Unload property page of Server Software Packages, 204–205
Preinstallation Requirements property page of Server Software Packages, 204
printing inventory reports, 383
product guides, 32
Products.dat property page of Server Software Packages, 214
Profile button, 345
Protocol Distribution command (View menu), 293
Pulling command (View menu), 327

R

RBS module objects, 43
RBS role objects, 44
RBS task objects, 44
Refresh Interval page of Search Policies, 70
Registry Settings property page of Server Software Packages, 214
remote servers
    Edit Security Parameters, 354
    managing, 351
    managing NetWare, 352–353
    managing NT, 354
Remote Web Console
    defined, 38, 179
    distributor functions, 182–185
    installing, 179
    objects, 44
    starting, 179–181
removing
    applications from scanning, 366
    columns, 232
renaming views, 234
reporting components, 224
Reporting page of Server Down Process Policies, 91–92
reports. *See also* inventory reports
    Computer Systems by Segment, 371–372
    detailed, 380
    health, *see* health reports
    history, 380
    NCP Servers, 371–372
    routers, 371–372
    segment, 371–372
    segment topology, 371–373
    TED (Tiered Electronic Distribution), 379–380
    topology, 371

INDEX

topology, creating, 384–385
troubleshooting, 405
Reports command (Tools menu), 385
Requirements property page of Server Software Packages, 196–197
Reset button, 62
resizing columns, 231
revision history reports
 creating, 396–397
 for failures, creating, 397
Rights to Files and Folders Property page of Container Policy Package, 60
RMON agent monitoring groups, 264–265
RMON lite agent monitoring groups, 265
RMON plus agent monitoring groups, 265–266
RMON2 agent monitoring groups, 266–267
role-based objects, 35
rollbacks, 189–190
routers reports, 371–372
Routing Hierarchy property page of distributor objects, 133–135
Run Selected button, 381

S

SAS service objects, 44
Save As command (View menu), 234
Save command (File menu), 291
saving
 trace files, 291
 views, 234
scalar objects, viewing tables of, 437–438
scanning
 adding applications for, 364–365
 editing file extensions for, 365–366

inventory, 361
inventory on NetWare, 362
inventory on Windows NT, 362–363
removing applications from, 366
Schedule Property page
 of channel objects, 178
 of distributor objects, 135–138
 of TED distribution objects, 162–165
 TED (Tiered Electronic Distribution) Polices, 78–80
Scheduled Down Policies, 85–86
Scheduled Load/Unload Policies, 86–88
scheduling health reports, 392
Script property page of Server Software Packages, 206–207
Search Policies
 overview, 67
 Refresh Interval page, 70
 Search Level features, 68–69
 Search Level page, 68
 Search Order page, 69–70
searching files, 210–212
Segment Dashboard command (View menu), 275
segment reports, 371–372
Segment Summary command (View menu), 279
segment topology reports, 371
 items within, 373
Segment Trends command (View menu), 275
segments
 alarm statistics, viewing, 276–277
 network statistics for, viewing, 272
 Segment Dashboard view, 274–275
 summary of, viewing, 276–279
 trends, 275–276
 views of, 273

475

Server Down Process Policies
　Broadcast Message page, 92
　Conditions page, 94–96
　Down Procedure page, 88–89
　Ordered Unload page, 90–91
　Reporting page, 91–92
　Targeted Messages page, 92–94
server inventory
　inventory gatherer, 361
　inventory manager database, 361
　inventory storer, 361
　reports for, 224
　scanning, 361
　scanning on NetWare, 362
　scanning on Windows NT, 362–363
　schema, 426–430
server management
　alarm notification agents, 335
　alarm thresholds, 337
　baseline documents, cache buffers, 336
　baseline documents, CPU utilization, 336
　baseline documents, creating, 336–337
　baseline documents, software, 337
　baseline documents, volume utilization, 337
　configuration management agents, 335
　console view, 335
　management console, 226–227
　monitoring agents, 334
　namespaces, 338
　overview, 224–225
　remote control components, 226
　sample intervals, setting, 355–356
　server configuration information, displaying, 338–339
　server inventory, 226

server parameters, configuring, 349–350
summary data, viewing, 339–342
summary view, 335
traffic analysis tools, 225–226
trend agents, 335
trend buckets, setting, 356
trend files, 357
trend values, setting initial, 355
trend view, 336
troubleshooting, 337, 410–414
utilization tracking, 337
server management agent for NetWare, 12
server package objects, 44
server parameters, configuring, 349–350
server policies reports, 224
Server Policy Package
　creating, 63
　General property page, 64–65
　NetWare Policies property page, 65–66
　policy page, 64
　Windows NT/2000 Policies property page, 66–67
server reports. *See* reports
Server Scripts Policies, creating, 96–97
server software package agents, 173–174
Server Software Packages
　adding components to, 202–203
　adding rules to, 197
　compiling, 215
　Copy File Property page, 207–208
　.cpk files, 189
　creating, 194–195
　disk space rules, 199
　file rules, 200–201
　Identification property page, 196, 203

INDEX

installation failures, 190
installation requirements, 188
installing on target servers, 216
memory rules, 198–199
operating system rules, 197–198
overview, 188
package management, 195–196
Preinstallation Load/Upload property page, 204–205
Preinstallation Requirements property page, 204
Products.dat rules, 201, 214
registry rules, 199–200
Registry Settings property page, 214
Requirements property page, 196–197
rollback, 189–190
Script property page, 206–207
Search File, 210–212
set commands rule, 199–200
.spk files, 189
Text Files property page, 209
updating, 217
variables, 193
Variables property page, 201–202
servers
    commands, executing, 351
    installation components, 26
    inventory, 4
    management site services, 34–35
    mapping drives to, 17
    packages, 37
    policies, 37
    policy management, 2–3
    remote, *see* remote servers
    roles of, 239
    Server Manager engine, 38
    software packages, 3–4
    Traffic Analysis, 36
    trending, 4

service location package objects, 44
Service Location Policy Package
    Associations page, 63
    creating, 60–61
    policy page, 62
Settings property page
    of channel objects, 178
    of distributor objects, 129–130
    I/O rate, 74
    maximum concurrent distributions, 74
    parent subscriber, 74
    of subscriber objects, 146–147
    Tiered Electronic Distribution policy, 73–74
    working directory, 74
Show Top Stations command (view menu), 281
Show View Title command (View menu), 231
SMTP Host Policies, 70–71
snap-ins, 39
SNMP Community Strings policies, 98–100
SNMP dialog box, 253
SNMP MIB Browser, 222
SNMP MIB Compiler, 222
SNMP services, 4
    monitoring, 222–223
SNMP trap receivers, 302
SNMP Trap Target Policies, 71–72
SNMP Trap Target Refresh policies, 101–102
software, 221
Software Scan Editor, 365
Sort command (View menu), 233
sorting
    alarms, 310–312
    views, 233
.SPK files, 189–190

starting
    capture packets, 286–287
    MIB browser, 436–437
    network discovery, 249–250
    Remote Web Console, 179–181
Stations command (View menu), 280
stopping
    capture packets, 287
    network discovery, 249–250
subscriber detail reports, creating, 395
subscriber distribution detail reports,
    creating, 395–396
subscriber objects
    Channels property page, 149–150
    Extract Schedule property page,
        150–153
    Messaging property page, 147–149
    overview, 143–144, 156
    Settings property page, 146–147
    Variables property page, 153–154
subscriber property page of channel
    objects, 178
subscribers
    defining configuration information
        for, 28–29
    function of, 40
    placing on Windows NT/2000,
        154–155
    schedules, 126
Summary command (View menu), 340
summary views, 229
    for server management, 335
support
    Cool Solutions, 456
    Novell Consulting Services, 457
    Novell Web site, 456
    support packs, 460–464
Switch Summary (View menu), 294

switch traffic, 293
    port statistics, 294
    summary data, 294

T

tabular views, 230
Targeted Messages page Server Down
    Process Policies, 92–94
TCO (total cost of ownership), 2
technical support. *See* support
TED agents, 167
    file, 174–177
    FTP, 171–172
    HTTP, 170–171
    NAL application distribution,
        168–169
    server software package, 173–174
TED distribution objects, 44, 158
    Agent property page, 161–162
    Channels property page, 160–161
    General property page, 159–160
    Schedule property page, 162–165
TED (Tiered Electronic Distribution), 3
    channel objects, 44
    complex tree example, 117–119
    components, relationship between,
        114–115
    components of, 40
    database schema, 432–435
    detail reports, 380
    distribution networks, 122–123
    distributor components, 112
    distributor objects, 45
    external subscriber objects, 45
    history reports, 380
    management of, 39
    NDS objects, 113–114
    parent subscriber components, 112

INDEX

reports, 224
simple tree example, 115–116
subscriber components, 112
subscriber objects, 45
system configuration, 123
system configuration, distributor validation, 124–125
system configuration, hierarchy routing construction, 124
system configuration, scheduler interactions, 125–127
TED agent components, 113
TED (Tiered Electronic Distribution) Policies
  Messaging property page, 75–77
  Schedule Property page, 78–80
  Settings Policy page, 73–75
  Variables property page, 77–78
template alarm archivers, 305
text, appending to files, 210
Text File Changes policies, 102
  append to file, 104
  creating, 102–103
  Policy Schedule page, 106
  pretend to file, 103
  search file, 104–106
Text Files property page of Server Software Packages, 209
Tiered Electronic Distribution. *See* TED
time spans, editing, 343–344
token rings, 248
  network profiles, 378–379
Tools menu commands
  Reports, 385
  Server Inventory Reports, 381
topology mapping, 221–222
topology reports, 224
  creating, 384–385
  types of, 371

total cost of ownership. *See* TCO
trace files, saving, 291
traffic analysis. *See also* LAN traffic analysis
traffic analysis agent for NetWare
  hardware requirements, 12
  software requirements, 13
traffic analysis agent for Windows NT, 13
traffic analysis tools, 225–226
transparent bridges, 248
tree
  activating distribution services in, 49–50
  existing objects modified in, 45
Trend Data view
  accessing, 275
  grid lines, 344
  legend, viewing, 342–343
  profile, editing, 345–346
  time spans, editing, 343–344
  viewing data, 342
trend parameters for Managed Servers, 374–377
trend views, 228
  for server management, 336
trends
  files, disabling, 357
  files, enabling, 357
  samplings, 346–347
  threshold alarm settings, 348–349
troubleshooting
  agent object associations, 400
  alarm management, 408–409
  distribution services, 400–405
  distributor building corrupt path files, 402
  distributor sending to concurrent connections, 401
  JVM installation, 405

(continued)

troubleshooting *(continued)*
  networks, using atlas, 260
  policy services, 400–405
  report printing, 405
  RWC ports, 405
  server management, 410–414
  software package distribution files, 402–403
  subscriber extraction failure, 404
  subscriber timing out, 401
  traffic analysis, 405–408
  ZFS agent installation, 404
Trustees of This Object page
  Container Policy Package, 56–57
  of distributor objects, 138–140

U

unloading
  Java Class, 206
  NLM, 206
updating Server Software Packages, 217

V

validating distributors, 124–125
variables for Server Software Packages, 193
Variables property page
  of Server Software Packages, 201–202
  of subscriber objects, 153–154
  TED (Tiered Electronic Distribution) Policies, 77–78
Vertical Grid button, 344

View menu commands
  Alarms History, 310
  Appearance, 230–231
  Column Selector, 232
  Conversations, 282
  Edit Saved Views, 234
  Filter, 232, 290
  List Segment, 274
  Monitor Nodes, 284
  Protocol Distribution, 293
  Pulling, 327
  Save As, 234
  Segment Dashboard, 275
  Segment Summary, 279
  Segment Trends, 275
  Show Top Stations, 281
  Show View Title, 231
  Sort, 233
  Stations, 280
  Summary, 340
  Switch Summary, 294
viewing
  capture packets, 288
  grid lines, 344
  health reports, 392–393
  inventory reports, 381
  tables of scalar objects, 437–438
views
  columns, adding, 232
  columns, changing order of, 232
  columns, removing, 232
  columns, resizing, 231
  deleting, 234
  exporting, 234
  font size, changing, 230–231
  graphical, 230
  grid lines, customizing, 231

INDEX

limiting with filters, 232–233
list of, 228–229
renaming, 234
saving, 234
server level, 229
site level, 229
sorting, 233
tabular, 230
titles, viewing, 231

W

WAN
  example tree, 118–119
  Hops for tree transmissions, 120
  segments, 248
Web sites
  Cool Solutions, 456
  Novell, 456
Windows NT/2000
  hardware requirements, 14–15
  placing subscribers on, 154–155
  software requirements, 15
Windows NT/2000 Policies property page of Server Policy Package, 66–67
workstations
  ensuring discovery of, 256–257
  hardware requirements for, 10
  software requirements for, 11

Z

ZENworks for Servers 2
  alarm management services, 4
  benefits, 6–7

installing, completion of, 29–30
installing, prerequisite steps for, 10–16
installing distribution services, 25–29
installing policy services, 25–29
installing server components, 16–19
installing site management Console snap-ins, 25
installing site management services and agents, 20–24
and ManageWise relationship, 5–6
migration tools, 30–32
objects, modified, 422–423
objects, new, 416–421
overview, 2
portal services, 5
server inventory, 4
server management, 2–3
server software packages, 3–4
server trending, 4
SNMP services, 4
TED (Tiered Electronic Distribution), 3
ZENworks for Servers License Policies, 82–83

481